CONIECTANEA BIBLICA · OLD TESTAMENT SERIES 31

CB
CONIECTANEA BIBLICA

OLD TESTAMENT SERIES 31

Present Editors:
Tryggve N.D. Mettinger (Lund) and Magnus Y. Ottosson (Uppsala)

Staffan Olofsson

GOD IS MY ROCK

A Study of Translation Technique and Theological Exegesis

in the Septuagint.

Almqvist & Wiksell International Stockholm

1990

BS
744
,O46
1990

Abstract

Olofsson, S., 1990. GOD IS MY ROCK - A Study of Translation Technique and Theological Exegesis in the Septuagint. Coniectanea Biblica. Old Testament Series 31. Revised edition of an earlier mimeographed dissertation submitted to the Theological Faculty of the University of Uppsala for the Degree of Doctor of Theology and publicly examined on September 23, 1988.

The present study seeks to make a valuable contribution within the field of theological exegesis and translation technique in the Septuagint. It devotes particular attention to a certain type of metaphorical divine epithets which are based on inanimate nature. These are contrary to other types of metaphorical as well as non-metaphorical designations of God translated with a vocabulary the basic aim of which is not to render the literal or the metaphorical meaning of the words in context. It is demonstrated that the Greek equivalents which are used are more or less restricted to the translation of these types of epithet and do not always express the difference between the individual words. On the other hand, the Hebrew words as a rule have a main equivalent which is employed in most cases. The use of an alternative rendering is based on the desire for variation and does not reflect contextual differences. Most of these metaphors are stereotyped expressions for the protection of God. One and the same translation technique pervades LXX as a whole, maybe because the choice of epithets is influenced by the prayer-language of the synagogue. To some degree, however, it also reflects the poetic vocabulary of the Hebrew of which these designations of God are a part. This technique is in line with a trait in the development of the Hebrew language. Theological and linguistic factors concur in the rendering of these epithets. Otherwise theological exegesis does not seem to be a distinctive feature of the LXX Psalms. The translation is not characterized by a negative attitude to anthropomorphisms nor does the translator generally seek to mitigate certain expressions which seem derogatory to the majesty and honour of God. As a rule unexpected translations are based on the translator's contextual interpretation or reflect his deficient knowledge of Hebrew.

Keywords:
Bible, Old Testament, Septuagint, Translation technique, Theological exegesis, Book of Psalms, Metaphors, Anthropomorphisms, God, Divine epithets, Prayer-language, Synagogue

Almqvist & Wiksell International, Stockholm, Sweden
ISBN 91-22-01394-6

ACKNOWLEDGEMENTS

The subject of this dissertation was given to me by my former supervisor, Professor Helmer Ringgren, who introduced me to the field of Old Testament studies. For this I owe him a deep gratitude. I am also obliged to my other supervisors, Doc. Agge Carlson, and especially to Professor Magnus Ottosson, who has constantly encouraged me in my work and not least helped me to finish it. I have been able to discuss some of the problems of Septuagint translation technique with the Old Testament seminar in Uppsala and I have learned a great deal from these seminar meetings. My position as assistant secretary in the Swedish Bible Translation Committee during many years has also had a stimulating effect on my dissertation work. I hope that experiences from the committee work has helped me to a better understanding of the translation process and thereby increased my ability to investigate the techniques of the Septuagint translators.

The present book is a revised edition of the main part of my dissertation submitted to the Faculty of Theology at Uppsala University on September, 1988. For valuable criticism, which aided me in the work of revison, I am especially indebted to the opponent in the public discussion, Professor James Barr, whose comments and suggestions have been a great help to me, as well as to Professor Magnus Ottoson, Professor Bertil Albrektson and Professor Lars Hartman, who shared with me their reactions to my thesis and submitted it to valuable criticism. A special word of thanks is due to B.A., B.D. Jean Theodosio Gray who undertook to correct my English.
Lastly, my heartfelt thanks go to my wife Agneta, without whose support this work could not have been completed.

God is my Rock is dedicated to my wife, Agneta, and my children, Anna, Mikael and Maria.

Uppsala, in May 1990

Staffan Olofsson

900543

TABLE OF CONTENTS

Chapter I

GENERAL INTRODUCTION

1.1 PROBLEM AND DEFINITIONS

This dissertation examines the influence of theological exegesis in the Septuagint, first and foremost in the Psalter. The investigation is further limited to certain anthropological expressions (antropomorphisms) in LXX Psalms and to metaphorical names or epithets of God in LXX as a whole, which, according to some scholars, reflect theologically motivated interpretations of the translators.

No clear distinction between divine epithet and divine name is made here, even though "name" is often used when the term expresses the relation between Yahweh and thĕ Psalmist or the people, while "epithet" is employed when it is apposed to designations such as "God", "Yahweh". See also p. 15 in this book. "Epithet" in less technical usage can, according to Yahweh and the Psalmist or the people, while designations such as "the Lord", "God" or "Yahweh", while "epithet" is employed when it English lexica, be employed as more or less synonymous with "name".[1] Regarding the definition of metaphor, see 6.4.3.

Anthropomorphism is sometimes distinguished from anthropopathism. It is then defined as the use of terms for the human body in the description of Yahweh while anthropopathism is the attribution to him of human feelings.[2] This is the general understanding of the terms but, according to J. Barr, the only true anthropomorphisms are those which are concerned with how Yahweh appears in human form, thus the description of God in a theophany,[3] since only there is a pictorial representation of Yahweh at issue. Indeed, the anthropomorphic imagery is seldom used in theophany texts such as Ex 33, Is 6 and Ez 1.[4] J. Barr suggests that most references to anti-anthropomorphisms, i.e. non-literal renderings of anthropomorphisms, in the OT are out of place, since the conventional anthropomorphisms, where various parts of the body are used in connection with Yahweh, in no way try to convey his appearance. Therefore it is a danger to exaggerate their importance. The real reason for the prominence of such anthropomorphisms in modern scholarly discussions is probably their offensiveness to rationalistic thought.[5]

"Anthropomorphism" is thus a controversial term in scholarly circles but if no attempt is made to read in any philosophical speculations concerning the corporeality of God it can hardly be discarded.[6] Even though the term is not ideal, "anthropomorphism" has retained its conventional meaning in this dissertation. Thus it is, for example, used for expressions such as "to see Yahweh", for the attribution of human feelings to God, and for the metaphorical employment of parts of the body in connection with God in all kinds of contexts.[7] In order to be

---

[1] See also the use in e.g. Freedman, **Divine Names**, passim.

[2] See Klein, **Pentateuch**, p. V n. 1. H.M. Erwin makes no distinction between them. See his definition in ibid., p. 23. The same is true for R.J.Z. Werblowsky. See Werblowsky, **Anthropomorphism**, col. 50, but cf. cols. 51-52. See also Jevons, **Anthropomorphism**, pp. 573-574.

[3] Barr, **Theophany**, pp. 31-32, 38. Cf. Bjørndalen, **Rede**, pp. 43-46.

[4] Cf. Caird, **Language**, p. 175.

[5] Barr, **Theophany**, p. 31. In OT times they were, according to Barr, regarded as trivial. Ibid., pp. 31, 38.

[6] For a criticism of the term, see especially Chester, **Revelation**, pp. 278-283 and n. 35-46, where he also quotes the opinions of other scholars.

[7] Cf. Chester, **Revelation**, pp. 289-292. For a discussion of the metaphorical character of the anthro-

able to discuss the different levels of meaning the term "literal meaning" or "literal sense" is used to refer to the image of the metaphor in contrast to the point of similarity.[8] The significance of "meaning" is crucial for the understanding of metaphors and figurative language as a whole, but it is more or less impossible to define.[9] "Meaning" and "sense" are thus used synonymously, even though "meaning" is the more generic. They refer to the connotation rather than the denotation of a term.

The use of anti-anthropomorphisms must be regarded as a non-literal translation technique, since the rendering of the metaphorical meaning, the point of similarity, is opposed to the literal tendency to preserve the image of the original.[10] Tov, on the other hand, emphasizes that the study of translation technique is "not involved with content exegesis".[11] But even Tov, in conformity with Barr, lists semantic accuracy, which may be regarded as a form of content exegesis, among the literal translation techniques.[12] The influence of theological exegesis on the choice of equivalents in LXX Psalms and in LXX as a whole is to be equated with translation technique proper, since translation technique is concerned with the actual equivalents themselves. But even theological motives, as well as the translator's knowledge of Hebrew, which are not part of the technique of translation, have a bearing on the evaluation of the LXX.[13]

Theological exegesis ought to be distinguished from both contextual and linguistic exegesis. Linguistic exegesis "is an integral part of the act of translation".[14] While theological exegesis may perhaps be regarded as a form of contextual exegesis, which is the ordinary type of exegesis in a translation,[15] it is contrary to the standard form of contextual exegesis, inasmuch as it introduces an interpretation of a phrase or a term in the Hebrew that is at variance with the literal meaning.[16] This is the usual understanding of theological exegesis, but it is an insufficient definition for my purpose since it does not take the situation of the LXX translators into account.

It may be taken for granted that even in the philological analysis of the Hebrew the translator was unconsciously influenced by the religious milieu of his time as well as by his own religious convictions. Particularly when he encountered words and expressions which he only vaguely comprehended, his choice of equivalents may have been affected by what he regarded as a reasonable interpretation from a theological point of view.[17] This kind of unconscious theological influence is more or less inherent in the translation process per se and I do not regard it as manifest theological exegesis. I deliberately restrict myself to the study of conscious theological exegesis reflected in the choice of equivalents, i.e. cases where the translation is more influenced by the theology of the translator than by the meaning of the words in their context. It is of course a complicated task to distinguish between conscious theological exegesis and mere theological influence, since it presupposes discernment of the translator's intentions.

---

pomorphisms, see Bjørndalen, **Rede**, pp. 37–64.

[8] Regarding this sense of the term, see **Nida, Taber**, pp. 210, 203.

[9] See e.g. Meier, **Metapher**, pp. 111–112. See also ibid., pp. 113–117.

[10] See Barr, **Typology**, p. 315. This aspect of literalism concerns the semantic accuracy and the level of semantic information. See Olofsson, **LXX Version**, pp. 21–22.

[11] Tov, **Analysis**, p. 3.

[12] Cf. Olofsson, **LXX Version**, p. 21 n. 171.

[13] For the definition of translation technique, see Olofsson, **LXX Version**, p. 65.

[14] Tov, **Septuagint**, p. 82. It is based on the semantic meaning of the texts without reference to the context. Aquila is an example of a translation which is more or less based on pure linguistic exegesis. Ibid., p. 82.

[15] Cf. Tov, **Septuagint**, p. 82.

[16] Tov, **Septuagint**, p. 82.

[17] See e.g. Barr, **Philology**, pp. 282, 285. He probably postulated that the Scriptures were consistent in the teaching of theological matters. Ibid., pp. 282, 285.

1.2 THE SITUATION OF THE TRANSLATORS

1.2.1 The translators' cultural and religious milieu

A translation never emerges in a social, cultural or religious vacuum.[18] Both the translators and the intended readers are to a certain extent influenced by the contemporary cultural situation. One of the aims of all translators is certainly to mediate the message to the readers in a way that they can understand. Therefore, in order to eliminate or at least reduce misinterpretations they may have taken into account what kind of associations were connected with different words and how they were used in religion and in secular life.[19] The translators may have viewed it, and probably rightly so, as a part of the transmission of the meaning of the text[20] to translate in such a way as to obviate misunderstandings.

The most frequent employment of free renderings for theological reasons probably consists in the choice of equivalents for certain cultic objects which were liable to be misinterpreted by the readers, such as, for example, certain trees that could easily be confused with sacred trees in pagan religions,[21] altars erected to Yahweh that could be taken for heathen altars,[22] and maybe also expressions about God that represented him more or less as a human being. This technique is compatible with a general tendency in the translation of religious texts in the Greco-Roman world; the translators of religious texts in Antiquity tried as a rule to illuminate the message of the original the way they understood it.[23]

Jewish and Hellenistic influences

In pursuing their task the Septuagint translators were to some extent influenced by the Judaeo-Hellenistic culture and religion, since the making of the Septuagint "bedeutet die Transponierung der Religionsurkunden Israels nicht nur in eine andere Zeit und Sprache, sondern auch in eine unendlich verschiedene Kultur- und Begriffswelt".[24] The translation was executed by Hellenistic Jews for Hellenistic Jews.[25] The Judaeo-Hellenistic cultural setting is thus of cardinal importance for the LXX. This does not mean that the Septuagint is only a vehicle of Hellenistic theological ideas, since the train of thought in the Hebrew Old Testament is its basic trait. But the translation obviously became "the most significant factor in the process of the Hellenization of Judaism".[26] On the other hand, this was hardly the purpose of the translators.

It is, however, no less important that the translation was made by Jews for Jews. Thus some scholars, as, for example, Marcus, emphasize the Jewish element in the LXX and minimize the Greek.[27] But Tov claims that "the Jewish

---

[18] Flashar, p. 86, Würtwein, **Text**, pp. 72-73.

[19] See the discussion and the examples in **Churgin**, pp. 41-65, Bertram, **Sprachschatz**, pp. 85-101 and **Arieti**, pp. 340-341, 347. But it is important to emphasize that this theological motivation competes with the aims of a literal translation technique, and the Septuagint is in many books a literal translation.

[20] Würtwein, **Text**, pp. 71-72.

[21] See Barr, **Wood**, pp. 11-20.

[22] See **Churgin**, pp. 44-47 and **Daniel**, pp. 13-32.

[23] Wigtil, **Religious Texts**, pp. 9-10, 336-338. See also ibid., pp. 340-341. Regarding the employment of an interpretative translation technique in Antiquity, see Herrmann, **Dolmetschen**, pp. 40-41 and n. 71.

[24] Flashar, p. 86.

[25] See e.g. Bertram, **Frömmigkeit**, p. 274. The Hellenistic background of the Jewish exegetical rules of interpretation codified in the middôt is stressed in Brooke, **Qumran**, pp. 8-17.

[26] Koester, **Hellenistic Age I**, p. 253.

[27] See Marcus, **Elements**, p. 244. For a discussion of the Judaeo-Palestinian influence in the LXX, see, above all, **Prijs**, pp. 1-75.

background of the translation is visible in a relatively limited number of technical terms in the area of the cult."[28] It is in any case essential that the influence from Jewish tradition and interpretation are taken into account when we are studying the Septuagint.[29] The type of translation and interpretation which were later employed in the Targums may have played a certain, albeit less significant, role.[30] For example, one sometimes encounters a feature which is best explained as an influence from the Targums, viz. to distinguish in the translation between different referents of a word.

One must, however, be aware of the facts that "Hellenistic" and "Jewish" are "labels too simple for extremely complex and diverse phenomena" and that "what we call 'Judaism' and 'Hellenism' has many profound points of contact in the religious and ethical field, so that it is often impossible to describe where a potential difference lies".[31]

The translators as pioneers

The Septuagint as a translation, not least the Pentateuch, was a pioneer work. Its translators thus had to cope with the basic problems of translation.[32] They had no previous translation model which they could imitate.[33] Furthermore, the translation technique which they adopted was hardly a matter of free choice: the lack of knowledge as well as of adequate tools excluded a good idiomatic translation.[34] The translators did not even have access to elementary linguistic tools such as lexica, concordances and grammars.[35] They did not employ footnotes to give alternative interpretations[36] or variant readings.

The choice of equivalents in LXX of course also depends on the possibilities of expression in the Greek language, grammatically,[37] as well as semantically. The lexical choices were limited by the translation technique as well as by the range of significance and the word field of the Greek words.[38]

---

[28] Tov, **Studies**, p. I.

[29] Barnes, **Recovery**, p. 131, Orlinsky, **The LXX**, p. 24. See also Thackeray, **Aspects**, pp. 36-37, Marcus, **Elements**, p. 243, **Roberts**, p. 185, Würtwein, **Text**, p. 72.

[30] Churgin, pp. 42-43, Rabin, **Character**, pp. 20-21.

[31] Gerhardsson, **Program**, p. 129. This is also emphasized by Marcus, **Elements**, p. 232, **Feldman**, p. 217, Orlinsky, **Holy Writ**, p. 108, Brooke, **Qumran**, pp. 6-8.

[32] Rabin, **Character**, p. 20, Harrison, **Introduction**, p. 231, Heller, **Grenzen**, p. 234, Brock, **Phenomenon**, pp. 541-542, ibid., **Septuagint**, p. 12, Lee, **Lexical**, p. 20.

[33] Rabin, **Character**, pp. 20-21, Brock, **Septuagint**, p. 12 and n. 4.

[34] Barr, **Typology**, pp. 289-290.

[35] Katz, **Übersetzungstechnik**, p. 267, Tov, **Impact**, p. 587. See also Caird, **Language**, p. 123, Aejmelaeus, **Parataxis**, p. 180, Tov, **Septuagint Translators**, p. 54 n. 1. Lexica are only known from a later period. Brock, **Septuagint**, p. 30 n. 1.

[36] Orlinsky, **Holy Writ**, p. 104.

[37] Heller, **Grenzen**, pp. 246-247. See also Wevers, **Versions**, p. 15, ibid., **Apologia**, pp. 23-24. The differences in language structure between Hebrew and Greek are outlined in Heller, **Grenzen**, pp. 246-248, Wevers, **Versions**, pp. 16-19.

[38] Bertram, **Sprachschatz**, pp. 87, 88, Barr, **Philology**, pp. 170-173, **Beekman, Callow**, pp. 175-211, Wevers, **Text History**, pp. 399-400.

1.3 PREVIOUS SCHOLARLY INVESTIGATIONS

1.3.1 Critical evaluation of previous methods

Investigations of influences from the theological views of the LXX translators and from their cultural and religious environment are not new. Influences from both Jewish and Hellenistic quarters have as we have seen been conjectured in both the LXX Psalms and in LXX as a whole. This applies not least to renderings of anthropomorphisms and anthropopathisms.[39] Another field where theologically motivated deviations from the ordinary equivalents, according to many scholars, are consistent in the LXX, comprises the metaphorical designations of God.[40] The passages where LXX paraphrases or alters textual references to God's human traits are, according to some scholars, balanced by those in which the translation is more anthropomorphic than the original.[41] It is also sometimes denied that an anti-anthropomorphic trait is visible at all.[42] The reason for the anti-anthropomorphisms is also disputed. Thus, for example, Orlinsky concluded that if the anthropomorphisms were "not reproduced literally, it was not for any theological reason".[43]

It is evident that two different schools of interpretation regarding the influence of theological presuppositions exist. One, which stresses the dominance of theological exegesis, is greatly indebted to the research of the famous scholar H.S. Gehman. The representatives thereof include C.T. Fritsch, especially in his studies of the Pentateuch, G. Bertram, G. Gerleman (the Book of Job), H.M. Erwin (the Psalms) and D.H. Gard (the Book of Job). The other, which minimizes theological influences behind the rendering of the anthropomorphisms in LXX, is represented by, among others, H.M. Orlinsky, A. Soffer, B.M. Zlotowitz and T.K. Wittstruck.[44] The methods and results of Orlinsky's investigations constitute the mainstream of LXX research[45] but the works of the other school of interpretation are not without significance.[46] While my investigation is in line with the methods employed by Orlinsky I seek to refine them and also isolate cases where conscious theological exegesis may have influenced the equivalents and show which theological presuppositions may have been involved.

Two studies of the LXX Psalms have most strongly emphasized that the translator often avoided a literal translation of anthropomorphisms for theological reasons, the investigations of Erwin and and Fritsch. Erwin says: "the LXX translator(s) frequently emended, paraphrased, or otherwise altered those expressions that violated his conception of the spiritual nature of God."[47] The point of departure of his investigation, which is the most comprehensive study extant of theological exegesis in the LXX Psalms, seems to be that all deviations from a strictly literal translation of the anthropomorphisms can be attributed to religious motives.[48] But there is in fact no such thing as a "normal" translation, an absolute

---

[39] See e.g. Briggs, **Psalms I**, p. XXV, **Erwin**, pp. 23-30, examples on pp. 30-55 and Fritsch, **Studies**, pp. 734-733.

[40] See e.g. Bertram, **Sprachschatz**, pp. 93-101, **Erwin**, pp. 56-78, Fritsch, **Studies**, pp. 739-734. Cf. Dell'Acqua, **Roccia**.

[41] Cf. **Soffer**, pp. 76-90, 96, Orlinsky, **Holy Writ**, p. 107 and n. 24.

[42] See especially **Soffer**, pp. 86-100, 106. He states that the renderings of anthropomorphisms and anthropopathisms closely follow the usual translation technique in the Book of Psalms. Ibid., p. 106. See also Levy, Review of Klein, **Pentateuch**, JBL 104 (1985), pp. 708-709.

[43] Orlinsky, **Holy Writ**, p. 107. See also the literature listed there. But e.g. Thackeray, **Aspects**, pp. 37-39, Würtwein, **Text**, p. 71, are of another opinion.

[44] For a more comprehensive description of the works of these schools, see Zlotowitz, **Jeremiah**, p. XI and the Introductory Essay by Orlinsky, pp. XV-XXI, in the same book.

[45] Cf. e.g. Jellicoe, **Septuagint**, pp. 270-271.

[46] See e.g. the presentation in Dorival, Harl, Munnich, **Septante**, p. 214.

[47] **Erwin**, p. 7.

[48] **Erwin**, pp. 23-24. The same is true for Fritsch, **Pentateuch**, according to Wittstruck,

model, from which all deviations, such as, for example, the renderings of anthropomorphisms, must be due to religious or other reasons.[49] This "normal version" is bound to be identical with a translation which is correct, according to modern standards, or a strictly literal translation.[50] Wigtil describes the type of method employed by Erwin only to reject it and disclose its inherent weaknesses. It runs several risks, chiefly that the tendency the student seeks becomes in practice his guideline so that the text is abandoned as the governing factor. This in turn impels the translator to overlook other important features of the text and fail to systematize the evidence on account of an inherent bias against proof to the contrary. The result is often unwarranted selectivity and incorrect findings.[51] With the suppositions of Fritsch and Erwin "the only way for the translator to be free of any accusation of Tendenz is for him to translate literally."[52]

The bases for Erwin's premises are that the "tenacity and conservatism of religious sanctions exerts tremendous pressure on the side of retaining anthropomorphic elements",[53] that Judaism is among the anthropomorphic religions and that the Semitic languages had a very vivid imagery.[54] This is, however, a somewhat outdated way of describing the properties of the Hebrew which has been severely damaged by the heavy linguistic artillery of J. Barr.[55] The whole idea of certain characteristics of Hebrew which are in opposition to other languages, not least Greek, exaggerates the way a language reflects the worldview and cultural idiosyncrasies of a people.[56] That the poetic medium is the most conservative literary form is, according to Erwin, a significant factor in the evaluation of the non-literal renderings in the Book of Psalms.[57] The only vital force which could explain examples of non-literal renderings of anthropomorphisms is the theological Tendenz of the translator.[58] Erwin does not maintain that all of them are altered, but that only theological motives can explain the appearance of occasional free translations of anthropomorphisms.[59] That other factors could have influenced the translator, such as his linguistic capacity,[60] the nature of the Hebrew text in question, the dependence on the Pentateuch,[61] or the resources and the demands of the target language[62] are rarely taken into account.

The methodology employed by Erwin has thus serious shortcomings, which exclude its use. It is true that an anti-anthropomorphic attitude may be conjectured even though there is no uniform tendency to make a free translation out of all anthropomorphisms which refer to God. Erwin admits that the anthropomorphic imagery is retained in most instances in the Psalter,[63] but emphasizes that the "retention of many anthropomorphic expressions in the Greek text of the Psalms is not a convincing argument against the principle of anti-anthropomorphisms".[64] But

---

Anti-Anthropomorphisms, p. 30, ibid., Pentateuch, p. 409.

[49] See e.g. Klein, Pentateuch, p. XIII.

[50] Cf. Wittstruck, Anti-Anthropomorphisms, p. 30.

[51] See Wigtil, Religious Texts, p. 26. Cf. ibid., p. 24.

[52] Wittstruck, Anti-Anthropomorphisms, p. 30.

[53] Erwin, p. 23.

[54] See Erwin, p. 23 and n. 3.

[55] See e.g. Barr, Semantics, pp. 30-31.

[56] See Barr, Semantics, pp. 8-20, and for that matter the whole discussion on pp. 21-205.

[57] Erwin, p. 24.

[58] Thus Erwin, pp. 23-24.

[59] Erwin, pp. 24-25. Erwin does not take into account that much of the imagery must have consisted of dead metaphors. See Olofsson, LXX Version, p. 22 n. 176. Concerning the background and function of dead metaphors, and how to distinguish them from live metaphors, see Beekman, Callow, pp. 131-136, Caird, Language, pp. 66-77, 152-197.

[60] See Olofsson, LXX Version, p. 11 and n. 98, pp. 28-32.

[61] Olofsson, LXX Version, pp. 26-28.

[62] Olofsson, LXX Version, pp. 11-12.

[63] Erwin, p. 24. Cf. Soffer, p. 106.

[64] Erwin, p. 23.

an anti-anthropomorphic trait must be more or less consistent if it is to be attributed to a specific theological tendency.[65] Fritsch's statement in this connection is at best only a half-truth: "Although the tendency to spiritualize the conception of God was active ... it was not strong enough to make itself felt consistently except in a few instances."[66] This applies to the LXX but the same is true for the Targums. Many methodologically adequate studies of both the Targums and the LXX convincingly show that neither consistently avoided a literal rendering of anthropomorphisms.[67] Studies of anthropomorphisms in the LXX have so far been limited to the Pentateuch, Joshua, Isaiah, the Minor Prophets, the Psalms and Job.[68]

To study the translation technique in general is in fact indispensable for the formation of an opinion on all types of theological exegesis. It is essential that the examples of a less literal translation be seen in relation to the general translation technique and the method of rendering the same terms when they do not refer to God.[69] This is also what Soffer has done. His occasionally schematical presentation is more than enough to convey the subjectivity with which a pronounced general anti-anthropomorphic trait in LXX Psalms has been conjectured.[70] We do well to heed the wise words of Orlinsky in this connection:

> It cannot be stressed enough that a sporadic exception or two within an otherwise consistent pattern of translation cannot by itself be seized upon as proof for the invalidation of that pattern; to the contrary, the exception must be studied both in the context of the translation of the entire book and per se, within its own immediate context.[71]

The rentention of a literal translation in so many instances is still the main obstacle to the use of the label "anti-anthropomorphic" simply of the Targums.[72] Some scholars suggest that, even though the translators of the Targums were not consistent, they followed a system of rendering different kinds of anthropomorphisms,[73] but in fact not even the individual Targums are congruous in their method of translation.[74]

The use of anti-anthropomorphisms in the Targum of the Book of Psalms, which Erwin often cites as an argument for the widespread influence of this technique in the LXX Psalter, is not invariable.[75] In fact some of the anthropomorphic expressions are always rendered literally, while none is translated by circumlocution in every case.[76] The lack of consistency in the Targum of the

---

[65] The lack of consistency in LXX is of course in itself a good argument against any strongly felt theological attitude and even more so here since non-literal renderings are in fact seldom employed. Cf. the discussion in Klein, **Pentateuch**, p. XI.

[66] Fritsch, **Studies**, pp. 730-729.

[67] Chester, **Revelation**, pp. 284-286 and n. 48-55.

[68] See Zlotowitz, **Jeremiah**, p. XI. Cf. the Introductory Essay by Orlinsky, pp. XV-XXI, in the same book.

[69] This is of course an indispensible requirement for any study of theological motives. See the excellent methodological description by Orlinsky in his review of Fritsch, **Pentateuch**, The Crozer Quarterly, 21 (1944), p. 159. Note also the criticism of the methodology of Fritsch in the same review on p. 157.

[70] Cf. the criticism of Soffer by Erwin. **Erwin**, p. 3. The same applies to the investigation of Job by Gard. See the critical evaluation of Gard, **Job**, by Orlinsky. Orlinsky, **Job**, pp. 70-71 and n. 63. The results from the study of Chronicles by Allen and of the Pentateuch by Wittstruck point in the same direction. Wittstruck, **Anti-Anthropomorphisms**, pp. 29-34, Allen, **Chronicles I**, pp. 120-124.

[71] Orlinsky, **Introductory Essay** in Zlotowitz, **Jeremiah**, pp. XIX-XX.

[72] See the discussion in Chester, **Revelation**, pp. 265-278.

[73] Cf. the references in Klein, **Pentateuch**, pp. IX, n. 20-22 and 35-36 n. 45-46.

[74] See Klein, **Converse Translation**, p. 515.

[75] See especially Shunary, **Psalms**, pp. 133-144.

[76] Shunary, **Psalms**, pp. 143-144. The same is in fact true for the Targums per se. Klein, **Pentateuch**, pp. X-XI and n. 11-12, pp. 10, 39. Concerning the theory of a systematic anti-anthropomorphic policy

Psalms may, however, be the outcome of revisions of the original translation towards a less literal rendering of the anthropomorphisms.[77]

In any case the non-literal translation of anthropomorphisms does not result from the compulsion of religious feeling"[78] since many passages employ "unmitigated anthropomorphic expressions in speaking of God".[79] Furthermore, the hermeneutics of the Targums do not represent a unified theological system. Rather a multiplicity of theological conceptions is involved, which may even include contradictory tendencies.[80] One reason for treating the LXX and the Targums on the same level, apart from the usage in Erwin's dissertation, is that, according to Orlinsky, they were derived from comparable Jewish communities and intended for a similar target group.[81] The original Sitz im Leben of the Targum as well as the LXX was the synagogue.[82] But the motivation for a non-literal translation of many of the anthropomorphisms in the Targums was not purely negative, to eliminate them in order to protect the readers from potentially misleading and improper expressions about Yahweh. The translators' main objective was probably positive; they were anxious to relate the biblical text to the everyday situation of ordinary people in a synagogue context, thus to edify and instruct. At the same time many non-literal renderings conformed to idiomatic Aramaic and were also used in connection with man.[83]

Erwin tries to explain the fact that most of the terms describing God with human attributes are rendered literally in LXX Psalms as the result of a tension between a literal and an allegorical interpretation, which, according to him, by definition are theological categories.[84] This tension is thus manifested in the work of one and the same translator.[85] Erwin offers some modifications: "This is not to say that the translator of the Septuagint is at one and the same time a strict literalist and an allegorist, an obvious paradox. He is rather the heir and perpetuator of a living theological tradition in which both literal and allegorical elements interact and modify each other."[86] This description does not tally with his guesses concerning the life of the Jewish community. He describes the allegorical and the literal school of interpretation as "fractions within the synagogue".[87] It is true that the understanding of anthropomorphisms was a controversial issue in rabbinic discussions, but to postulate a strict polarization between two schools of interpretation from an early date is open to criticism.[88]

The origin of Jewish anti-anthropomorphism is also obscure. We know that in the 1st–2nd century A.D. two distinct schools had emerged; one interpreted biblical anthropomorphisms literally, while the other regarded them as allegorical.[89] But as a matter of fact, the tension which can and often does exist in a translation rather concerns different aspects of literality, because literal and free techniques of translation were not fundamentally contradictory tendencies in ancient biblical translation. All aspects of literalism are not necessarily interrelated and some of

---

in the Targums, now an antiquated view, see especially the references in Klein, op. cit., p. IX n. 12-19, pp. 9 n. 12 and 22 n. 1-3.

[77] Shunary, **Psalms**, pp. 142, 144.

[78] Shunary, **Psalms**, p. 133.

[79] Shunary, **Psalms**, p. 133.

[80] Patte, **Hermeneutic**, pp. 74-76.

[81] Orlinsky, **Introductory Essay** in Zlotowitz, **Jeremiah**, p. XXIII.

[82] Patte, **Hermeneutic**, pp. 54-55.

[83] Chester, **Revelation**, pp. 284, 289-291, 374-382.

[84] See Erwin, pp. 24-25. The term allegorical interpretation gives, however, a wrong impression of the freer aspects of the translation technique in LXX Psalms, and for that matter, in LXX as a whole.

[85] I presuppose that LXX Psalms is the work of a single translator. See **Flashar**, p. 85 n. 1, **Soffer**, pp. 96-97.

[86] **Erwin**, p. 25.

[87] **Erwin**, p. 40 n. 1. Cf. ibid., pp. 24-25.

[88] See Chester, **Revelation**, pp. 288-289 and n. 58.

[89] See Klein, **Pentateuch**, p. VI. Cf. **Erwin**, p. 25 n. 2.

them are in fact at variance with each other.[90] This is perhaps what puzzles Gehman when he suggests that one may find "in the same verse or in adjacent verses both literalism and extreme freedom of translation side by side ... as if the interpreter was working under a tension between literalism and freedom of rendering".[91]

The use of anti-anthropomorphisms seems to be a fairly common characteristic of both Alexandrian and Palestinian exegesis,[92] even though the main concern of the Rabbis was not to avoid anthropomorphism.[93] An anti-anthropomorphic tendency is clearly evidenced in the Jewish Apocryphal and Apocalyptic literature from the 2nd century B.C. onwards, with the exception of Jubilees, Ethiopian and Slavonic Enoch and 3 Maccabees.[94] It may have started much earlier, maybe even during the exile. In particular attempts were made to avoid statements considered derogatory to God, not least those implying that he could be literally seen.[95] But the conventional understanding of an early, steadily growing, opposition to anthropomorphisms in the OT itself is not shared by all.[96] The religious outlook with reference to the rendering of anthropomorphisms which is sketched by Erwin is by no means impossible a priori in the time and the milieu of the translator. But the Jewish congregations in Egypt hardly constituted a milieu characterized by a unified theological approach. As in Palestine the divergence of theological views was great.[97]

The cultural milieu of the translator of the Psalms

In an investigation of theological exegesis it is advisable to take the translator's cultural environment into account. The translation in one way or another reflects the milieu of the translator. This milieu certainly affected his choice of equivalents and of general translation technique.[98] A highly specialized, purely linguistic, approach to the issues of translation technique as well as textual criticism is not to be recommended.[99] Translation cannot be reduced to a question of certain techniques which were consistently carried out and can be described in detail, even though some of the translators and revisers of the LXX did their best to fulfil such a description. The translators were after all human beings and the art of translation has many irrational aspects.

Thus it is reasonable that Erwin has tried to give a plausible religious background to the suggested anti-anthropomorphic tendency in LXX Psalms.[100] It is important to find an environment in which the translator can be placed. But a conjectured theological milieu must, apart from being documented at the place and time of the translation,[101] be confirmed by an analysis of the translation technique

---

[90] See Olofsson, **LXX Version**, pp. 15–26. The Targums are good examples of the combination of different aspects of translation technique. See Rabin, **Character**, p. 24, and Olofsson, op. cit., p. 20 and n. 167, 168.

[91] Gehman, **Adventures**, p. 102.

[92] Olofsson, **LXX Version**, p. 5 n. 37.

[93] See Dahl, Segal, **Philo**, p. 26 and n. 72.

[94] Erwin, pp. 28–30.

[95] Caird, **Language**, pp. 73–75, 127, 176.

[96] See e.g. Barr, **Theophany**, pp. 33–38. Cf. **Erwin**, p. 37 and n. 4–5.

[97] For a discussion of the LXX translators and their environment, see Olofsson, **LXX Version**, pp. 2–5.

[98] See e.g. **Sailhamer**, pp. 1–6, 9, 222–225, Olofsson, **LXX Version**, pp. 1–2. Cf. Tov, **Septuagint**, p. 83, Tov, **Bibelübersetzungen**, pp. 145–146.

[99] Cf. the justified warnings of Goshen-Gottstein concerning the negative effect of a too marked specialization in text critical work. Goshen-Gottstein, **Textual Criticism**, pp. 379–384, 385 and n. 70.

[100] Erwin, pp. 25–30.

[101] It cannot be taken for granted that all LXX books were translated in Alexandria. Some books may have had a Palestinian origin. See Olofsson, **LXX Version**, p. 54 and n. 32, 33. The project of trans-

or at least not be inconsistent with it. The influence from a cultural milieu can hardly be regarded as plausible if the general translation technique and choice of vocabulary consistently negate it.

Erwin's criticism of Soffer on the ground that his study does not deal with the cultural background and the motives behind the translation[102] is, however, ill-founded since the basic investigation of translation technique must be complete before questions concerning theological exegesis can be raised and adequately answered.[103] This is not least important as regards the translation of the Psalms since both the place[104] and the time of the translation are open to discussion.[105]

Erwin tried to connect the theological attitude of the translator with that of Hellenistic Jewry in Egypt, especially Philo. It is hard to tell whether Philo's outlook was really representative of the religious climate of the Jews of Alexandria when the translation of the Psalms was made.[106] Although Philo often allegorized the Scriptures he was not among the most radical allegorizers in Alexandria, but rather held an intermediate position.[107] Thus his preference for an allegorical or mystical interpretation of the OT generally did not signify that he rejected the literal meaning.[108] The allegorical interpretation which Philo represented flourished in the first century A.D.,[109] even though isolated examples of this approach appear at the time of the translation of the Psalter, e.g. Aristobolus' commentary on the Pentateuch.[110]

But allegory was only one of Philo's methods. He came to terms with the anthropomorphic imagery in three ways; through allegorization, through ascription of the anthropomorphisms to the pedagogical wisdom of Moses, or by referring them to subordinate powers of God.[111] Not even Philo tried to abandon the anthropomorphic imagery of the OT completely.[112]

It is a matter of dispute how much his interpretation of the Scriptures, not least his theories concerning the meaning of the designations יהוה and אלהים, are based on well-established Midrashic traditions.[113] The Sitz im Leben of the Midrash, especially the Haggaic Midrash, was the preaching of the synagogue,[114] which could serve as a link with LXX, since its use in the synagogue service was one of the major reasons for this translation.[115] Erwin also suggests that both

---

lating the Hebrew OT was protracted since the Palestinian Jews' canonical books may have taken at least 150 years to complete from the beginning in 275-250 B.C. If the Apocrypha are included the translation was hardly finished before the turn of the era. For a modern discussion regarding the dating of the translation project, see e.g. Caird, **Ben Sira**, pp. 95-100.

[102] See **Erwin**, p. 3.

[103] Unfortunately, Erwin has done the reverse, or wholly disregarded the ordinary translation equivalents to the Hebrew terms he studies. See also below.

[104] See especially Venetz, **Quinta**, pp. 80-84, and van der Kooij, **Origin**, pp. 68-74, which state that the Book of Psalms was translated in Palestine, even though the arguments are far from convincing. See Munnich, **La Septante**, pp. 75-89.

[105] The Book of Psalms may have been translated in 150-100 B.C. See Olofsson, **LXX Version**, p. 43 n. 8. But e.g. Briggs suggests the first part of the second century B.C. Briggs, **Psalms I**, p. XXV.

[106] See Goodenough, **Philo**, pp. 796, 798. Orlinsky denies this. Orlinsky, **Holy Writ**, p. 108. But Erwin seems to take it for granted. See **Erwin**, pp. 25-28, 39-43. Cf. also pp. 45-46, 51-55 and passim. For a discussion of the religious milieu in Alexandria, see Olofsson, **LXX Version**, pp. 2-5.

[107] See Dahl, Segal, **Philo**, p. 26.

[108] Goodenough, **Philo**, p. 797.

[109] Hamerton-Kelly, **Allegorical Commentary**, pp. 51-52.

[110] See **Wacholder**, pp. 59, 262 n. 9.

[111] Dahl, Segal, **Philo**, p. 26. See also ibid., pp. 6-9.

[112] Caird, **Language**, p. 176.

[113] See Marmorstein, **Doctrine**, pp. 44, 49, Dahl, Segal, **Philo**, pp. 1-3 and n. 4-6. For arguments in favour of Philo's dependence upon Jewish traditions, see ibid., pp. 3-28. Cf. Brooke, **Qumran**, p. 18 with references.

[114] Hamerton-Kelly, **Allegorical Commentary**, pp. 48-49 and n. 10, 11.

[115] See Olofsson, **LXX Version**, p. 9 and n. 77.

Mishna and the Targums could shed light on the theological presuppositions of the translators.[116] Although the immediate antecedents of Mishna cannot be traced further back than 30 A.D., it is not improbable that it included traditions of great antiquity.[117] The tradition behind the Targums also seems to be pre-Christian.[118]

Thus one can hardly confine Philo solely to the role of exponent of Greek philosophy in the Alexandrian Jewish community.[119] Philo's exegetical method is neither essentially Greek nor Jewish since the Hellenistic culture set the scene for similar exegetical techniques in both Palestine and Alexandria.[120]

But one may seriously question whether it is possible to see a connection between the literal translation of the Psalter[121] and the hermeneutics of Philo and other more or less allegorical interpreters. Indeed, LXX Psalms as a translation is in opposition to the allegorical interpretations of Philo and the anthropomorphisms are as a rule rendered literally. Unfortunately one cannot avoid the impression that the religious and cultural background of the translation as outlined by Erwin is not proven by a few, isolated, renderings which deviate from a "neutral", "natural" translation, especially since some of them are, as we shall see later in this dissertation, in perfect harmony with the translation technique of LXX Psalms.

1.4   METHODICAL BACKGROUND TO THE STUDY OF THEOLOGICAL EXEGESIS

The investigation of the possible theological motivations of the LXX translators is an interesting, but complicated task. As we have seen many scholarly studies of theological exegesis in the LXX lack an adequate methodological basis. In consequence few previous studies were firmly based on a comprehensive knowledge of the translation technique adopted.[122] The investigations sometimes pay no attention to the situation of the LXX translators and frequently conclude with premature references to later interpretations and traditions. Discussions of theological motives for a certain rendering must derive from a familiarity with the translator's method and the basic problems which he faces. This task has been been much neglected.[123] A thorough study of the translator's knowledge of Hebrew and the translation technique employed is a prerequisite for the investigation of conscious theological exegesis in the LXX. In many cases the translator did not know the meaning of the Hebrew text in question.

Since my study seeks to examine conscious theological exegesis I must be able to distinguish between kinds of theological exegesis. It is possible to separate conscious theological exegesis from the kind of influence from the cultural milieu which is part of the ordinary translation process by tracing a difference between the translation equivalents as regards certain terms when they are used of God and when they are used of man; but also to consider the translation technique in

---

[116] Cf. Olofsson, **LXX Version**, pp. 4-5 and n. 31-35.

[117] Erwin, p. 4.

[118] McNamara, **Targums**, p. 860. The written forms of most of the Palestinian Targums probably antedate the second Jewish revolt in A.D. 132. Ibid., p. 859. But cf. p. 858. An investigation of Brown, based on the foreign vocabulary in both the LXX and the Targums, suggests that the literary relationship is vice versa, i.e. the Targums are dependent on the LXX. Brown, **Loan-words**, pp. 196-197, 216.

[119] Brooke, **Qumran**, p. 25. Some interaction with contemporary Judaism can certainly be demonstrated. Ibid., p. 25. For parallels with Targumic interpretations, see ibid., p. 27 and n. 124, and for the use of pre-Rabbinic exegetical methods, see ibid., p. 11.

[120] Brooke, **Qumran**, p. 18. Cf. Olofsson, **LXX Version**, pp. 4-5, n. 29, 36.

[121] See Olofsson, **LXX Version**, p. 77 n. 26.

[122] Cf. Olofsson, **LXX Version**, p. 2 n. 11, 12. Flashar's article, albeit not exclusively concerned with the theological exegesis in the translation, is an exception. See **Flashar**, passim. For a better approach to the study of the influence from theological exegesis in the Book of Psalms, see **Soffer**, pp. 85-105.

[123] Cf. e.g. the deficiences in this respect in Fritsch, **Studies**.

the rendering of metaphors in contrast to words with a literal meaning. Particularly divergences from the ordinary translation equivalents may reveal theological motives for the choice of rendering.

It is true that the ordinary counterparts to Hebrew words may sometimes have been chosen on account of specific theological tenets, but this is hard to demonstrate with any certainty, at least without a profound knowledge of the religious connotations of certain terms in the environment of the translators. This knowledge presupposes access to a very extensive background material of original Hellenistic texts outside the LXX.

The deviation of a rendering from an adequate interpretation from a modern perspective or from a literal translation is not per se a reason for postulating theological motives behind the translation. On the contrary, it is only natural that the LXX translator has an interpretation distinct from what we would have expected in a modern translation; if the situation of the translators is taken into account. The choice of an odd rendering from the semantic point of view often accords with the translation technique in use or can be attributed to a lack of lexical or grammatical knowledge on the part of the translator.[124]

Methodologically speaking it is of paramount importance to leave all possibilities of interpretation open, in order to prevent specific presuppositions from influencing the results of the investigation. If theological exegesis in the translation is discussed no attempt should be made thus to interpret all renderings which can be explained as theologically motivated, but the probability of this interpretation should be weighed against other possible interpretations.[125] Many of the expressions which are not literally translated, and have been adduced as evidence of an anti-anthropomorphic tendency, are idioms, frequently employed also when God is not involved. This is true for the Targums as well as the Septuagint.[126]

Thus other possible explanations must be investigated before we can approach with confidence the complex problems concerning ideology and theology reflected in the Septuagint:[127]

> Methodologically speaking, however, an argument based on the formal aspects of a given text should take precedence over an argument based on its possible 'Tendencies'. Tendenzkritik is very much exposed to the fantasies and the biases of each exegete.[128]

1.4.1 Theological exegesis in the ordinary choice of equivalents

In some cases it might be reasonable to find a theological motivation for the employment of a certain vocabulary in the translation, even if it is not an exception to the general translation technique since most of the exegetical elements are reflected in the lexical choices.[129] One example might be the use of the term τὸ ἅγιον for the temple in Jerusalem, instead of the more natural τὸ ἱερόν, which was often reserved for heathen temples.[130]

---

[124] Regarding the translation techniques employed in LXX and the standard of Hebrew knowledge among the translators, see especially Olofsson, **LXX Version**, pp. 12–32.

[125] See Wigtil, **Religious Texts**, p. 26.

[126] Klein, **Pentateuch**, pp. XIII, XX. For examples, see ibid., pp. XIII–XIX.

[127] By the term Septuagint (or LXX), I refer to the original translation, the so-called "Old Greek". For the misuse of the term "LXX" in modern scholarship, see Greenspoon, **LXX**, passim. It is self-evident that the Old Greek must as far as possible be the basis for a study of the intentions of the translator. See e.g. Pace, **Tendenz**, p. 15.

[128] Trebolle, **Redaction**, p. 25. For a more detailed description of the kind of methodical approach employed in this dissertation, see Olofsson, **Jer 2,18**, pp. 169–200.

[129] See Tov, **Septuagint**, p. 83.

[130] See Flashar, p. 245 n. 2, Schrenk, ἱερός, p. 232:32–47. This does not apply to 1–4 Macc. Ibid.,

But Barr strongly criticizes the opinion that τὸ ἱερόν was avoided for theological reasons. His main objections are that the choice of ἅγιος for קדוש is natural from a semantic point of view, since the meanings of the two words largely coincide, and that the LXX translators would hardly be embarrassed by its pagan associations since ἱερός is sometimes employed in connection with the temple in Jerusalem.[131] The difference in the frequency of the term τὸ ἱερόν for the Jerusalem temple in LXX and in non-Septuagintal Jewish literature, including the NT, may partly be explained by the translation character of the LXX, especially the frequent employment of stereotyped renderings. Barr also suggests the appearance of a general bias in ThWNT towards finding a Hebrew-Greek theological contrast or even a prejudgement of how the choice of equivalents in LXX was influenced by the use of certain words in a pagan context.[132]

A similar but more convincing case is the distribution of θυσιαστήριον, a word which may even have been coined by the LXX translators.[133] It is a rendering of מזבח as referring to an altar dedicated to Yahweh, while in many books a heathen altar[134] was designated with one of the usual Koine terms for an altar, βωμός. In the Hellenistic epoch the term was especially employed for an altar with a base, an erected altar, used for offerings to the Olympic gods.[135] θυσιαστήριον could without distinction be employed for different kinds of altar, in line with the use of מזבח in MT.[136] Another common word for an altar ἐσχάρα, which originally referred to a "sacrificial heart (hollowed out in the ground)", but was often employed as a generic term for an altar,[137] was never used as an equivalent to מזבח in LXX. But this can hardly be justified on theological grounds since it rendered, inter alia, different details in the tabernacle such as מִכְבָּר "grating", רֶשֶׁת "network", Ex 27:4,[138] כַּרְכֹּב "edge", "rim (of altar)", 27:5, and גָּג "top slab (of altar of incense)", 30:3.

In some of the cases discussed above it is not possible to exclude a direct theological influence on the choice of equivalents for different objects, but it is not easy to prove the involvement of conscious theological exegesis. Without the support of a semantic and a translation technical analysis the postulation of a specific theological motive remains pure conjecture. A theological interpretation of the choice of a certain vocabulary in the LXX must be based on a thorough investigation of the religious and cultural milieu.[139] Cf. the statement of Sailhamer:

---

pp. 232:40-233:3. Josephus and NT employ τὸ ἱερόν for the temple in Jerusalem without hesitation. Schrenk, ἱερός, pp. 233:26-236:26. See also Borse, τὸ ἱερόν, col. 430. For the avoidance of ἱερός with cognates for קדוש generally, see especially Schrenk, op. cit., pp. 225:46-226:15. Regarding the employment of the Greek term among the Hellenistic Jews and in the Old Testament, see ibid., pp. 226:16-229:30, and for its religious use in non-biblical Greek, see ibid., pp. 222:25-225:45, 230:32-232:30.

[131] Furthermore, ἅγιος was in fact a term as deeply involved in the terminology of pagan cults as ἱερός. For the use of ἅγιος in a pagan religious context, see especially Procksch, ἅγιος, pp. 87:15-88:21.

[132] Barr, Semantics, pp. 283-286.

[133] Daniel, p. 27, Lee, Pentateuch, p. 52.

[134] The Pentateuch, Joshua, Isaiah and Jeremiah. Daniel, pp. 16-22. See also Barr, Homoeophony, pp. 23-27, Dohmen, מזבח, cols. 789, 798, Behm, θύω, p. 182 n. 8. Philo and Josephus, who lived in a period more open to Hellenism, do not make any distinction in the use of these terms. Ibid., p. 182 n. 8.

[135] Daniel, p. 26, LSJ. Cf. Barr, Homoeophony, p. 23.

[136] Dohmen, מזבח, cols. 792, 793-799, Behm, θύω, p. 182:30-38.

[137] See LSJ, Daniel, p. 26. ἐσχάρα had a fairly wide semantic range. See LSJ.

[138] Cf. BHS where it is suggested that the LXX translator had מִכְבָּר, a mis-spelling of מִכְבָּר, instead of רשת in his Vorlage, but this is hardly necessary since ἐσχάρα renders nine different Hebrew words out of 13 occurrences with a Hebrew Vorlage. See HR.

[139] Cf. Barr, Semantics, p. 276.

14

The study will also help lay the basis for the control of the contribution of the LXX to an understanding of the social and religious history of the period of the translation ... Only a close study and description of as many factors as possible lying behind the translation can hope to uncover this subjective moment in the text.[140]

1.4.2 Delimitations and methodical procedure

My investigation of theological exegesis concerns two areas of research, anthropomorphisms and inanimate metaphorical names or epithets. First I shall investigate the most convincing cases of suggested theological exegesis from the examples of Erwin and Fritsch. I shall discuss selected anti-anthropomorphisms and anti-anthropopathisms in LXX Psalms but concentrate my efforts on some of the examples of theological toning down discussed by Erwin and Fritsch. A sector where the theology of the translator seems to have had a great influence is the rendering of metaphorical divine titles, and the main part of my dissertation is devoted to the different designations of God. The investigations of Erwin and Fritsch list equivalents in LXX Psalms to metaphorical names of God.[141] A theological motivation of the choice of equivalents has been suggested as regards צור, סלע, מגן, מעוז, מעון, מחסה מצודה and משגב. It is hardly the question of anti-anthropomorphisms proper, but Erwin says that the rendering of divine titles is "characterized by reverence and restraint"[142] and that "anti-anthropomorphisms will be found in the section under Divine Titles and Liturgy."[143]

To give an indication of the translation technique as regards these inanimate metaphorical names I shall present the Greek equivalents, first in the Book of Psalms but also in LXX at large, and contrast them with the renderings of these Hebrew terms in other contexts, first and foremost in the Book of Psalms, and draw preliminary conclusions regarding the translation technique. The text-critical issues, the meaning of the Hebrew metaphors per se and in context, the interpretation of these terms in the LXX as well as the technique adopted in the choice of equivalents generally and in the individual passages is taken into account. A background for the use of certain of the names will be given. Later on the translation technique of these divine designations as a whole is discussed and a possible Sitz im Leben suggested.

In order to investigate which factors are involved in the choice of non-literal equivalents of names or epithets based on inanimate nature, in this dissertation often called inanimate metaphorical names or inanimate metaphorical epithets, I shall study the choice of vocabulary in LXX for diverse designations of God; names or epithets based on inanimate nature, עז, אבן, קרן, מרום, צבאות, an epithet or a name which may have had a metaphorical character in the eyes of the translators, שדי, a metaphor based on the activities or capacity of man, i.e. what may called an anthropological metaphor, עזר, a designation of Yahweh which may have referred to a bull, i.e. a theriomorphic name, אביר, and a non-metaphorical name or epithet, עליון. Tentative conclusions regarding the choice of equivalents and the translation technique are drawn and possible sources of influence discussed.

I shall examine the relation between the Greek equivalents to inanimate metaphorical designations of God and to a certain degree both the frequency and the distribution of literal and metaphorical senses of the Hebrew terms, since these may throw light on certain aspects of the semantic development of Hebrew words. Further, I shall relate LXX:s translation technique to the renderings of these names

---

[140] Sailhamer, p. 9.
[141] Erwin, pp. 56-78, Fritsch, **Studies**, pp. 741-730. See also **Flashar**, pp. 243-244, Bertram, **Sprachschatz**, pp. 93-101, Dell'Acqua, **Roccia**.
[142] Erwin, p. 56.
[143] Erwin, p. 6.

or epithets in other Greek versions in order to see whether similar equivalents or translation techniques are evidenced there or whether LXX, primarily the Book of Psalms, is isolated in this respect. The question of the influence from theological exegesis on the non-literal renderings of certain names or epithets is compared with the role which may have been played by linguistic factors. Eventually, a proposed Sitz im Leben of the Greek renderings of inanimate metaphorical names or epithets of God will be discussed.

Three categories of metaphorical divine names are considered; the metaphor used as a form of address, as a designation, and as a characterization of the actualization of Yahweh ("charakterisierung einer Selbstaktualisierung Jahwes").[144] But I shall not differentiate these categories. They will all be termed variously "divine names", "names of God", "designations of God" without discrimination. Eichhorn divides צור into several different classes. But since he himself concludes that none of these divisions have a bearing on the function of this Hebrew word as a divine name, he does not continue with the classification.[145] Furthermore, the choice of equivalents in LXX has no relation whatsoever to these categories. I therefore refrain from a subdivision of the material on that basis. The only distinction made from the outset concerns passages in which the Hebrew word is regarded as a designation of God, according to my definition, and borderline cases where the metaphor is closely connected with Yahweh. Eichhorn's work is used in order to determine which passages to include under the designation "divine names or divine epithets" and not for any classification thereof. The opinions of other scholars are of course also reflected. In HAL the inclusion of passages seems to be more restricted, but otherwise no systematic difference is visible.

In general Rahlfs' edition of LXX is the textual basis of this dissertation, but for the Book of Psalms the Göttingen edition, i.e. Psalmi cum Odis, is used, and for Jeremiah, which will be thoroughly discussed in 5.9, the text of Ziegler. Texts in which recensional activity may be suspected will also be noted. For convenience sake the translations of Hebrew texts are taken from RSV (1st ed.) and Greek texts from the translation by Brenton, unless otherwise stated. But misleading translations and renderings based on an inferior text will be corrected. The order of the books is that of RSV not the Hebrew Bible. The connotation and denotation of the Hebrew and Greek words in context will also be discussed wherever pertinent.

---

[144] This description is based on the work of Eichhorn and only comprises the names discussed in chap. 3. Eichhorn, pp. 30, 89-91.
[145] Eichhorn, p. 92.

Chapter II

THEOLOGICAL EXEGESIS IN THE BOOK OF PSALMS

2.1   THE AVOIDANCE OF ATTRIBUTING PHYSICAL FORM TO GOD

A field where theological presuppositions may have exerted an influence comprises expressions for "seeing God". The textual traditions of the OT, including the versions, reveal a growing suspicion of expressions which suggest that Yahweh could be seen by the ordinary Israelite or leaders among the people or by cultic functionaries.[1] This may be part of a theological development which is manifest in both Palestinian and Hellenistic Judaism, to emphasize the invisibility of God.[2] The rendering of these expressions in the passive in LXX is often attributed to a conscious theological exegesis on the part of the translator.

One of the reasons for this theological tradition is probably that "to see God" originally meant to see the image of God in the temple so that the expression could be misinterpreted, especially in a pagan context, even though it in OT is often a stereotyped phrase for visiting the sanctuary.[3] Thus it is a common understanding that the translator of the Book of Psalms shrinks from saying "to see God", 62 (63):3, or "to see the face of God", 16 (17):15, for theological reasons when that was the meaning of the text in MT.[4] The same is true of cases where the original, contrary to MT, may have said "to see the face of God". See, for example, 41 (42):3, where the active voice is evidenced in both Peshitta and the Targum and in some Hebrew manuscripts,[5] and 83 (84):8, where an original with the expression "to see God" may be conjectured. See, for example, BHK.

It is possible that the renderings in LXX reflect some kind of theological exegesis, but I shall try to modify this assertion with the situation of the translator as the point of departure. Thus if a rendering only presupposes a different pointing from that of MT one may not assume that it reflects a deliberate attempt to avoid an anthropomorphism which was offensive for the theology of the translator. One must be aware that he was dealing with an unpointed, even if not unvocalized, text; the vocalization or at least the interpretation was partly implied by the employment of matres lectionis at an early date.[6] The verb could often be understood as either active or passive; both would have been justified by the unpointed Hebrew text. This may suggest that the translator has written down what he regarded as the meaning of the Hebrew, or that he has based the rendering on a reading tradition at his disposal. His interpretation would then in practice reflect a later stage in the development of a theological tradition which is evidenced in MT too, but not be the result of deliberate theological exegesis.

---

[1] Cf. **Eichhorn**, pp. 85–87.

[2] Cf. **Erwin**, pp. 25–30.

[3] See e.g. Gunkel, **Psalmen**, p. 41, Anderson, **Psalms**, pp. 330, 605, Michaelis, ὁράω, p. 325 n. 58. Cf. Olofsson, **LXX Version**, p. 1 and n. 2, 3.

[4] **Mozley**, pp. XV, 100, Flashar, p. 247, Wutz, **Psalmen**, p. 247, **Erwin**, p. 38, Fritsch, **Studies**, pp. 734–733.

[5] See BHK, BHS, **Baetgen**, p. 630, Briggs, **Psalms I**, p. 372, Wutz, **Psalmen**, pp. 106–107, Fritsch, **Studies**, p. 733 n. 28, Kraus, **Psalmen**, p. 472.

[6] See Tov, **Septuagint**, p. 161. Concerning the problem of vocalization and interpretation generally, see Olofsson, **LXX Version**, pp. 31–32. For the relation between the translation technique and the level of the text, i.e. a pointed or an unpointed text, see ibid., pp. 24–25.

Another factor which may have been of some importance is that the translator, in line with Jewish tradition generally, understood the Scriptures as a theological unit. He was then to some extent obliged to make a translation which was in harmony with religious logic and expressed some kind of theological consistency. See 1.1. He could hardly be expected to believe that the Holy Writ contained texts which ought to be interpreted contrary to the important theological doctrine in Ex 33:20:

ויאמר לא תוכל לראת את-פני כי לא-יראני האדם וחי

But, "he said", you cannot see my face; for man shall not see me and live".

καὶ εἶπεν οὐ δυνήσῃ ἰδεῖν μου τό πρόσωπον; οὐ γὰρ ἴδῃ ἄνθρωπος τό πρόσωπόν μου καὶ ζήσεται

God said, Thou shalt not be able to see my face; for no man shall see my face, and live.[7]

The translator cannot be accused of an anti-anthropomorphic attitude if he was only writing down his natural linguistic and exegetical interpretation of the Vorlage in front of him.[8] That theological aspects are not always involved may be surmised from the translation of Ex 10:29 where the same passive understanding of the phrase ראה פנים as we have seen in Ps 41 (42):3 is in fact evidenced in LXX with reference to men.[9]

The translator's interpretation was naturally influenced by passages in the Pentateuch where MT says the "sight of God" rather than "to see God". See Ex 23:15, 17; 34:20, 23, 24; Deut 16:16; 31:11, where both MT and LXX have a passive voice.[10] Even if the right interpretation of the original text demanded the use of an active verb in 41 (42):3 the LXX translators only shared the presuppositions behind the Massoretic text, which are of course inherent in the linguistic interpretation, i.e. through the pointing of MT.[11] That the development is not unequivocal is shown by Ps 83 (84):8 where LXX had a more anthropomorphic interpretation than MT: ילכו מחיל אל חיל יראה אל-אלהים בציון "They go from strength to strength; he appears before God on Zion"[12] is translated by πορεύσονται ἐκ δυνάμεως εἰς δύναμιν, ὀφθήσεται ὁ θεὸς τῶν θεῶν ἐν Σιών "They shall go from strength to strength: the God of gods shall be seen on Zion."[13]

But how should one understand passages where the translator had to alter the consonants in order to be able to translate in the passive voice. This may be the case in, for example, Ps 62 (63):3, according to many scholars, where חזיתיך is rendered by ὤφθην σοι "appeared before thee".[14] But that חזה only occurs in qal in MT is not an insuperable obstacle to the understanding in LXX since the translator was not equipped with modern lexica and could thus have understood it as pual. In fact he had no access to any elementary linguistic tools, such as lexica, concordances and grammars. See 1.2.1. There are certainly passages in the Pentateuch

---

[7] For the use of the Pentateuch as a textbook and commentary for later LXX translators, see Olofsson, **LXX Version**, pp. 26–28. Not least the choice of interpretation in the Pentateuch influenced the wording of the other LXX books. Tov, **Impact**, p. 590.

[8] This may apply to at least 16 (17):15 and 62 (63):3. See the careful discussion in **Soffer**, pp. 89–92, especially p. 91.

[9] See BHS, Rahlfs and **Mozley**, p. 30, **Soffer**, p. 90. In 10:28 it is, on the other hand, translated in an active voice.

[10] Cf. **Soffer**, p. 90.

[11] This text is the implicit or explicit point of departure for the translation technical investigations of the LXX. See the discussion in Olofsson, **LXX Version**, pp. 65–67.

[12] Since RSV emends in v. 8b I have made a literal translation of this passage. Cf. Anderson, **Psalms**, p. 605.

[13] Cf. **Mozley**, pp. XV, 30, **Soffer**, p. 92.

[14] Flashar, p. 247. Cf. **Baetgen**, pp. 419–420, **Mozley**, p. 100, **Erwin**, p. 38.

where the text was paraphrased in order to avoid the plain meaning of the Hebrew. One of the best examples is the LXX rendering of Ex 24:11: ויחזו את-האלהים "they beheld God" is translated by καὶ ὤφθησαν ἐν τῷ τόπῳ τοῦ θεοῦ "and they appeared in the place of God".[15]

The rendering in 62 (63):3 may also have been based on a variant reading which only existed in the translator's mind, a so-called pseudo-variant.[16] This pseudo-variant could reflect an unconscious influence from the passages where MT or LXX had the verb in a passive voice. Ps 63:3 is, however, difficult to interpret. The meaning of the verb חזה in this context is far from obvious. It must signify "to watch for" rather than "to see", "to behold" if emendations should be avoided.[17] Thus it is not to be taken for granted that the text included an expression which must be interpreted as "to see God".

Four important reservations can be made to the interpretation that the renderings under discussion are examples of a deliberate theological exegesis on the part of the translator.

1. The unpointed Hebrew could be understood in either the passive or the active sense.

2. The rendering is based on a, theologically motivated, deviating Vorlage, or on a reading tradition deeply rooted in the milieu of the translator.

3. The rendering is a pseudo-variant.

4. The translator based his interpretation on the authority of the Pentateuch without having a theological motivation of his own.

2.2   THE TONING DOWN OF GOD'S DESTRUCTIVE ACTIVITIES

Erwin and Fritsch suggest that there are signs in LXX Psalms of a softening of expressions for God's punishment of man and nature, because such activities were repugnant to the translator's religious outlook.[18] This tendency is examplified by Ps 50 (51):10; 71 (72):4. First we shall examine 50 (51):10: תגלנה עצמות דכית "Let the bones rejoice which Thou hast crushed" is translated by ἀγαλλιάσονται ὀστᾶ τεταπεινωμένα "They shall rejoice, the bones which have been humbled."[19] According to Erwin, דכה "crush" is not translated literally here because it "carried a connotation of anthropomorphic violence offensive to the translator's concept of the spirituality and perfection of God's character."[20] Fritsch emphasizes that the

---

[15] Cf. also v. 10. But even here the possibility that the Vorlage of the translation had this theologically motivated change cannot be excluded since the translation involves an unexpected Hebraism. See Michaelis, ὁράω, p. 332 n. 85.

[16] See Olofsson, **LXX Version**, p. 73 n. 67-69. For a comprehensive discussion, see Tov, **Septuagint**, pp. 228-240.

[17] See Baetgen, **Psalmen**, p. 189, Kraus, **Psalmen**, p. 600, who with hesitation keeps MT. Cf. Dahood, **Psalms II**, p. 97. He interprets the verb as a precative perfect in a circumstantial clause. See also ibid., **Psalms I**, p. 50. Others emend, see Gunkel, **Psalmen**, pp. 267-268, Herkenne, **Psalmen** p. 215. For further references, see Gunkel, op. cit., p. 268, **Soffer**, p. 91. Regarding the translation in the LXX, see especially **Soffer**, pp. 91-92.

[18] Erwin, p. 7, Fritsch, **Studies**, pp. 732-729.

[19] Concerning 50 (51):10; 71 (72):4, see **Erwin**, pp. 11-12, Fritsch, **Studies**, p. 732. In order to do justice to the interpretations of Erwin and Fritsch their renderings are taken as point of departure for all examples. Brenton has the translation "afflicted bones".

[20] Erwin, p. 11. The translator changed the meaning of the verse when he used ταπεινοῦν as equivalent to דכה. Ibid., p. 11. Erwin also suggests that he rendered the finite verb with a circumstantial participle in order to eliminate the personal pronoun which referred to God. Ibid., p. 11. Surely

physical action by God in MT is avoided through the rendering of the finite verb in Hebrew with a participle in Greek, and through the change of the meaning of the original.[21]

The choice of grammatical equivalent is unusual. Hebrew perfect is seldom rendered by a perfect participle in LXX Psalms. Sailhamer could find only one example in the first book in the Psalter, 18 (19):10.[22] But in reality it is only a question of pointing, since וֹ, וֹ could hardly be distinguished in the Hebrew manuscripts from Qumran which are contemporary with the LXX Psalms.[23] This is also evidenced in the LXX translation of the Psalter.[24]

The reluctance to ascribe the destructive activity of דכה "crush" to Yahweh also applied to the 'ideal king', i.e. the Messiah, who, according to an interpretation of the Hellenistic Jews, is mentioned in 72:4:[25] וידכא עושק "And he will crush the oppressor" is rendered by καὶ ταπεινώσει συκοφάντην "And he will humble the slanderer."[26] It is of course impossible to postulate that the linguistic knowledge of the translator equals the knowledge of Hebrew today, or that his understanding as a rule is in line with the meaning suggested in modern Hebrew lexica,[27] which unfortunately seems to be the implicit point of departure for Erwin's interpretation.

In order to form an opinion of the lexical choice of the translator, i.e. the use of ταπεινοῦν for Hebrew דכה and דכא, one should study the ordinary equivalents and if they cannot explain the rendering one could go further and investigate how the translator regarded the destructive activities of Yahweh generally. The translator did not distinguish between דכה and דכא. These verbs are also closely related in meaning. Both mean "crush". Only the participle in niphal of דכא is employed in the sense of "humiliated". See Is 57:15, where probably the whole phrase דכא ושפל-רוח "contrite and humbled spirit" (RSV) or "crushed and humbled spirit"[28] is rendered by ὀλιγόψυχος "faint-hearted". Cf. also דכאי רוח "crushed in spirit" rendered by τοὺς ταπεινοὺς τῷ πνεύματι "the lowly in spirit" in Ps 33 (34):19.

דכה occurs in 10:10; 38:9; 44:20; 51:10, 19 and דכא in 72:4; 89:11; 94:5; 143:3.[29] They are both rendered in the same way. Obviously they were regarded as variant spellings of one and the same verb. This interpretation is further strengthened by the fact that דכה is a word that is found only in poetic texts.[30]

In three instances God is the subject of דכה or דכא in LXX Psalms, 43 (44):20; 50 (51):10; 88 (89):11, and they are always translated by ταπεινοῦν "to humble". This seems to strengthen Erwin's position, because here is an obvious case of a destructive word which is never rendered literally in the Book of Psalms when Yahweh is the subject. But as a matter of fact ταπεινοῦν is also employed as equivalent to דכה, דכא when God is not the subject, 9:31 (10:10); 37 (38):9; 50 (51):19; 93 (94):5; 142 (143):3. The king is the subject of the verb in 71 (72):4, further specified as Solomon in both MT and LXX, v. 1. There is nothing in the

he must mean the subject of the verb since no personal pronoun is involved.
[21] Fritsch, Studies, p. 732.
[22] See Sailhamer, pp. 53–54. Mozley has another solution of the grammatical problem. The translator could have read the verb as דְּבֻּוֹת. Mozley, p. 89.
[23] For a graphical illustration, see the table of scribal alphabets at the end of Martin, Character.
[24] Ottley, Handbook, p. 113.
[25] Thus Erwin, p. 12 n. 1.
[26] Erwin, p. 11. Or "the false accuser" (Brenton).
[27] See Olofsson, LXX Version, p. 11 n. 98.
[28] See HR and Ottley, Isaiah I, p. 290, Isaiah II, p. 358.
[29] See Lisowsky, BHS, Rahlfs, HR and Tsevat, pp. 14, 81 n. 37. The vocalization in 89:11 is that of דכה. See Tsevat, pp. 31, 118 n. 325. This suggests that the Massoretic tradition did not distinguish strictly between the two. The reason for this pointing may be that the Massoretes wanted to exclude דכא from the Psalter. But it may equally well reflect the reading tradition which they adopted. Ibid., p. 118 n. 325.
[30] It only occurs in the Psalter. See Lisowsky, Tsevat, pp. 14, 81 n. 37. Moreover, it seems to be part of a specific psalm language. Ibid., pp. 2–12.

translation of the LXX to suggest that the translator intended a different interpretation. This Hebrew verb is thus always translated by ταπεινοῦν in the Psalms.
What at the outset resembles a deliberate avoidance of an anthropomorphic interpretation proved to be the ordinary, and in fact stereotypical, representation of the
verb. The choice of equivalent may seem slightly odd to us. The expression
"humbled bones" is not really apposite. But the translator did not strive primarily
for an expression which suited the context. In any case it was obviously a term
which fitted his linguistic exegesis.[31] Klein calls such examples of alleged anti-
anthropomorphisms, pseudo-anthropomorphisms.[32]

Thus the choice of equivalent cannot have had the theological motivation
postulated by Erwin. The theory of the translator's theological bias can also be
challenged in more general terms since, according to Flashar, Yahweh,'s
destructive activities especially against his enemies, is in fact rather underlined
than softened in the interpretation of the LXX Psalms.[33] Two religious motives
seem in fact to predominate in the translation of the Psalms; "the centrality of the
law for religious life and the hope of a future judgment for the wicked and reward
for the righteous".[34]

On the other hand, the rendering diverges from the usual equivalents outside
the Psalter, including the Pentateuch. This translation is in fact restricted to the
Psalms, with one exception, Lam 3:34: לדכא תחת רגליו כל אסירי ארץ "To crush
under foot all the prisoners of the earth" is translated by Τοῦ ταπεινῶσαι ὑπὸ
τοὺς πόδας αὐτοῦ πάντας δεσμίους τῆς γῆς "To humble under his feet all the
prisoners of the earth." Except for the Greek term under discussion the translation
is that of Brenton, who has the free rendering "to bring down", in accordance with
the Hebrew, instead of "humble". See LSJ. The translator may have taken over this
interpretation from the LXX Psalms, but there are no signs of assimilation to a
certain passage in the Psalter.[35] The various renderings in LXX as a whole clearly
indicate that the translators generally guessed at the meaning of דכא in piel. See
e.g. ἀδικεῖν "to wrong", Is 3:15, ἀτιμάξειν "dishonour", Prov 22:22, καθαίρειν
"destroy", Job 19:2, παίειν, "smite", Job 4:19, τιτρώσκειν "injure", "wound",
"dispatch", Job 6:9.[36]

ταπεινοῦν is a so-called favourite word in LXX as a whole.[37] It renders nine
different Hebrew terms. Favourite words is a technique frequently employed by the
translator of the Psalms,[38] despite the general literality of the version. The
consistent use of ταπεινοῦν as an equivalent to דבה or דכא reflects two different
translation techniques, consistency, a literal translation technique, and favourite
words, a free translation technique.[39] Favourite words were often used when the
translator could not understand the meaning of the Hebrew[40] and this seems to be
the case here too. The number of mistranslations due to a deficient knowledge of
the Hebrew is much greater than formerly assumed.[41]

It is thus evident that the choice of equivalent to the verb in 50 (51):10 and 71
(72):4 is in line with the translation technique of LXX Psalms. This technique
depends in turn on the somewhat defective knowledge of Hebrew on the part of

---

[31] For a definition of this term, see 1.1. Cf. Barr, **Typology**, pp. 290-293.
[32] See Klein, **Pentateuch**, p. XIII. See his examples from the Targums. Ibid., pp. XIII–XIX.
[33] For an informative description, see Flashar, pp. 259-265, especially p. 263.
[34] **Sailhamer**, p. 223. Cf. **Flashar**, p. 263.
[35] See HR. There are no close Hebrew parallels. See Mandelkern.
[36] See LSJ, Brenton, Rahlfs and Heater, **Job**, p. 103.
[37] For the definition of favourite words, see Barr, **Philology**, pp. 251-253
[38] See Olofsson, **LXX Version**, p. 20 n. 165.
[39] See Olofsson, **LXX Version**, pp. 16-20. Favourite words as a translation technique has in fact many
similarities with the stereotyping tendency. See Olofsson, **LXX Version**, p. 20 n. 165.
[40] See Tov, **Dimensions**, pp. 538, 541-542, Tov, **Septuagint Translators**, pp. 66-67, and Olofsson, **LXX
Version**, p. 20 and n. 163-165. Cf. Olofsson, **LXX Version**, p. 35.
[41] Tov, **Septuagint Translators**, p. 70. See the examples on pp. 55-70 in the same article.

the translator.[42] The rendering of the term in 50 (51):10 is an obvious example of a Verlegenheitsübersetzung,[43] which indirectly confirms the translator's fidelity to the text. Instead of making a free translation which suited the context, he adhered to his stereotypical equivalent.[44] The same technique seems to be applied when the translator of the Psalter was confronted with unique meanings of common verbs,[45] or unusual employment of tenses. He then resorted to a so-called formal equivalency (formal correspondence), rather than guess at the meaning.[46]

Another example of the same theological tendency is found by some scholars in 59 (60):14: והוא יבוס צרינו "And He will tread down our adversaries",[47] which in LXX is interpreted as καὶ αὐτὸς ἐξουδενώσει τοὺς θλίβοντας ἡμᾶς "And He Himself will treat with contempt those afflicting us."[48] An identical Hebrew text appears in 108:14. According to Erwin, the translator deliberately treats בוס "tread down" as if it equals בוז "to despise"[49] in order to avoid the idea that Yahweh would tread down his enemies, a metaphor repugnant to Hellenistic Judaism.[50] The Targum also avoided the anthropomorphism by making the Memra of Yahweh the subject of the clause: "With the Memra of Yah, we will do mightily, and He will tread down our oppressors."[51] But the Memra in the Targums seems to appear "arbitrary and unmotivated by theological considerations", at least in the Pentateuch.[52] It is "a term presumably devoid of any theological content".[53] On the other hand, according to Chester, the use of Memra may have undergone a complicated development in the Targums so that what was once a mere exegetical device has sometimes acquired theological significance.[54]

As regards LXX, the rendering of בוס by ἐξουδενοῦν in 43 (44):6 is probably enough to rule out Erwin's suggestion. בך צרינו ננגח בשמך נבוס קמינו "Through thee we push down our foes; through thy name we treat with contempt our assailants" is translated by ἐν σοὶ τοὺς ἐχθροὺς ἡμῶν κερατιοῦμεν καὶ ἐν τῷ ὀνόματί σου ἐξουθενώσομεν τοὺς ἐπανισταναμένους ἡμῖν "In thee will we push down our enemies, and in thy name will we bring to nought them that rise up against us." In this case it is the Israelites who will "set at naught" (LSJ) their enemies. The explanation must evidently be sought elsewhere. Mozley proposes that the translator confused בוס with a cognate Aramaic or Syriac verb which means "despise".[55] He may be right since the translator sometimes resorted to Aramaic when he did not understand, or did not want to understand, the Hebrew

---

[42] Regarding the LXX:s translators' knowledge of Hebrew generally, see Olofsson, **LXX Version**, pp. 28–32.

[43] A phrase or an idiomatic expression that is rendered by the words which are the most frequent equivalents for the separate terms, even if the meaning of the phrase is obscure. **Mozley**, p. XV, **Flashar**, p. 94, Rabin, **Character**, pp. 23–24.

[44] See **Flashar**, p. 114, Barr, **Typology**, pp. 290, 292–293. Cf. also Olofsson, **LXX Version**, pp. 16–20.

[45] See **Flashar**, pp. 96–114.

[46] **Sailhamer**, pp. 199–205. For the definition of these terms, see e.g. **Nida, Taber**, pp. 200–201.

[47] The translation is that of Erwin. **Erwin**, p. 9. Fritsch has "He will tread upon our foes." Fritsch, **Studies**, p. 732.

[48] **Erwin**, p. 9. Cf. Fritsch, **Studies**, p. 732 "and He will bring to nought those who afflict us". See LSJ.

[49] There are some indications of deliberate mistranslations in the LXX Psalms. See **Erwin**, p. 10. Cf. **Flashar**, p. 251.

[50] **Erwin**, p. 10. Fritsch has the same interpretation. Fritsch, **Studies**, p. 732.

[51] See **Erwin**, p. 9. Erwin suggests that both the Targum and the LXX are trying to avoid an anthropomorpic expression for theological reasons. Ibid., p. 10.

[52] This quotation from another author is cited in Klein, **Pentateuch**, p. XVIII and n. 43.

[53] Klein, **Pentateuch**, p. 125 n. 5. See also the conclusion in **Strack, Billerbeck**, p. 333, regarding the use of Memra in the Targums that it "ist ein einhaltloser, rein formelhafter Ersatz für das Tetragram gewesen". Some scholars suggest that it has a theological sense in some contexts, e.g. creation, revelation and salvation. Klein, op. cit., p. X.

[54] Chester, **Revelation**, pp. 308–313.

[55] **Mozley**, pp. 78, 98. His suggestion is based on the authority of G.R. Driver.

text.[56]

The most probable explanation is, however, that בוס "to tread down" is regarded as a variant form of בוז "to despise" by the translator. בוז is always rendered by ἐξουδενοῦν "set at nought" in LXX Psalms, 43 (44):6; 59 (60):14; 107 (108):14 and בוז as a noun has without exception the equivalent ἐξουδένωσις, 30 (31):19; 118 (119):22; 122 (123):3, 4. It does not occur as a verb in the Psalms. ἐξουδενοῦν is also the most common rendering of בוז in the LXX as a whole. See 2 Kgs 19:21; Songs 8:1, 7; Zech 4:10.

Even though other LXX translators may have had a similar interpretation sporadically, it is only in the Book of Psalms that the two words are identified with each other. In Songs 8:7, where both of them occur, the noun is rendered by ἐξουδένωσις and the verb by ἐξουδενοῦν. בוז is translated by ἐμπαίζειν "mock at" in Prov 27:7: ψυχὴ ἐν πλησμονῇ οὖσα κηρίοις ἐμπαίζει "A full soul scorns honey-combs."[57] See also Jer 12:10 which has μολύνειν "defile": ἐμόλυναν τὴν μερίδα μου "they have defiled my portion". This rendering is, however, in line with the meaning here suggested by the lexica. See KBL, HAL "desecrate".

Only a couple of the translators knew the meaning of בוס. It is rendered by καταπατεῖν "trample down" in Is 18:2, 7; 63:6, 18 and in Zech 10:5 by πατεῖν "tread", "walk". That at least the same theological motives were not involved in the choice of equivalents in Isaiah is obvious from the rendering in Is 63:6 where God is the subject of בוס in MT and of καταπατεῖν in LXX. Remarkably enough, the translator of Isaiah, who otherwise is an unreliable guide to the meaning of the Hebrew, has the most adequate renderings. It cannot be excluded that the Book of Psalms was translated before Isaiah and Zechariah. The lack of knowledge on the part of the translator is then understandable.

Another example of toning down of Yahweh's destructive activities for theological reasons consists in the rendering of 20 (21):10 where יהוה באפו יבלעם "Yahweh will swallow them in His wrath" is rendered by κύριος ἐν ὀργῇ αὐτοῦ συνταράξει αὐτούς "The Lord in His anger will throw them into confusion".[58] Erwin maintains that בלע is translated by συνταράσσειν in order to avoid the anthropomorphism that Yahweh "swallows" someone, which is at variance with the concept of God in Hellenistic Judaism.[59]

In order to evaluate this suggestion one has to consider the meaning of בלע in this connection. According to Erwin, it means "swallow (up)"[60] and that is the point of departure for his argument. This is indeed one meaning of the word, but not the only one. It can also be interpreted as "confuse" and "destroy".[61] In this passage the verb has, according to KBL, HAL, Gesenius, the meaning "destroy" (vertilgen). Cf. Lisowsky, who has it under the heading "to swallow", "to destroy". Maybe also BDB can be interpreted in this way. There are marked differences in the understanding of the word here in the modern translations[62] and to a lesser extent in the commentaries.[63]

---

[56] See **Flashar**, p. 251 and n. 1. Cf. Olofsson, **LXX Version**, p. 29 and n. 241-242.

[57] Cf. BHS and HAL, which read תבוה.

[58] The translations are those of Erwin. **Erwin**, p. 7.

[59] **Erwin**, p. 7. See also **Baetgen**, p. 612, Fritsch, **Studies**, p. 732.

[60] See **Erwin**, p. 7.

[61] See e.g. BDB, Lisowsky. According to some lexica, "confuse" is confined to בלע III, see KBL, HAL, Lisowsky, and "destroy" is regarded as one of the meanings of בלע I piel. See Lisowsky. The existence of a בלע II, with the meaning "reach", "communicate", "spread abroad" is often taken for granted. See KBL, HAL. Cf. Albrektson, **Lamentations**, p. 115, and the references in n. 1.

[62] ASV, RSV have "swallow up", JerB "engulf", NEB "strike down", TEV "devour".

[63] For example, Kissane, **Psalms I**, p. 92, has "destroy", referring to 2 Sam 20:19, 20, Weiser, **Psalmen**, ad loc. "consume", Briggs, **Psalms I**, pp. 183, 188, "swallow ... up", Baetgen, **Psalmen**, p. 61, Gunkel, **Psalmen**, p. 85, Kittel, **Psalmen**, p. 79, Herkenne, **Psalmen**, p. 103 and Kraus, **Psalmen**, p. 314, all have the literal rendering "verslingen".

The commentaries and translations which have the rendering "destroy" can hardly be accused of a conscious softening of the anthropomorphisms of the original for theological reasons.[64] If בלע means "destroy" in this context, which is very probable, there is no such offensive metaphor involved, at least from the standpoint of the modern translator; this in fact is the implicit point of departure for both Erwin and Fritsch. But the crux is of course the translator's understanding of this verb generally.[65] One must therefore delineate the ordinary equivalents to בלע in LXX Psalms. The translator was acquainted with the meaning "swallow (up)", since his ordinary translation of בלע in qal, piel and hithpael is καταπίνειν "drown", "devour", 34 (35):25; 68 (69):16; 105 (106):17; 106 (107):27; 123 (124):3, but he was evidently unaware of the sense "destroy", 20 (21):10 (KBL, HAL), or "confuse", "be confused", 54 (55):10; 107 (108):27, (KBL, HAL and Lisowsky). It is rendered by καταποντίζειν "throw into the sea", "drown" in 54 (55):10 and in 107 (108):27 it has the equivalent καταπίνειν, which ought to be translated "drown", "drowning". The rendering in Brenton "destroy", "destruction" does not have the support of LSJ.

On the other hand, בלע in 51 (52):6, where it is translated by καταποντισμός, and probably also in 54 (55):10 means "communicate", "report", i.e. it is to be put under the root בלע II in KBL, HAL.[66] The translator of the Psalms seems as a rule to follow the ordinary rendering in the LXX, καταπίνειν, even though καταποντίζειν is also common.

In fact none of the LXX translators knew of any other meaning than "swallow (up)", "devour". In Is 3:12; 9:15; 19:3; 28:7 (KBL, HAL, Lisowsky) and Eccles 10:12 (KBL) the Hebrew term in question means "confuse" or "be confused". It is rendered by ταράσσειν, Is 3:12,[67] καταπίνειν 9:15; 28:7, διασκεδάξειν, 19:3.

In cases where בלע, according to KBL, HAL, ought to be interpreted as "destroy", Num 4:20 (KBL); Job 2:3; 7:19 (KBL, which reads qal); 8:18; Prov 19:28 (KBL); 21:20; Is 25:7, 8 (conj.); Lam 2:2 (HAL), 5a (HAL), 5b (HAL), 8, it is as a rule translated by καταπίνειν, Job 7:19; 8:18; Prov 19:28; 21:20 or καταποντίζειν, Is 25:8; Lam 2:2, 5a, 5b, 8. Num 4:20 ought to be excluded since here the meaning is probably "a moment".[68] LXX has correctly ἐξάπινα "suddenly" in Num 4:20. In Job 10:8 LXX may have had a different Vorlage. See BHK, BHS. The translator has also misunderstood בלע which is translated by παίειν "smite".

One rendering that shows a sign of the meaning "destroy" occurs, ἀπολλύειν, Job 2:3.[69] But the equivalent here is unique in LXX. In fact even in the other places in Job where בלע ought to be interpreted as "destroy", 7:19; 8:18, the literal translation καταπίνειν is employed. Job is the book which has the most varied renderings of בלע. See 10:8; 20:18; 37:20.[70] The meaning "communicate", which, according to Lisowsky and KBL, occurs only in 2 Sam 17:16; Job 37:20 and, according to HAL, also in Prov 19:28, is not recognized at all. All these meanings, "communicate", "destroy" and "confuse" are, without sufficient reason, denied by Schüpphaus, even though he emphasizes the destructive element of the Hebrew term.[71] The meaning "confuse" is in fact now confirmed by occurrences in 1QpHab

---

[64] Idiomatic translations are of course more prone to spell out the meaning of metaphors, see Olofsson, **LXX Version**, p. 21, but there are no theological motives involved. Cf. **Soffer**, pp. 101–102.

[65] It is the intention of the translator that decides the meaning of the metaphor in the translation. See Olofsson, **LXX Version**, p. 39.

[66] Cf. Albrektson, **Lamentations**, p. 115. This meaning is not attested in the Psalms, according to Lisowsky, KBL, HAL.

[67] Here it is obviously the question of a generic term which suited the context, rather than an indication that the translator knew the sense "confuse" of the word. This Greek term is a favourite word in Isaiah and in LXX as a whole. Cf. Ottley, **Isaiah II**, p. 119 "an easy paraphrase".

[68] See HAL and Schüpphaus, בלע, cols. 660–661. Cf. the qal entry in KBL.

[69] See Albrektson, **Lamentations**, p. 87, who contrasts it with the literal, misleading translation in Lam 2:2, 5a, 5b, 8.

[70] See BHS, Rahlfs and Heater, **Job**, p. 28 n. 53.

[71] See Schüpphaus, בלע, cols. 658–659.

and 1QH.

Venetz asserts that the rendering of בלע piel by καταποντίξειν is typical of the Kaige recension.[72] This would be in line with a trait visible in the choice of equivalents in this recension and in Aquila.[73] Aquila employs καταποντίξειν in Job 2:3; 10:8; Ps 34 (35):25; Prov 19:28; Is 3:12; 25:7, 8, and καταπίνειν in Hab 1:13. He thus takes over one of the two main equivalents in LXX, which is a common procedure in Aquila. But Venetz's arguments are far from convincing, even though καταποντίξειν is often employed in Eccles, Lam and 2 Sam, books in which the Kaige recension has influenced Rahlfs' text.[74]

The use of συνταράσσειν thus appears to be an exception to the ordinary translation technique in the Book of Psalms. This is true also for LXX as a whole. Only once is בלע rendered by ταράσσειν with cognates, the complicated Is 3:12: ודרך ארחתיך בלעו "and confuse the course of your paths" is translated by καὶ τὸν τρίβον τῶν ποδῶν ὑμῶν ταράσσουσιν "and pervert the path of your feet". The fact that the translator did not employ the usual rendering, but chose a favourite word may reveal an uncertainty as to its meaning. See above. ταράσσειν with cognates is a favourite word in LXX as a whole and not least in the Book of Psalms. It is never a consistent equivalent to a certain Hebrew word (except in Dan Th). Already in Genesis where it occurs six times it has six different Hebrew equivalents. In the LXX as a whole it has 46 equivalents. This Greek term occurs 36 times in the Psalms and renders 16 Hebrew words.[75]

Whereas translation technical or linguistic factors can hardly explain the rendering here, theological motivations cannot be excluded, even though there are no signs thereof outside the Book of Psalms, since a literal rendering is employed also when Yahweh is the subject and a different equivalent would have been more appropriate, e.g. Job 8:18; 10:8; Lam 2:2, 5a, 5b. Yahweh is also the subject of the verb בלע in 54 (55):10. The word is, as we have seen, literally rendered, but the object is probably the enemies' tongue, rather than the enemies themselves and the passage is corrupt. See, for example, BHK and the commentaries generally.

If the kind of theological motivation proposed by Erwin is involved in the translation of 21:10 it contradicts a supposed development in the transmission history of the Hebrew, since, Kraus, among others, suggests that the original spoke of the king's power to destroy the enemy, using terms associated with the holy war. The king was thus given a privilege which was reserved for Yahweh.[76]

Maybe the unusual translation συνταράσσειν can be explained as an assimilation to Ps 2:5 which has a similar wording in Greek: בחרונו יבהלמו "terrify them in his fury" is translated by ἐν τῷ θυμῷ αὐτοῦ ταράξει αὐτούς "trouble them in his fury". One should certainly not propose a Vorlage יבהלמו in accordance with 2:5. ταράσσειν can hardly be employed as an indication of a certain Hebrew Vorlage, not identical with MT. Cf. Wutz, who thinks that the translator had תבלעם in (the transcribed Vorlage), but reads it as תבהלם, i.e. it is a so-called pseudo-variant.[77]

---

[72] Venetz, **Quinta**, p. 68.

[73] See O'Connell, **Greek Versions**, p. 378.

[74] See the lucid argumentation in Munnich, **La Septante**, p. 76.

[75] See HR, Fritsch, **Studies**, p. 732.

[76] Kraus, **Psalmen**, p. 319. Cf. BHK. Note the immediate context, 21:8–12, and the unexpected shift from the second to the third person here. The imagery may have a Canaanite background. Dahood, **Psalms I**, p. 134.

[77] Wutz, **Psalmen**, pp. 44–45. This suggestion must also be based on an inferior Greek variant συνταράξεις. See Rahlfs, Psalmi, Wutz, **Psalmen**, p. 45.

2.3 THE ELIMINATION OF ASSOCIATIONS OF HUMAN UTENSILS WITH GOD

Fritsch asserts that the person is changed in Ps 55 (56):9 in order to avoid the idea that God keeps count:[78] "Thou hast kept count of my tossings; put my tears in thy bottle. Are they not in thy book?" (RSV) is translated in LXX by "O God, I have declared my life to thee; thou hast set my tears before thee, even according to thy promise" (Brenton). נֹדִי סְפַרְתָּה אָתָּה "Thou hast kept count of my tossings" is translated by τὴν ζωήν μου ἐξήγγειλά σοι "I have declared my life to thee."

In order to give a comprehensive description of the understanding in LXX it is necessary to delineate the ordinary translation equivalents in the Book of Psalms. ἀριθμεῖν and ἐξαριθμεῖν are the most common renderings of ספר in qal in LXX as a whole, and only here is it translated by ἐξαγγέλλειν. In LXX Psalms, however, ספר is, according to HR, never rendered by ἀριθμεῖν, but twice by ἐξαριθμεῖν, 21 (22):18; 138 (139):18. It is thus obvious that the translator knew of the meaning "count" for ספר. On the other hand, ἐξαγγέλλειν is always equivalent to ספר piel in LXX Psalms, 9:15; 70 (71):15; 72 (73):28; 78 (79):13; 106 (107):22; 118 (119):13, 26. Apart from Sir 18:4; 39:10; 44:15, this verb is only employed in the Psalms and in Prov 12:16.

Evidently the translator interpreted the verb סְפַרְתָּה as 1 p. sg. piel.[79] It was a question of a linguistic interpretation on his part, since the Vorlage had no vowel-points. The ה as termination is simply a matter of orthography.[80] אָתָּה can, as suggested by Briggs, be a dittography of the of the verb ending in MT.[81] Others suggest that the translator interpreted the pronoun as a dative object.[82]

נוד is a hapax legomenon with an uncertain meaning. Its most probable significance is "unstetes Leben", often rendered by "Elend".[83] Cf. "tossing" in RSV. Other interpretations are "wanderings" (BDB), possibly "agitation".[84] Dahood proposes "lament" and refers to Ps 69:21 (emended text) and Jer 22:10.[85] The word is often emended, e.g. Oesterley and Duhm read נְדֹד instead of נֹד in MT.[86] That LXX had a different Vorlage here cannot be excluded a priori. For example, Berg and Wutz suggest that the original behind the Old Greek had another wording, but in neither case are the proposals worthy of consideration.[87] Baetgen and Mozley try to explain the interpretation in LXX by the rendering of the Targum.[88]

Not only LXX and the Targum had a divergent interpretation here. None of the versions seem to have understood the meaning of the Hebrew. Briggs sketches a complicated development from the original text and tries to explain the renderings in the old versions from a common original.[89] Symmachus has τὰ ἔνδον μου, the Vulgate "vitam meam", Jerome "secretiora mea", the Targum "dies vagationis

---

[78] Fritsch, **Studies**, p. 731.

[79] Cf. **Baetgen**, p. 637, Briggs, **Psalms II**, p. 35. This is true for Peshitta as well. Briggs, op. cit., p. 35.

[80] Cf. **Baetgen**, p. 637.

[81] See Briggs, **Psalms II**, p. 35.

[82] **Baetgen**, p. 637. See also **Mozley**, p. 94. Wutz rather postulates the existence of an inner-Greek corruption here. Wutz, **Psalmen**, p. 141.

[83] See KBL, HAL, Baetgen, **Psalmen**, p. 165, Kraus, **Psalmen**, p. 565. Cf. Wutz, **Psalmen**, p. 141 "meine Unstetigkeit" or "mein Elend". But the original had, according to him, נֹהִי with the same meaning.

[84] Briggs, **Psalms II**, p. 35.

[85] See Dahood, **Psalms II**, pp. 45, 162. Cf. Anderson, **Psalms**, p. 423, who also mentions "homelessness".

[86] Oesterley, **Psalms**, ad loc., Duhm, **Psalmen**, ad loc. See also BHK.

[87] See **Berg**, p. 110. Wutz's explanation in his commentary on the Psalms presupposes both his transcription theory and an inner-Greek corruption. Wutz, **Psalmen**, p. 141. For another proposal, no less improbable, see Wutz, **Transkriptionen**, p. 491, ibid., **Wege**, p. 985.

[88] **Baetgen**, p. 637, Baetgen, **Psalmen**, p. 165, **Mozley** p. 94. Mozley also refers to 36 (37):7, where דֶּרֶךְ is translated by ζωή in B'', 2013 '. **Mozley**, pp. 66, 94. But neither of these explanations is adequate. Rahlfs, **Psalmi** has ὁδός in 36 (37):7 with R'' Ga L'' Cyp, which is evidently the original reading. דֶּרֶךְ is in fact never rendered by ζωή in the LXX as a whole.

[89] See Briggs, **Psalms II**, p. 35.

meae" and the rendering of Peshitta can be translated "my confession".[90] But all may be guesses seeking to make sense of an unfamiliar word. The number of guesses in the LXX has been greatly underestimated.[91] The equivalent in the LXX is thus a word that suited the context, i.e. a noun that fits in with ἐξαγγέλλειν. Otherwise ζωή is a stereotype equivalent to חי with cognates in LXX.Psalms.

The phrase in the Hebrew is far from certain textually. Cf. the suggestion in BHK to read בספרתך instead of the verb and delete the phrase "Are they not in thy book? at the end of verse. As we have seen, neither the Vorlage of the LXX nor the exact meaning of the Hebrew is obvious. The confusion evidenced in the interpretations of the versions in this passage is striking. In this situation it is really to beg the question to propose that a certain theological motive can explain the translation in LXX.

The phrase שימה דמעתי בנאדך "Put my tears into Thy bottle" was in the eyes of the translator also unworthy of God and the text was therefore rendered by ἔθου τὰ δάκρυά μου ἐνώπιόν σου "Put my tears before Thee".[92] Fritsch and Erwin translate LXX as if it had imper., in accordance with MT, but the Greek text has aor. ind. med. The LXX translator probably understood the Hebrew as part. pass.[93]

נֹאד is an unusual word which means "skin-bottle".[94] Dahood suggests, contrary its significance in other passages, but in line with the context here, that it denotes "parchment",[95] but this is less probable. The LXX translators probably knew the meaning of נאד. Otherwise it is always rendered by ἀσκός "skin", "wine-skin" in LXX. In 32 (33):7 it probably was in the Vorlage of the old versions, except in Quinta.[96]

Outside the Book of Psalms the context could indicate the right interpretation, but the renderings in Ps 32 (33):7 and 118 (119):83 show that the translator of the Psalter was well aware of the meaning of the word. This means that if he had the text of MT in 60:9 in front of him his translation may well have been based on theological exegesis. But the text of MT is uncertain. LXX, Peshitta and Vulgate had, according to the majority of scholars, a different text with נֶד in some form.[97]

The evaluation of the propositions regarding the Vorlage of the LXX depends to a great extent on the analysis of the translation technique. According to Santos, נגד is only once translated by ἐνώπιον in LXX. The usual equivalent is ἐναντίον. Trommius, on the other hand, contains 16 cases where נגד is rendered by ἐνώπιον, and five of them in the Book of Psalms. There are also nine where ἐνώπιον is equivalent to לנגד in the Greek Psalter. Rahlfs has ἐνώπιον for נגד or לנגד in 11 cases and ἐναντίον in 13.[98] The differences depend on the vacillation

---

[90] See Baetgen, p. 637, Briggs, **Psalms II**, p. 35. See also Oliver, **Syriac Psalms**, p. 109.

[91] See Tov, **Septuagint Translators**, p. 70. Regarding the position of LXX Psalms in this respect, see **Flashar**, p. 255.

[92] The translation is that of Erwin. God was not in the possession of a "tear-bottle". **Erwin**, p. 22. Cf. Fritsch, **Studies**, pp. 731-730.

[93] Cf. **Baetgen**, p. 637, Baetgen, **Psalmen**, p. 167, Briggs, **Psalms II**, p. 35, BHK. This may be in line with the intention of the original. Others suggest that LXX read שַׂמְתָּ. **Mozley**, p. 94, Kittel, **Psalmen**, p. 201. Cf. BHK. That accords with the translation of Brenton: "thou hast set".

[94] See e.g. BDB. It was probably a 'bottle' of leather or skin, a container of animal skin, made for wine, Josh 9:4, 13; 1 Sam 16:20, or for milk, Judg 4:19 (with an unusual spelling in MT). Here it is employed for tears. Cf. the simile in Ps 119:83. See BHS, HAL. Cf. Fritsch, **Studies**, p. 730 n. 33.

[95] Dahood, **Psalms II**, p. 46.

[96] See BHK, BHS, HAL, Briggs, **Psalms I**, pp. 285, 293. MT has נֵד.

[97] The Vorlage may have been נֶגְדָּ, BHS, **Mozley**, p. 94, Briggs, **Psalms II**, p. 35, Wutz, **Psalmen**, pp. 140, 142, ibid., **Transkriptionen**, pp. 226, 347, or לנגד, Oesterley, **Psalms**, p. 288. Wutz suggests an original בגאדך, Arab. "Beim Gebet zu Dir", with some support from LXX. Ibid., **Wege**, p. 985. But that is out of the question. נֶגְדָּ, even though closest paleographically to the MT, can perhaps be ruled out since this construction does not occur in Hebrew. See Mandelkern. Mozley has ב within brackets, but BHS is not even that cautious. See BHS, **Mozley**, p. 94.

[98] See Pietersma, **Manuscripts**, pp. 40-41.

between ἐνώπιον and ἐναντίον in the Greek manuscript tradition.[99]

Symmachus' rendering strengthens the suggestion that LXX had another Vorlage. It was probably not identical with the Hebrew text behind Symmachus, since he renders נאד by ἔνδον "within", which is always a translation of בְּקֶרֶב, 54 (55):5, 11, 12; 77 (78):28; 109 (110):2,[100] and בקרב is mostly rendered by ἔνδον or ἐν μέσου in his Psalter.[101] Symmachus probably knew the meaning of the Hebrew word.[102] On the other hand, both נוֹד and נֹאד are rendered by ἔνδον and ספרה as well as ספר are translated with different forms of the verb ἐξαριθμεῖν "count".[103] It is unlikely that the Vorlage of the LXX is original here.[104] MT is lectio difficilior, without being impossible. The rendering of the LXX translator was as we have seen hardly based on theological exegesis. On the other hand, it cannot be ruled out that theological factors influenced the transmission of the Hebrew text behind LXX, even though they played no part in the translation process.

The last clause in this verse has also, according to Fritsch, been subjected to theological exegesis:[105] הלא בספרתך "are they not in thy book"? (RSV) is translated by ὡς καὶ ἐν τῇ ἐπαγγελίᾳ σου "and in thy promise".[106] Fritsch suggests that the translator found the thought that Yahweh kept records of the tears of the pious improper or unbecoming,[107] and therefore renders it loosely with "in thy promise".[108]

The Hebrew phrase is, however, far from certain textually, since it is contextually inappropriate.[109] Some scholars assert that it is an explanatory gloss to the difficult and unusual word נאד, which occurs six times in MT, but only here in the Book of Psalms.[110] But this is hardly an adequate solution, even though glosses can be highly illogical, since ספרה is neither a suitable explanation of נאד nor was it more easily understood by the old translators or for that matter by the modern interpreters. See below. Others suggest that it was a gloss without specified function.[111] Briggs in fact presents many alternative explanations. It is "doubtless a gl. or txt. err. by dittog. of ספרתה above or conflation".[112]

The meaning of the expression is not a matter of course either. ספרה is a hapax legomenon which probably means book[113] or "scroll".[114] The sense "book" is also supported by the fact that variation between forms in the masculine and in the feminine is a common phenomenon, if not in the Hebrew, at least in the cognate languages.[115]

[99] See the comments in Rahlfs, Psalmi to Ps 21:26. See also Johannessohn, Präpositionen, p. 194.

[100] See Saiz, Simaco, p. 504.

[101] See Saiz, Simaco, p. 720.

[102] See 32 (33):7 where ἀσκός renders נוד, which the translator understood as נֹאד. See Saiz, Simaco, pp. 474, 684.

[103] See Field II and Saiz, Simaco. It cannot therefore be excluded that he guessed at the meaning of the unusual Hebrew words נוד, נֹאד and ספרה.

[104] Thus Briggs, Psalms II, p. 35, Wutz, Psalmen, pp. 140, 142.

[105] See Fritsch, Studies, p. 730.

[106] הלא is rendered by ὡς καὶ rather than καὶ. Cf. Fritsch, Studies, p. 730. Brenton has the translation "even according to thy promise". Cf. "as also in Thy promise". Erwin, p. 22.

[107] Fritsch, Studies, p. 730.

[108] Fritsch, Studies, p. 730.

[109] Gunkel, Psalmen, p. 244.

[110] See e.g. Anderson, Psalms, p. 423.

[111] Briggs, Psalms II, p. 33, Kittel, Psalmen, p. 201, Oesterley, p. 287, Kraus, Psalmen, p. 565. Cf. Herkenne, Psalmen, p. 198. See also BHK.

[112] Briggs, Psalms II, p. 35. Cf. ibid., p. 31. Since he is so fully covered he can easily afford to write "doubtless".

[113] Thus KBL, HAL, Baetgen, Psalmen, pp. 165-166, Kittel, Psalmen, p. 200, Anderson, Psalms, p. 423. See also Briggs, Psalms II, p. 35, Herkenne, Psalmen, p. 198. That it had the meaning "reckoning" (BDB, Gesenius, Gunkel, Psalmen, p. 244) is less probable.

[114] Dahood, Psalms II, p. 46.

[115] See Dahood, Psalms II, pp. 46-47.

For most of the ancient translators the meaning of the word seems to have been unknown, even though Peshitta has "book".[116] The book under discussion is maybe the ספר זכרון in Mal 3:16, in which the sufferings of the godly and their perseverance are recorded.[117] ἐπαγγελία made good sense in the context, even though it is not a commonplace term in the LXX. With the exception of the Apocrypha, it is only employed here and in Ezra 4:7 and Amos 9:6.[118] Maybe the rendering of LXX is an indication that the translator of the Psalms, when he could not understand the meaning of the Hebrew, tried to reflect an etymological connection between ספר and ספרה in MT.[119] On the other hand, he does not seem to be interested in demonstrating etymological connections of the original generally. Mozley only suggests that the translator loosely renders a difficult expression.[120]

The Hebrew text of the whole psalm is in poor condition. This is clearly stated in the commentaries: "The text seems to have suffered seriously in course of transmission, though both the Septuagint and Peshitta sometimes offer a useful alternative text,"[121] or "Der Text des Psalms ist sehr verderbt und nur annähernd herzustellen."[122] Cf. Herkenne who speaks about its "trostlos entstellte Zustand".[123] One of the reasons for this state of affairs is that the psalm contains many rare words and rare uses of words.[124]

To propose a theological motivation behind the choice of equivalents in the LXX, without discussing the condition of the text, the translator's understanding of the Hebrew and his translation technique is, to say the least, inadequate. Apparently the translator had to guess at the meaning of נוד and ספרה and rendered them with generic terms that suited the context. This was a common expedient when he came across difficult expressions.[125] The only words in the text which were completely understood were given their ordinary equivalents, e.g. ספר, שים and דמעה. On this basis he tried to make sense of the verse. הלא and אתה were probably paraphrased in order to facilitate a reasonable translation.[126]

It has also been suggested that theological motives were involved in the rendering of the first part of 60:10, מואב סיר רחצי "Moab is my wash-pot" by Μωαβ λέβης τῆς ἐλπίδος μου "Moab is the cauldron of my hope" or "Moab is the pot of my hope". Several scholars have suggested that the translator shunned a literal translation because he took offence at the thought that Moab is the wash-pot of the Lord.[127] The translator knew the meaning of רחץ. It is rendered by νίπτειν "to wash (oneself)" in 25 (26):6; 57 (58):11; 72 (73):13. He was also acquainted with the meaning of the noun. They are both common words in LXX. The syntactical construction of the phrase is also easy. But the translator's interpretation is based on the Aramaic word רְחַץ "trust".[128] סיר "pot", on the other hand, is translated literally by λέβης, which in fact is the ordinary equivalent in LXX as a whole. The rendering is hardly based on the vocabulary of the Pentateuch, as Tov suggests, since λέβης is only employed in Ex 16:3, other equivalents being used in 27:3 and

---

[116] See Oliver, **Syriac Psalms**, p. 109, **Erwin**, p. 22.

[117] Baetgen, **Psalmen**, p. 166.

[118] The Hebrew equivalent is uncertain. See HR. MT has אֲגֻדָּה "vault" (RSV), "firmament" (Hol).

[119] Cf. Symmachus, who renders both of them with different forms of ἐξαριθμεῖν.

[120] **Mozley**, p. 94.

[121] Oesterley, **Psalms**, p. 287.

[122] Gunkel, **Psalmen**, p. 43.

[123] Herkenne, **Psalmen**, p. 198.

[124] See Briggs, **Psalms II**, p. 31. This is not least the case in v. 9, e.g. נוד and ספרה.

[125] Cf. Tov, **Septuagint Translators**, p. 66.

[126] Cf. **Mozley**, p. 94.

[127] Fritsch, **Studies**, p. 731. Cf. **Mozley**, p. 97, **Flashar**, p. 95 n. 1.

[128] See, inter alia, **Mozley**, p. 97, **Flashar**, p. 251, Wutz, **Psalmen**, pp. 152-153, Barr, **Philology**, pp. 54-55, Fritsch, **Studies**, p. 731, Barr, **Typology**, p. 320 n. 1, Tov, **Septuagint**, p. 250. Cf. Dan 3:95 (28) where רחץ in hithpael is rendered by ἐλπίζειν. See BHS, Rahlfs. Prijs has found a counterpart to this translation in a Midrash. **Prijs**, p. 105.

The Episcopal Theological Seminary of the Southwest
Austin, Texas

38:3.[129]

The metaphor per se is incongruous, since the comparison between a wash-basin and a country is problematic.[130] For this reason modern commentators often emend the text to מֵי מוֹאָב "the water of Moab"[131] or יָם מוֹאָב "the sea of Moab".[132] These emendations, which lack textual support, do not commend themselves. The Hebrew expression is of course derogatory for Edom. He is reduced to a simple wash-basin. Even though the expression "God's wash-pot" causes the translator to depart from a natural interpretation of רחץ, his fidelity to the Hebrew text kept him from removing the whole metaphor. The lack of congruity between the image and the reference is not solved by the rendering in LXX so that semantic problems of this type can hardly have been the reason for the choice of equivalent. This supports the suggestion that theological motives are involved in the choice of rendering.[133] The stumbling-block is obviously not that the picture is too anthropomorphic or derogatory to God either, since the anthropomorphic expression "upon Edom I cast my shoe" in the same verse is more or less literally translated in LXX: "over Idumea will I stretch out my shoe". This phrase is best understood as a symbol of the right of possession,[134] but this does not restrain the LXX translator from a literal translation.

Kissane understands the metaphor rather as a pars pro toto. The congruity between the metaphors is thereby increased, i.e. Moab will have the status of a slave who washes his master's feet,[135] which may be the best understanding of MT. It was one of the duties of a slave to wash the feet of his master.[136] See 1 Sam 25:41. Cf. Joh 13:4-14. Thus the metaphor switches are reduced in number. They may be limited to only two (or three). The images in v. 9 are obviously taken from the battle-field; Yahweh is pictured as a warrior with a helmet. If the interpretation "sceptre" is used the second metaphor implies kingship and royalty, but it could equally well denote the commander's staff.[137] The image in v. 10 probably refers to a slave who takes care of his master's sandals and washes his feet, i.e. a metaphor of humility and subordinate status. That Yahweh as a warrior had a wash-basin for washing his feet on the battle-field and that Moab is described as the slave who washes his master's feet is not an improbable interpretation.[138] The last expression would, if Yahweh is understood as the implicit or explicit subject of the clause, refer back to the military metaphors of v. 9. Yahweh shouts in victory; the enemy is defeated. This would be in line with the military metaphors of v. 9. See below.

What may have been offensive to the translator is that Yahweh instead of Edom could be understood as the slave, since the relation between Yahweh and his "wash-pot" is not developed in the text. The risk of such a misinterpretation should not be underestimated. That expressions which might be understood in such a way that it gave Yahweh a subordinate position could offend scribes during the transmission history of the text is illustrated by the tiqqune sopherim in Gen 18:22, where the expression that "Yahweh stood before Abraham" is changed to "Abraham stood before Yahweh", since the Hebrew phrase could suggest that Yahweh was a servant to Abraham. As a literal translation could easily be misun-

---

[129] Tov, **Impact**, p. 582.

[130] Cf. Gunkel, **Psalmen**, p. 259.

[131] See Kraus, **Psalmen**, p. 586.

[132] See Herkenne, **Psalmen**, p. 210. Cf. Kraus, **Psalmen**, p. 586.

[133] LXX could, for example, have followed the rough paraphrase in the Targum. See Barr, **Philology**, pp. 54-55.

[134] See e.g. Gunkel, **Psalmen**, pp. 257-258, Kraus, **Psalmen**, p. 589. Cf. Ruth 4:7-8.

[135] Kissane, **Psalms I**, p. 260. See also **Psalms II**, p. 60. Cf. Baetgen, **Psalmen**, p. 179. He refers to 2 Sam 8:2 where the Moabites were called David's servants.

[136] See e.g. Toombs, **Bathing**, p. 365.

[137] Briggs, **Psalms II**, p. 60.

[138] See e.g. Baetgen, **Psalmen**, pp. 181-182.

derstood the translator based his translation on the Aramaic.[139] Otherwise the division between Aramaic and Hebrew was as a rule well maintained by the translators.[140] At the same time it is a Verlegenheitsübersetzung, since the rendering "cauldron of my hope" does not make sense.[141] This example shows that there are probably cases where the translator shunned a literal interpretation because he took offence at the plain meaning of the Hebrew text or a certain interpretation thereof, but was not thereby prompted to paraphrase. He strictly followed his literal translation technique, but interpreted a word with reference to a cognate language in order to avoid a fatal misunderstanding of the text.

2.4 THE AVOIDANCE OF ATTRIBUTING HUMAN FEELINGS TO GOD

The translator may also have departed from a literal rendering on account of theological presuppositions in the last part of 59 (60):10:[142] עלי פלשת התרעעי "Philistia, shout because of me" is translated by ἐμοὶ ἀλλόφυλοι ὑπετάγησαν "to me the Philistines are subjected".[143] V. 10 is part of a Salvation oracle, v. 8–10, which actualizes Yahweh's ownership of the whole country of Canaan and proclaims his right of possession over the neighbouring countries:[144]

> God has spoken in his sanctuary: "With exultation I will divide up Shechem and portion out the Vale of Succoth. Gilead is mine; Manas'seh is mine; E'phraim is my helmet; Judah is my sceptre. Moab is my wash-basin; upon Edom I cast my shoe; over Philistia I shout in triumph (RSV).[145]

רוע in MT has the less adequate equivalent ὑποτάσσειν in LXX. The translation in LXX is, according to Fritsch, intended to avoid the expression "God shouts".[146] This can only be true for 107 (108):10. Unfortunately Fritsch's whole presentation is very confusing since his argumentation seems be derived from the translation of RSV: "over Philistia I shout in triumph", which in 60:10 is based on a text identical with that of 108:10. This is in line with the proposition of BHK and BHS concerning the original Hebrew, which had the text of 108:10. The identical expression אתרועע in both passages is supported by Peshitta and the Targum in 59 (60):10, according to BHK and the commentaries generally. This in turn is an emendation made in order to avoid a contextual, and partly, a theological problem. God does not shout at all in the text of MT in 60:10. It is Philistia that is urged to shout for joy over Yahweh.

If there is a theological motive involved in LXX:s translation then it must be based on the fact that the call to the Philistines to rejoice seems somewhat out of place, since the foreign nations are objects of Yahweh's sovereignty in this context. Some commentators suggest that it is the question of an ironical exhortation, i.e. "shout in triumph" (if you can). For this interpretation, see the translation of JerB "Now shout 'Victory', Philistia!" Others consider it a shout of pain, as in Is 15:4, or try to read it in the infinitive in order to make Yahweh the subject,

---

[139] It seems to be a characteristic trait of the translator to resort to Aramaic when he did not understand, or did not want to understand, his Vorlage. See **Flashar**, p. 251 and n. 1.

[140] See e.g. Barr, **Philology**, pp. 54–55.

[141] Cf. **Flashar**, p. 95 n. 1.

[142] Thus Fritsch, **Studies**, p. 731.

[143] The parallel passage, 107 (108):10, is rendered in the same way even though the Hebrew is different, עלי פלשת אתרועע "over Philistia I shout in triumph". In BHK, BHS, however, it is suggested that LXX had a Vorlage in 107 (108):10 which was identical with 59 (60):10 in MT.

[144] Kraus, **Psalmen**, pp. 588–589.

[145] This is an emended text. MT has rather "Philistia, shout because of me".

[146] Fritsch, **Studies**, p. 731.

which is exactly the opposite to what Fritsch regarded as the objective of the LXX translator.[147] The theological and contextual motive behind the emendation which is proposed in BHK and BHS[148] thus runs contrary to the supposed theological exegesis in the LXX. The emended text corresponds to the text which the LXX translator avoided rendering literally, i.e. what for him, according to Fritsch, was a theological problem has by the modern commentators been regarded as the solution to such an obstacle in the transmission history of the Hebrew. Admittedly the LXX translator may have understood the Hebrew verb as an infinitive.

Finally, apart from the theological considerations, two reasons for this rendering have been suggested. The translator could have derived the word from רעע I.[149] But רעע I is as a rule rendered in the LXX by κακός or πονηρός with derivatives,[150] and ὑποτάσσειν is never, whether in the Book of Psalms or elsewhere, a rendering of רעע I or II.[151] Another possibility is that the verb is derived from רעע II hithpael "to be broken" in LXX.[152] But the translators hardly knew of a רעע II. Of the two instances of the verb in hithpael which are recorded in KBL and Lisowsky, Is 24:19 and Prov 18:24, the former is rendered by ταράσσειν "be confused" in LXX; this may also be a good description of the translator's state of mind when he met this word. See the employment of favourite words in 2.2. LXX has no counterpart to Prov 18:24 in MT. In the other instances of רעע II (qal), Job 34:24; Ps 2:9; Jer 15:12; Mic 5:5, the LXX translators have never caught its meaning. ποιμαίνειν "rule" or more literally "tend as a shepherd" is employed in Ps 2:9; Mic 5:5, i.e. the translators obviously derived the Hebrew verb from רעה "to tend", "to keep flocks".[153] Different forms of these two types of verb were often confused by the LXX translators which was not astonishing, because certain of them were more or less identical, especially in an unpointed text, and the analysis of the Hebrew was rather undeveloped in the last centuries B.C.[154] This word is sometimes used of political and religious leaders and therefore fits the context. See 2 Sam 5:2. Cf. Is 44:28. In Jer 2:8 רעה "shepherd" is employed. The LXX translator obviously based his rendering on a form of ידע in Jer 15:12, a derivation supported by some Hebrew manuscripts and most of the versions. See BHK, BHS, BDB. Job 34:24 seems to have been completely misunderstood in LXX and the Hebrew may also be in doubt. See BDB. According to BDB and KBL, the original text in Is 8:9 may be included here.[155]

How can the identical translation of 59 (60):10; 107 (108):10 be explained? It is probably a case of assimilation to a parallel passage in the LXX, since these passages are in fact parts of longer texts with a wording that, apart from minor variations, is identical in MT. Compare Ps 59 (60):7-14 and 107 (108):7-14. Parallel texts are easily assimilated to each other in both the Hebrew and the Greek. There are also in 107:7-14 obvious signs of assimilation to the parallel text in 59:7-14 (and vice versa) in the Greek textual tradition. Admittedly, this does not explain the choice of equivalent. Perhaps the LXX translator expresses the implicit

---

[147] For this suggestion, see e.g. Herkenne, **Psalmen**, p. 210, Dahood, **Psalms II**, pp. 75, 80. Dahood regards it as hithp. inf. with 1 sing. suffix, while the parallel has the finite form of the same verb. Dahood, **Psalms II**, p. 81. For a description of different proposals, see Baetgen, **Psalmen**, p. 182.

[148] The same emendation is made in Baetgen, **Psalmen**, p. 182, Briggs, **Psalms II**, p. 64, Herkenne, **Psalmen**, p. 210, Kraus, **Psalmen**, p. 586.

[149] Cf. **Mozley**, p. 97. It would then be interpreted as "to be worsted". See ibid., p. 97. No other examples of the hithpolel form exist, however.

[150] See Dodd, **Bible**, p. 76, Santos, **Index**.

[151] See HR. HR has ? in both 59 (60):10 and the parallel passage. ὑπετέγεσαν in Fritsch, **Studies**, p. 731 is obviously a simple typing error.

[152] Thus Briggs, **Psalms II**, p. 64.

[153] KBL, HAL. This is supported by the equivalents in LXX as well as by the commentaries. See also BHS, Santos, **Index**.

[154] See Weissert, pp. 39-44, and Olofsson, **LXX Version**, p. 32.

[155] LXX read a form of ידע. See BHS, Santos, **Index**.

significance of the military metaphor. That Yahweh is a warrior[156] who shouts in jubilation over the victory, presupposes that the enemy is defeated. See also below. The Greek term is employed for the subordination of countries in the Book of Psalms, 17:48; 143:2. Nevertheless the translator as a rule rendered the metaphors literally, with the divine epithets as an exception. It may also have been a guess from the context of an unknown word since the LXX translator derived it from רעע and he only knew the meaning of רעע I which did not fit the context.

The other examples of theological exegesis which are cited by Erwin and Fritsch are even less convincing. They may concern the toning down of God's destructive activities. 59 (60):4; 82 (83):16, the substitution of an abstract for a concrete term, 56 (57):2, the avoidance of actions offensive to the translator's idea of God's transcendence and spirituality in the creation and support of life, 70 (71):6; 138 (139):13, and the elimination of the association of human weapons and utensils with God, 20 (21):13. The translation technique, the translator's knowledge of Hebrew or the Vorlage of the LXX can easily explain the choice of equivalents in these cases.

---

[156] This is based on the reading of the verb in the infinitive or on the usual emendation.

Chapter III

THE TRANSLATION OF METAPHORICAL DESIGNATIONS OF GOD

3.1 THE TRANSLATION OF ṢÛR AS A DIVINE NAME

3.1.1 The equivalents in LXX

The equivalents in LXX Psalms

צור as a divine title in LXX Psalms is as a rule translated by θεός, 17 (18):32, 47; 27 (28):1; 30 (31):3; 61 (62):3, 7, 8; 70 (71):3; 72 (73):26; 91 (92):16; 94 (95):1; 143 (144):1. Tsevat does not include 62:7 in his statistics of צור as a divine name which only concern the Hebrew text.[1] In 74 (75):6 צַוָּאר "neck" is rendered by θεός, which suggests that LXX had a Vorlage with צור in this context.[2] The text in 18:3 shows a break-up of a phrase otherwise employed as a divine name, צור ישעי, 89:27; 95:1. It now occurs in two designations of God: אלי צורי, קרן ישעי צורי. Cf. 62:3, 7, where the words are different divine names.[3]

θεός, which can be regarded as the main equivalent of צור as a title of God in the Psalms, is (among the metaphors discussed in chapter 3) reserved for this Hebrew word. It is, however, used for other divine names or epithets as well. See 5.1, 5.7. The discrepancy between this equivalent and the general sense of the Hebrew term in both the literal meaning "rock" and the most common metaphorical meaning "refuge", "protection" immediately strikes the eye. The main equivalent is thus a word which reflects neither the metaphorical nor the literal sense of the Hebrew term. Only the referent is clearly marked. Delekat calls this a Targumic type of translation.[4]

Delekat's suggestion that צור in 71:3 and in 92:16, in contrast to the other passages, refers directly to the temple-rock in Jerusalem is hard to accept.[5] It would be more reasonable to argue that צור in Ps 28:1 refers, at least indirectly, to the holy rock. Cf. the mention of the holy of holies in v. 2.[6] The context in 144:1 is partly characterized by offensive war which shows that צור as a divine name is not exclusively employed as a term of protection:[7] "Blessed be the LORD, my rock, who trains my hands for war, and my fingers for battle." This deviating context

---

[1] **Tsevat**, p. 97 n. 156. Nor are Flashar's or Dell'Acqua's statistics complete. **Flashar**, pp. 243-244, Dell'Acqua, **Roccia**, pp. 421-422. The unique expression צור לבבי in 73:26 is regarded as corrupt and mostly emended to צורי for metrical reasons. See Briggs, **Psalms II**, pp. 147, 149, Wutz, **Transkriptionen**, p. 354, Kraus, **Psalmen**, pp. 664, 673. Cf. **Eichhorn**, p. 41 and n. 72a. In e.g. BHK the whole phrase is deleted.

[2] See BHK, BHS, **Baetgen**, p. 646, **Mozley**, p. 124, Briggs, **Psalms II**, p. 164, Gunkel, **Psalmen**, p. 328. Cf. **Eichhorn**, p. 75 and n. 190, Fritsch, **Studies**, p. 738. This was probably also the original text. See BHK, Baetgen, **Psalmen**, p. 237, Briggs, **Psalms II**, pp. 160, 164, Gunkel, **Psalmen**, p. 237, **Eichhorn**, p. 75 and n. 190, Kraus, **Psalmen**, pp. 683-684. Cf. van der Woude, צור, col. 542. The same corruption in MT exists in Hab 3:13. Gunkel, op. cit., p. 237. See also BHK, BHS.

[3] Regarding this type of break-up of stereotype expressions in MT generally, see Melamed, **Break-up**, passim.

[4] Delekat, **Asylie**, p. 379.

[5] See Delekat, **Asylie**, pp. 209-211, 379.

[6] See also Kraus, **Psalmen**, p. 373.

[7] See below for a further discussion. Cf. Kraus, **Psalmen**, p. 1123.

has thus not influenced the choice of equivalent in LXX.

The main equivalent is not always employed, being sometimes superseded by other renderings. βοηθός is the most common of these. It occurs in 17 (18):3; 18 (19):15; 77 (78):35; 93 (94):22. We have here an equivalent which reflects neither the literal meaning of the Hebrew nor the referent (even though the context clearly identifies the referent). On the other hand, it bears an obvious relation to the metaphorical meaning of the Hebrew original. צור in Ps 88 (89):44, which is rendered by βοήθεια in LXX, may thus have been regarded as a form of designation of God:[8] אף תשיב צור חרבו "Yea, thou hast turned back the edge of his sword" is rendered by ἀπέστρεψας τὴν βοήθειαν τῆς ῥομφαίας αὐτοῦ "Thou hast turned back the help of his sword". The translator did not know the meaning "edge" of צור and has probably interpreted צור חרבו as referring to God. See 4.1. "Edge" is, however, not the only possible understanding.[9]

ἀντιλήμπτωρ is used as equivalent only once, 88 (89):27. It has a meaning similar to that of the previous rendering. The phrase צור ישועתי is rendered by ἀντιλήμπτωρ τῆς σωτηρίας μου. The same expression, but with a suffix in the 3rd person translated by θεοῦ σωτῆρος αὐτοῦ, occurs in Deut 32:15.[10]

צור is thus not rendered in a stereotypical fashion. This applies to most of the divine titles. According to Berg, θεός is the only equivalent to צור as a divine title in the Book of Psalms.[11] As we have seen this is not true. צור is in the opinion of Erwin once rendered by πέτρα when it is employed as a divine name, 60 (61):3.[12] But the translator in this case evidently thought of the temple rock in Jerusalem. LXX is here in harmony with most of the modern interpreters.[13] This identification is also clearly suggested by the context. Note especially the close connection between צור v. 3, and אהלך בנפיך, סתר, v. 5. Briggs, however, infers, with reference to 27:5; 31:3; 62:8, that the rock in this case is the usual refuge in early Psalms. His evaluation is based on his conception of the original text. He deletes 62:5 as a late gloss.[14] Nevertheless it is not convincing, since the reference in the only good parallel adduced, 27:5, is to the temple:[15]

> One thing have I asked of the LORD, that will I seek after; that I may dwell in the house of the LORD all the days of my life, to behold the beauty of the LORD, and to inquire in his temple. For he will hide me in his shelter in the day of trouble; he will conceal me under the cover of his tent, he will set me high upon a rock (27:4-5).

צור stands in parallel with סכה "his shelter" and אהלו "his tent", which are archaizing metaphors for the temple, that is explicitly mentioned in v. 4.[16] This interpretation is certainly convincing, even though the parallelism is not direct. In Briggs' reconstruction of the original text in 27:5 even the rock has disappeared, because he reads בַּצַּר "in straits".[17] Ps 27 and 61 reflect a tradition from Jerusalem where צור is the place where Yahweh lives and reveals himself. The term refers

---

[8] Cf. Bertram, Sprachschatz, p. 99.

[9] See Briggs, Psalms II, p. 270, Anderson, Psalms, pp. 645-646, Kraus, Psalmen, p. 781. It rests on the analogy with Josh 5:2. Other interpretations are also possible. Anderson, op. cit., p. 646 with references. HAL p. 953, follows a suggestion in BHK, BHS to read מְצָר. See צור II.

[10] Cf. Briggs, Psalms II, p. 268, Anderson, Psalms, p. 642. A similar expression in Ps 94 (95):1 is translated in conformity with Deut 32:15. This is easily explained by the translation technique in LXX as a whole. See below.

[11] Berg, pp. 62-63.

[12] Erwin, p. 78.

[13] See e.g. Eichhorn, p. 84, Kraus, Psalmen, p. 592.

[14] Briggs, Psalms II, p. 66.

[15] Cf. Haag, סלע, col. 879. In both 31:3 and 62:8 צור is in fact a divine title.

[16] Eichhorn, pp. 83-84 with references.

[17] Briggs, Psalms I, pp. 239-240, 243. Cf. the rendering in NEB "in distress".

here to דביר, the holy of holies.[18] Thus there are no examples of a literal rendering of צור as metaphor when applied to God.

The equivalents outside LXX Psalms

θεός is also the main equivalent to צור as a name of God outside the Psalms, Deut 32:4, 15, 18, 30, 31, 37; Is 30:29. But other translations occur, e.g. φύλαξ, 2 Sam 22:3, 47, 47; 23:3. The rendering of צור here, φύλαξ, although it is included in Rahlfs' text, comes from the Kaige recension.[19] The Lucianic recension has πλάστης "creator", "sculptor" as a rendering of צור as a divine name.[20] Probably neither of them is the original translation, even though the (Proto)Lucianic recension is usually closer to the Old Greek.[21] In Hab 1:12 the name is rendered by πλάσσειν, which suggests that the tradition behind the Lucianic recension was known to the original translators. On the other hand, it is more probable that צור is read as a verb. Cf. Ps 138 (139):5. In any case it is not understood as a divine name in LXX:

> Art thou not from everlasting, O LORD my God, my Holy One? We shall not die. O LORD, thou hast ordained them as judgement; and thou, O Rock, (צור) hast established them for chastisement (MT).

> Art not thou from the beginning, O Lord God, my Holy One? and surely we shall not die. O Lord, thou hast established it for judgment, and he has formed me (ἔπλασέ με) to chasten with his correction (LXX).

This is the only place outside the Psalms or parallel passages to occurrences in the Psalms where the name is employed as an invocation of God. This may be one of the reasons why the term was not understood by the translator. In 1 Sam 2:2 δίκαιος is perhaps the equivalent. This is a complicated passage which has conflated readings in all witnesses. On the other hand, the Greek term may reflect a Hebrew variant with צדיק and MT another with צור. In that case, MT:s variant is probably the older. Cf. 4QSam-a.[22] κτίστης is employed in 2 Sam 22:32. It may, however, reflect a form of יצר, according to Bertram.[23] But his supposition regarding the hyponym[24] here is in fact less probable, since traditions which understood צור as a name of God as צייר "artist" or "sculptor" are evidenced in later Jewish writings, for example, Talmud, Midrash and among Jewish commentators.[25] This interpretation is also reflected already in the Lucianic manuscripts in 2 Sam 22:3, 47; 23:3,[26] which have πλάστης, 22:3; 23:3 or the cognate verb, 22:47.[27]

---

[18] Eichhorn, pp. 83–84, 88.

[19] See e.g. Venetz, **Quinta**, p. 85. In Venetz it is entitled the Palestinian recension. It is probably also the ordinary equivalent of Theodotion. Ibid., pp. 74–80, 85.

[20] McCarter, **2 Samuel**, p. 455. But cf. Venetz, **Quinta**, p. 77.

[21] See e.g. the discussion in Olofsson, **LXX Version**, pp. 60–61 with references.

[22] See McCarter, **1 Samuel**, pp. 68–69. In that case צור was missing in the Vorlage of the LXX.

[23] See Bertram, **Sprachschatz**, p. 100 n. 2.

[24] Hyponym is that unit of language of which the expression is a translation, both in the invidual case (= Vorlage) and generally. McGregor, **Ezekiel**, p. 24 and n. 3.

[25] Wiegand, **Gottesname**, pp. 88–93.

[26] Cf. McCarter, **2 Samuel**, pp. 455, 462.

[27] See further Wiegand, **Gottesname**, pp. 85, 87, Bertram, **Sprachschatz**, p. 100 n. 5. Cf. Rahlfs. A similar interpretation occurs in Deut 32:4, 15, in Syrohexapla. See Bertram, op. cit., p. 100 n. 5. The translation of Is 44:8 in Vulgate, formator, can depend on the same tradition. Some associations to the root יצר are probably also involved. Cf. v. 9. See van der Kooij, **Textzeugen**, p. 303.

צוּר may have been translated by μέγας in Is 26:4,[28] but the relation between MT and LXX is not easy to grasp. MT:s בִּי בְיָה יהוה צוּר עולמים is rendered by ὁ θεὸς ὁ μέγας ὁ αἰώνιος. θεός is probably a rendering of בְיָה יהוה, an unusual combination.[29] One may also argue that בִּי בְיָה was absent from the Vorlage, of the LXX text, since it can be a corruption of בְּיהוה, a correct marginal variant of יהוה, the ordinary name of the Lord.[30] θεός is in fact a very common equivalent to יהוה in the Book of Isaiah.[31] Seeligmann less convincingly suggests that θεός is a rendering of צוּר as a divine name here.[32] Bertram's proposal that μέγας is a colourless replacement for צוּר as a name of God,[33] is in line with the employment of alternative renderings when the ordinary equivalent is already in use. μέγας, although never otherwise a designation of God in LXX, is sometimes employed as a name or an epithet of the sun-god, especially in Egypt.[34]

Once צוּר is rendered by κύριος, Is 17:10.[35] The non-use of θεός may be due to the parallelism, but the fact that the most common alternative equivalent in the Book of Psalms, βοηθός, was not employed can also be explained on similar grounds. κύριος as a name of God is not reserved for Yahweh in Isaiah. It is an equivalent also for other terms for God. This free usage is unique for Isaiah in LXX, if the Hagiographa is excluded.[36] צוּר as a divine name in Is 44:8 is not recognized in LXX. It is probably lost through haplography. Cf. יצר in the beginning of v. 9.[37] On the other hand, both the Hebrew and the Greek texts are doubtful.[38] Here, as in most of the texts where צוּר occurs as a name of God outside the Book of Psalms, the incomparability of Yahweh is stressed.[39]

The term as a divine name in Deut 32

Since Deut 32 gives important clues for the understanding of צוּר as a divine name I shall discuss it in more detail. צוּר occurs six times in this chapter and it is always rendered by θεός in LXX. It stands in parallel with אֵל, v. 4, 18, אֱלוֹהַ, v. 15, or יהוה, v. 30. The usual metaphorical meaning of צוּר, connected with refuge and salvation, occurs in Deut 32 (v. 31, 37), but a different accent is also conspicuous, particularly in v. 4. Here God is depicted as the rock in a context where his moral character and his righteousness is emphasized. God "the rock" is connected with words as מִשְׁפָּט, אֱמוּנָה, צַדִּיק and יָשָׁר, rather than terms for protection. צוּר occurs in a similar context in 1 Sam 2:2 and Ps 92:16.[40] Also in v. 15 and 18 a partly different emphasis is apparent, since even though v. 15 has "Rock of his salvation" it parallels "God who made him" and in v. 18 "the Rock that begot you" is in perfect parallel with "the God who gave you birth". Thus the image of the rock is here tied to the motif of creation or generation rather than protection. This

---

[28] Thus HR, p. 905. See also e.g. Bertram, **Sprachschatz**, p. 100.

[29] Cf. HR, p. 643, Goshen-Gottstein, **Isaiah**, ad loc. It can also render only יהוה. Cf. BHK, BHS. See also HR, p, 905.

[30] See Gray, **Isaiah**, p. 440, who notes the remarkable use of בְּ in the text under discussion.

[31] See Baudissin, **Kyrios I**, pp. 156-158, p. 157 n. 1, HR, pp. 643-644.

[32] Seeligmann, **Isaiah**, p. 100.

[33] Bertram, **Gottesnamen**, p. 244.

[34] Baudissin, **Kyrios III**, pp. 71, 72 and n. 5. Cf. Ibid., p. 76 n. 2.

[35] See BHS, Rahlfs and Bertram, **Sprachschatz**, pp. 99-100, Baudissin, **Kyrios I**, p. 172.

[36] See Baudissin, **Kyrios I**, pp. 169-173, 453-454.

[37] See Goshen-Gottstein, **Isaiah**, ad loc. Cf. Bertram, **Sprachschatz**, p. 98.

[38] See especially the discussion in Ziegler, **Untersuchungen**, pp. 155-156. Elliger assumes that either the Vorlage of LXX did not include צוּר or the term was so corrupt that it was rendered by τότε. Elliger, **Deuterojesaia**, p. 397. Seeligmann understands θεός as equivalent. Seeligmann, **Isaiah**, p. 100.

[39] van der Woude, צוּר, col. 542. Cf. **Eichhorn**, pp. 75-77.

[40] Cf. Knowles, **Rock**, pp. 311-312.

is also a major theme in the first part of the poem.[41] In neither of these cases the context has influenced the choice of counterpart.

θεός as a translation of צור always refers to Yahweh except in Deut 32:31, 37, where it is also employed as a name of other gods, which are in opposition to Yahweh. We shall take a closer look at the Hebrew and the Greek texts of Deut 32:31: כי לא כצורנו צורם "For their rock is not as our Rock" is rendered by ὅτι οὐκ ἔστιν ὡς ὁ θεὸς ἡμῶν οἱ θεοὶ αὐτῶν "For their gods are not as our God." Wittstruck's suggestion that this translation was only "a non-figurative rendering of a metaphor",[42] without any motivation apart from the translation practice, does not do justice to the consistently pursued policy in the LXX, that "rock" as divine name is generally rendered by θεός, save when it is employed in a literal sense or is a general metaphor. See below. Note also the conscious use of the plural for צור when it refers to other gods here.

Delekat's assumption that "rock" is not only a divine name but also refers to a literal rock in 32:37[43] is probably to a certain extent true since there is an obvious interplay between the two levels of meaning, i.e. the name of God is used ironically with reference to the literal meaning of the term[44] in order to drive home the lesson in v. 31 that there is no true rock except Yahweh. See 32:37–38:

> Then he (the Lord) will say, "Where are their gods, the rock in which they took refuge, who ate the fat of their sacrifices, and drank the wine of their drink offering? Let them rise up and help you, let them be your protection!" (MT).

The translation in LXX is very interesting here:

> and the Lord said, Where are their gods on whom they trusted? the fat of whose sacrifices ye ate, and ye drank the wine of their drink-offerings? let them arise and help you, and be your protectors (LXX).

Both texts emphasize that Yahweh is the true "rock", the only "rock" worthy the name, i.e. only he can protect the people, while the foreign gods are mere cultic stones on which the Canaanites offered sacrifices, rocks in which none can find shelter. They are unable to "rise up and help". But in LXX the Israelites ate the offerings and not the foreign gods (the rock). Thus much of the irony in the passage may have escaped the translator. Contrary to the usual technique in LXX "rock" is not given an alternative equivalent here when the ordinary equivalent is already employed. צור is consistently rendered by θεός, whether it is in parallel with אל with cognates or not. In this case theological consistency was perhaps the main motivation for the change of subject in the text since a literal understanding of v. 37–38, without the image of the rock and the irony, would contradict the implicit thought in the chapter that the foreign gods are unable to be active in any way.

The reference to the offerings of fat and wine on the cultic stone, the מצבה, to the foreign gods is in the Hebrew opposed to Yahweh's gifts to the Israelites, fat and wine, v. 14, as well as honey and oil from the rock, v. 13. See also v. 32–33 where the bitter, poisonous grapes and wine of the Canaanites stands in direct antithesis to the beneficial wine from the blood of grapes in v. 14. Thus not only the contrast between the God of Israel and the foreign gods is evident, the ironical accent in Deut 32 is also conspicuous.[45] The whole chapter depicts Yahweh as the

---

[41] Knowles, **Rock**, pp. 312–313.

[42] Wittstruck, **Anti-Anthropomorphisms**, p. 32. Unfortunately the whole article is simplistic, even though the basic methodological approach is right to the point. Wittstruck, op. cit., p. 32.

[43] Delekat, **Asylie**, pp. 209, 379. Cf. v. 38.

[44] Cf. Is 8:14 where the divine name is used with an ironical accent, even though only on a metaphorical level.

[45] Cf. Knowles, **Rock**, p. 314.

living rock and emphasizes his goodness to the Israelites. 32:4-14, in contrast to the attitude of Israel, who has abandoned her God and turned to other gods, v. 15-18, variously termed "strange gods", "demons", "no god" and "idols", v. 16-17, 21, and with an ironical accent "rock", v. 31, 37, a rock, which in opposition to the "Rock of Israel", could not offer refuge. This explains the metaphorical meaning of the term here, further specified by the statement that they cannot rise up and help, since they, contrary to the "Rock of Israel", are pure stone, v. 37-38.[46] The contrast between the rock of the people, the foreign god, and the true rock, the God of Israel, which is explicit in v. 31, is implicit in the whole of Deut 32 from v. 4.

Perhaps even a further irony occurs in the chapter, which as a rule is not recognized by the modern translators, but the text is admittedly hard to interpret adequately. פלילים ואיבינו in 32:31 is usually translated "even your enemies themselves being judges" (RSV).[47] The translation relates the text to the principle which recurs in the later prophets, that the enemies of the Israelites could execute God's judgement on his own people.[48] But the best interpretation of the text in the context of the whole chapter is that even the enemies themselves would have to agree that their god is inferior to the God of Israel.[49] LXX has misunderstood the passage "their enemies are stupid", ἀνόητοι.

Deut 32:37 is the only place in this chapter where the metaphorical meaning of the "rock" is made explicit and the image mentioned in the context so that the metaphor is undisputably a living one,[50] at least when the Hebrew text was written. Nevertheless the LXX translator has not recognized the ironical accent or at least not reflected it in his translation through a reference to a literal stone here. Perhaps he regarded an identical rendering of צור as more important. The non-literal rendering is unexpected if only linguistic factors decided the choice of equivalent. Cf. 6.4.3. "Rock" as a name of God expresses a motive in Deut 32, which may explain its translation in the same way throughout the chapter, notwithstanding that it is sometimes parallel with ordinary terms for "God". See above.

The poem in Deut 32 is derived from the domain of cultic prophetical traditions from Zion.[51] It is, according to Eichhorn, a programmatic didactic poem from the prophetic circles in the sanctuary of Jerusalem, which adopted terminological and ideological motives from the Canaanite religion,[52] mainly for polemic purposes.[53] The text has clear affinities with Ps 78 as regards both form and substance,[54] but these similarities between the texts[55] did not prevent the translator of the Psalter from using an alternative equivalent for צור. He has thus followed the ordinary translation technique in the Book of Psalms. Cf. Ps 78:35.

---

[46] Cf. Craigie, **Deuteronomy**, pp. 377-387.

[47] Cf. Craigie, **Deuteronomy**, p. 385. For example, in JerB it is interpreted in another way "our enemies are no intercessors".

[48] Craigie, **Deuteronomy**, p. 386. This understanding also has some justification within the text itself. Cf. v. 21, 30.

[49] Cf. HAL. This interpretation probably lies behind the rendering in TEV "Their enemies know that their own gods are weak", but the ironical accent is missing.

[50] Regarding the criteria for living metaphors, see **Beekman, Callow**, pp. 133-136.

[51] Eichhorn, p. 53. For references to the prophetic form and content of Deut 32, see ibid., pp. 51-52 and n. 107a-111. See also Craigie, **Deuteronomy**, p. 374. It may be a covenant lawsuit associated with a ceremony of covenant renewal. See Knowles, **Rock**, p. 321.

[52] Eichhorn, p. 52 and n. 114, p. 53 and n. 117 with references, Knowles, **Rock**, pp. 316-321.

[53] Cf. **Eichhorn**, pp. 52-53 and n. 115, where the Canaanite population is regarded as the enemy in v. 21-35.

[54] See especially Eichhorn, pp. 54, 67-68, Cf. Freedman, **Divine Names**, p. 77.

[55] **Eichhorn**, pp. 67-68.

The term as divine name in Is 8:14

Is 8:14 is the only text outside the Psalter in which the actualization of Yahweh as צור occurs. In this function צור is always employed in a status constructus relationship, usually with another divine name, and as a rule in a context where an individual is strongly pressed by enemies and appeals to Yahweh for help.[56] The only exception is Is 8:14:

> And he will become a sanctuary, and a stone of offense, (אבן נגף)
> and a rock of stumbling (צור מכשול) to both houses of Israel, a trap
> and a snare to the inhabitants of Jerusalem (MT).

> And if thou shalt trust in him, he shall be to thee for a sanctuary; and
> ye shall not come against him as against a stumbling-stone, (λίθος
> πρόσκομμα) neither as against the falling of a rock: (πέτρα πτῶμα)
> but the houses of Jacob are in a snare, and the dwellers in Jerusalem
> in a pit (LXX).

The LXX translator has only recognized the function of the first of the five divine names in the text, "sanctuary",[57] which is also the only one with positive connotations, but not "stone of offence", "rock of stumbling", "trap", "snare". As we have seen צור as a divine metaphor signifies protection. Note that in 31:3; 71:3; 94:22, where Yahweh is actualized as צור, the term is combined with other divine names, משגב and מצודה, which are also associated with protection. Here it is employed in exactly the opposite meaning. Yahweh will not be a צור מעוז, 31:3; 71:3 (emend. text) nor a צור מחסה, 94:22, but a צור מכשול "stumbling–rock" for his people. In this way the threat to Israel is expressed in the harshest possible terms: Yahweh, the "rock", will be an obstacle instead of a rock in which they could find protection.[58] מכשול is sometimes employed in connection with worship of idols, Ez 14:3; 44:12, which makes the severity of the punishment even more pronounced. Yahweh will himself be an obstacle like a pagan god. The LXX translator, however, has misunderstood, deliberately or not, the Hebrew text, which incorporates several problems and may partly be corrupt.[59] That Yahweh is described as both a "sanctuary" and a "stone of offence", "stumbling rock" is of course hard to understand. The translator resolves this discrepancy by making the people instead of Yahweh the subject, negating a part of the verse and changing some of the metaphors into similes. In consequence he also translates "stone of offence" and "stumbling rock" literally.

Neither צור nor אבן are thus divine names in LXX:s interpretation.[60] It is there rather a question of an exhortation to the people not to treat Yahweh as an obstacle in Israel's way, but as a positive factor, "sanctuary". The translator may have been influenced by his understanding of the text as a prophecy which is fulfilled in his time.[61] That the Targum has the same interpretation may show that the LXX translator was dependent on an ancient exegetical tradition.[62] Presumably

---

[56] Eichhorn, pp. 78, 82.

[57] The original text may have had a term which was synonymous with the other metaphors. See e.g. Bjørndalen, **Rede**, p. 140 and n. 811, 812.

[58] Eichhorn, pp. 82–83. This ironical employment gives life to the metaphor. Cf. Nielsen, **Håb**, p. 63.

[59] See e.g. Duhm, **Jesaia**, pp. 83–84. See also Bjørndalen, **Rede**, p. 140.

[60] Cf. the discussion in Ziegler, **Untersuchungen**, pp. 95–96. See also 5.2.

[61] See especially Koenig, **L'Herméneutique**, pp. 46–47, 125–130. For the use of the fulfilment of prophecy as an element in the interpretation of LXX Isaiah, see van der Kooij, **Textzeugen**, pp. 36–47. Goshen-Gottstein also supports an exegetical rather than a textual solution to the rendering here. See Goshen-Gottstein, **Isaiah**, ad loc., who refers to v. 17 in LXX and Is 28:16. Ziegler also pays regard to Is 28:16 but proposes that the negation in v. 14a depends on a dittography. Ziegler, **Untersuchungen**, p. 95.

[62] Ziegler, **Untersuchungen**, p. 96.

he is responsable for the negation in LXX since it seems to be a common device of the translator of Isaiah to add a negation to a text which he does not understand or in which he tried to avoid ideas which offend him.[63]

3.1.2   The general and tradition-historical background of the metaphor

צור in literal meaning in the OT, not least in the Book of Psalms, forms a suitable background for the employment of this term as divine name since it is tied to a specific tradition with positive connotations, for example, the water which flowed from the rock in the desert, Ex 17:6; Deut 8:15. See Ps 78:15, 20; 105:41. Cf. Is 48:21; Ps 114:8. The watering rock is a motive of blessing which is developed in later Jewish traditions.[64] The rock is identified through an allegory with Christ in 1 Cor 10:4,[65] and connected with the so-called well tradition built on Num 21:16-20.[66] צור is also a site of the theophany of God, Ex 33:21, 22, as well as a place for sacrifice and a place of revelation of the angel of the Lord (who is often more or less identified with Yahweh himself), Judg 6:21; 13:19.[67] Thus the word in literal meaning sometimes has clear cultic associations with positive connotations, which may have facilitated its use as divine name. The ordinary metaphorical use of צור also favours this usage.[68] In Deut 32:13; Job 29:6 and Ps 81:17 צור signifies abundance and blessing and in Job 24:8; Ps 27:5; 61:3; Is 2:10, 19, 21 it is a place of shelter.[69] "Rock" as a designation of Abraham and Sarah in Is 51:1 is unique. They are described as the rock from which the faithful Israelites were hewn.[70] The positive connotations of the word evident here also accords with the metaphorical meaning of the term in Deut 32:4. The reference was, however, not understood by the translator or he may have had a different text in front of him.[71]

The significance of the metaphor is underlined by the occurrences in the beginning of a psalm (four times), as part of an opening appeal (three times), at the end (two times), or near the end as part of the conclusion (three times).[72] That the metaphoric uses outnumber the literal (ca. 44x to 34x) also speaks in the same direction.[73]

צור is a common divine name in the religious traditions of Jerusalem.[74] It is especially connected with the cultic traditions where Yahweh's saving and protecting function is emphasized, not least the Zion-tradition. These traditions are, according to Eichhorn, as a rule mediated by the king, or by appointed functionaries of the temple in Jerusalem.[75] צור as divine name shows clear connections with the temple rock.[75] Note especially the more or less explicit identity between the rock and the temple in Ps 27:5 and 61:3-5. God is of course not identified with the temple rock, but the metaphor is used with reference to the temple in

---

[63] Seeligmann, **Isaiah**, p. 57. Cf. Ottley, **Isaiah I**, pp. 52-53.

[64] Cullman, πέτρα, p. 96:28-33.

[65] Cullman, πέτρα, pp. 96:40-97:5.

[66] See Olsson, **Structure**, pp. 162-173.

[67] Cf. van der Woude, צור, col. 539, **Eichhorn**, pp. 84-87.

[68] Knowles, **Rock**, p. 322.

[69] van der Woude, צור, col. 539. Cf. Stolz, **Kult**, p. 163 n. 58.

[70] The implicit suggestion in the verse is that Yahweh is the real rock but Abraham and Sarah function as a rock in derivative sense. Cf. Knowles, **Rock**, p. 308 n. 3.

[71] Fabry, צור, col. 982.

[72] Cf. Knowles, **Rock**, p. 307 n. 2.

[73] Knowles, **Rock**, p. 307.

[74] Or at least in a southern tradition. See Davies, **Psalm 95**, pp. 189-190.

[75] See Wildberger, **Jesaia**, p. 338, **Eichhorn**, pp. 83-88, 91, Kraus, **Psalmen**, pp. 287-288, 373-374 with references, Haag, סלע, col. 879. For the symbolic meaning of the temple rock, see Cullman, πέτρα, pp. 95:17-96:12 and n. 17-23.

Jerusalem as the place where Yahweh reveals himself as protector of his people.[76]
This is one explanation of the number of references to God as "rock" in the
Psalms, since the cultic traditions from Jerusalem played an important role in this
prayer- and hymn-book of the temple cult, while another is the poetic language.
"Rock" is often employed in poetic passages where the incomparability of Yahweh
is stressed.[77] Another, less plausible explanation, is also possible, that Yahweh's
power to protect, experienced in the history of the people, inspired the choice of
metaphor.[78] There are no exact parallels to the use of the term צור as divine name
in the cultures of the Orient,[79] although mountain, rock and crag were used as
divine epithets in the cultures of the Ancient Near East. On the other hand,
Eichhorn, inter alia, suggests that the cultic tradition of the holy rock in Jerusalem
is pre-Israelitic.[80] The rock had generally a rich symbolic meaning in the cultures
of the Orient and in the Jewish traditions.[81] The image is thus ultimately derived
from other cultures in the Ancient Near East. This is also reflected in Deut 32
where the metaphorical meaning partly deviates from the usual connotations of צור
as designation of God but accords with fertility associations which often accompa-
niates El, Baal and Anath and their sacred mountains. Thus attributes of Canaanite
deities are applied to Yahweh. This is also understandable in the polemic context.[82]
In conclusion: the metaphor has derived its function from three different domains,
the natural rock, Yahweh as the covenant God, with a special emphasis on his
protection, and, especially in Deut 32, from Near Eastern religion, where the fertility
associations are prominent.

3.1.3 The equivalents of the term as a metaphor and in the literal sense

The usual equivalent of צור in LXX Psalms, when it is not employed as a divine
name, is $\pi\acute{\epsilon}\tau\rho\alpha$. $\pi\acute{\epsilon}\tau\rho\alpha$ is mostly used of a large, solid rock, but may also denote
an individual cliff as well as a stony mountain chain.[83] This makes it a suitable
rendering for both צור and סלע, which is also clearly seen by the choice of equiv-
alents in LXX. $\lambda\acute{\iota}\theta\sigma\varsigma$ "stone" is never a translation of either of these Hebrew
words, and is thus only employed in the literal sense, contrary to the use in the NT
where it sometimes is an epithet of Christ, Mt 21:42; Rom 9:32-33; 1 Pet 2:6. Thus
the semantic meaning of the terms in a literal sense is well reflected in LXX.
$\pi\acute{\epsilon}\tau\rho\alpha$ is employed in Ps 26 (27):5; 60 (61):3; 77 (78):15, 20; 80 (81):17; 104 (105):41;
113 (114):8. The occurrence of $\pi\acute{\epsilon}\tau\rho\alpha$ in 26 (27):5; 60 (61):3; 80 (81):17 shows that
when צור is used as an ordinary metaphor, it is rendered literally in LXX Psalms.
The same is true of passages outside the Psalter. See, for example, Deut 32:13.
This equivalent is used despite the fact that "rock" has positive connotations.
Regarding the metaphorical meaning of $\pi\acute{\epsilon}\tau\rho\alpha$, see 3.2.3. צור in Jer 21:13 is
transcribed. See further 3.6.3.

Outside the Book of Psalms too $\pi\acute{\epsilon}\tau\rho\alpha$ is as a rule employed (31x) for צור in
the literal sense, but sometimes $\pi\acute{\epsilon}\tau\rho\iota\nu\sigma\varsigma$, Josh 5:2, 3, or $\sigma\tau\epsilon\rho\epsilon\grave{\alpha}\ \pi\acute{\epsilon}\tau\rho\alpha$, Is 2:21;
51:1. In Is 5:28 the same equivalent is used for צר "flint", which was obviously
read as צור "rock".[84] $\acute{o}\rho\sigma\varsigma$ is sporadically employed, Num 23:9; Job 18:14 (a variant

---

[76] Eichhorn, p. 91. He even suggests that צור as address or designation only occur in theophanies of
Yahweh in the temple. **Ibid.**, p. 83.

[77] See e.g. Deut 32:31; 2 Sam 22:32 = Ps 18:32. Cf. van der Woude, צור, col. 542.

[78] Cf. Haag, סלע, col. 879.

[79] Eichhorn, p. 30. But cf. ibid., p. 30 n. 2. See further 5.7.2.

[80] Eichhorn, p. 88.

[81] See Cullman, $\pi\acute{\epsilon}\tau\rho\alpha$, pp. 95:18-96:12.

[82] See the discussion in Knowles, **Rock**, pp. 316-321, where comparative material are also presented.

[83] Cullman, $\pi\acute{\epsilon}\tau\rho\alpha$, p. 94:23-25 and n. 1.

[84] See Rahlfs and HR. 1Qls-a has in fact צור. See Goshen-Gottstein, **Isaiah**, ad loc., BHS, Tov,
Septuagint, p. 173. According to Goshen-Gottstein, the rendering is more or less in agreement with

has ἡ γῆ A+); 29:6.

3.1.4 Preliminary conclusions regarding the translation technique

A clear structure can be seen in the diverse renderings. θεός is the ordinary equivalent, while βοηθός and ἀντιλήμπτωρ are alternative renderings which are employed, except in 18 (19):15, only when θεός stands in close proximity, 17 (18):3; 77 (78):35; 88 (89):27; 93 (94):22. The reverse sometimes applies in the Book of Psalms; θεός is used, except in 17 (18):32, 47; 61 (62):8; 72 (73):26, only when it is not employed as the semantically correct equivalent of a Hebrew term for "God" in the vicinity. Flashar has observed this technique in 17 (18):3 where אלי צורי is rendered by ὁ θεός μου βοηθός μου, but has not understood that it is a more or less consistently executed translation technique as regards the rendering of metaphorical designations of God.[85] This is not least the case with this designation of God.

The impression that the metaphorical meaning of the Hebrew term in context is not reflected in the renderings of LXX is confirmed by a scrutiny of the texts. צור is in 18:47; 62:3; 89:27; 95:1 used for the help of God, in 28:1; 31:3; 62:8; 71:3 for the protection he grants, in 18:3, 32; 94:22; 144:1 for the security in his presence, in 19:15; 78:35 for his saving actions and in 73:26; 92:16 for his faithfulness.[86] These shades of meaning are of course hardly indisputable, as is obvious from the renderings in, for example, TEV, 18:47 "defender", 31:3; 89:27; 94:22; 95:1 "protect", 18:3; 62:8; 78:35; 92:16 "protector", 28:1 "protection", 71:3 "secure (shelter)", 18:32 "defence", 19:15 "refuge", 73:26 "strength" (צור לבבי). In any case van der Woude's opinion that the LXX rendering seeks to convey the meaning of the metaphor is hardly adequate.[87] Apart from the fact that the translation technique clearly speaks against it, the ordinary rendering, θεός, is obviously too neutral a designation for the Lord as rock.[88] צור as a divine name in general means "support", "defence" (BDB) or "place of protection", "security" and "refuge" (HAL), but it is also used for God as creator of man and for his moral character, his righteousness, especially in Deut 32.[89] Perhaps also it has the connotations "power", "strength", "reliability" and "unchangeableness".[90] The only relation to the divine names in LXX consists in the reflections of the positive connotations of the metaphor. Both the Targum and Peshitta have non-literal renderings of God as "rock". Peshitta as a rule has "the mighty" as equivalent and the Targum "strength", even though the former twice has a word for "God".[91] The renderings in these two versions are thus similar to those in LXX as regards the use of non-literal equivalents, but they do not follow LXX in the choice of interpretation.

The general choice of terminology for the metaphorical use of צור outside the Psalter is in line with the equivalents in LXX Psalms. This applies especially to θεός, the main equivalent. On the other hand, the alternative equivalents are not the same, e.g. βοηθός, ἀντιλήμπτωρ do not occur; instead κύριος, Is 17:10,

---

Vulgate, Targum, Peshitta and the Arabic version. Goshen-Gottstein, **Isaiah**, ad loc. That the LXX translator read MT as צַו is not probable. This Hebrew word is seldom so rendered in LXX. Only once has it the equivalent πέτρα, Ez 3:9.

[85] Flashar, p. 103. See 6.3.1 and Tables 1, 2.

[86] See van der Woude, צור, col. 542.

[87] van der Woude, צור, col. 543.

[88] Cf. Begrich, **Vertrauensäusserungen**, p. 255 n. 3, who speaks of the divine metaphors generally as symbols of Yahweh's protection. Eichhorn also rightly stresses the protective function of these metaphors. **Eichhorn**, p. 24 and passim.

[89] Knowles, **Rock**, pp. 311–312.

[90] Anderson, **Psalms**, p. 228. Cf. Caird, **Language**, p. 154, where he emphasizes the security of the rock in 31:3.

[91] Schwarzenbach, **Geographische Terminologie**, p. 114. Cf. **Erwin**, pp. 74–75.

μέγας, Is 26:4, and δίκαιος, 1 Sam 2:2,[92] are used. All of the alternative renderings outside the Psalter are employed when θεός is in close proximity. This is the reason why θεός is regarded as the main equivalent also outside the Book of Psalms. The employment of alternative equivalents in the recensions thus accord with expectations in the Old Greek. These renderings may indicate knowledge of this translation technical device in LXX, even though the alternative equivalents are not the same as in the Book of Psalms. But it is more probable that these are the main equivalents in the recensions. On the other hand, θεός is, contrary to the main translation technique in the Psalter, employed in Deut 32 when θεός also renders אל or אלוה in the same verse.

That θεός is the main equivalent of this divine name in LXX as a whole can be partly explained by the passages where צור stands in parallel with אל, Deut 32:4, 15, 18, 37; 2 Sam 22:32, אלוה, Ps 18:32, 47; Is 44:8, or אלהים, 2 Sam 23:3; Is 17:10. or in close association with אל, Ps 18:3; 78:35; 89:27, or אלהים, Ps 62:8; 73:26; 94:22, passages which, ironically enough, therefore often have an alternative equivalent. Another explanation could be based on Delekat's suggestion that צור as a divine name has been replaced by אלהים in Ps 24:5; 25:5; 27:9; 32:23; 51:16; 65:6; 79:9; 85:5 and outside the Book of Psalms in Is 17:10; Mic 7:7; Hab 3:18; 1 Chr 16:35 in MT. This is at least a possibility in view of the differences between the parallel texts, 2 Sam 22:47 and Ps 18:47.[93] But the more speculative reconstruction of Delekat, which presupposes that an original צור in 73:28 has been amended to יהוה in some manuscripts and אדני in others,[94] and the two readings are combined in MT into the overburdened text we now have[95] is hardly convincing, even though אדני is probably secondary.[96] Ps 73:28 in MT באדני יהוה מחסי has ἐν τῷ κυρίῳ τὴν ἐλπίδα μου as counterpart in LXX. Similar expressions are in fact common, especially in the Book of Psalms. The use of צור as a divine name is more or less confined to the Book of Psalms or psalms in other parts of the Bible, not least in prophetic literature.

The translator of the Book of Psalms always treated צור as a divine title differently from its literal and its ordinary metaphorical meaning and the same is true of the translators of the other LXX books. A literal rendering of צור was consistently avoided when it referred to God.[97]

3.2   THE TRANSLATION OF SELAʿ AS A DIVINE NAME

3.2.1   The equivalents and the translation technique of the name in LXX

סלע is another term used as a designation of God in LXX Psalms. It mostly occurs in connection with other divine names, especially צור, and also depicts God's power to protect, further emphasized through the accumulation of divine epithets in 18:3; 31:3–4; 71:3. Thus it often serves as a synonym for צור as a name of God.[98] The reason for its use is probably the variation of the divine metaphorical names in the Hebrew which the LXX translator sought to provide in the Greek. The

---

[92] Apart from the fact that LXX may have had a different Vorlage here, cf. BHK, BHS, codex A has another rendering. See Rahlfs. HR and Dell'Acqua suggest ἅγιος as equivalent but it can hardly be regarded as a rendering of צור. Cf. Dell'Acqua, **Roccia**, p. 421. See Bertram, **Sprachschatz**, p. 100 n. 1.

[93] Delekat, **Asylie**, p. 380 and n. 2. Even though he assumes that an original צור has in most cases been kept. Ibid., p. 211 n. 1.

[94] The proposed original phrase (צור מחסי) occurs in 94:22.

[95] See Delekat, **Asylie**, p. 211 n. 1.

[96] Briggs, **Psalms II**, pp. 147–150. It is missing in a few Hebrew manuscripts as well as in LXX and Peshitta. See BHS.

[97] Cf. Bertram, **Sprachschatz**, pp. 99–101, Fritsch, **Studies**, p. 738 n. 13.

[98] Eichhorn, p. 93, Haag, סלע, col. 879.

interchangeability of צור and סלע as names of God is strengthened by the fact that when סלע once is employed in isolation, 42:10, the literary form is one in which צור also occurs, the Prayer of individuals.[99] This is also clearly seen by the composition of 31:3-4 (and 71:3):

> Be thou a rock (צור) of refuge for me, a strong fortress to save me!
> Yea, thou art my rock (סלע) and my fortress (31:3-4) (MT).

Thus the Psalmist in Ps 31:4, when he refers back to v. 3, replaces צור with סלע.

Contrary to most of the other names under discussion, סלע has no stereotyped equivalent in LXX. It is translated by ἀντιλήμπτωρ in Ps 41 (42):10. The rendering wholly benefits the situation, whereby the Psalmist cannot return to Zion without a revelation from God to whom he appeals in his positive function as the one who ought to help and protect the vulnerable suppliant.[100] On the other hand, this term would have been as suitable in the other places where the name occurs. It is also rendered by κραταίωμα, Ps 30 (31):4, and στερέωμα, 17 (18):3; 70 (71):3.[101] The equivalents of 17 (18):3; 30 (31):4; 70 (71):3 suggest that the differences are sometimes haphazard, since when סלע as a divine name occurs in the Hebrew phrase סלעי ומצודתי it is in 17 (18):3 and 70 (71):3 rendered by στερέωμα μου καὶ καταφυγή μου and in 30 (31):4 by κραταίωμα μου καὶ καταφυγή μου. (On the translation of 2 Sam 22:2, see below). The contexts in Ps 31 and 71 are also identical; 31:2-4 and 71:1-3 are parallels. On the other hand, ἀντιλήμπτωρ may have been avoided in 17 (18):3 because it renders משגב in the same verse, and could therefore be regarded as the main equivalent.

However, Rahlfs' text contains one exception to the non-literal rendering of "rock" as a divine name, viz. 2 Sam 22:2, where סלע is translated by πέτρα. This passage is exceptional in its treating of divine names generally. The parallel text, Ps 17 (18):3, which was evidently in liturgical use, has a more conventional rendering, στερέωμα, Ps 17 (18):3.[102] But Rahlfs' text obviously reflects the Kaige recension and not the Old Greek in 2 Sam 22:2.[103] The renderings of the divine names in 22:2-3 in B show a close affinity with the equivalents in Aquila. In fact all equivalents here, with the exception of ἀντιλήμπτωρ for משגב, and ὑπερασπιστής for מגן, are also found in Aquila. See 6.2.1.

3.2.2 The background for the use of the term as a divine name

סלע was often used in a literal sense as a place where man could find shelter from enemies in holes or caves of the rock, 1 Sam 13:6; 23:25. Cf. Is 2:21; Jer 16:16. Ps 141:6 too could be understood in this perspective.[104] It was also a lair and thus a shelter for animals, 104:18, and a place where things could be hidden, Jer 13:4. Note that the theme of protection, refuge, is explicitly mentioned in 104:18 by the use of the word מחסה, rendered by a term which also occurs as an equivalent of divine metaphorical names, καταφυγή. This is of course a suitable

---

[99] See **Eichhorn**, pp. 31-34, 45-46, 95. These individuals are, according to Eichhorn, cultic functionaries trusted with the mediation of the current revelation of Yahweh's salvation at the temple of Zion. In this case it is probably the question of a temple singer or a cultic prophet. Ibid., p. 95.

[100] **Eichhorn**, pp. 93-94. The interpretation that the Psalmist is seriously ill is also possible and does not alter the impression from the context. See Kraus, **Psalmen**, p. 476. The character of the distress is not reflected in the text. Anderson, **Psalms**, p. 330.

[101] Tsevat's statistics are not completely reliable since he does not count Ps 70 (71):3. **Tsevat**, pp. 15, 83 n. 53. Regarding the renderings in LXX, see Bertram, **Sprachschatz**, p. 100 n. 5, Erwin, pp. 72-73, Fritsch, **Studies**, pp. 735-734.

[102] See Bertram, **Sprachschatz**, p. 100.

[103] See e.g. Muraoka, **Samuel-Kings**, pp. 28-30.

[104] Haag, סלע, cols. 873-874. For a different interpretation, see e.g. Anderson, **Psalms**, p. 921.

background for the word's significance as a metaphor of the protection of God. Another factor behind the use of סלע as a divine name is that it can be employed literally in cultic contexts as a place of offering, Judg 6:20.[105] It is also used, along with צור, in the traditions of the watering rock in the desert, Ex 17:1-7; Num 20:1-13, a blessing-motive, echoed in Ps 78:16; Neh 9:15, and as part of a description of God's blessings of Israel, "honey out of the rock", Deut 32:13.[106] The similarities with the previous designation of God are striking.

The distinction between סלע as a divine title and a literal rock, whether it occurs in metaphorical language or not, is consistently maintained in LXX Psalms.

3.2.3   The equivalents of the term as a metaphor and in the literal sense

סלע is literally a crag or a cliff, i.e. a solitary rock.[107] As a literal rock in the Psalter it is rendered by πέτρα, Ps 39 (40):3; 77 (78):16; 103 (104):18; 136 (137):9; 140 (141):6. πέτρα is predominantly a large, solid rock,[108] which makes it a suitable equivalent for both סלע and צור. סלע is sometimes regarded as a metaphor in 137:9, since a literal rock stands in opposition to the character of Babylon:[109] "Happy shall he be who takes your little ones and dashes them against the rock!" But that may be an overinterpretation,[110] even though the language could be described as figurative, i.e. to illustrate the fate of the defeated. In Ps 40:3 too the metaphorical element is conspicuous: "He drew me up from the desolate pit, out of the miry bog, and set my feet upon a rock, making my steps secure." "Rock", as well as "desolate pit" or perhaps "muddy pit" and "miry bog" are, strictly speaking, metaphors, and all of them, except "rock", refer to the chaotic world of the dead.[111] A literal translation could, however, hardly have been avoided in any of these cases. See e.g. the rendering in TEV. The term in Ps 141:6 could also be regarded in a similar way, i.e. as a metaphor.

סלע in its literal meaning is thus mostly rendered by πέτρα, sometimes by κρημνός "beetling cliff", "crag" (LSJ), 2 Chr 25:12 (2x), and צחיח סלע "the top of the rock" (RSV), or rather "the bare rock",[112] is translated by λεωπετρία "smooth rock", Ez 24:7, 8, or "bare rock", 26:4, 14 (Brenton). This is an extremely unusual word which probably only occurs here. The meaning "rock of plundering", λεία πέτρα, or something similar, is suggested in LSJ.[113] The LXX translator thus probably regarded the expression as a metaphor and translated it accordingly. He hardly tried to reflect the specific character of a literal rock as Haag assumes.[114] סלע in these passages is sometimes looked upon as a metaphor also in MT.[115] See below.

The "rock" as an ordinary metaphor[116] is often rendered by πέτρα, Ps 39 (40):3; 136 (137):9; Is 31:9; 33:16; Jer 5:3; 23:29; 28 (51):25; Amos 6:12 but sometimes other equivalents are employed, Is 32:2; Ez 24:7, 8; 26:4, 14. In Ps 40:3;

---

[105] Haag, סלע, col. 874. In v. 21 the same rock is called צור.

[106] Haag, סלע, cols. 874-875. See 3.1.2.

[107] See KBL, HAL. It is thus more or less a synonym to צור also in the literal sense. Cf. Haag, סלע, col. 873, van der Woude, צור, cols. 539-540.

[108] Cullman, πέτρα, p. 94:23-24, Haag, סלע, col. 879.

[109] Haag, סלע, col. 878. See also Anderson, **Psalms**, p. 900.

[110] See e.g. Hartberger, **Psalm 137**, pp. 211, 225.

[111] See Briggs, **Psalms I**, p. 151 "fig. of security", Anderson, **Psalms**, p. 315, "symbol of security and safety". See also Kraus, **Psalmen**, p. 460. Cf. Haag, סלע, col. 878.

[112] Haag, סלע, col. 874.

[113] See LSJ, pp. 1034, 1043. Other lexica seem to base the sense of the Greek word on the meaning of the Hebrew, rather than the Greek.

[114] Haag, סלע, col. 880.

[115] Haag, סלע, col. 878. See also BDB. But cf. Zimmerli, **Ezechiel**, pp. 565-566, 615, 619, who obviously regarded the description of the fate of Tyre as literal.

[116] See Haag, סלע, cols. 878-879. Cf. BDB.

Is 31:9; 32:2; 33:16; Jer 51:25 סלע means protection and security in line with the use of this word as a name of God.[117] But in Ps 137:9; Jer 5:3 and 23:29 the hardness of the rock is in focus in a negative context.[118] In Amos 6:12 the expression "do horses run upon rocks" suggests destruction and decay of righteousness in the society.[119] But even though the word is used in expressions with a metaphorical meaning סלע has a literal sense in these passages.

Sometimes the meaning "hardness" is emphasized and sometimes "protection". But these differences are not reflected in LXX. In the latter cases, where the meaning accords with that of סלע as a divine name, it often refers to a leader of the people or a pagan god. We shall examine two instances where סלע refers to persons, Is 31:9; 32:2. In both cases it means protection but is rendered in two different ways in LXX. Is 31:8-9:

> And the Assyrian shall fall by a sword, not of man; and a sword, not of man, shall devour him; and he shall flee from the sword, and his young men shall be put to forced labour. His rock shall pass away in terror, and his officers desert the standard in panic (MT).

> And the Assyrian shall fall: not the sword of a great man, nor the sword of a mean man shall devour him; neither shall he flee from the face of the sword: but the young men shall be overthrown: for they shall be compassed with rocks as with a trench, and shall be worsted; and he that flees shall be taken (LXX).

וסלעו ממגור יעבור in Is 31:9 "His rock shall pass away in terror" is rendered by πέτρᾳ γὰρ περιλημφθήσονται ὡς χάρακι "for they shall be compassed with rocks as with a trench".[120] This may be an example of the employment of סלע of a foreign god in line with the use of צור in Deut 32:31, 37, but the parallelism with שר "prince", "officer" favours the reference to the king of Assyria,[121] or maybe one of his officers (HAL). Even though the king is the probable referent the difference between gods and kings was often vague in the Ancient Near East.[122] The diverging interpretation in LXX, as regards the function of the "rock", may be due to a different Vorlage, i.e. מָצוֹר "siege", "bulwark" (cf. Deut 20:19-20) instead of מָגוֹר "terror", "horror",[123] a word which was never adequately interpreted in LXX.[124] Cf. Is 30:32. Note also Jer 46:5. The Targum has evidently grasped the metaphorical character of סלע, while Peshitta has a different interpretation.[125] In all probability the use of the term סלע in this connection was strange for certain of the translators, since it was otherwise only employed for Yahweh in the meaning "protection". Obviously the translator of Is 32:2 did not understand the Hebrew:

והיה-איש כמחבא-רוח וסתר זרם כפלגי-מים בציון כצל סלע-כבד בארץ עיפה

---

[117] See Haag, סלע, cols. 878-879. Cf. Caird, **Language**, p. 48.

[118] Jer 23:29, which primarily emphasizes the strength of the word of God, indirectly bears witness to the hardness of the rock. Polak, **Jer 23:29**, pp. 119-123. It is a simile rather than a metaphor.

[119] Haag, סלע, col. 878. It can also depict pure futility. Caird, **Language**, p. 48.

[120] Or "palisade". See Ottley, **Isaiah I**, p. 185.

[121] See Haag, סלע, cols. 878-879, Eichhorn, p. 92 n. 2, Kaiser, **Jesaia**, p. 319 n. a. In LXX the officers have disappeared altogether.

[122] Cf. **Eichhorn**, p. 92 n. 2.

[123] Cf. Duhm, **Jesaia**, p. 235, Goshen-Gottstein, **Isaiah**, ad loc. The meaning of the Hebrew is not self-evident. Cf. the different understanding in NEB. But Ziegler also supports this suggestion. Ziegler, **Untersuchungen**, p. 102.

[124] See Santos, **Index**. As a rule the translators derived this term from the root גור. For a different solution, see Ottley, **Isaiah II**, p. 262.

[125] Ziegler, **Untersuchungen**, p. 102. Cf. the similar use of מגן for the king of Israel and maybe also for the princes of foreign nations. See 3.3.1.

(Behold, a king will reign in righteousness, and princes will rule in justice.) Each will be like a hiding place from the wind, a covert from the tempest, like streams of water in a dry place, like the shade of a great rock in a weary land (32:1-2 MT).

καὶ ἔσται ὁ ἄνθρωπος κρύπτων τοὺς λόγους αὐτοῦ καὶ κρυβήσεται ὡς ἀφ' ὕδατος θερομένου καὶ φανήσεται ἐν Σιων ὡς ποταμὸς φερόμενος ἔνδοξος ἐν γῇ διψώσῃ

(For, behold, a righteous king shall reign, and princes shall govern with judgement.) And a man shall hide his words, and be hidden, as from rushing water, and shall appear in Sion as a rushing river, glorious in a thirsty land (LXX).

Thus in MT the king and the princes are compared with the shade of a great rock. But בצל סלע "like the shade of a rock" is rendered by ὡς ποταμὸς φερομένους "as a rushing river". סלע is translated by φερόμενος. φέρεσθαι was a favourite word of this translator, who often resorted to it when he did not know the meaning of the Hebrew word or construction.[126] But Koenig has a different interpretation. He maintains that צלסלע was regarded as a form סלל by the translator and that it is reflected by φανήσεται "shall appear".[127] But סלל "heap up", "lay out" is in fact never rendered by φανήεσθαι, nor even a synonym thereof, in LXX as a whole. φανήσεσθαι is probably a plus in LXX Isaiah, which is added as a form of contrast to κρυβήσεσθαι "hide" in v. 2a.[128] בצל סלע is the last in a series of four (or three) similes[129] in MT, only one of which is recognized in LXX, "streams of water".

סלע in the description of the fate of Jerusalem, Ez 24:7, 8, and of Tyre, Ez 26:4, 14, may as we have seen be understood literally but could equally well be a metaphor.[130] If the latter is the case the same negative meaning of סלע is evidenced here as in Ps 137:9; Jer 5:3; 23:29 since in Ez 24:7, 8 the innocent blood is spilled on the rock where it could not be hidden and there cries for revenge, and in Ez 26:4, 14 the bare rock testifies to a total devastation. Thus as an ordinary metaphor, where it does not refer to man, negative points of similarity are emphasized in contrast to the use of סלע as divine metaphor.

πέτρα in non-biblical Greek could be employed as a metaphor of firmness and immovability but also hardness and lack of feeling, callousness.[131] Thus πέτρα was a suitable equivalent when the hardness of the rock was emphasized, but not for "rock" as a name of God, since the Greek word is not employed in the meaning "refuge", "security". In fact negative connotations seem to dominate its use.[132] If the image was employed metaphorically in the target language the translators as well as the readers of their translation of course interpreted it in line with the metaphorical meaning in their own tongue since the point of similarity was implicit

---

[126] See Ziegler, **Untersuchungen**, pp. 142-143. It was as a rule used in the form φερόμενος in apposition to a noun. Ibid., p. 143. The reason for the choice of translation may be the parallelism. Ottley, **Isaiah II**, p. 263, Ziegler, **Untersuchungen**, p. 143. זרם "tempest" was not understood by the translator and therefore differently rendered on every occasion, 4:6; 25:4; 28:2 (2x); 30:30; 32:2. Ibid., p. 143. The lack of knowledge is not astonishing since the Hebrew word only occurs twice outside Isaiah, Job 24:8; Nah 3:10, and is never understood by the translators of the Old Greek. The rendering in Job 24:8 "heavy rain" is in a Hexaplaric addition.

[127] Koenig, **L'Herméneutique**, pp. 146-147.

[128] Cf. the criticism of Koenig in van der Kooij, **Accident**, p. 371. For the interpretation of 32:2 in general, see Koenig, **L'Herméneutique**, pp. 76, 146 n. 14.

[129] זרם is formally not a simile. Similes in fact often come in series of four or more in the Bible. Watson, **Poetry**, p. 259.

[130] Haag, סלע, col. 878.

[131] See LSJ, Cullman, πέτρα, p. 94:26-28, Haag, סלע, cols. 879-880.

[132] Bertram, στερεός, p. 610:10-12.

in these divine designations.[133] Concerning the ordinary metaphors in the Hebrew this distinction is not consistently maintained, even though Is 31:9 is misunderstood by the translator and a literal translation of 33:16 could hardly be avoided.

This state of affairs, even though it does not contradict the assumption that the choice of terminology had a theological motivation, i.e. to ward off the, not least in the Hellenistic world, easy misunderstanding of the rock as a place where God lived or even his incarnation,[134] shows that other factors were also of importance for the non-use of the literal equivalent. Irony is invariably involved when foreign gods or man are given the title "rock". This ironical use as a rule presupposes the meaning "refuge" or maybe "saviour" for "rock" as a designation of Yahweh. This is also evident in Jer 2:27.[135]

3.3 THE TRANSLATION OF MĀGĒN AS A DIVINE NAME

3.3.1 The equivalents of the name in LXX

The equivalents of the name in LXX Psalms

מגן as a name of God is rendered by ὑπερασπιστής, Ps 17 (18):3, 31; 27 (28):7; 32 (33):20; 58 (59):12; 83 (84):10; 113:17, 18, 19 (115:9, 10, 11); 143 (144):2, or ἀντιλήμπτωρ, 3:4; 118 (119):114.[136] מגן in 83 (84):12 is paraphrased; שמש ומגן יהוה is rendered by ἔλεον καὶ ἀλήθειαν ἀγαπᾷ κύριος. ἔλεον must correspond to שמש and מגן to ἀλήθεια. The translation here is unique in LXX Psalms since the translator otherwise renders the Hebrew word for word.[137] But the suggestion of a textual corruption in Hebrew and/or Greek is hardly warranted.[138] The proposal that שמש denotes a buckler or a sun-formed shield,[139] or that the two terms are a hendiadys which refers to a small, circular shield is of no avail for the understanding of the LXX translation.[140] מגן is thus employed 13x as a designation of God in the Book of Psalms. The term is in 7:11 sometimes regarded as a divine name or epithet in line with the rest.[141] It is always used with other designations of God, not least metaphorical names based on inanimate nature, 18:3, 31; 28:7; 84:12; 144:1, especially צור, מצודה and משגב, but also with divine names or epithets generally, 3:4; 7:11; 33:20; 115:9, 10, 11; 119:114. This trait is visible wherever divine metaphorical names are encountered. See especially the cluster of names in Ps 18:3 (= 2 Sam 22:2-3) and Ps 144:1-2.

מגן is used with words where the active meaning "save", "give" is conspicuous, but also with others where a more passive nuance "protection", "shelter" can be seen.[142] It is evident that the LXX translator does not always reflect, nor indeed try

---

[133] Cf. **Beekman, Callow**, pp. 138-139.

[134] Bertram, **Sprachschatz**, p. 101 n. 1, 2, Haag, סלע, col. 880, van der Woude, צור, col. 543. The cultic veneration of stones was still prevalent when the LXX was translated. Keel, **Bildsymbolik**, p. 161. Cf. Jer 2:27 where this popular belief in stone as the incarnation of gods was rejected. Bertram, op. cit., p. 101 n. 2. Jirku even suggests that this was the original meaning of the metaphor. See the description in Begrich, **Vertrauensäusserungen**, p. 255 n. 3. Cf. Keel, op. cit., p. 161. But that is hardly the case. See e.g. Caird, **Language**, passim.

[135] Cf. v. 27d-28. See also Watson, **Poetry**, p. 311.

[136] Cf. HR, Flashar, p. 243, **Erwin**, pp. 62-64 and n. 2, Fritsch, **Studies**, pp. 737-738 and n. 14, 15. Cf. **Tsevat**, pp. 16, 88 n. 91, who has missed a few occurrences in MT, viz. 115:10, 11. Erwin fails to notice 17 (18):31.

[137] Cf. **Mozley**, p. XV.

[138] For suggestions, see e.g. **Flashar**, pp. 242-244, Walters, **Text**, p. 59.

[139] See **Flashar**, p. 242, Gunkel, **Psalmen**, p. 372, Anderson, **Psalms**, p. 606. Cf. the Targum.

[140] Cf. Hugger, **Zuflucht**, p. 99.

[141] Freedman, O'Connor, מגן, col. 657. But see below.

[142] Freedman, O'Connor, מגן, col. 658.

to reflect, the semantic meaning of the metaphors since the renderings in cases where the meaning "refuge" is clearly favoured by the context, e.g. 118 (119):14; 143 (144):2, are ἀντιλήμπτωρ and ὑπερασπιστής. "Refuge", "protection" is in fact never reflected by the equivalents in LXX. On the other hand, the renderings reproduce the general understanding of the metaphor as a positive expression, which signifies "help", "salvation". The interpretation of the Hebrew term as "salvation", rather than "protection" is perhaps especially pronounced in 7:11 and 33:20. That the different shades of meaning of the metaphor in the individual cases are not obvious is seen by the renderings in TEV: 7:11; 119:114 and probably also 144:2 (inverted word order) "protector", 18:31 "like a shield" and 33:20 "help".

It could be understood as a participle "giver" in 7:11; 18:31; 47:10; 59:12 in accordance with the meaning of the root in many Semitic languages.[143] The interpretation proposed by Dahood, "suzerain", in this and related passages is not probable.[144] The same sense may apply to passages such as 2 Sam 1:21; Is 21:5, according to some scholars. The meaning in Nah 2:4 is extremely uncertain.[145] Dahood's proposal, even if it is not acceptable from a linguistic point of view, fits the proposed metaphorical meaning of מגן "protection", since it designates one who bestows gifts, a suzerain who provides protection for his vassals in return for obediance and service.[146] Even though nothing implies that the LXX translators knew of another meaning than "shield", these suggestions call for caution since the new interpretations are on the whole restricted to passages where מגן is commonly regarded as a divine name.

The equivalents of the name outside the Psalms

A non-literal translation of מגן as a divine name in MT is consistently carried out also outside the Book of Psalms. It is rendered by the indicative of ὑπερασπίζειν, Gen 15:1; Deut 33:29; Prov 2:7; 30:5 (and thus not regarded as a designation of God in LXX), ὑπερασπιστής, 2 Sam 22:3, 31, or ὑπερασπισμός, 2 Sam 22:36.[147] In Deut 33:29; 2 Sam 22:36 = Ps 18:36 it is better to understand מגן as an epithet closely associated with Yahweh,[148] rather than a divine name. Deut 33:29 can be interpreted in both ways. In NEB "shield" is obviously regarded as a name of God.[149] Regardless of the right interpretation of the Hebrew text in Deut 33:29 the LXX translator could equally well have read מגן piel, which is always rendered by ὑπερασπίζειν. This is true also for Gen 15:1; Prov 2:7; 30:5. Thus the equivalents of the term as a name of God in LXX are in line with those in the Book of Psalms.

---

[143] Freedman, O'Connor, מגן, cols. 658-659. The same meaning may apply to 84:10; 89:19. Ibid., col. 659.

[144] Dahood, **Psalms I**, pp. 16-17. See Freedman, O'Connor, מגן, col. 658 and Loretz, **Psalmenstudien III**, pp. 178-183. McCarter suggests the translation "sovereign" instead. McCarter, **2 Samuel**, p. 465.

[145] Freedman, O'Connor, מגן, col. 659.

[146] See McCarter, **2 Samuel**, p. 465, where he discusses 2 Sam 22:3, which is not included among Dahood's examples. See Dahood, **Psalms I**, p. 17, where the background of this term is described.

[147] See HAL, BHS, Rahlfs and HR. The texts from 2 Sam 22 may reflect the Kaige recension here, notwithstanding that the equivalents in 22:3, 31 are the same as in the Book of Psalms. Cf. Venetz, **Quinta**, pp. 75-76.

[148] Cf. Freedman, O'Connor, מגן, col. 659.

[149] But cf. Freedman, O'Connor, מגן, col. 651.

The term employed in close connection with God

מגן, even when not exactly a divine name, but used in close connection with God is not rendered literally. In Ps 7:11 the term is translated by βοήθεια "help": מגני על־אלהים "My shield is with God" is in LXX rendered by ἡ βοήθειά μου παρὰ τοῦ θεοῦ "(Righteous) is my help from God".[150] The text of MT is probably corrupt. For example, Kraus reads עלי, which makes the shield a divine name here.[151] Cf. the translation in NEB "God, the High God, is my shield", which must be based on the conjecture אֵל. But the rendering in LXX is obviously built on the text of MT. God was maybe pictured here as the shield-bearer of the Psalmist.[152]

מגן is rendered by ὑπερασπισμός in Ps 17 (18):36: ותתן־לי מגן־ישעך "And Thou hast given to me the shield of Thy salvation", καὶ ἐδωκάς μοι ὑπερασπισμὸν σωτηρίας μου "And Thou hast given to me the protection of my salvation".[153] In this case the Targum, which often renders the figure literally, has departed from a literal translation, while Peshitta keeps the metaphor.[154]

The literal translation of the weapons, including מגן, in Ps 34 (35):2-3 where Yahweh fights for the Psalmist,[155] suggests that it was hardly the anthropomorphic imagery per se that caused the LXX translator to refrain from a literal rendering of מגן as a name of God.

צנה, another word for shield, is twice employed in close connection with God, Ps 5:13 and 91:4.[156] Hugger's rendering of 5:13 "Du bist eine Deckung über ihm wie eine צנה, Huld gibst du ihm als seine Krone",[157] which implies that it is a simile for God here, is misleading. RSV has a more traditional and more adequate translation. In neither case is it rendered by a term employed for designations of God, instead the ordinary equivalent of מגן in literal sense, ὅπλον, is used. See below. But these are exceptions, otherwise the Hebrew term was not employed in poetical texts. It did not have an independent role in the cultic language.[158]

The term employed as a name of man

On three occasions מגן may have been employed as a metaphorical designation of man, 47:10; 84:10; 89:19. It invariably denotes the king of Israel or other kings.[159] Wanke, on the other hand, declares that in the only place where the king is clearly meant, 89:19, the text is secondary and the original Hebrew referred to the Lord.

[150] Cf. **Erwin**, p. 63, **Flashar**, p. 243. Dahood's proposal that it is a designation of God preceded by an emphatic lamed is hardly probable. Dahood, **Psalms I**, p. 143, ibid., **Psalms II**, p. 309.
[151] Gunkel, **Psalmen**, p. 26, Kraus, **Psalmen**, pp. 191, 198. Cf. HAL. Peshitta does not reflect the preposition. See e.g. BHK. Dahood suggests that על is a name of God, "the Most High". Dahood, **Psalms I**, pp. 45-46.
[152] **Erwin**, p. 63. Erwin asserts that this was too bold a picture for the translator of Peshitta who has "(the righteous) God is my helper". Ibid., p. 63. Both the Targum and Aquila have a literal rendering of the metaphor. See Field II, ad loc., **Erwin**, p. 63 and n. 3.
[153] The translation is that of Erwin. **Erwin**, p. 64. See also **Flashar**, p. 243.
[154] See **Erwin**, p. 64. Even Aquila, Symmachus and Theodotion may have employed the same equivalent as LXX, according to Reider, Turner, **Index**, p. 244. Thus also Field II, ad loc. But Aquila probably used his ordinary translation. See Mercati, **Hexapli**, p. 5, Schenker, **Hexapla**, pp. 400-404. The same is true for Ps 32 (33):20.
[155] Yahweh is hardly pictured here as the shield-bearer of the Psalmist, as Keel suggests, Keel, **Bildsymbolik**, p. 201, in that case only צנה would have been appropriate but rather as an offensive warrior of the first century B.C. Cf. Freedman, O'Connor, מגן, cols. 648-649, 652, 654. Cf. 1 Sam 17:7. See below.
[156] Hugger, **Zuflucht**, p. 100.
[157] Hugger, **Zuflucht**, p. 100.
[158] Hugger, **Zuflucht**, p. 101.
[159] See Kraus, **Psalmen**, p. 507, Freedman, O'Connor, מגן, col. 659.

In 84:10 too the original text, according to Wanke, described Yahweh as king and shield.[160] Even though the meaning of 47:10 is obscure[161] most scholars rightly see an allusion to leaders of some kind in these passages.[162] The parallels in 47:10 "nobles of the peoples", 84:10 "your Messiah" and 89:19 "our king" clearly favour the reference to kings.[163]

In all these cases the connection with God is emphasized. See Ps 46 (47):10: "For the shields of the earth belong to God; he is highly exalted" is rendered by "for God's mighty ones of the earth have been greatly exalted".[164] Even though LXX partly deviates from the usual understanding of the Hebrew, "the shields of the earth" obviously refers to men in LXX as well as in MT. The parallelism between מגני ארץ and נדיבי עמים "nobles of the peoples" or "princes of the peoples" is reflected in LXX. This is also clearly seen in the choice of translation, οἱ κραταιοὶ τῆς γῆς "the powerful (or the mighty ones) of the earth". Cf. also Peshitta "the powers of the earth".[165] κραταιός is never employed as a rendering of מגן as a divine name, or for that matter of any of the metaphorical names of God. Loretz suggests that the right meaning here is "gift", "present". It is also the expected ending of the Psalm.[166] Both this and Driver's propositions with reference to Arabic are, however, far from convincing.[167] The metaphorical character of the term is thus recognized in LXX and the Hebrew word is given a suitable equivalent.[168]

In Ps 89:19 it clearly refers to the king in MT while LXX avoids such an interpretation: "For our shield belongs to the LORD, our king to the Holy One of Israel" is translated by "for our help is of the Lord; and of the Holy One of Israel, our king". On the other hand, it is not regarded as a name of God in LXX, as is reflected also in the choice of equivalent, ἀντίλημψις, "help",[169] which is never employed for מגן as a divine name in LXX Psalms, even though the cognate ἀντιλήμπτωρ is sometimes so used.

"Behold our shield, O God; look upon the face of thine anointed!" in the Massoretic text of 84:10 is interpreted as "Behold, O God our defender, and look upon the face of thine anointed." "Our shield" and "thine anointed" are parallel word pairs in the Hebrew. In LXX the term is obviously applied to God, since it is in vocative case and thus a direct address to God, rather than a parallel to "thine anointed". Furthermore, it is also rendered by ὑπερασπιστής, which is only employed as a designation of God in LXX. See 4.1. "The anointed one" here may have been understood in a Messianic sense, but this does not alter the translation equivalents in LXX.[170]

The use of מגן to express trust in Yahweh was probably a royal prerogative (with clear religio-historical parallels)[171] from the beginning, which has been

---

[160] Wanke, **Zionstheologie**, pp. 20-21.

[161] See Anderson, **Psalms**, p. 366. Cf. Wanke, **Zionstheologie**, p. 20.

[162] See e.g. Anderson, **Psalms**, p. 366. According to Briggs, the reference is to shield bearers, warriors, here. "Shield" is thus used as pars pro toto. Briggs, **Psalms I**, p. 400, Barr, **Philology**, pp. 241-242, HAL. Cf. Gunkel, **Psalmen**, pp. 203-204.

[163] See Freedman, O'Connor, מגן, col. 659. Cf. BDB "rulers".

[164] Aquila and Hieronymus agree with LXX in reading the verb in plural. See Briggs, **Psalms I**, p. 400. Cf. BHK, BHS.

[165] See Barr, **Philology**, p. 241.

[166] See Loretz, **Psalmenstudien IV**, p. 214.

[167] Cf. Barr, **Philology**, pp. 241, 330.

[168] Cf. Barr, **Philology**, pp. 241-242.

[169] Cf. HR, **Flashar**, p. 243, **Erwin**, p. 63. Peshitta also avoids a literal translation. See **Erwin**, p. 63.

[170] Later on the psalm was in Jewish tradition obviously interpreted with reference to the days of the Messiah. See e.g. Braude, **Midrash**, p. 66 and n. 10.

[171] Hugger, **Zuflucht**, p. 99. The parallels from the countries surrounding Israel suggest that the choice of this metaphor, in contrast to other terms for a specific weapon which could have been employed, was a heritage from the cultural environment in the Ancient Near East.

debased.[172] This also seems to be true for other metaphorical designations of God.[173] But some divine names, e.g. מעוז and מחסה, do not occur at all in the mouth of the king in the OT texts.[174] On the other hand, these designations were, according to Eichhorn, restricted to appointed functionaries of the cult. They were not used by ordinary people in OT.[175]

3.3.2   The translation of the term as a metaphor and in the literal sense

מגן as an ordinary metaphor, i.e. a metaphor which does not refer to God, is at least once rendered literally by ἀσπίς, Job 15:26, which concerns a sinner's defence against the judgments of Yahweh. This is, however, in the Hexaplaric addition, i.e. it was not part of the original LXX. It is also employed in metaphorical sense in Songs 4:4, rendered by θυρεός, and in Job 41:7, rendered by ἀσπίς. Thus a literal translation of the metaphor predominates.[176] The specific employment of the term for "scales (of a crocodile)", according to HAL, in Job 41:7 was not recognized by the translator of Job.[177] But here, as in Songs 4:4, where the neck of a woman is likened to the tower of David, covered with shields, the term probably refers to the so-called testudo, rather than the ordinary shield.[178]

The rendering in Hos 4:18, φρύαγμα "insolence", may reflect a Hebrew מגן II "insolent".[179] In two other cases of metaphorical use HAL proposes a מגן II, Prov 6:11; 24:34. But the meaning suggested, "insolent", does not fit the equivalent in 6:11: איש מגן is rendered by ἀγαθὸς δρομεὺς "swift courier" in LXX. Nor does it agree with other proposals. The sense "beggar" is also often suggested.[180] Loretz even argues that the phrase should be translated "shield-bearer" and that the metaphor reflects the swift approach of a lightly armed soldier.[181] 24:34 is not translated at all. מגנה in Lam 3:65 is understood as "insolence" in HAL, an interpretation which does not really suit the context.[182] It is rendered by ὑπερασπισμός in LXX, i.e. interpreted as "shield", even though the Greek word in itself could also mean "protection". See LSJ. The same word is used in 2 Sam 22:36 = Ps 17 (18):36 for מגן. According to Albrektson, the right interpretation of the Hebrew term is, "covering".[183] In all probability the translators did not know the meaning "insolent" of מגן.

The ordinary meaning of מגן "shield", "round shield"[184] was well known to the translators of the LXX. Hugger, on the other hand, less convincingly equates מגן with צנה in the OT, although he admits that they may once have signified different kinds of shield.[185] ἀσπίς is a common translation of מגן, Job 15:26 (Hexaplaric

---

[172] Keel, **Bildsymbolik**, p. 201.

[173] See **Eichhorn**, pp. 89-91, 123-125.

[174] **Eichhorn**, pp. 113, 120.

[175] **Eichhorn**, pp. 123-125 and passim.

[176] Freedman, O'Connor, מגן, col. 655, who wrongly has 41:6.

[177] In BDB it is regarded a metaphor, which presupposes the ordinary sense of the word. Thus also Dhorme, **Job**, p. 634, Habel, **Job**, p. 572, Gordis, **Job**, pp. 484-485, Freedman, O'Connor, מגן, col. 655.

[178] See Pope, **Job**, p. 468, Freedman, O'Connor, מגן, col. 655.

[179] See e.g. Lisowsky, ad loc. Cf. HAL where a Hebrew מגן "gift", "present" is suggested here. In BDB it is regarded as a metaphorical use of the ordinary מגן and BHS suggests a Vorlage with גאון "arrogance", "pride".

[180] See Freedman, O'Connor, מגן, col. 659 with references.

[181] Loretz, איש מגן, p. 477.

[182] Cf. Albrektson, **Lamentations**, p. 170.

[183] See Albrektson, **Lamentations**, p. 170. See also BDB, Gesenius.

[184] See e.g. Anderson, **Psalms**, p. 72. Regarding the appearance and the material of this shield, see Freedman, O'Connor, מגן, col. 649. Cf. col. 647. See also Galling, **Reallexikon**, pp. 279-280.

[185] Hugger, **Zuflucht**, pp. 99-101.

addition); 41:7,[186] 1 Chr 5:18; 2 Chr 9:16 (twice); although θυρεός is the main rendering.[187] Neither of them are equivalents of מגן in LXX Psalms. θυρεός is in fact more adequately employed for צנה, since it best covers the semantic meaning of this word[188] and צנה also mostly has θυρεός as equivalent. But צנה is also often rendered by more generic terms.

מגן and צנה have many different equivalents within one and the same book (Ezekiel). On the five occasions where מגן and צנה occur in close connection, Ps 35:2; Jer 46:3; Ez 23:24; 38:4; 39:9, the LXX translators never have the same rendering of both. צנה ומגן in Ez 23:24 is rendered by θυρεοὶ καὶ πέλται and in 38:4 by πέλται καὶ περικεφαλαίαι, מגן וצנה is in 39:9 translated by πέλταις καὶ κοντοῖς, in Jer 26 (46):3 by ὅπλα καὶ ἀσπίδας and in Ps 34 (35):2 by ὅπλου καὶ θυρεοῦ. Cf. also 2 Chr 14:7. Some of the differences in Ezekiel may be due to the fact that this book is not a homogeneous translation, thus 23:24 and 38:4; 39:9 had different translators.[189] There are also doubts about the Vorlage of LXX in some cases. In Ez 38:4 περικεφαλαίαι may render כובה "helmet" as in v. 5.[190] In that case πέλτη is probably a rendering of מגן and צנה is omitted by the trans- lator.[191] Despite the differences, πέλτη is then the most common translation of מגן in Ezekiel, since it also occurs in 27:10. The interpretation of צנה in Ez 39:9 κοντός "lance" is also reflected in other old versions.[192]

The generic term ὅπλον "arms" is a fairly common equivalent to מגן in LXX as a whole. The many different Hebrew equivalents to ὅπλον, 1 Sam 17:7; Ps 5:13; Amos 4:2, צנה, Ps 45 (46):10; 56 (57):5; Nah 3:3 and Hab 3:11, חנית, to mention a few, accord with the supposition that technical terms are seldom stereotypically rendered in LXX. Other weapons are also translated by the generic term ὅπλον. For further examples, see HR. מגן in its literal sense is always rendered by ὅπλον in LXX Psalms, 34 (35):2; 75 (76):4, in contrast to the equivalents as a name of God. Mozley suggests that the translator regarded the literal translation of specific weapons as prosaic.[193] But ὅπλον is a usual rendering of מגן also in non-poetic contexts. Weapons are in fact often rendered by more or less generic words and seldom stereotypically translated in LXX. Examples of different interpretations of specific weapons abound.[194] A good example is חרב, which is sometimes rendered by πόλεμος, Lev 26:6, 36, 37; Num 14:3; 20:18.[195] πελταστής is equivalent to two different Hebrew phrases. It is a translation of נשׂא מגן, 2 Chr 14:7, and נשׁק מגן, 17:17.

---

[186] See BHS, Rahlfs. Cf. HR, Dhorme, **Job**, p. 220, Freedman, O'Connor, מגן, col. 659.

[187] It occurs 13x, according to HR, Santos, **Index**. But cf. Freedman, O'Connor, מגן, col. 659, who only notes nine occurrences.

[188] Freedman, O'Connor, מגן, col. 647. Cf. Anderson, **Psalms**, p. 276.

[189] See especially McGregor, **Ezekiel**, pp. 197-199. It is probable that at least chapters 1-25 and 26-39 were rendered by different hands. Ibid., pp. 197-199.

[190] Thus Zimmerli, **Ezechiel**, pp. 925-926. It is perhaps a misplaced gloss. Cooke, **Ezekiel**, p. 410. Thus also BHK.

[191] See Cooke, **Ezekiel**, p. 423.

[192] See Zimmerli, **Ezechiel**, p. 930.

[193] **Mozley**, pp. XVI, 12-13. But ὅπλον sometimes refers to a large shield. See LSJ.

[194] See e.g. Wevers, **Weapons**, pp. 823-825. Cf. Pope, **Songs**, pp. 468-469, Freedman, O'Connor, מגן, cols. 657, 659.

[195] Cf. Caird, **Language**, p. 136. This term thus functions as a kind of metonomy. For the definition of metonomy, see e.g. Caird, op. cit., pp. 136-137.

3.3.3 Preliminary conclusions regarding the translation technique

The distinction between the term when it means a literal shield and when it refers to God is maintained. Different equivalents are also employed when it refers to God and when it refers to man in LXX Psalms. Even though the translator does not render the semantic meaning of the metaphors in context, the generic term chosen adequately reflects the positive meaning in most passages. ὑπερασπιστής was the favourite rendering of מגן as a divine name in LXX, probably because it contains an element denoting "shield", ἀσπίς, i.e. a connection with the literal meaning of the metaphor has been kept,[196] or in terms of the conventional metaphor theory, the image. But ἀσπίς rarely renders מגן in the literal sense in LXX. HR lists only five examples and Trommius three. An etymological interest is also evident since גנן is always, and מגן as a verb mostly, rendered by ὑπερασπίζειν.

The choice of main equivalent is thus an example of both literal and free trans-lation technique; the relative consistency in the use of the rendering ὑπερασπιστής for מגן as a divine name is a literal trait,[197] as is also true of the "etymological" translation technique.[198] On the other hand, the non-literal rendering of the metaphors of course contradicts a literal method.[199] The use of ἀντιλήμπτωρ in Ps 3:4; 118 (119):114 instead of the ordinary ὑπερασπιστής seems to be arbitrary, since it neither accords with the probable semantic meaning of the metaphor in context nor does it depend on the usual endeavour for variation. These passages do not even occur in similar contexts.[200] That the translation in 119:114 is based on the Hebrew phrase rather than the individual word can probably be excluded since the Hebrew expression is unique. The Greek expression is not a set phrase either. Cf. especially Ps 27 (28):7, where עזי ומגני is rendered by βοηθός μου καὶ ὑπερασπιστής μου, and 118 (119):114, where סתרי ומגני is translated by βοηθός μου καὶ ἀντιλήμπτωρ μου. The difference can hardly be explained by the context since both עז, 28:7, and סתר, 119:114, are as divine names, contrary to their semantic meaning, rendered by βοηθός. That מגן rather functions as a kind of metrical woof in 28:7; 33:20 and 84:12[201] has had no effect on the choice of equivalent. On the other hand, the translator distinguishes between passages in which the metaphor is used in close connection with God and those where it is employed as a divine name. In the few passages where מגן is a metaphor in other contexts it has one of the ordinary equivalents as a rule. See below.

An interesting question for the evaluation of the influence from theological exegesis in the rendering of this metaphor concerns the validity of the metaphor when the Hebrew Scriptures were translated into Greek. Was it a dead metaphor for the LXX translators? In that case how would it have influenced their translation? Nevertheless even though it may have been intuitively understood as a dead metaphor the translator could for translation technical reasons, possibly as a question of fidelity to the Holy Scriptures, have rendered it literally. For a more comprehensive discussion, see 6.4.3. The expression in 3:4 "But thou, O Lord, art a shield about me" suggests that the metaphorical element, at least in this phrase, had faded,[202] but evidently this has not influenced the rendering in 3:4. If the metaphor was live, one would at least have expected the term צנה, since this was larger and often had a concave–convex form in order to better encompass the

---

[196] Cf. Fritsch, **Studies**, p. 737.

[197] See Olofsson, **LXX Version**, pp. 16–20.

[198] Olofsson, **LXX Version**, pp. 22–24.

[199] Olofsson, **LXX Version**, pp. 21–22.

[200] Cf. Hugger, **Zuflucht**, p. 100. The description of the context by Hugger is, however, not reliable in detail.

[201] Thus Hugger, **Zuflucht**, p. 100.

[202] Cf. Keel, **Bildsymbolik**, pp. 201–202.

body.[203]

3.4 THE TRANSLATION OF MĀ'ŌZ AS A DIVINE NAME

3.4.1 The equivalents of the name in LXX

The equivalents of the name in LXX Psalms

מעוז is, according to HAL, a divine name in Ps 27:1; 28:8; 31:5; 43:2, but this hardly includes all passages in the Book of Psalms.[204] 31:3; 37:39; 52:9 should also have been mentioned.[205] It is rendered by ὑπερασπιστής in Ps 26 (27):1; 27 (28):8; 30 (31):3, 5; 36 (37):39. In 70 (71):3 the Vorlage of LXX probably had צור מעוז instead of צור מעון. This is clearly implied by the equivalents of the divine metaphors.[206] Fritsch must have built on this emended text in his statistics.[207] ὑπερασπιστής is thus the most common rendering of מעוז in LXX Psalms and it never has that equivalent outside the Psalter. See Table 2.

An equivalent which occurs only once in LXX Psalms is βοηθός, 51 (52):9:

> See the man who would not make God his refuge, (מעוזו) but trusted in the abundance of his riches, and sought refuge (יעז) in his destruction.[208] (MT).

> Behold the man who made not God his help; (βοηθὸν αὐτοῦ) but trusted in the abundance of his wealth, and strengthened himself in his vanity (LXX).

κραταίωμα in 42 (43):2 is also an uncommon equivalent.[209] BHS suggests עז as Vorlage of LXX, the Targum and Jerome, but this is extremely far-fetched, at least as regards the Septuagint. κραταίωμα is only once a rendering of עז, 27 (28):8, where it may be regarded as a name of God. Neither עז nor מעוז are translated stereotypically in LXX Psalms, especially not as designations of God. See Table 1.

מעוז as a metaphor used as a designation of God mostly occurs in the Laments in the Psalter, according to Zobel.[210] On the other hand, this name is confined to Ps 1-72, i.e. the first and second books of the Psalter. This is astonishing since the other divine names, which mean "fortress", "stronghold", have not replaced מעוז in the second part of the Book of Psalms. They are evenly spread through the Psalms, even though the majority of the metaphorical divine names are to be found in the first part of the Psalter.

---

[203] See Freedman, O'Connor, מגן, col. 648. This is the usual understanding of the word. Both צנה and מגן refer, according to Hugger, to the great shield that covered the whole body. Hugger, **Zuflucht**, p. 99.

[204] See e.g. Bertram, **Sprachschatz**, p. 95.

[205] Cf. **Eichhorn**, pp. 115-120. See also BDB.

[206] See Table 1. The emendation is supported by many Hebrew manuscripts including 4QPs-a, but also by Peshitta, the Targum and Ps 31:3. BHK also mentions Symmachus, which in a retranslation of Syrohexapla by Field has the same equivalent as in 30 (31):3. See BHK, BHS, HAL, Skehan, **Qumrân**, p. 175. See also **Baetgen**, p. 644, Baetgen, **Psalmen**, p. 218, **Mozley**, p. 113, Briggs, **Psalms I**, p. 272, Wutz, **Transkriptionen**, pp. 223, 351, Anderson, **Psalms**, p. 511, **Eichhorn**, p. 121.

[207] See Fritsch, **Studies**, p. 737 n. 18. See also Zobel, מעוז, col. 1022.

[208] RSV has "wealth", which is an emendation based on Peshitta and the Targum.

[209] See Fritsch, **Studies**, p. 736, HR and BDB.

[210] See Zobel, מעוז, col. 1026. But that is hardly the case. See Wagner, עזז, col. 12.

The equivalents of the name outside the Psalms

Apart from 2 Sam 22:33, מעוז as a designation of God in MT is only employed in prophetical texts outside the Book of Psalms.[211] It is, according to BDB, a name of God in Prov 10:29; Is 17:10; 25:4; 27:5; Jer 16:19; Nah 1:7 and Joel 3 (4):16. MT in 2 Sam 22:33 is probably corrupt.[212] Since the first layer of the Lucianic text in 1 Kgs 21 – 2 Kgs 25 is closest to, if not identical with, the Old Greek, according to the majority of scholars,[213] מעוז does not occur in the Vorlage of LXX.

מעוז is rendered by βοήθεια in Jer 16:19 and βοηθός in Is 17:10, the two places where the LXX translators have, without doubt, understood it as a divine name:

> O LORD, my strength and my stronghold, (מעוזי) my refuge in the day of trouble ... (Jer 16:19 MT).

> O Lord, my strength, and mine help, (βοήθειά μου) and my refuge in a day of evil ... (LXX).

The phrasing of Jer 16:19-21 is typical of both Personal Laments and Thanksgivings.[214] This text echoes other passages in Jeremiah.[215]

> For you have forgotten the God of your salvation, and have not remembered the Rock of your (מעוזך) refuge ... (Is 17:10 MT).

> Because thou hast forsaken God thy Saviour, and hast not been mindful of the Lord thy (τοῦ βοηθοῦ σου) helper ... (LXX).

This refers to the Jews who have abandoned Yahweh, the rock, and turned to other gods for protection.[216] Here the same Hebrew expression as in Ps 31:3 (MT) and probably in the Vorlage of 70 (71):3 (see above) is employed, צור מעוז, but rendered by κυρίου τοῦ βοηθοῦ.

In Prov 10:29 it is not a name of God, but a description of the security of the righteous.[217] The text of Is 25:4 is understood by the translator differently from the traditional interpretation: כי היית מעוז לדל מעוז לאביון בצר־לו "For thou hast been a stronghold[218] to the poor, a stronghold to the needy in his distress" is rendered by ἐγένου γὰρ πάσῃ πόλει ταπεινῇ βοηθός, καὶ τοῖς ἀθυμήσασιν διὰ ἔνδειαν σκέπη "For thou hast been a helper to every lowly city, and a shelter to them that were disheartened by reason of poverty." At least one of the two occurrences of מעוז may be interpreted as a divine name also in LXX. It is rendered by βοηθός, a term which as a rule pertains to Yahweh in LXX.[219] The textual problems of the verse are, however, complicated and not adequately

---

[211] Cf. Eichhorn, p. 114.

[212] Most scholars now read מָאֻזְּנִי with 4QSam-a, the Lucianic text of LXX, Peshitta, Vulgate, Old Latin and Ps 18:33. Smith, **Samuel**, p. 380, McCarter, **2 Samuel**, p. 459. See also BHK, BHS. Wagner, מעוז, col. 12, keeps MT with reference to v. 32 and translates the phrase מָעוּזִּי חָיִל with "starke Festung" (strong fortress).

[213] See Olofsson, **LXX Version**, pp. 60-61 with references. See also McCarter, **1 Samuel**, pp. 7-9, ibid., **2 Samuel**, p. 3.

[214] See Holladay, **Jeremiah**, p. 480. Eichhorn calls it a "Liturgie". Eichhorn, p. 115.

[215] See e.g. Holladay, **Jeremiah**, p. 481, Carroll, **Jeremiah**, p. 347.

[216] Cf. Eichhorn, pp. 70, 118. In this case it is probably the question of Tammuz. Gray, **Isaiah**, pp. 296, 302, Eichhorn, pp. 70, 118, Wildberger, **Jesaia**, pp. 656-657.

[217] Zobel, מעוז, col. 1023.

[218] Maybe מעוז should be understood as "shelter" here. See Zobel, מעוז, cols. 1023-1024. Cf. Wagner, מעוז, col. 12 "shelter and protection".

[219] Ottley has tried to understand the interpretation in LXX in light of the Hebrew. See Ottley, **Isaiah II**, p. 225. For a background to the interpretation of LXX, see Ziegler, **Untersuchungen**, pp. 82-83.

solved.[220]

In Joel 3 (4):16 מעוז is rendered by ἐνισχύειν "strengthen". מחסה, the A word in the pair, is also rendered verbally, by φείδεσθαι "spare". Regarding the interpretation of this verse, see 3.5.1. The translation thus diverges from the usual rendering of מעוז as a divine name in LXX, notwithstanding that the Hebrew text is obviously dependent upon cultic phraseology where Yahweh is depicted as a shelter in which the people can find protection in times of danger. Cf. texts as Ps 14:6; 31:4; 43:2; 47:1.[221] The exact parallel between מעוז and מחסה otherwise only occurs in Is 25:4.[222] It is striking that the translation has no connection with the equivalents in LXX Psalms, despite these Hebrew parallels. Instead the translator alludes to two earlier passages in Joel, 2:27 and 3:5.[223] The choice of ἐνισχύειν must evidently be understood as a conscious reference to the wording in 2:27 where ולא־יבשו עמי לעולם "and my people shall never again be put to shame" is rendered by καὶ οὐ μὴ καταισχυνθῶσιν οὐκέτι πᾶς ὁ λαός μου εἰς τὸν λαός μου εἰς τὸν αἰῶνα "No more will my whole people be humiliated." Cf. 3:16 "the Lord will strengthen (ἐνισχύσει) his people".

The interpretation of Is 27:5 varies widely. בְּמָעֻזִּי "in my stronghold" is rendered by οἱ ἐνοικοῦντες ἐν αὐτῇ "they that dwell in her (shall cry)". מעוז probably refers to the temple in MT and is not a name of Yahweh.[224] But other interpretations are also possible. Cf. the translation in RSV of the expression או יחזק במעוזי "Or let them lay hold of my protection." The LXX translator has understood the song of the vineyard, 27:3–5, an admittedly obscure text, as a song over a destroyed city.[225] Perhaps he saw a root מעון* "live" in מעוז read as מעון. Cf. the rendering of ענה in 13:22.[226] Thus no divine name existed in the interpretation of the LXX translator and it is not even probable that the Hebrew term refers to Yahweh in MT.

In Nah 1:7 where למעוז "a stronghold" is rendered by τοῖς ὑπομένουσιν αὐτὸν "to them that wait on him" it is disputable whether it is the question of a divine name or a divine characteristic at all in MT, despite the reference in e.g. BDB and the rendering in NEB and RSV.

> The LORD is good, a stronghold in the day of trouble; he knows those who take refuge in him. (MT).[227]

> The Lord is good to them that wait on him in the day of affliction; and he knows them that reverence him (LXX).

The LXX translator has not seen a divine name here. He probably only read the verb קוה "wait".[228]

---

[220] Gray, Isaiah, p. 428.
[221] See Smith, Waard, Bewer, Micah, p. 138, Allen, Joel, p. 121.
[222] Cf. Wolff, Joel, p. 98.
[223] See Rudolph, Joel, p. 85, Allen, Joel, p. 121.
[224] See Zobel, מעוז, col. 1025. Cf. 1 Kgs 1:50. For a reasonable interpretation of Is 27:5, see also Procksch, Jesaia I, pp. 338–339. Thus it is not mentioned among the divine names in Eichhorn, pp. 114–120.
[225] Ziegler, Untersuchungen, pp. 87, 91, Seeligmann, Isaiah, pp. 26–27. See also Goshen-Gottstein, Isaiah, ad loc.
[226] Ziegler, Untersuchungen, p. 91.
[227] The translation is taken from RSV. The inclusion of מעוז in Nah 1:7 among the divine names by Eichhorn partly depends on an emendation to לְקֹוָיו מָעוֹז on the authority of LXX. Eichhorn, p. 114 n. 2. This is a common emendation, but it in fact derives from a combination of the renderings of the LXX and the Targum. Cf. Smith, Waard, Bewer, Micah, p. 300 with references.
[228] Smith, Waard, Bewer, Micah, p. 300. Another suggestion is that he had למקוין in his Vorlage. Thus Rudolph, Micha, p. 152. The text of MT is probably corrupt. See BHS, Rudolph, Micha, p. 152.

3.4.2 The background for the use of the term as a divine name

מעוז is a term with different referents which, apart from its use as a divine name, is frequently employed in its literal sense in MT. It occurs in both recent and in older texts.[229] I shall therefore briefly describe its use and distribution in the Old Testament as a basis for an understanding of its employment as a divine name and thereby also shed light on the metaphorical use of the other names with a similar meaning.

The military referents clearly dominate the secular usage. They pertain mainly to castles and fortresses. In Is 23:4 the word refers to the fortress of the sea, "Sidon", in 23:11 to "fortresses" or "castles".[230] Nah 3:11 could be interpreted in an abstract way as a shelter from the enemy but in view of כל מבצריך "all your fortresses" in v. 12, the meaning "fortress" best fits the context.[231] The same could be said of Dan 11:7, 10, 19.[232] Judg 6:26 is not easy to interpret, but the word may here signify a mountain-fortress[233] or a mountain-peak.[234] The term refers to the city of Sin, i.e. Pelusium, in Ez 30:15 (see e.g. RSV), described as the fortress of Egypt.[235] In Dan 11:39 it probably denotes a fortified castle[236] or maybe a garrison.[237] מעוז refers to Sidon as a secure harbour, a shelter, in Is 23:14. Cf. v. 1. Sometimes, however, this word denotes the temple, Ez 24:25[238] and Is 27:5. In Dan 11:31 too the temple, regarded as a fortress, is obviously the referent.

The general idea behind מעוז in literal sense is thus protection, mostly military, such as fortresses and castles, but also in the form of the temple, as a place where people could find refuge.[239] This is evidently also the main reason for the use of the word as a name of God. The same is in fact true for the other designations of God with a similar meaning, מצודה and משגב, except that they never refer to the temple.

The LXX translators seem to have had vague ideas concerning the meaning and referents of מעוז. Mostly a general term for strength, ἰσχύς, is employed, whether it is the question of fortresses, cities or the temple in Jerusalem, Is 23:4, 11; Ez 24:25; 30:15; Dan 11:1 (Th), 7, 10 (Th), 19 (Th). The term is interpreted as a metaphor in Nah 3:11 and στάσις is therefore used instead. But ὀχύρωμα once occurs as equivalent, Is 23:14. This is the only place where a rendering in LXX clearly reflects the referent of the Hebrew term.

---

[229] Zobel, מעוז, col. 1025, Wagner, עזז, col. 11.

[230] This translation is based on the reading of 1QIs-a. Wagner, עזז, col. 11, Talmon, **Aspects**, p. 124. The form in MT is a contamination of מעוזיה with an alternative reading מעוניה. Otherwise the plural of מעוז is as a rule מעונות. Talmon, op. cit., p. 124 n. 89.

[231] Wagner, עזז, col. 11. Cf. Zobel, מעוז, col. 1021.

[232] Zobel, מעוז, col. 1021.

[233] Wagner, עזז, col. 11.

[234] Zobel, מעוז, col. 1022. This interpretation could perhaps be supported by the frequent parallelism between צור, סלע and מעוז.

[235] See e.g. Zimmerli, **Ezechiel**, pp. 736-737.

[236] Thus HAL, Zobel, מעוז, col. 1021.

[237] Wagner, עזז, col. 13.

[238] Thus Zimmerli, **Ezechiel**, p. 575, Zobel, מעוז, col. 1025. But Wagner rather suggests that the city of Jerusalem is intended. Wagner, עזז, col. 11.

[239] In Ez 24:25 the preciousness of the temple is also emphasized.

3.4.3 The equivalents of the term as an ordinary metaphor

מעוז is used twice of the personified people, Ephraim, in the Book of Psalms, the parallel passages 60:9 and 108:9. Here it is part of a description where Yahweh is depicted as a warrior:[240]

> God has spoken in his sanctuary: "With exultation I will divide up Shechem and portion out the Vale of Succoth. Gilead is mine; Manas'seh is mine; E'phraim is my helmet; (מעוז ראשי) Judah is my sceptre" (60:8–9).

The reference is to a helmet, as a symbol of power.[241] Thus Yahweh is depicted as a warrior whose helmet is northern Israel and whose commander's staff is Judah.[242] ואפרים מעוז ראשי is rendered by καὶ Εφραιμ κραταίωσις τῆς κεφαλῆς μου "Ephraim is the strength of my head" (59:9) and by καὶ Εφραιμ ἀντίλημψις τῆς κεφαλῆς μου "Ephraim is the help of my head" (107:9).

There seems in fact to be a minor distinction in LXX Psalms between the translation of מעוז as a name of God and its use as a metaphorical expression in connection with God. Thus neither κραταίωσις nor ἀντίλημψις render מעוז as a designation of God, even though both terms sometimes occur as divine names. See Table 1. ἀντίλημψις also renders the metaphor מגן in connection with God in 88 (89):19.

Outside the Book of Psalms, מעוז as an ordinary metaphor has the equivalent σκέπη "protection", "shelter", Is 30:3 and in 30:2 the phrase in which it occurs is not translated or it is paraphrased:

> "Woe to the rebellious children", says the LORD, … who set out to go down to Egypt, without asking for my counsel, to take refuge in the protection (מעוז) of Pharaoh, and to seek shelter in the shadow (צל) of Egypt. Therefore shall the protection of Pharaoh turn to your shame, and the shelter in the shadow of Egypt to your humiliation (30:1–3 MT).

> Woe to the apostate children, therefore thus saith the Lord: … even they that proceed to go down into Egypt, but they have not inquired of me, that they might be helped by Pharao, and protected by the Egyptians. For the protection of Pharao shall be to you a disgrace, and there shall be a reproach to them that trust in Egypt (30:1–3 LXX).

לעוז במעוז פרעה "to take refuge in the protection of Pharaoh" is rendered by τοῦ βοηθηθῆναι ὑπὸ Φαραω "that they might be helped by Pharao", Is 30:2. The parallel term to מעוז in the word pair, צל, is left untranslated in v. 2 and in v. 3, even though the translator knew the meaning of both words.[243] Terms which are usually employed for God are here with an ironical purpose transferred to Egypt.[244] The LXX translator's failure to catch the irony of the text may have contributed to the omission.

---

[240] See Bertram, **Sprachschatz**, p. 95, Kraus, **Psalmen**, pp. 588–589. Cf. HAL.

[241] Zobel, מעוז, col. 1023.

[242] Anderson, **Psalms**, p. 445. The translation "sceptre" is less probable in this context.

[243] See Ziegler, **Untersuchungen**, p. 55. This type of expression was often rendered without the noun in LXX Isaiah. Ibid., pp. 53–55. Cf. Wagner, עזז, col. 12.

[244] Cf. Kaiser, **Jesaia**, pp. 285–286.

The derivation of the term in MT and LXX

מעוז can be derived from either עזז or עוז, according to the lexica and grammars.[245] The most probable solution is that מעוז is derived from both roots, even though עוז clearly dominates.[246] This is also the general impression of the renderings of the divine names in LXX.[247] מעוז in both the literal and the metaphorical sense has many Greek equivalents, but few occur more than once. The Hebrew term, when not employed as a designation of God, often seems to be derived from עזז by the LXX translators.[248] Cf. these renderings of עזז: βοηθεῖν (1x), κραταιοῦν (3x), δυναμοῦν (2x), κατισχύειν (2x), ἰσχύειν (1x). מעוז had similar equivalents: βοήθεια (1x), βοηθός (3x), δύναμις (1x), ἰσχύς (9x), κραταιοῦν (1x), κραταίωσις (1x), κραταίωμα (1x) in LXX.[249] But the two roots cannot be strictly differentiated in LXX, since they have many equivalents in common. Either the LXX translators could not distinguish between the two or they thought that both had a similar meaning. Even lexica and concordances (such as Gesenius, Lisowsky, HAL) have different divisions between the two verbs.

The interpretation of the term in MT and LXX

The literal meaning of מעוז is "stronghold", "place of refuge", "defence".[250] According to Hugger, contrary to Zobel and Wagner, מעוז is not to be understood in the meaning "fortress" or "bulwark" employed as a metaphor in the Book of Psalms.[251] Cf. the translation "Zuflucht", "Schutz". Zobel, on the other hand, has the rendering "Bollwerk", "Burg".[252] If Hugger's theory is correct the literal meaning of מעוז is "place of refuge" in the Psalms. But in view of the words in the word field this is not probable.[253] The significance of the term in places where it is commonly regarded as a metaphor in MT is thus not self-evident. It may also have been derived from עוז, whereas when it refers to a fortress it stems from עזז.

On the other hand, the interpretations of the LXX translators are of course the most adequate point of departure for the study of translation technique and not the meaning of MT.[254] It is thereby needful to investigate whether the renderings of מעוז as a divine title stand out from the equivalents of the term generally.

מעוז is seldom or never interpreted as a fortress in LXX.[255] Therefore מעוז may not have been regarded as a metaphor by the translators since they make no distinction between a literal and a figurative meaning. The term is often rendered by ἰσχύς in metaphorical language – see e.g. Is 23:11; Ez 24:25[256] and Neh 8:10 – but once by καταφυγή, Dan 11:39 (Th). But it is hard to distinguish between a

---

[245] See HAL, Anderson, **Psalms**, p. 220. The vocalization of MT rather suggests עזז, but, according to BDB, the right derivation is עוז. See also Bertram, **Sprachschatz**, pp. 93 n. 4, 95 n. 1, Ringgren, עוז, col. 1130.

[246] Hugger seems, however, to exaggerate this dominance. Hugger, **Zuflucht**, p. 91.

[247] Thus translations concerned with protection and help outnumber equivalents where strength is the dominant motive. See e.g. Zobel, מעוז, col. 1021.

[248] Bertram, **Sprachschatz**, p. 93 n. 4.

[249] The figures are based on Santos, **Index**.

[250] Thus Fritsch, **Studies**, p. 737. See HAL "Bergfeste", "Zufluchtstätte", BDB "place or means of safety", "protection", Erwin, p. 70, Wagner, עזז, col. 11 "fortress".

[251] Hugger, **Zuflucht**, p. 91.

[252] Zobel, מעוז, cols. 1022-1023. See also Wagner, עזז, cols. 11-12.

[253] Zobel refers to other metaphorical names of God such as מצודה and סלע. Cf. Zobel, מעוז, cols. 1022-1023.

[254] Cf. Olofsson, **LXX Version**, pp. 39-40.

[255] See Santos, **Index**, Zobel, מעוז, col. 1021.

[256] It may have a literal referent here. Even though Cooke renders this word with "refuge" the suggested referent is the same. Cooke, **Ezekiel**, pp. 273, 276.

literal and a metaphorical sense of the word. Most of these passages could equally well be understood literally. See 3.4.2.

3.4.4 Preliminary conclusions regarding the translation technique

The equivalents of מעוז as a divine name; the ordinary rendering ὑπερασπιστής and the alternatives βοηθός, κραταίωμα, clearly differ from those used for the term in literal sense and as an ordinary metaphor, even though the equivalent in 59 (60):9, κραταίωσις, is a cognate term with an alternative rendering of מעוז as a name of God. On the other hand, it is not self-evident that the translators were acquainted with the literal meaning of the word, since it only once had an equivalent which refers to a stronghold or a fortress, Is 23:14. The two alternative renderings of the term as a designation of God in LXX Psalms are not due to variation and the use of κραταίωμα suggests that the LXX translators sometimes derived מעוז as a divine name from עזז rather than from עוז.

There are some differences in the translation of the term as a divine name inside and outside the Psalms. It is true that the equivalents in Jer 16:19 and Is 17:10, βοηθός, occur as a designation of God in the Psalter, but only as an alternative rendering to מעוז. Otherwise it is a semantically accurate translation of עזר generally in the Psalter and in LXX as a whole. See 5.5. The alternative renderings of מעוז as a divine name in LXX as a whole do not depend on a desire for variation, even though other names of God occur in e.g. Jer 16:19, viz. ἰσχύς as a translation of עז and καταφυγή as a rendering of מנוס. Both are semantically accurate renderings, and καταφυγή in particular is a common divine name in LXX Psalms. On the other hand, neither in Is 17:10 nor in Jer 16:19 is the main equivalent of מעוז as a name of God in the Psalms employed.

The equivalents in Isaiah and Jeremiah are thus not identical with those in the Psalter, even though renderings which are used for metaphorical designations of God in LXX Psalms are employed. This suggests either that the translator of Isaiah was independent of the translation in the Book of Psalms in this respect or that his version is the earlier and the equivalents of the divine names under discussion were not yet crystallized. See 4.1. The choice of a term which does not reflect the literal meaning of the name and is employed for other metaphorical designations of God favours the second alternative. The same is true for Jeremiah. See further Table 2.

3.5 THE TRANSLATION OF MAHĂSÊ AS A DIVINE NAME

3.5.1 The equivalents of the name in LXX

The equivalents of the name in LXX Psalms

מחסה in the Book of Psalms is mostly a figurative description of the function of the temple as a place of refuge. It is the protective sphere which Yahweh himself guarantees with his presence.[257] The term as a divine title is as a rule rendered by ἐλπίς, 13 (14):6; 60 (61):4; 61 (62):8; 72 (73):28; 90 (91):9; 93 (94):22 and 141 (142):6.

מחסה in 62:8 has, according to Tsevat, a general religious sense, even though it is employed in close connection with Yahweh. The same is true for 73:28.[258] In 73:28 it is regarded as a designation of God in HAL but not its similar employment in 62:8 and 94:22, notwithstanding that משגב and צור in the same verses are

---

[257] See e.g. Kraus, **Psalmen**, pp. 498, 805.
[258] **Tsevat**, pp. 17, 92 n. 110,

understood as names of God. מחסה is a designation of God in 94:22 in analogy with משגב and צור. See 3.1.1 and 3.8.1. מחסה in 73:28 is also a designation of God.[259] We shall compare these passages.

> But the LORD has become my stronghold, (משגב) and my God the rock of my refuge (צור מחסי) (94:22 MT).

> But the Lord was my refuge; (καταφυγὴν) and my God the helper (βοηθὸν) of my hope (ἐλπίς) (93:22 LXX).

The translator evidently made little attempt to express even the metaphorical meaning of the terms. Other aims than semantic accuracy are prominent here.

> He only is my rock (צורי) and my salvation, my fortress; (משגבי) I shall not be shaken. On God rests my deliverance and my honour; my mighty rock, (צור עזי)[260] my refuge (מחסי) is God (62:7-8 MT).

> For he is my God (θεός μου) and my Saviour; my helper, (ἀντιλήμπτωρ μου) I shall not be moved. In God is my salvation and my glory: he is the God of my help, (ὁ θεὸς τῆς βοηθείας μου) and my hope (ἡ ἐλπίς μου) is in God (61:7-8 LXX).

A different Vorlage, חֲסוּ, for מחסי, is hesitantly suggested in HAL. See also BHK. But this must be out of the question. The proposition in BHK and BHS that LXX read צור-עזרי instead of MT:s צור-עזי is difficult to accept too since βοήθεια is not only equivalent to עזר as a divine name but also renders מגן in close association with God, 7:11, and the cognate βοηθός is sometimes used for עז as a designation of God.[261] Furthermore, although צור-עזי occurs only here the phrase צור-עזרי is also unique in the Hebrew. But different metaphorical divine names are often combined with צור in MT. Cf. 94:22 צור מחסי, 31:3 צור-מעוז, 71:3 צור מעון. This emphasizes the interchangeability of the metaphorical divine names in the Hebrew, which probably also influenced the choice of translation technique in LXX for them.

> But for me it is good to be near God; I have made the LORD GOD my refuge, (מחסי) that I may tell of all thy works (73:28 MT).

> But it is good for me to cleave close to God, to put my trust (τὴν ἐλπίδα μου) in the Lord; that I may proclaim all thy praises (72:28 LXX).

מחסה in both 72:28 and 94:22 refers to the asylum and protective function of the sanctuary,[262] which is here in fact identified with Yahweh.

Even though מחסה as a rule has ἐλπίς as equivalent it is also rendered by βοηθός, 61 (62):9; 70 (71):7. ἐλπίς and ἐλπίζειν are equivalents to מחסה and בטח in 61 (62):8-9. This probably explains the use of βοηθός in 61 (62):9. The Greek equivalent in 70 (71):7 also seems to be employed for the sake of variation. מחסי עז, 70 (71):7, is better rendered βοηθὸς κραταιός "strong helper" in this context since ἐλπίς translates מבטח in v. 5.

ἀντιλήμπτωρ is employed only once, 90 (91):2:

---

[259] For the inclusion of these passages, see also Briggs, **Psalms I**, p. 24, Eichhorn, pp. 38-42, 78-79, 109, 113. The employment in 94:22 is to be regarded as a characterization of the actualization of Yahweh as מחסה. Eichhorn, p. 77.

[260] According to some scholars, the expression means "protecting rock" and thus עז has the meaning "protection", "refuge". Thus e.g. Gunkel, **Psalmen**, p. 265. See 5.4.1.

[261] See 5.4.1 and Table 1. Cf. Tsevat, p. 92 n. 110. See also Wutz, **Psalmen**, p. 156.

[262] Kraus, **Psalmen**, p. 826.

He who dwells in the shelter of the Most High, who abides in the shadow of the Almighty, will say to the LORD, "My refuge (מחסי) and my fortress; (מצודתי) my God, in whom I trust" (91:1-2 MT).

He that dwells in the help of the Highest, shall sojourn under the shelter of the God of heaven. He shall say to the Lord, Thou art my helper (ἀντιλήμπτωρ μου) and my refuge: (καταφυγή μου) my God; I will hope in him (90:1-2 LXX).

ἐλπίς is not used since ἐλπίζειν renders בטח in the same verse. The translator's basic aim with this rendering was to avoid repetition. Note also the conscious parallelism between "help", "helper" and "shelter", "refuge" in LXX, which may have influenced the choice of this specific equivalent. In MT the semantic parallelism is within each verse, "shelter" // "shadow" and "refuge" // "fortress". Both סתר "shelter" and צל "shadow" in v. 1 refer directly to the temple and the holy of holies.[263] The shadow of the Almighty is probably the shadow of the wings of the cherubim in the holy of holies, even though the thought is here more or less spiritualized.[264] It is evident that in this text as in many other passages the LXX translator has not reflected or indeed even tried to reflect the semantic meaning of the names as metaphors.

καταφυγή is also employed once, 45 (46):2. The main equivalent ἐλπίς was perhaps avoided because this term was hardly suitable where the Hebrew expresses the characterization of the actualization of Yahweh as מחסה. The Hebrew אלהים לנו מחסה ועז could hardly be rendered ὁ θεὸς ἡμῶν ἐλπὶς καὶ δύναμις.

מחסה is more or less cultic term which is reserved for Yahweh. Thus none is a true refuge except the Lord. When this name refers to man it is ironic. See below. This word is hardly part of the everyday language.[265] מחסה as an address to God occurs with one exception, 73:28, in noun clauses and often in similar expressions, even though it is hardly a question of formulas. As a rule the word order is one and the same. Note the similarity between Ps 71:7; 91:2, 9; 142:6 and Jer 17:17,[266] which does not seem to have had any effect on the choice of equivalents in LXX.

When the Hebrew word by way of exception has its literal meaning it is rendered by καταφυγή, 103 (104):18:[267] סלעים מחסה לשפנים "the rocks are a refuge for the badgers" is rendered by πέτρα καταφυγὴ τοῖς χοιρογρυλλίοις "the rock is a refuge for the rabbits". καταφυγή is thus employed in both its literal and its metaphorical meaning as a rendering of מחסה in the Book of Psalms.

The equivalents of the name outside the Psalms

מחסה as a designation of God occurs in MT in Prov 14:26; Jer 17:17; Joel 4:16, but also in Is 25:4.[268] The equivalents vary, but a literal translation is never employed.

Jer 17:17 and Joel 3 (4):16 have φείδεσθαι, "spare", i.e. it is hardly interpreted as a divine name in LXX and is perhaps derived from חום, which in Joel and Jeremiah sometimes has this Greek equivalent.[269] This is more probable than that

---

[263] Hugger, Zuflucht, p. 149. For the use of these terms in OT and outside Israel, see ibid., pp. 147-152.

[264] Cf. Anderson, Psalms, p. 656.

[265] See Hugger, Zuflucht, p. 64. Cf. Tsevat, pp. 17, 92 n. 110-111.

[266] Here the word order is inverted. See Hugger, Zuflucht, pp. 63-64.

[267] The only examples of this term in a non-religious context are the passage under discussion and Job 24:8. Cf. Hugger, Zuflucht, p. 64.

[268] Thus Tsevat, p. 92, p. 17 n. 110 and Eichhorn, pp. 108-109, 114. See also HAL, BDB.

[269] See HR. Note that Aquila reflects MT in Jer 17:17. See Reider, Turner, Index, p. 78.

it is a free translation.[270] Cf. Jer 17:17: "Be not a terror (מחתה) to me; thou art my refuge (מחסי) in the day of evil" (MT). Cf. LXX "Be not to me a stranger, but spare me (φειδονός μου) in the evil day." LXX, according to McKane, also paraphrases the first part of the verse, but this is hardly true.[271] The rendering "stranger" is probably a guess from the context.[272] The prophet clings to the fact that Yahweh is characterized by מחסה in an extreme situation where the Lord threatens his own people.[273] That the designation of God is used with a prepositional qualification "in the day of evil" is unique for this text. It never occurs in the Book of Psalms.[274]

In Prov 14:26 it is rendered by ἐρεισμα "support" because ἐλπίς was used for the parallel מבטח in the first half of the verse. "In the fear of the LORD one has strong confidence, and his children will have a refuge" (מחסה). Cf. the translation of Brenton "In the fear of the Lord is strong confidence: and he leaves his children a support." On the other hand, the context may indicate a different interpretation. In any case it is not a divine name in LXX and there is doubt as to whether it is a name of God in MT. Despite the parallelism, מחסה does not refer to Yahweh but rather to the whole expression "fear of the LORD". Note especially the function of this phrase as a catch-word to v. 27: "The fear of the LORD is a fountain of life."[275] The LXX translator did not grasp the meaning of the Hebrew in Is 25:4 but has a different interpretation of the whole passage.[276] The occurrences of מחסה outside the Psalter are as a rule in the context of a language akin to that of the Book of Psalms.[277]

3.5.2   The equivalents of the term as a metaphor and in the literal sense

מחסה as an ordinary metaphor, according to HAL, occurs in Is 28:15, 17. It is rendered by ἐλπίς in Is 28:15:

> Because you have said, "We have made a covenant with death, and with Sheol we have an agreement[278] when the overwhelming scourge passes through it will not come to us; for we have made lies our refuge, (מחסנו) and in falsehood we have taken shelter" (סתר) (MT).

> Because yea have said, We have made a covenant with Hades, and agreements with death; if the rushing storm should pass, it shall not come upon us: we have made falsehood our hope,(τὴν ἐλπίδα ἡμῶν) and by falsehood shall we be protected (LXX).

The use of ἐλπίς, which otherwise occurs only when the term is a divine name, in this negative context is surprising. Both here and in v. 17 it is the question of lies as a refuge. Perhaps the translator tried to reflect the irony of the Hebrew since מחסה and סתר, traditional words which signify a good relation with Yahweh,

---

[270] This is suggested concerning Jer 17:17 in McKane, **Jeremiah**, p. 413.

[271] McKane, **Jeremiah**, p. 413.

[272] Cf. the translation of מחתה in Jer 31 (48):39 "object of anger". Confusion regarding the meaning of this Hebrew word recurs throughout LXX. See Santos, **Index**.

[273] Eichhorn, p. 113.

[274] Gamberoni, חסה, col. 80.

[275] Cf. Gamberoni, חסה, col. 80.

[276] See 3.4.1 and Goshen-Gottstein, **Isaiah**, ad loc. Even though מחסה may be regarded as a designation of God it is rendered by σκέπη, a word which is employed for מעוז as an ordinary metaphor in 30:2 and for מחסום in literal meaning in Job 24:8.

[277] Compare, for example, Is 25:4 with Ps 46:2 and 62:9. See Gamberoni, חסה, col. 80.

[278] The meaning of the Hebrew word is extremely uncertain, but the parallelism favours this rendering. See the commentaries.

are shown to be nothing but lies and deceit when they are confronted with the hail and waters as instruments of God's judgement, v. 17.[279] מחסה in Is 28:17 may be rendered by πείθειν, but the relation between the Hebrew and the Greek is extremely uncertain:

> And I will make justice the line, and righteousness the plummet; and hail will sweep away the refuge (מחסה) of lies, and waters will overwhelm the shelter (סתר) (MT).

> And I will cause judgement to be for hope, and my compassion shall be for just measures, and ye that trust vainly in falsehood shall fall: for the storm shall by no means pass by you (LXX).

מחסה in a literal or a metaphorical sense "shelter", "place of refuge",[280] is rendered by σκέπη "shelter" in the LXX, Job 24:8; Is 4:6; 25:4. The text of Is 25:4 is completely misunderstood by the LXX translator, even though מחסה is employed as a metaphor here, notwithstanding the opinion in HAL. Both the Hebrew word (in its second occurrence) and its Greek equivalent are in fact divine names. See 3.4.1.

In Is 4:6, which is also metaphorical, it occurs in close connection with God, since manifestations of his presence from Ex 40:35–38, cloud, smoke and fire, are a shelter and refuge for the people of God in the restored Jerusalem.[281] Is 4:5–6 is hard to interpret in detail since metaphors from two conceptual fields are mixed, i.e. a theophany motive[282] "cloud by day", "smoke and the shining of a flaming fire by night" and motives from the Feast of Tabernacles, "canopy", "booth". The LXX translator obviously understood 4:5–6 in the light of Ex 40:35.[283] He emphasized the theophany motive rather than the connection with the Feast of Tabernacles. Cf. the translation of וברא "and (the Lord) will create" by καὶ ἥξει "and he shall come" and the rendering of סכה "booth" with "defence". In MT both of the connections are clearly reflected.[284] This text is probably part of a more comprehensive concept which is evidenced in 3:16–4:6, the restoration of the covenant between Yahweh and the people of Israel in terms of a marriage.[285] Gray also points out the close relation with Ps 91:1–2, where the same or cognate names are used of Yahweh.[286]

The term in Job 24:8 probably refers to a literal place of refuge where the poor could find shelter from the rain.[287] This is also the interpretation in LXX:

> They are wet with the rain of the mountains, and cling to the rock for want of shelter (מחסה) (MT).

> They are wet with the drops of the mountains: they have embraced the rock, because they have no shelter (σκέπη) (LXX).

---

[279] Thus Wildberger, **Jesaja**, p. 1077. Cf. Kaiser, **Jesaia**, p. 252, where it is emphasized that the leaders' reliance upon human aid, instead of Yahweh, is in itself a lie.

[280] See e.g. HAL, Fritsch, **Psalter**, p. 736.

[281] The function of the metaphors is one and the same in both texts even though this passage is rhetorically overloaded. Cf. Gamberoni, חסה, col. 80. It is hardly a designation of God here, since the "refuge" does not refer directly to Yahweh. Cf. **Eichhorn**, p. 108.

[282] It is the question of how the Lord through external signs of his presence leads the Israelites on their journey through the wilderness. Cf. Ex 13:21–22; Num 14:14.

[283] See Koenig, **L'Herméneutique**, pp. 54–55. Cf. Ziegler, **Untersuchungen**, p. 62.

[284] Koenig, **L'Herméneutique**, p. 54.

[285] See the detailed argumentation in Wiklander, **Prophecy**, pp. 131–142, 239–241.

[286] Gray, **Isaiah**, p. 81.

[287] The only examples of this term in a non-religious context are Ps 104:18 and Job 24:8. Cf. Hugger, **Zuflucht**, p. 64.

On the other hand, in the light of chapters 23–24, Yahweh is depicted as the real refuge which the poor so desperately need. See especially 24:1–12. Note v. 12 "From out of the city the dying groan, and the soul of the wounded cries for help; yet God pays no attention to their prayer."

3.5.3 Preliminary conclusions regarding the translation technique

The distinction between a literal and a metaphorical sense of the Hebrew term does not seem to be consistently followed in LXX, even though as a divine name it is mostly interpreted as "hope" while as a rule in literal and often in metaphorical sense it is understood as "shelter". It is rendered by σκέπη, Job 24:8; Is 4:6; 25:4, or καταφυγή, Ps 103 (104):18 when it is not a divine name. Thus the word is understood as more or less abstract in all its occurrences in LXX. Therefore, it cannot be taken for granted that the metaphorical character of the Hebrew term was recognized by the LXX translators.

The choice of ἐλπίς as the main equivalent of מחסה as a divine name in LXX Psalms is probably based on the ordinary rendering of the cognate verb. The alternative equivalents βοηθός and ἀντιλήμπτωρ are employed for the sake of variation, while καταφυγή is used in order to avoid a contextually inadequate translation. καταφυγή can thus render מחסה in both its literal and its metaphorical meaning in the Book of Psalms. ἐρεισμα in Prov 14:26 also seems to be employed for the sake of variation. The use of ἐλπίς, which is otherwise only employed when the term is a divine name, in Is 28:15 is surprising. The translator may have tried to catch the irony of the Hebrew. This is, however, an exception, since the irony in MT when metaphorical designations of God are used for others than Yahweh is seldom reflected in LXX.

3.6 THE TRANSLATION OF MĀ'ŌN AS A DIVINE NAME

3.6.1 The equivalents of the name in LXX

מעון, which in literal sense refers to a "lair (of animals)" or "God's abode", is as a designation of God translated by καταφυγή, Ps 89 (90):1; 90 (91):9, or ὑπερασπιστής, 70 (71):3. The original wording of all these texts in the Hebrew is disputed. This is not least the case in 70 (71):3 where LXX seems to have had a different Vorlage:

> Be thou to me a rock of refuge, (צור מעון) to come continually thou hast commanded, to save me, for thou art my rock (סלעי) and my fortress (מצודתי) (MT).[288]

> Be to me a protecting God, (θεὸν ὑπερασπιστήν) and a strong hold (τόπον ὀχυρὸν), to save me: for thou art my fortress[289] (στερέωμά μου) and my refuge (καταφυγή μου) (LXX).

HR wrongly suggests that τόπος is equivalent to מעון in 70 (71):3 and Preuss repeats this mistake.[290] מעון is usually emended to מעוז with many Hebrew manuscripts, LXX, Symmachus, the Targum and Ps 31:3,[291] but Preuss rightly

---

[288] The translation is that of RSV and of RSV margin where RSV deviates from MT.

[289] A more natural translation, which is also in line with the translation technique of the divine names, is "strength". See LSJ.

[290] See Preuss, מעון, col. 1028.

[291] Thus BHK, BHS and the majority of the commentators. See also HAL.

pleads for caution regarding this emendation since מעון is an adequate name of God.[292] Furthermore, Symmachus' rendering can hardly be taken as an indication of a different Vorlage here, since ἰσχυρός has many different Hebrew equivalents in the Psalms, including קדוש, Ps 77 (78):41.[293]

Some of the old versions may have read מעוז in 70 (71):3, but the opposite also applies since Quinta's κατοικητήριον clearly reflects מעון in the parallel passage, 30 (31):3.[294] On the other hand, ὑπερασπιστής is the most common equivalent to מעוז as a divine name in LXX. See Table 1. This word occurs also in the parallel text 30 (31):3 and the graphical appearance is very close. The suggestion regarding LXX is reasonable even though an assimilation in LXX to the rendering in 30 (31):3 cannot be excluded.

Goiten's proposal that מעון in 91:9 is derived from עוון "sin" and thus refers to Yahweh as a God who makes us conscious of our sins is hardly valid. His argument for introducing this new interpretation is that מעון is always used when God is invoked for preservation against enemies, Ps 71, or against illness or other evils, Ps 91, whereas Ps 90 does not contain any prayer for protection.[295] But the number of passages is too small to allow of any conclusions regarding the deviating context in Ps 90.

According to BHK, BHS and HAL, LXX had מעוז in its Vorlage also in Ps 89 (90):1 and 90 (91):9, a text which is often regarded as the original. Briggs proposes that LXX read מעוז, even though he himself preferred MT.[296] מעוז is supported by some Hebrew manuscripts in 90:1 and in 90 (91):9 Quinta reflects this term.[297] These texts may, on the other hand, have inserted a correction to the usual employment of מעוז as a name of God.[298] καταφυγή is certainly never used as equivalent to מעוז, if Dan 11:39 (Th) is disregarded, notwithstanding that it well reflects the semantic meaning of the Hebrew term in most instances and often renders metaphorical divine names in LXX.[299]

This is a further indication that the equivalents of these designations of God do not in the first place convey the metaphorical or the literal meaning of the terms. It can only partly be explained by the fact that the metaphorical names of God are mostly confined to poetry. It is thus not necessary, although probably correct, to point out that the rendering in LXX reflects the etymology of מעון, which may be "place of refuge".[300] Kraus, however, seems to be uncertain regarding the Vorlage of LXX but admits that מעון has the specific meaning "refuge" in 71:3; 90:1 and 91:9,[301] which is adequately rendered in LXX by καταφυγή in 90:1 and 91:9.

The designation of God in 90:1 may be based on Deut 33:27.[302] But the LXX translator has not taken over the wording or interpretation of his predecessor who does not understand מעונה as a divine name:[303] "The eternal God is your dwelling

---

[292] Preuss, מעון, cols. 1028-1030.

[293] Saiz, Simaco, p. 527. As a matter of fact, מעון and מעוז as divine names have different Greek equivalents in every instance. Ibid., p. 679 and 6.2.3.

[294] See Venetz, Quinta, pp. 29-30, Schenker, Hexapla, pp. 108-109, 256. See also Baetgen, Psalmen, p. 86, Briggs, Psalms I, p. 86, Kraus, Psalmen, p. 393.

[295] Goitein, מעון, p. 52.

[296] Briggs, Psalms II, pp. 276, 282. Cf. Briggs, Psalms I, p. 236. Regarding 90 (91):9, see also Kraus, Psalmen, p. 803. He asserts that the emendation in 89 (90):1 is not "unbedingt erforderlich". Ibid., p. 795.

[297] See BHK, Kraus, Psalmen, p. 803. Cf. Eichhorn, p. 121.

[298] Eichhorn, p. 121.

[299] Cf. Hugger, Zuflucht, p. 45 and n. 23.

[300] See Hugger, Zuflucht, pp. 46, 152. Cf. Kraus, Psalmen, p. 795 and the translation of Ps 90:1 on p. 794 "Zuflucht". Eichhorn has a similar interpretation. Eichhorn, p. 121.

[301] Kraus, Psalmen, pp. 795, 797.

[302] See Briggs, Psalms II, p. 272. The psalm shows an affinity with Deut 32 in many respects. Ibid., p. 272.

[303] Regarding the interpretation of Deut 33:27, see e.g. Hugger, Zuflucht, p. 155, Preuss, מעון, col. 1029.

place, (מעונה) and underneath are the everlasting arms."[304] The translator renders the Hebrew as follows: "And the protection[305] (σκέπασις) of God is a beginning, and that under the strength of the everlasting arms." The meaning of the Greek is not clear. The Hebrew term is thus once used as a designation of God outside the Book of Psalms.[306]. Since there is no difference in meaning[307] between מעון and מעונה and the LXX translators do not distinguish between them, they are both taken into consideration without always discussing them separately.

The attested confusion between מעון and מעוד in 31:3; 71:3 does not only depend upon graphical similarity.[308] מעון is a good parallel to מחסה in 90 (91):9 and the same is true for מעוד. That they clearly function as synonyms can be seen by the fact they occur in parallel with a third synonym, מחסה, in Ps 91:9 מעון, and in Joel 4:16 מעוד. Cf. also Is 25:4; 30:2-3.[309] מעוד and מחסה are also in close proximity in Jer 16:19.[310] Stolz does not support the emendation to מעוד in any of the cases where מעון is a divine name in MT.[311]

Hugger proposes that two further cases of מעון as a divine metaphor occurred in the Psalter, Ps 84:7; 87:7. In 84:7 he conjectures מעון for MT:s מַעְיָן "spring" and in 87:7 reads מְעוֹנַי instead of מַעְיָנַי "my springs" in MT.[312] Both retroversions are in fact disputable, even though LXX may have had a different Vorlage. Hugger does not base his emendation of 84:7 on LXX, but BHK gives the same term as Vorlage of LXX. BHK is more uncertain regarding the Vorlage in 87:7. The Hebrew-Greek alignment of E. Tov and B. Kraft supports the retroversion in 87:7 but not in 84:7. But the equivalent in 86 (87):7, κατοικία, does not render מעון at all in LXX, even though it reflects the semantic meaning of the Hebrew, and τόπος, 83 (84):7, is never employed for מעון as a name of God. Once it is used for his habitation, 67 (68):6, in LXX Psalms.

מעון is in fact both a possible and a reasonable designation of God but, apart from Deut 33:27, confined to the Book of Psalms. The world around Israel was well acquainted with "abode" as a name of the gods.[313] מעון was at least used as a designation of God during the exile. When the people did not have access to the temple, Yahweh himself became their living temple. See especially Ez 11:16:

> Though I removed them far off among the nations, and though I scattered them among the countries, yet I have been a sanctuary to them for a while in the countries where they have gone.[314]

But the use of מעון as a designation of God is probably much older. Indeed, מעוד seems to be the latecomer, which replaces an original מעון in the Book of Psalms.[315]

---

[304] For a similar understanding and translation, see Craigie, **Deuteronomy**, p. 402. NEB has a totally different interpretation of the text: "who humbled the gods of old and subdued the ancient powers; who drove out the enemy before you". "Subdued" is, however, based on an emendation to מְעֻנֶּה.

[305] See LSJ. This is the only example of this word in LSJ.

[306] See e.g. Stolz, **Kult**, p. 213 n. 178, Craigie, **Deuteronomy**, pp. 402-403. An emendation to מעוד is not warranted here. Stolz, **Kult**, p. 213 n. 178.

[307] See apart from the standard lexica also Hugger, **Zuflucht**, p. 152, Preuss, מעון, col. 1028.

[308] Cf. Hugger, **Zuflucht**, p. 45. For the rare alternation between ד and נ, see Wutz, **Transkriptionen**, p. 223, Talmon, **Aspects**, p. 125 n. 91.

[309] Cf. Hugger, **Zuflucht**, p. 65 n. 37.

[310] Cf. Talmon, **Aspects**, pp. 124-125.

[311] Stolz, **Kult**, p. 213 n. 178. See also Preuss, מעון, cols. 1029-1030.

[312] Hugger, **Zuflucht**, p. 142 n. 95, p. 154. See also BHK and **Mozley**, pp. 138-140, Briggs, **Psalms II**, p. 229 with references. Cf. Kraus, **Psalmen**, p. 765.

[313] See Hugger, **Zuflucht**, p. 154 n. 107, Preuss, מעון, col. 1029. מעון as a divine name is especially discussed in Hugger, **Zuflucht**, pp. 152-155.

[314] Cf. Briggs, **Psalms II**, p. 272. See also Preuss, מעון, col. 1030.

[315] Cf. **Eichhorn**, p. 121. Note especially the use of this term in Deut 33, which may be an old text. Cf. Freedman, **Divine Names**, p. 70.

3.6.2 The equivalents of the term as a habitation of God

The Hebrew word is often employed for God's abode in the Book of Psalms, 26:8; 68:6; 76:3,[316] but also elsewhere, Deut 26:15; 2 Chr 30:27; 36:15; Jer 25:30; Zech 2:17.[317] Cf. also Judg 6:26; 1 Sam 2:29, 32.[318]

As a rule the phrase קדוש מעון is employed for God's abode, heaven, or the temple. As we have seen מעון as the habitation of God is once rendered by τόπος, Ps 67 (68):6. מעון קדוש here probably refers to the temple[319] as a meeting point between heaven and earth.[320] εὐπρέπεια is used in Ps 25 (26):8:

> O LORD, I love the habitation of thy house, and the place where thy glory dwells (MT).

> O Lord, I have loved the beauty of thy house, and the place of the tabernacle of thy glory (LXX).

מעון ביתך "the habitation of thy house" is here rendered by εὐπρέπειαν οἴκου σου "the beauty of thy house". This term may have been used since τόπος occurs in the same verse, and must therefore have been regarded as the main equivalent of מעון as the habitation of God in LXX Psalms. On the other hand, a synonymous term would then have been expected. Otherwise, except in 2 Chr 36:15, when מעון is employed of heaven or the temple the attribute קדוש is added. But this is not necessary here since it is qualified through ביתך and further defined through the parallelism with "the place where your glory dwells". It is not probable that the LXX translator made an error of transposition for an original נעם "kindness".[321] It is true that the roots correspond in 2 Sam 1:23; 23:1; Job 36:11.[322] But εὐπρέπεια has in fact different equivalents in every instance in the Book of Psalms, 49 (50):2; 92 (93):1; 103 (104):1, and נעם is only interpreted as λαμπρότης, "brightness", 89 (90):17, in the Psalter. The seemingly distinct phrase מעון ביתך is, however, ambiguous. It probably means "the house which is God's habitation", but may refer to the worshipper and could thus be translated "the abiding (worshipper) in God's house".[323] In the interpretation of LXX the phrase clearly refers to the temple.

In Ps 75 (76):3 the dwelling place of God is rendered by κατοικητήριον. In this case מעון may be employed as a metaphor where God is pictured as the lion of Judah.[324] Cf. Is 31:4. Note the parallelism with סך which could be understood as "lair".[325] סך refers to a lion's den in 9:30 (10:9), where, however, it is rendered by μάνδρα "den". A closer parallel is Jer 25:38 where Yahweh is depicted as a lion who goes out from his covert (סך). This Hebrew term may sometimes also refer to the temple. Cf. Ps 42:5.[326] It may not be a question of animal imagery in 76:3 inasmuch as all other texts where Yahweh is depicted as a lion occur in a context of judgment, which is also true of the use of מעון as a lair of animals. See below. LXX interprets מעונה as referring to a den since κατοικητήριον is employed, which, except in 2 Chr 30:27, is always used of an animal's lair. This is also the understanding in most of the ancient versions. מעון never occurs in a purely literal

---

316 Kraus, **Psalmen**, p. 797, Preuss, מעון, col. 1030.
317 Briggs, **Psalms I**, p. 236, Hugger, **Zuflucht**, pp. 152–153 and n. 104. Cf. Preuss, מעון, col. 1029.
318 Hugger, **Zuflucht**, p. 153 and n. 105.
319 See Stolz, **Kult**, p. 213 n. 178, Hugger, **Zuflucht**, p. 153 n. 104.
320 Anderson, **Psalms**, p. 485. It may also be said to refer to both heaven and the temple at the same time. Preuss, מעון, col. 1029.
321 Thus **Mozley**, p. 46, Briggs, **Psalms I**, p. 236.
322 See HR, **Mozley**, p. 46.
323 Anderson, **Psalms,** p. 217.
324 Briggs, **Psalms II**, p. 166. Cf. Anderson, **Psalms**, pp. 551–552, who is more uncertain, since this term sometimes denotes the habitation of Yahweh, the temple.
325 Cf. the translation in Briggs, **Psalms II**, pp. 165–166.
326 The meaning of the word here is disputed. See the commentaries.

sense in LXX Psalms, but מעונה is so employed in Ps 103 (104):22. It is translated by μάνδρα.

In other books of the LXX where it refers to the dwelling of God, מעון is rendered by οἶκος, Deut 26:15, ἁγίασμα, 2 Chr 36:15, νεφέλη, Zech 2:13 (17)[327] and by κατοικητήριον, 2 Chr 30:27.[328] The liturgical addition Zech 2:17 as well as Ps 68:6 do not allow of distinction between Yahweh's heavenly and earthly dwelling.[329]

In Jer 32:16 (25:30) Yahweh's habitation is depicted in metaphorical language: "The LORD will roar from on high, and from his holy habitation (וממעון קדשו) utter his voice" is rendered by "The Lord shall speak from on high, from his sanctuary, (ἀπὸ τοῦ ἁγίου) he will utter his voice". The LXX translator has obviously omitted מעון "habitation" or more probably it was never in the Vorlage of the LXX.[330] Thus MT had ממעון קדשו while LXX had only מקדשו "from his sanctuary".[331]

מעון קדוש, with different suffixes, only refers to heaven, according to Holladay.[332] This is probably also true for Jer 25:30.[333] But, according to Carroll, מעון in Jer 25:30, in line with the use in Amos 1:2; Joel 4:16, refers to the sanctuary in Jerusalem.[334] Both views are possible, but in LXX, in Peshitta, Vulgate and the Targum, it is probably a question of heaven.[335] This is evidently an adequate interpretation. Yahweh has removed his presence from the Jerusalem temple and threatens Jerusalem from heaven.[336]

God is here depicted as a lion in the description of the coming of the Lord in his heavenly abode, which is likened to a lion's den.[337] He roars from heaven. This interpretation is supported by Amos 3:4 where a literal lion roars, שאג, which here also stands in parallel with נתן קול "cry out". Yahweh is also pictured as a lion "who roars" // "cries out his voice" in Amos 1:2; Joel 4:16. More or less the same text occurs in Jer 25:30 as in Amos 1:2; Joel 4:16, but there it explicitly refers to Zion and Jerusalem. The lion metaphor is not reflected by the equivalents chosen in the LXX here or in Amos 1:2; Joel 3 (4):16, even though the similar passage in Amos 3:4, which refers to a literal lion, has ἐρεύγεσθαι.

מעון is disputed in Judg 6:26; 1 Sam 2:29, 32.[338] The text of MT in 1 Sam 2:29, 32 is a corrupt and highly conflated tradition. LXX reflects an older text, but the term is in neither MT nor the LXX original. צר מעון in 2:32 in MT is a correction of צרת עין, which was in the text of LXX.[339]

---

[327] See HR. It is hardly a literal translation of a different Vorlage. Thus e.g. Wutz, **Transkriptionen**, p. 225.

[328] Apart from "lair" this term can refer more generally to a "dwelling-place", an "abode". See LSJ. מעון קדוש is probably in 2 Chr 30:27, as mostly, God's dwelling in heaven. Preuss, מעון, col. 1029.

[329] Preuss, מעון, col. 1029. Cf. the equivalents in LXX. The temple is in fact the only place where the distinction between heaven and earth is obliterated. Metzger, **Wohnstatt**, p. 154, Mettinger, **Sabaoth**, p. 30 and n. 45, p. 31. See also Preuss, מעון, col. 1029.

[330] See BHK, BHS, Ziegler, **Ieremias**, p. 329. The term was maybe lost through haplography. Holladay, **Jeremiah**, p. 680. Even though die Catenen-Gruppe and 613, which are identical with MT here, as a rule did not follow the Hebrew, the reading can hardly reflect the Old Greek here. Ziegler, **Ieremias**, pp. 10, 94.

[331] See BHS, Carroll, **Jeremiah**, p. 505.

[332] Holladay, **Jeremiah**, p. 679.

[333] See Thompson, **Jeremiah**, p. 519, Holladay, **Jeremiah**, pp. 679-680, Preuss, מעון, col. 1029.

[334] Carroll, **Jeremiah**, p. 505, McKane, **Jeremiah**, p. 648.

[335] McKane, **Jeremiah**, p. 648. Holladay has the opposite interpretation of the reference in MT and LXX. Holladay, **Jeremiah**, p. 679. He proposes that the rendering in LXX refers to the temple.

[336] Thus McKane, **Jeremiah**, p. 648. See also his exposition of the different interpretations of this passage.

[337] Stolz, **Kult**, p. 213.

[338] Cf. Preuss, מעון, col. 1028. For the textual problems of Judg 6:26, see Zobel, מעון, cols. 1021-1022.

[339] See McCarter, **1 Samuel**, p. 87, where an attempt to reconstruct the original text is made. Cf.

3.6.3 The equivalents of the term as an animal's lair

מעון or מעונה, where it refers to a lair (of an animal) or a dwelling-place of man, is translated by κατοικητήριον, Jer 9:11 (10); 21:13, Nah 2:12, 13; or διατριβή "haunt" or "pastime",[340] Jer. 30:11 (49:33), and κοίτη "lair", Jer 10:22. One and the same phrase, מעון תנים "lair of jackals" occurs in 9:10; 10:22; 49:33 and 51:37 in Hebrew, but is missing in the Vorlage of the LXX in 51:37. Jer 49:33 appears to consist of phrases from the other passages. It is probably an editorial conclusion of the poem in v. 28-33.[341] But also 10:22 and 51:37 are probably secondary texts established on the analogy of 9:10.[342] When the Hebrew phrase occurred in the Vorlage of the LXX it was rendered in three different ways: 9:11 (10) κατοικτήριον δρακόντων, 10:22 κοίτην στρουθῶν, and 30:11 (49:33) διατριβὴ στρουθῶν.

While κατοικητήριον and κοίτη are adequate equivalents to מעון in this sense, the use of διατριβή is probably at least partly a consequence of the misunderstanding of חצור "Hazor" as "palace" in this chapter, v. 28, 30, 33. στρουθός is an extraordinary rendering of תן "jackal".[343] Otherwise it is translated by δράκων, except in Gen 1:21 where κῆτος is used for both תן and תנין. מעון as a lair of animals is always used in words of judgment over specific places, Jer 9:10 Jerusalem, 10:22 the cities of Judah, 49:33 Hazor, 51:37 Babylon, Nah 2:12 Nineveh.[344]

The use of מעונה for the habitation of man in Jer 21:13 is unique:[345]

> Behold, I am against you, O inhabitant of the valley, O rock (צור) of the plain, says the LORD; you who say, "Who shall come down against us, or who shall enter our habitations? (מעון)" (MT).

> Behold, I am against thee that dwellest in the valley of Sor; in the plain country, even against them that say, Who shall alarm us? or who shall enter into our habitation? (LXX).

In view of our previous experiences Holladay's suggestion that Jerusalem is arrogating to herself names and claims appropriate only for Yahweh is feasible. "Habitations" in MT may then be an ironical way of exceeding the prerogatives of Yahweh who has only one מעון, the Jerusalem temple.[346] On the other hand, מעונה could also be understood as "lair" here.[347] The use of צור referring to a city or its inhabitants is also unique. Therefore it is wrongly regarded as a place-name in LXX.

BHK. BHS has no comments.

[340] This is the most suitable interpretation in the context. See LSJ. Brenton suggests "resting-place", a meaning that is not supported by LSJ.

[341] Carroll, **Jeremiah**, p. 810. Cf. Bright, **Jeremiah**, p. 336.

[342] Preuss, מעון, cols. 1028-1029.

[343] Cf. HR, p. 1297, which has ? here.

[344] Preuss, מעון, cols. 1028-1029.

[345] Cf. Hugger, **Zuflucht**, p. 152. In Zeph 3:7, where the term may refer to a habitation of man LXX reads מֵעֵינֶיהָ "her eyes". See Rudolph, **Micha** p. 286. See also BHK, BHS.

[346] Holladay, **Jeremiah**, p. 579.

[347] This interpretation is only based on the use of the expression "her forest" in v. 14. See Holladay, **Jeremiah**, p. 579.

3.6.4   Preliminary conclusions regarding the translation technique

The distinction between מעון when it refers to God and when it denotes the place where God lives or a den of an animal, is reflected in LXX as a whole. Thus καταφυγή is never employed as a rendering of this term when it means the habitation of God or the lair of an animal, even though many different equivalents are used for the word in these senses. The choice of καταφυγή as the main, and probably the only, equivalent of the term as a divine name in the Old Greek may have been based on etymology, which in these cases (Ps 90:1; 91:9) fit the context.

As a rule the distinction between the use of the term for a lair and for the habitation of God is reflected in the choice of translation equivalents. The only exceptions are Ps 75 (76):3 and 2 Chr 30:27, where מעון as the place where God lives is rendered by the most common equivalent of the term as a lair, κατοικητήριον. 75 (76):3 may in LXX have been understood as a description of God with animal imagery where God is pictured as a lion in his lair. This interpretation was facilitated by the translator's understanding of "Salem" and "covert". The rendering then accords with the choice of equivalents in LXX as a whole, even though the lion imagery is not otherwise reflected in LXX. See Amos 1:2 and Joel 3 (4):16. The use of the same term for the habitation of God in 2 Chr 30:27, where the animal metaphor did not influence the choice of terminology, is, however, unique. On the other hand, it fits the meaning of this Greek word generally, since, apart from the sense lair, it can be employed also as a neutral word for "habitation".

3.7   THE TRANSLATION OF MEṢÛDÂ AS A DIVINE NAME

3.7.1   The equivalents of the name in LXX

מצודה as a name of God is always translated by καταφυγή. See Ps 17 (18):3; 30 (31):3, 4; 70 (71):3; 90 (91):2; 143 (144):2. The same is also true for Symmachus.[348] The term as a designation of God is thus restricted to the Psalter.

Schunck suggests the meaning "place of shelter" for all the occurrences of the term in the Book of Psalms.[349] If he is right, LXX only expresses the semantic meaning of the term. But there is no reason to depart from the traditional understanding in lexica and commentaries, viz. "fortress", "stronghold".[350] As a designation of God it only occurs in psalms where individuals pray.[351] In Ps 70 (71):3 where לבוא תמיד צוית "to come continually thou hast commanded" (RSV margin) is rendered by καὶ εἰς τόπον ὀχυρὸν "and to a strong hold" the Vorlage of the LXX was, according to nearly all scholars, לבית מצודות as in 30 (31):3, where it, however, is rendered by καὶ εἰς οἶκον καταφυγῆς. Symmachus, Peshitta, Jerome and the Targum support MT.[352] It is not included among the divine designations in HAL, but in BDB.[353] The text of MT in 71:3 is probably corrupt, but it is not to be taken for granted that the Vorlage of the text of Rahlfs was identical with that of 30 (31):3, despite the authorities in favour.[354]

[348] See Saiz, **Simaco**, p. 680.

[349] See Schunck, מצודה, cols. 1084–1085.

[350] Cf. the rendering in Briggs, **Psalms I**, p. 151 "stronghold". Even as a divine name it is always to be understood as "fortress", employed as a metaphor. Ibid., pp. 137, 263, Briggs., **Psalms II**, pp. 126, 279, or maybe "fastness", 144:2. Ibid., p. 521.

[351] **Eichhorn**, p. 96.

[352] See **Baetgen**, p. 644, Baetgen, **Psalmen**, pp. 218–219, **Mozley**, p. 113, Briggs, **Psalms I**, p. 272, Gunkel, **Psalmen**, p. 302, Wutz, **Transkriptionen**, p. 351. See also BHK, BHS, Kraus, **Psalmen**, p. 651.

[353] That the text in 31:3 is the original is also underlined by Michel, **Tempora**, p. 252. Briggs suggests that 31:3 and 71:3 are different interpretations of a common original. Briggs, **Psalms I**, p. 272.

[354] Delekat has a different reconstruction which lacks textual support. Delekat, **Asylie**, p. 210 and n. 5.

The variation in the rendering of these two parallel passages in the LXX are greater than could be expected from the translation of formulas generally in the Psalter. Moreover, מצודה as a divine name is always rendered by καταφυγή in LXX Psalms. בית is as a rule translated by οἶκος and very seldom by τόπος in LXX as a whole. The exceptions are 1 Sam 24:23; 1 Kgs 8:42; 2 Chr 6:32; Ps 118 (119):54; Jer 7:14. Thus this correspondence occurs only once in the Book of Psalms, 118 (119):54. ὀχυρός, which lacks Greek variants here, is never an equivalent to מצודה in LXX as a whole. Once it is employed for משגב, Is 33:16, but B and S have ἰσχυρός, and twice for נשגב, Is 26:5; 30:13, but never as a divine name. In fact it is not used as a designation of God at all in the LXX, even though it is employed in connection with him in Prov 10:29.[355]

This is not surprising since ὀχυρός always has a literal meaning in classical literature and papyri.[356] NT has taken over the figurative use of ὀχυρός in the OT, which is reflected especially in Aquila and Symmachus, in 2 Cor 10:4, the only place where it occurs in NT. There it is used of spiritual weapons.[357] The cognate ὀχύρωμα is used three times figuratively in LXX, for מצודה, 2 Sam 22:2, for מצוד, Job 19:6 and for מעוז, Prov 10:29.[358] Since this is the ordinary translation of מצודה, מצוד in Aquila, some of the occurrences of the term in figurative sense may be due to Hexaplaric influence. This at least true for 2 Sam 22:2. Se below.

ὀχυρός is as a rule employed in connection with πόλις, viz. as many as 51 out of 63 occurrences.[359] This combination was so established that πόλις could even occur modified by ὀχυρός without foundation in the Hebrew text.[360] This is in fact a very significant trait in the use of this word. In a few passages it modifies or is used in close connection with πύργος, 1 Macc 1:33; 4:60; 6:37 and 2 Macc 10:18, or τεῖχος, Deut 28:52; Jer 1:18 (second occurrence); 15:20, and once to τόπος, 1 Macc 6:57.[361] ὀχυρός and ὀχύρωμα thus never acquaired the same religious significance as, for example, καταφυγή in LXX.[362]

The non-use of the expected equivalent καταφυγή (if the text of 31:3 was the Vorlage of 70 (71):3), could not be explained by the fact that it appears in the next line, for מצודה, since this did not as a rule prevent the LXX translator from repeating the word. See 6.3.1. In the parallel 30 (31):3 καταφυγή is employed for מצודה in both of its ocurrences. Furthermore, it is the only one of the metaphorical designations of God under discussion that really is stereotypically rendered in LXX Psalms. In no way could the translator of the Psalms have had the text of 30 (31):3 as Vorlage. If the Greek text is original it appears to be a Verlegenheitsübersetzung, of an unintelligible Hebrew text.[363] Talmon has tried to sketch the textual development from the original text, written in the old script, to MT.[364]

Another possibility is that Rahlfs' text in this case reflects an Aquila-like revision, but hardly Quinta of the Psalter. See 6.2.2. The rendering of מצודה as a divine name in Aquila is perfectly in line with Rahlfs' text in Ps 71:3. ὀχυρός is

---

He reads מצדת לביא (מעון) "ein Löwen(versteck), eine Bergfeste" with reference to Nah 2:12 and Ps 26:8. In the last-mentioned, however, מעון refers to the temple.

[355] See Rahlfs. Cf. Michaelis, πύργος, p. 954:9.

[356] Heidland, ὀχύρωμα, p. 590:21-22, Dell'Acqua, Roccia, p. 439.

[357] Cf. Heidland, ὀχύρωμα, p. 591:8-11, Balz, Schneider, ὀχύρωμα, col. 1356.

[358] See Heidland, ὀχύρωμα, p. 590:28-29 and n. 1-2, Dell'Acqua, Roccia, p. 439.

[359] Thus HR. Heidland notes 73 occurrences in LXX. Heidland, ὀχύρωμα, p. 590.

[360] See Is 27:3. Ziegler, Untersuchungen, p. 89. ὀχυρός has in fact here brought with it πόλις. πόλις ὀχυρά is a favourite expression in the LXX translation of Isaiah. See 25:2; 26:1; 36:1; 37:26. Ziegler, Untersuchungen, pp. 89, 93.

[361] Jer 1:18; 1 Macc 1:33; 4:60 and 6:57 have the variant reading ἰσχυρός. In Is 33:16 ὀχυρός, according to a variant reading, modifies πέτρα.

[362] Se e.g. Dell'Acqua, Roccia, p. 439.

[363] A good illustration of the state of confusion in the Hebrew text is given in 4QPs-a, which has לבי, probably for MT:s לבוא. Cf. Skehan, Qumrân, p. 175.

[364] Talmon, Alphabet, pp. 510, 513, 514-516.

employed in both of the parallel passages, 30 (31):3 and 70 (71):3. בית is trans-
lated by τόπος in 118 (119):54. In Symmachus it is so rendered also in 30 (31):3.[365]
The rendering in LXX thus resembles a combination of the texts of Aquila and
Symmachus in the parallel text.[366] This only applies to the words under discussion.
The Greek is then in harmony with the usual reconstruction, even though it was
not part of the Proto-Septuagint, a text no longer extant.

מצודה is used as a divine name in 2 Sam 22:2, the only case in LXX where it,
as a designation of God, is rendered literally by ὀχύρωμα "fortress". The parallel
passage, Ps 17 (18):3, has, as we have seen, the expected equivalent καταφυγή.
The rendering in 2 Sam obviously reflects the Kaige recension and not the Old
Greek.

3.7.2   The equivalents of the term as a metaphor and in the literal sense

The literal sense of מצודה II is traditionally "fortress", "stronghold". See e.g. HAL.
But, according to Schunck, this is a special use of the word, restricted to four
passages, 2 Sam 5:7, 9; 1 Chr 11:5, 16, where it refers to Zion, the city of David.
These passages can be distinguished from the rest of the occurrences of the word
by the defective writing.[367] מצודה is nearly always a divine name in the Psalter. It
is in its literal sense (this applies to both מצודה I and II) translated by περιοχή, 1
Sam 22:4, 5; 2 Sam 5:7, 9, 17; 23:14; 1 Chr 11:5, 16; Ez 12:13; 17:20, and once by
στενός "narrow", 1 Sam 24:23. See LSJ. Brenton wrongly has "strong-hold" in line
with the meaning of the Hebrew.

Hugger suggests that מצודה in the everyday language went out of use just
before or during the exile, that it was mostly employed in the early period of the
kings of Israel, but that it was later replaced by משגב and מעוז in the literal
sense.[368] On the other hand, משגב is in fact very seldom employed in a purely
literal sense, which suggests that it may have been the other way around. Cf.
3.8.1 and 6.3.2.

מצודה is once employed in the sense of "net" as a metaphor of the Lord's
judgement, Ps 65 (66):11.[369] God is here depicted as a hunter who catches the
wicked in his "snare" or "net".[370] LXX has the equivalent παγίς "snare". Peshitta,
the Targum and Vulgate have a similar understanding. Aquila, Symmachus and
Quinta have "prison".[371] The Hebrew text is dubious.[372] That some of the versions
had a different text cannot be excluded. HAL reads מצור, as do Symmachus, Quinta
and Hieronymus, according to BHK. BHS is more uncertain, and rightly so, because
πολιορκία is in fact only employed here in Symmachus Psalms, and although
καταφυγή is as a rule a translation of מצודה, 30 (31):3, 4; 70 (71):3, the Hebrew
word is then a divine name. Moreover, מצור is only rendered by περιφράσσειν, 30
(31):22, or φράσσειν, 59 (60):11, in Symmachus Psalms.[373]

---

[365] See Reider, Turner, **Index**, p. 239 and Saiz, **Simaco**, p. 593.

[366] For the most instructive view of the renderings, see Mercati, **Hexapli**, p. 31. See also Schenker,
Hexapla, pp. 253-256.

[367] Schunck, מְצוּדָה, col. 1083. The basic meaning of the term is "a place difficult to access", cf. Job
39:28, but in the majority of the cases it denotes a "hiding-place", "den". Ibid., col. 1083.

[368] Hugger, **Zuflucht**, pp. 101-102.

[369] Thus BDB, but not KBL, HAL. Dahood argues for a totally different meaning here, "wilderness", but
that is hardly warranted. See Dahood, **Psalms II**, p. 122.

[370] Cf. Anderson, **Psalms**, p. 476.

[371] See Baetgen, **Psalms**, p. 198, Briggs, **Psalms II**, p. 92, Gunkel, **Psalmen**, p. 279, Kraus, **Psalmen**, p. 66
with reference.

[372] Briggs, **Psalms I**, p. 151. Cf. ibid., **Psalms II**, p. 92.

[373] See Saiz, **Simaco**, p. 680.

The equivalent in LXX of the term in 65 (66):11 may have been a guess from the context, since only here does it render מְצוּדָה in LXX. The usual translation of the literal meaning of the word, περιοχή "stronghold", was too neutral in this context. Obviously something negative was implied by the Hebrew. Note the parallelism with מוּעָקָה "affliction". A more or less correct interpretation "trap", "snare" in the wrong place is, however, a weak ground for the supposition that the translator knew the meaning "hunting-net" of the Hebrew term under discussion.[374] On the other hand, παγίς seems to be too specific rendering to be a mere guess. It is not the kind of generic term that one would have expected if the translator was at loss as to the meaning of the Hebrew.[375] παγίς otherwise as a rule reflects the semantic meaning of the Hebrew terms it renders. See HR. The LXX translator may have derived the word from מְצוּד "snare", "net",[376] even though he cannot be assumed to have known the meaning of this word. In other cases, where מְצוּד with a similar meaning occurs, Job 19:6; Eccles 7:26 and maybe Ez 19:9, it hardly ever has an adequate equivalent. The translator may have guessed at the meaning of the term in 19:9 since he renders it by φυλακή "prison".[377] The text of MT is doubtful. Zimmerli emends to "Gewahrsam", which well reflects the rendering in LXX.[378] Only once do we find a reasonably adequate rendering, Eccles 7:26, θήρευμα "spoil", "prey" (LSJ). Cf. the rendering of Brenton, "snare", which must be based on the Hebrew.

The meaning "prey", "net", "hunting-net" (מְצוּדָה I in KBL, HAL) was obviously not known to the LXX translators, since the Hebrew term is rendered by περιοχή in Ez 12:13 and 17:20.[379] In Ez 13:21 the Hebrew word, which here probably means "prey",[380] has the equivalent συστροφή "confounded" (Brenton).[381] The translator of Eccles 9:12, who employs the equivalent ἀμφίβληστρον "net", "drag", may have guessed at the meaning of מְצוֹדָה (note the different vocalization), since the context clearly implies a net.[382] In all these cases it is the question of metaphorical language, and man is described as the prey. Yahweh captures king Zedekiah in his net, Ez 12:13; 17:20. In Ez 13:21 it is not as closely connected with Yahweh.

3.7.3 Preliminary conclusions regarding the translation technique

The difference between the equivalent of מצודה as a name of God, καταφυγή, and the usual rendering where it has a literal referent, περιοχή, is obvious, especially if the LXX as a whole is taken into account. καταφυγή is also the ordinary translation of מעון as a name of God. The choice of equivalent is demonstrably not based on etymological speculations since the cognate verb is employed for totally different Hebrew words. Evidently, the LXX translators were acquainted with the traditional interpretation of the term in literal sense, "fortress", and could thus understand the metaphorical character of the term as a name of God. That the Hebrew word means "hiding-place" in the majority of its occurrences in MT, and that the translator of the Psalms only tried to reflect this meaning in his rendering

---

[374] See especially Barr, **Philology**, p. 272. Cf. ibid., pp. 243-245. See below.

[375] See especially Tov, **Septuagint Translators**, p. 66. None of the other usual ways of handling a deficient knowledge of the Hebrew applies here.

[376] מְצוּד II in HAL. This is supported by BDB. See also RSV "net".

[377] He may also have read מְמוּרָה. See BHK, BHS, HAL.

[378] Zimmerli, **Ezechiel**, p. 419. But the equivalent in LXX rather indicates that MT was derived from צרר or נצר. See ibid., p. 419 with references.

[379] The translator could have been helped by the parallelism with רֶשֶׁת "net" here and in 12:13a, which are exact parallels, except for the word order.

[380] See e.g. RSV, HAL and the translation in Zimmerli, **Ezechiel**, p. 282.

[381] The meaning of the word here is not a matter of course. See LSJ.

[382] The meaning "net" of the Hebrew word is suggested in BDB. See also RSV.

of the term as a name of God is hardly probable. In that case one would have expected the same equivalent in literal sense and as a designation of God, i.e. περιοχή, or at least a synonym, but this diverges from the translation technique adopted. The translators did not know the meaning of the homonym מצודה I "prey", "net" nor the cognate words of similar import.

3.8 THE TRANSLATION OF MIŚGĀB AS A DIVINE NAME

3.8.1 The equivalents of the name in LXX

משגב as a divine name, which only ocurs in the Psalter, is as a rule rendered by ἀντιλήμπτωρ, Ps 17 (18):3; 45 (46):8, 12; 58 (59):10, 17, 18; 61 (62):3, 7; 143 (144):2, but once by ἀντιλαμβάνεσθαι, 47 (48):4. Even though the term in 47 (48):4 is rendered by a cognate word, it cannot be regarded as a divine name: "Within her citadels God has shown himself a sure defence" is interpreted in LXX as "God is known in her palaces, when he undertakes to help her." משגב is rendered as from an Aramaic infinitive.[383] The ל before משגב, which signifies a condition,[384] could have misled the translator. Cf. 68 (69):30 where ἀντιλαμβάνεσθαι renders שגב piel. Flashar suggests that it is a free translation with an independent, but wrong interpretation of the original.[385] משגב in 18:3 may be an inner-textual Hebrew variant.[386]

That one and the same equivalent of משגב is employed in both 58 (59):10, 18 and 45 (46):8, 12 is to be expected, but this equivalent also occurs in a variety of other contexts. The use of ἀντιλήμπτωρ in 61 (62):3, 7, apart from being the ordinary rendering, is not unexpected in view of the preceding designation of God ישועתי "my help". The identical translation of צור and משגב in v. 3 and 7 is also natural because the Hebrew wording is the same.

משגב as a divine name is also rendered by βοηθός, 9:10b. βοηθός is employed here partly for variation (even though ἀντιλήμπτωρ could have been chosen), since משגב is rendered by καταφυγή in the first part of the parallelism, but also since the translator read משגב in conjunction with לעתות "a seasonable (help)": ויהי יהוה משגב לדך משגב לעתות בצרה "The LORD is[387] a stronghold for the oppressed, a stronghold in times of trouble" is rendered by καὶ ἐγένετο κύριος καταφυγὴ τῷ πένητι, βοηθὸς ἐν εὐκαιρίαις ἐν θλίψει "The Lord also is become a refuge for the poor, a seasonable help, in affliction." Thus καταφυγή was sometimes employed, 9:10a; 93 (94):22. Since צור in 94:22 was rendered by βοηθός in the word pair this term could not be employed there. But no reason for the non-employment of the ordinary equivalent can be detected. The parallelism (with a liberal definition) between καταφυγή and βοηθός sometimes occurs in LXX Psalms (always in that order). It is, apart from Ps 9:10; 93 (94):22, employed in 17 (18):3; 45 (46):2. This may have influenced the choice of equivalent for משגב in 9:10 and 93 (94):22.

The metaphorical meaning of the Hebrew term is probably "place of refuge". Weiss argues that the metaphor in 46:8 means not only protection but, in accordance with the etymology, also exaltation. He uses a structural argument which, however, is hardly convincing.[388]

---

[383] Mozley, p. 84. Cf. 126 (127):2 where מַשְׁכִּימֵי is translated by τοῦ ὀρθρίζειν "to rise early". Mozley, p. 175. See also BHS.

[384] See Num 22:22 לשטן לו "as his adversary". Cf. Baetgen, Psalmen, p. 113.

[385] See Flashar, p. 93. The suffix αὐτῆς is supplied to suit the interpretation. Cf. Mozley, p. 84.

[386] Kraus, Psalmen, p. 283. Cf. BHK and Eichhorn, p. 31 n. 8.

[387] This rendering presupposes the emendation to ויהי.

[388] Weiss, Bible, p. 343.

משגב is used only once as divine name outside the Psalter, 2 Sam 22:3. The equivalent in 2 Sam 22:3 is ἀντιλήμπτωρ, exactly as in the parallel passage, Ps 17 (18):3. It reflects the usage of the Old Greek since none of the other versions (except Quinta) have this correspondence. See 6.2. Thus the usage of משגב as a divine name is confined to psalms,[389] and is in fact more or less reserved for the Psalter.

The equivalents of the term in literal sense

משגב in literal sense means "high spot", "height".[390] It always functions as a refuge, according to HAL.[391] The word is as a rule used in close connection with God. Only three times is it employed in the literal sense, Is 25:12; 33:16 and Jer 48:1.[392] משגב is rendered by καταφυγή in Is 25:12, where it refers to walls:

> And the high (משגב) fortifications of his[393] walls he will bring down, lay low, and cast to the ground, even to the dust (MT).

> And he shall bring down the height of the refuge (καταφυγή) of the wall, and it shall come down even to the ground (LXX).

The context implies that "high fortifications" are a sign of pride rather than of protection. Cf. v. 11 "the LORD will lay low his pride together with the skill of his hands". καταφυγή can thus be used in both a literal and a metaphorical sense, but only appears as an alternative rendering of משגב as a divine name. It is the best translation of the metaphorical meaning of the word, but is employed for the term in the literal sense in a context which rather suggests that it is an expression for pride.

It is translated by ἰσχυρός "strong" in Is 33:16. Cf. the variant ὀχυρός. The term is employed as an adjective referring to a rock:

> he will dwell on the heights; his place of defense will be the fortresses of rocks; his bread will be given him, his water will be sure (MT).

> he shall dwell in a high cave of a strong rock: bread shall be given him, and his water shall be sure (LXX).

The LXX translator obviously understood the reference to the literal rocks, but it is not certain that he recognized the metaphorical function of the rocks as a defence.[394]

In Jer 31 (48):1 the word also has a literal referent.[395] משגב probably refers to

---

[389] **Tsevat**, pp. 15, 84 n. 70, **Eichhorn**, p. 100.

[390] See HAL. Cf. Fritsch, **Studies**, p. 735. Other suggestions are "high tower", Briggs, **Psalms I**, p. 151, or "fortress", Kraus, **Psalmen**, p. 215.

[391] Cf. Kraus, **Psalmen**, p. 215.

[392] Here it may also be regarded as a metaphor, even though it is connected with the actual life in the liberated Jerusalem. Kaiser, **Jesaia**, p. 347.

[393] Emended text.

[394] Cf. the rendering "Zuflucht" in Wildberger, **Jesaia**, p. 294.

[395] See e.g. Giesebrecht, **Jeremia**, p. 233, Thompson, **Jeremiah**, p. 699 and n. 2. The reason for the inclusion of 48:1 among the divine names in HAL, with reference to BHK, is not easy to see. Dell'Acqua also wrongly includes Jer 48:1 in his statistics of metaphorical divine names. Dell'Acqua, **Roccia**, p. 426.

[396] Thompson, **Jeremiah**, p. 699 and n. 2. It is hardly a place-name, even though Carroll suggests that this is implied by the feminine form of the verb. See Thompson, **Jeremiah**, p. 699 n. 2. Cf.

the fortress of Kiriathaim.[396] The text is, however, probably corrupt:[397]

> Woe to Nebo, for it is laid waste. Kiriatha'im is put to shame, it is taken; the fortress (המשגב) is put to shame and broken down; the renown of Moab is no more (MT).

> Woe to Nabau! for it has perished: Cariathaim is taken: Amasagab and Atath are put to shame. There is no longer any healing for Moab (LXX).

In the texts of Rahlfs and Ziegler משגב is transcribed, but S and many minuscules have κραταίωμα, alone or in combination with a transcription.[398] This may imply that in certain Greek manuscripts the Hebrew word is regarded as a designation of God (see 4.1), but the context makes this, to say the least, less plausible. It is more probable that these texts reflect stages in the Greek textual transmission where the term κραταίωμα is no longer reserved for Yahweh.

3.8.2   Preliminary conclusions regarding the translation technique

No definite distinction, reflected in the vocabulary, is made between the literal and the figurative meaning of the term, contrary to the usual translation technique in LXX in this regard. On the other hand, it cannot be taken for granted that the translators of the Psalms and 2 Samuel regarded the term as a metaphor, since the literal sense of the word is hardly recognized in LXX. But only terms which are used as equivalents of metaphorical divine names are employed. The ordinary equivalent of the term as a divine name, ἀντιλήμπτωρ, is a common alternative rendering of metaphorical names of God, but does not reflect the metaphorical meaning of the Hebrew which is probably "place of refuge". The LXX translator can hardly have chosen the main equivalent in order to reflect the significance of the word as a metaphor, since καταφυγή is only employed as an alternative rendering and not as the ordinary equivalent. Another alternative equivalent is βοηθός. Etymological considerations have probably not influenced the choice of equivalent either, since the cognate Hebrew verb is only once rendered by ἀντιλαμβάνεσθαι, Ps 68 (69):30. Otherwise the Greek verb has many different Hebrew equivalents. The preference for variation can also be seen here, but the variation is rather between the two alternative equivalents, than between the ordinary translation and the alternative equivalents.

Carroll, **Jeremiah**, pp. 778-779. See also NEB.

[397] Giesebrecht, **Jeremia**, p. 233, Volz, **Jeremia**, p. 405. The wealth of variants in the Greek confirm the state of the text. See Ziegler, **Ieremias**, ad loc.

[398] This is wrongly regarded as the translation of the LXX by Dell'Acqua. Dell'Acqua, **Roccia**, p. 426.

Chapter IV

CONCLUDING REMARKS REGARDING THE TRANSLATION TECHNIQUE

4.1 THE EQUIVALENTS OF INANIMATE METAPHORICAL DIVINE NAMES

The Greek terms used for the divine names under discussion are few being restricted to ὑπερασπιστής with cognates, βοηθός, ἀντιλήμπτωρ with cognates, ἐλπίς, καταφυγή, θεός, κραταίωμα and στερέωμα. One and the same word often renders many Hebrew metaphors. ἀντιλήμπτωρ is thus equivalent to סלע, 41 (42):10, צור, 88 (89):27, מגן, 3:4; 118 (119):114, מחסה, 90 (91):2, and משגב, 17 (18):3; 45 (46):8, 12; 58 (59):10, 17, 18; 61 (62):3, 7; 143 (144):2. βοηθός is equivalent to צור, 17 (18):3; 18 (19):15; 77 (78):35; 93 (94):22, מעוז, 51 (52):9, מחסה, 61 (62):9; 70 (71):7 and משגב, 9:10b. καταφυγή translates both משגב, 9:10a; 93 (94):22, and מעון, 89 (90):1; 90 (91):9. The suggestion that καταφυγή is a rendering of מעוז in 89 (90):1; 90 (91):9 is not warranted. See 3.6.1. ὑπερασπιστής renders מעוז in 26 (27):1; 27 (28):1, 8; 30 (31):3, 5; 36 (37):39 and probably in 70 (71):3, even though MT has מעון, and מגן in 17 (18):3, 31; 27 (28):7; 32 (33):20; 58 (59):12; 83 (84):10; 113:17, 18, 19 (115:9, 10, 11); 143 (144):2. ἐλπίς is only equivalent to מחסה, 13 (14):6; 60 (61):4; 90 (91):9; 141 (142):6, while κραταίωμα renders סלע, 30 (31):4 and מעוז, 42 (43):2. θεός is the most common rendering of צור in LXX Psalms and στερέωμα is equivalent to סלע, 17 (18):3; 70 (71):3. See Table 1.

It is interesting to point out that the same Greek terms are also employed for other designations of God, which are more or less metaphorical, thus ἀντιλήμπτωρ renders סמך (or to be more specific בְּסֹמְכֵי) in 53 (54):6 with God as subject and man as object: "the LORD is with those who uphold my life" (RSV margin). Note the parallelism with עזר. סמך is often used for God as he who upholds and sustains his people[1] and is once rendered by a cognate verb, e.g. 3:6. But many different equivalents occur. Indeed, ἀντιλήμπτωρ is, with a single exception, employed only in connection with God. It once translates משך חסד "extend kindness" in 108 (109):12[2] in a more neutral context where it is negated: "Let there be none to extend kindness to him, nor any to pity his fatherless children." The use of this word is in fact confined to the Book of Psalms, except 2 Sam 22:3 (= Ps 18:3) and Sir 13:22. The same is true of the cognate ἀντίλημψις (the Apocryphal books are excluded), which, however, is not only employed for divine names. See 3.3.1. ἀντιλήμπτωρ is extremely rare outside the LXX.[3]

βοηθός is a translation of סתר in 118 (119):114 and the same is true for βοήθεια in 90 (91):1. סתר in its religious sense occurs only in the Book of Psalms, 27:5; 31:21; 32:7; 61:5; 81:8; 91:1 and 119:114. The equivalents are mostly in line with its semantic meaning, "hiding-place", "refuge", but as a divine name it is only translated by terms which are more or less reserved for different designations of God.[4] Such a name is then rendered directly by βοηθός, 118 (119):114, or

---

[1] See Briggs, **Psalms I**, p. 27.

[2] Cf. **Mozley**, p. 163. See BHS, Rahlfs and HR. Occurrences outside MT such as Sir 13:22 are not included in this description.

[3] See **Flashar**, p. 243 n. 2 and LSJ.

[4] For similar designations of gods in other religions in the countries surrounding Israel, see Hugger, **Zuflucht**, p. 148.

indirectly by καταφυγή, 31 (32):7.[5] Even the verb סתר in hiphil is as a rule employed with God as subject (see Lisowsky) and man as object. Sometimes it occurs in this connection in the sense of protection, Job 14:13; Ps 17:8; 27:5; 31:21; 64:3.[6]

βοηθός renders עז "strength", "power" in connection with God, Ex 15:2; Ps 27 (28):7; 58 (59):18; 80 (81):2, and עזר "helper", Gen 2:18, 20; Ex 18:4; Deut 33:7, 26, 29; 1 Sam 7:12; Ps 32 (33):20; 69 (70):6; 113:17-19 (115:9-11); 145 (146):5. It is also equivalent to עזרה "support", "help", Ps 26 (27):9; 39 (40):18; 45 (46):2; 62 (63):8.

The roots עזר, עזרה nearly always refer to God in MT, and are as a rule rendered by βοηθός in LXX, when it applies to God, passim or Eve, Gen 2:18, 20, but also when it is sporadically used in a profane context, Nah 3:9; Ez 12:14. βοηθός is also as a rule employed of God both in LXX and in NT. Büchsel's statement "oft von Gott" is thus an understatement.[7] βοηθεῖν is the ordinary rendering of both the verb עזר and the noun עזרה in LXX as a whole. It is seldom used for עזז or עוז, and the same is true for βοήθεια. The suggestion in HR that βοήθεια renders נצל hiphil in Ps 69 (70):2 is definitely wrong and the reference to אילות in 21 (22):20 in HR is hardly correct either. The word order of the Hebrew was probably inverted here. See e.g. the Hebrew-Greek alignment which is created by E. Tov and B. Kraft.

ἐλπίς is nearly always employed as a designation of God, 13 (14):6; 60 (61):4; 61 (62):8; 64 (65):6; 70 (71):5; 72 (73):28; 90 (91):9; 93 (94):22; 141 (142):5, or in close connection with him, 4:9; 15 (16):9; 21 (22):10; 39 (40):5; 69 (70):2; 77 (78):7, 53; 145 (146):5. The only exception is the Verlegenheitsübersetzung in 59 (60):10 = 107 (108):10. ἐλπίς does not mean "hope", "expectation" generally in LXX, as in non-biblical Greek, but rather refers to "die auf Gott gerichtete Hoffnung".[8]

Outside the Book of Psalms ἐλπίς is once employed without counterpart in MT, Is 30:32:

> And every stroke of the staff of punishment which the LORD lays upon them will be to the sound of timbrels and lyres; battling with brandished arm he will fight with them (MT).

> And it shall happen to him from every side, that they from whom their hope (ἐλπίς) of assistance was, in which he trusted, themselves shall war against him in turn with tabrets[9] and with harp (LXX).

"Their hope of assistance" probably refers to the enemies of Israel, presumably the Assyrians, in whom Israel had put its faith. The meaning may be ironical, viz. that to trust the Assyrians will bring no good since only Yahweh, the true ἐλπίς, is worthy of confidence. Instead they will fight against Israel. Other interpretations of the referents are also possible. But such an understanding would accord with the use of other metaphorical divine names, at least in MT. On the other hand, the LXX translators have often misunderstood the ironical accent in MT in these places. In the Hebrew it is rather the Lord who will punish the Assyrians.[10] The translator may have understood the text in relation to chap. 31 where the Israelites are accused of seeking help from Egypt instead of the Lord, and here they are reproached for relying upon the Assyrians. Note that v. 29 in LXX, contrary to MT, is an accusation against Israel rather than a continuation of the promise in v. 19-26.

---

[5] Cf. Hugger, **Zuflucht**, p. 148.

[6] See **Tsevat**, pp. 18, 94 n. 132.

[7] Büchsel, βοηθέω, p. 627:26.

[8] See Bultmann, ἐλπίς, p. 519:9-10.

[9] Cf. Ottley, **Isaiah I**, p. 183.

[10] For the problematical relation to the Hebrew and the other versions, see Wildberger, **Jesaia**, p. 1209. Cf. Wutz, **Wege**, p. 856.

καταφυγή, if we disregard its literal employment for the cities of refuge, Num 35:27, 28; Deut 19:3 (implicit in MT), for the walls in Is 25:12, and for a heathen god in Dan 11:39 Th, always occurs in connection with the Lord, rendering; apart from the metaphors previously discussed, also מנוס "place of refuge", 2 Sam 22:3; Ps 58 (59):17; Jer 16:19. It is well in line with the meaning of the Greek. מנוס, in contrast to מעוז, never refers to a concrete place.[11] Thus it is hardly an ordinary metaphor. Perhaps it might be labelled a "conceptual metaphor" since it is based on an abstract rather than a concrete imagery.[12] מנוס, especially as a divine name, belongs to the poetic language.[13] In non-religious use it is, in contrast to its employment as a divine name, always rendered by φυγή "flight", Job 11:20; Ps 141 (142):5; Jer 26 (46):5; 32:26 (25:35); Amos 2:14. The LXX translators thus equate this word in literal sense with the cognate מנוסה "flight". In Jer 46:5 and Amos 2:14 the rendering is in line with the meaning of the Hebrew in the context.[14]

καταφυγή is once equivalent to נס "banner", "standard", Ex 17:15. Here the phrase יהוה נסי "the Lord is my banner" is a name of an altar. The naming of the altar bears witness to Yahweh's role in the battle. Yahweh himself is the standard beneath which the Israelites should fight.[15] Otherwise the Hebrew term is not used in a religious sense being mostly rendered by σημεῖον in LXX.[16] καταφυγή can thus be employed both in its literal meaning and as a divine name.

κραταίωμα is as a rule a name of God in LXX Psalms (see above), but is once a translation of סוד "confidential conversation", "friendship" in close connection with Yahweh, 24 (25):14:

The friendship of the LORD is for those who fear him, and he makes known to them his covenant (MT).

The Lord is the strength of them that fear him; and his covenant is to manifest truth to them (LXX).

Mozley suggests that the translator associated the Hebrew word with יסד "found firmly", "lay foundations of",[17] but actually he used an ordinary rendering for a term which he (contrary to the natural understanding of MT) considered more or less as a divine name. Otherwise the translator has employed various equivalents of סוד which generally reflect the meaning of the Hebrew. See 63 (64):3; 82 (83):4; 88 (89):8; 110 (111):1.

In 1 Sam 2:32 κραταίωμα may be used for the מעון "dwelling" of God in certain manuscripts of the LXX. It is here an unexpected, albeit not wholly impossible, rendering. κραταίωμα with cognates is regarded as a favourite word group in LXX Psalms.[18] This is true for the majority of the equivalents to divine metaphorical names. But they do not share one of the main functions of favourite words, to disguise words unknown to the translator.[19]

Contrary to most of the other equivalents under discussion στερέωμα is rarely a divine name in LXX, but the usual rendering of רקיע "firmament", Gen 1:6, 7, 8, 14, 15, 17, 20; Ps 18 (19):2; 150:1; Ez 1:22, 23, 25; 10:1; Dan 12:3 (Th). As a designation of God it is twice a rendering of סלע, Ps 17 (18):3; 70 (71):3. The translation of סלע by στερέωμα, which is not a common divine name in LXX, may have

---

[11] See HAL, Reindll, נוס, cols. 312–313.

[12] Watson, **Poetry**, p. 264.

[13] See Tsevat, pp. 15, 28 n. 50, 298.

[14] Reindll, נוס, cols. 312–313.

[15] Hyatt, **Exodus**, p. 185, Childs, **Exodus**, p. 315.

[16] Fabry, נס, col. 470.

[17] Mozley, p. 45. In Briggs, **Psalms I**, p. 228 the exact form יסוד is proposed. But only in Ps 27 (28):8 does this Greek term express the semantic meaning of the Hebrew word it renders. It has became a cultic term.

[18] Barr, **Philology**, p. 251.

[19] See Tov, **Septuagint Translators**, p. 67.

been intended to avoid the misunderstanding of an objectivation of God.[20] Apart from Ez 1:26 and Dan 12:3 רקיע is always rendered by στερέωμα in LXX. στερέωμα in the meaning "firmament" is sometimes employed without an adequate Hebrew counterpart,[21] Ex 24:10; Ezra 9:29, 30; Ps 72 (73):4; Ez 13:5.

This Greek word seems in the course of time to have acquired transcendental associations in LXX. See e.g. Sir 43:1, 8. This is a natural development for a term referring to the firmament, to which the use of οὐρανός as a name of God in intertestamental literature and in the NT can testify. στερεός has not undergone the same development although some of the associations of στερέωμα are also probably tied to στερεός, since it is often employed as an attribute of God.[22] The use of στερεός as a divine name for צור in Aquila bears out this reasoning.[23]

4.2   THE BACKGROUND FOR THE CHOICE OF EQUIVALENTS IN LXX

The specific vocabulary, which is more or less reserved for metaphorical divine names, is rarely employed in religious contexts in non-biblical Greek. Thus the terms are in a way devoid of pagan religious associations. καταφυγή, ἐλπίς and βοηθός are common in non-biblical Greek but refer as a rule to man or to inanimate objects.[24] στερέωμα is not a specific religious term in ordinary Greek, but its employment for "heaven", "firmament" in LXX has parallels in non-biblical Greek.[25] Other names, such as ὑπερασπιστής, ὑπερασπισμός, ἀντιλήμπτωρ and κραταίωμα seldom occur outside the Bible. ἀντιλήμπτωρ is at least once employed as a name of a pagan god in an Egyptian document from the second century B.C. (UPZ 14.18).[26] ὑπερασπιστής only occurs in literature influenced by the LXX, e.g. works by Philo, Josephus and Jerome.[27] κραταίωμα is a neologism in LXX which is later on sometimes employed in Christian literature. These terms are in any case not employed regularly as titles or epithets for man or gods in Greek papyri.[28] It thus appears that the translators consciously chose non-religious words as renderings of divine metaphorical names, rather than established religious terms, perhaps in order to avoid religious associations from the pagan environment.

Some of the renderings suggest that the translator tried to convey the connotations of the original metaphors. Note especially the different equivalents of מגן in the LXX Psalms, all of which mean "protection" or "help".[29] In fact most of the divine names in the Hebrew are, as we have seen, connected with the theme of protection. The general picture is, however, that semantic accuracy was not one of the primary aims in the translation of divine names. Bertram's conclusion that "Weder philologische Genauigkeit noch auch theologische Begriffsschärfe sind

---

[20] Bertram, στερεός, p. 610:10–12.

[21] Bertram, στερεός, p. 609 n. 9.

[22] Bertram, στερεός, p. 612:19–20.

[23] Cf. Bertram, στερεός, p. 610 n. 16.

[24] See the lexica. But βοηθός occasionally refers to gods. See Herodian 3,6,7; PLond 410,8; POxy 1381,83. Arndt, Gingrich, ad loc.   βοηθός is common in military contexts, but is also used as a designation for an official, often a civil servant. See Preisige III, pp. 98–99. Cf. Preisige II, p. 335. καταφυγή is used also in pagan religions for the asylum in the temple, e.g. UPZ 1.18; P. Ent. 82.6. Cf. Dell'Acqua, Roccia, p. 433.

[25] See LSJ. Once it is used in a religious context, in a magical papyri, P. Warr. 21.14. See Dell'Acqua, Roccia, p. 433.

[26] See LSJ and Dell'Acqua, Roccia, p. 431.

[27] See Dell'Acqua, Roccia, p. 434.

[28] Preisige II, pp. 342–344. For a comprehensive presentation of the use of these terms in non-biblical sources, see Dell'Acqua, Roccia, pp. 430–434.

[29] Cf. Flashar, pp. 243–244.

dabei von bestimmendem Einfluss gewesen"[30] is to the point. We have seen that the terms employed as equivalents of the metaphorical names from inanimate nature were hardly taken from the ordinary religious vocabulary of the Greek. It is possible that the choice of terms was influenced by the designations of God in the liturgical language of the synagogue.[31] A religious vocabulary in Greek employed in the synagogue probably existed before the translation of the Pentateuch:

> Il est en tout cas possible que le vocabulaire religieux se soit peu à peu fixé, en grec, dans la communauté juive alexandrine, par la pratique orale.[32]

The differences between the rendering of these Hebrew names as designations of God and in literal versus ordinary metaphorical meaning are on the whole consistently maintained in the Septuagint. Only $\kappa\alpha\tau\alpha\phi\upsilon\gamma\dot{\eta}$ and $\sigma\tau\epsilon\rho\dot{\epsilon}\omega\mu\alpha$ are not always employed in connection with God. The avoidance of a literal rendering of the divine metaphors from inanimate nature is thus not confined to the Book of Psalms; indeed it is representative for the LXX as a whole, but the majority of metaphorical designations of God in MT occur in the Psalter. This is easy to understand since these names of God are as a rule limited to the poetic language. The comment of Thackeray is to the point here "The translators were at one in their treatment of Divine titles."[33]

---

[30] Bertram, **Sprachschatz**, p. 98. See e.g. $\kappa\alpha\tau\alpha\phi\upsilon\gamma\dot{\eta}$, which as a divine name renders as different words as מעון, משגב, ס and סתר. See above.

[31] See Bertram, **Sprachschatz**, pp. 97–98.

[32] Harl, Dorival, Munnich, **Septante**, p. 228.

[33] Thackeray, **Worship**, p. 34.

Chapter V

THE TRANSLATION OF DIFFERENT TYPES OF METAPHORICAL NAMES

5.1 THE TRANSLATION OF 'ĀBÎR AS A DIVINE NAME

5.1.1 The equivalents of the name in LXX

This chapter will examine the translation of different divine names or epithets. The translation of אלֿיון, שדי, מרום, עֻזֹר, עז, קרן, אבן, אבֿיר and יהוה צבֿאות in LXX will thus be scrutinized. They are chosen in order to show the degree to which divine metaphorical names or epithets from animate or inanimate nature have equivalents different from those usually employed for these terms both in literal and metaphorical meaning.

Another suggested example of theological exegesis in the rendering of divine names consists in the translation of אבֿיר יעקב in LXX, which has been interpreted as both "the Strong One of Jacob" and "the Bull of Jacob". Erwin is of the opinion that the translators tried to avoid the meaning "bull" or associations with this term, since animal worship of not least bulls was widespread in Egypt. These kinds of equivalent in LXX are called anti-theriomorphisms by Erwin.[1] He also refers to the Mithra liturgy where the bull-motive was the dominant feature.[2] The Apis bull was sacred in Egypt. It is also symptomatic that the episode with the golden calf in Ex 32 was tantamount to Apis worship, according to Philo.[3] This implies that the LXX translators, or at least those who were resident in Egypt, generally had strong theological motives for avoiding a translation that could be misunderstood as a reflection of animal worship.[4]

The translation of the term in Isaiah and in the Psalter

The expression אבֿיר יעקב is translated in many different ways in the LXX. The rendering of the term in the Pentateuch, δυνάστου Ιακωβ "the mighty one of Jacob", Gen 49:24, is not followed by the translator of Isaiah. See 5.2.1. The phrase is there translated by ἰσχύος Ιακωβ "the strength of Jacob", Is 49:26, θεὸς Ισραηλ "the God of Israel", Is 60:16 and אבֿיר ישראל by οἱ ἰσχύοντες Ισραηλ "the mighty ones of Israel", 1:24.

Is 60:16 and 49:26 are closely related. Thus the same expression in the Hebrew occurs in both.[5] In Is 60:16 כֿי אני יהוה מושיעך וגֹאֲלך אבֿיר יעקב "(and you shall know) that I, the LORD, am your Saviour and your Redeemer, the Mighty One of Jacob" is rendered by ὅτι ἐγὼ κύριος ὁ σῴζων σε καὶ ἐξαιρούμενός σε θεὸς Ισραηλ "(and shalt know) that I am the Lord that saves thee and delivers thee, the God of Israel",[6] and in 49:26 by ὅτι ἐγὼ κύριος ὁ ῥυσάμενός σε καὶ

---

[1] Erwin, p. 79.
[2] But the validity of the Mithra liturgy is questionable in this context since it is of later date.
[3] Regarding the worship of animals in Egypt, see **Erwin**, pp. 81-83 with references.
[4] Erwin, p. 81.
[5] The wording in Is 60:16 is in fact dependent on 49:26. See Kapelrud, אבֿיר, col. 45.
[6] Brenton's rendering "the Holy One of Israel" is misleading.

ἀντιλαμβανόμενος ἰσχύος Ιακωβ "(and all flesh shall perceive) that I am the Lord that delivers thee, and that upholds the strength of Jacob." It is astonishing that not only is the divine name rendered differently, both passages have a double translation of גאל, a word which is often employed in connection with this name as well as with "the Holy One of Israel". It occurs in the phrase "the Holy One of Israel is your Redeemer", with small variations in 41:14; 43:14; 47:4; 48:17; 54:5 (cf. 49:7), which are parallels to the expression in 60:16. גאל in 47:4; 48:17; 54:5 is translated solely by ὁ ῥυσάμενος and in 41:14; 43:14 by ὁ λυτρούμενος. Thus the rendering in 60:16 does not combine the translation of two parallel passages. "The strength of Jacob" in Is 49:26 is not a name of God in LXX but rather a quality of Jacob.[7]

The phenomenon of double translation is a common trait in the LXX version of Isaiah. It is often a combination of two different renderings of the same Hebrew expression, either by the translator or as part of a, mostly anonymous, revision,[8] sometimes based on the later Greek versions.[9] In the case of 60:16, where a single Hebrew word is rendered by two Greek synonyms, it is probably a question of the original translation.[10]

In the translation of אביר ישראל in Is 1:24 the interpretation was, according to Erwin, twisted in order to avoid a literal understanding of אביר as a bull:[11]

> Therefore the LORD says, the LORD of hosts, the Mighty One of Israel:
> "Ah, I will vent my wrath on my enemies, and avenge myself on my
> foes" (Is 1:24 MT).

> Therefore thus saith the Ruler, the lord Sabaoth, Woe to the mighty
> ones of Israel; for my wrath shall not cease against my adversaries,
> and I will execute judgment on my enemies (LXX).[12]

אביר ישראל is rendered by οἱ ἰσχύοντες Ισραηλ "the mighty ones of Israel" and הוי "woe" is placed before this phrase instead of after where it occurs in the Hebrew. Thus the reference is changed from God to a group in Israel with whom God was displeased.

The reason for the translation in 1:24 is probably that the translator was so imbued with the ideas preached by the prophets that he naturally understood the unusual name as a qualification of a certain influential class of persons among the people of Israel, even by altering the word order.[13] אביר was often employed as a name of influential people in a neutral or a negative context. See below.

It is true that the LXX of Isaiah is free, paraphrastic and strongly affected by the exegetical understanding and translation techniques of the translator and his personality as well as the Sitz im Leben of the version as regards both time and place,[14] therefore it is legitimate "to take the difference between the original and the translation as a basis for an attempt to reconstrue the complex of theological ideas behind the translation."[15] But one must also be aware that "any attempt on our part to conclude as to a given tendency on the part of the translator should, therefore, be made with the greatest caution, and can, moreover, be made only after a thorough study of certain preliminary problems."[16]

---

[7] The rendering in Erwin, p. 80 "the Strength of Jacob" as a divine name is thus misleading.

[8] Seeligmann, Isaiah, pp. 33, 35, 36–37.

[9] Ziegler, Untersuchungen, p. 57.

[10] Cf. Seeligmann, Isaiah, p. 41.

[11] Erwin, pp. 79–80.

[12] The translation of Brenton is here partially based on the Hebrew and therefore greatly modified.

[13] Seeligmann, Isaiah, p. 104.

[14] For these and other aspects of the translator's attitude, see Ziegler, Untersuchungen, pp. 1–31, 175–212, Seeligmann, Isaiah, pp. 3–5, 39–69, 95–121. Cf. van der Kooij, Textzeugen, pp. 25–29, 33–64.

[15] Seeligmann, Isaiah, p. 4.

[16] Seeligmann, Isaiah, p. 4.

Inconsistencies in the rendering of words and phrases is a common feature in the LXX translation of Isaiah,[17] and as Seeligmann says "the great majority of the inconsistencies ... must be imputed to the translator's unconstrained and carefree working method, and to a conscious preference for the introduction of varia-tions."[18] Thus "we shall, on the one hand, feel sceptical towards the probability of their (scil. the inconsistencies) being particularly ingenious and particularly purposeful efforts to discover logical connexions in any chapter or part of a chapter in our Septuagint-text, but ... they also entitle us to try ... to discover, in isolated, free renderings, certain ... expressions of the translator's own views and ideas."[19] Furthermore, the LXX of Isaiah has suffered from numerous, partial revisions. It is therefore seldom advisable to base the nature of the Hebrew text on divergences in the LXX.[20] In neither of these passages do BHS or BHK or the commentaries suggest that the LXX reflects a different Vorlage.

In the Book of Psalms this name occurs twice, 132:2, 5.

> Remember, O LORD, in David's favour, all the hardships he endured; how he swore to the LORD and vowed to the Mighty One of Jacob, "I will not enter my house or get into my bed; I will not get sleep to my eyes or slumber to my eyelids, until I find a place for the LORD, a dwelling place for the Mighty One of Jacob" (132:1–5).

אביר יעקב "the Mighty One of Jacob" is in LXX rendered by θεὸς Ιακωβ in both v. 2 and v. 5.[21] It is thus treated in a similar way to the metaphorical designations based on inanimate nature in the Book of Psalms, especially צור. The identical translation of the two names can partly be explained by the context in which they occur and by their relation to other names.

Thus the reason for the rendering in Ps 131 (132):2, 5 and Is 60:16 is hardly that a literal interpretation of the Hebrew could give associations to the sacred bull or to worship of bulls, as was suggested by Erwin. This understanding is out of the question for the translator of the Psalms as well as the translator of Isaiah, since the name under discussion was rendered by δυνάστου Ιακωβ in the Pentateuch.[22] אביר יעקב always stands in parallel with יהוה in the Book of Psalms and its character of a divine name is thereby underlined. This parallel and the frequent occurrence of the phrase "the God of Jacob" may also to a certain degree explain the choice of θεός as equivalent, while the other renderings are rather based on the semantic meaning of the Hebrew. Thus two types of equivalent were operative in the translation of this expression. Cf. 6.4.1. The equivalent of the phrase in Is 1:24; 49:26 reflects the semantic meaning of this name even though the translation is twisted. What may be of interest is why the translators did not employ the wording of Gen 49:24. One possibility is that they tried to avoid a common name of different gods in their cultural environment.[23]

[17] See the discussion and the examples in Ziegler, **Untersuchungen**, pp. 32–46, Seeligmann, **Isaiah**, pp. 39–44.

[18] Seeligmann, **Isaiah**, p. 41.

[19] Seeligmann, **Isaiah**, p. 41.

[20] See especially Seeligmann, **Isaiah**, pp. 12, 22–38, 59.

[21] Peshitta has the same interpretation, but the Targum is more literal. Concerning 131 (132):2, 5, see also Baetgen, **Psalmen**, pp. 401–402, Gunkel, **Psalmen**, pp. 564–565, 568.

[22] For the dependence on the Pentateuch generally, see Olofsson, **LXX Version**, pp. 26–28, Isaiah, Ziegler, **Untersuchungen**, p. 103, Seeligmann, **Isaiah**, pp. 45–49.

[23] Cf. Grundmann, δύναμαι, p. 288:15.

5.1.2   A tradition-historical background for the term as a divine name

The divine name under discussion is obviously connected with the Zion tradition. It only occurs in passages connected with Zion, Ps 132:2, 5; Is 1:24; 49:29; 60:16, apart from the archaic text, Gen 49:24.[24] Like צבאות יהוה it was probably originally associated with Shiloh and the ark.[25] This applies to the most common form of the name and the variant, אביר ישראל in Is 1:24.[26] It was probably adopted during the early monarchy in Israel, but retained the associations with the worship at Jerusalem.[27]

אביר יעקב is in itself a variant of the title אלהי יעקב or אל יעקב "the God of Jacob",[28] one of the ancient Israelite divine names, which is probably a designation from northern Israel.[29] But when the name is part of psalm texts or texts from the prophets the original traditions had lost their significance.[30] "God of Jacob" is always employed in poetic texts, not least in the Book of Psalms, 20:2; 46:8, 12; 75:10; 76:7; 81:2, 5; 84:9; 94:7; 114:7; 146:5.[31] In the Vorlage of LXX this name may have occurred also in 23 (24):6, since the phrase מבקשי פניך יעקב is there rendered by ζητούντων τὸ πρόσωπον τοῦ θεοῦ Ιακωβ. But it may also interpret a difficult expression in MT "those who seek thy face, Jacob". Cf. the description of MT by Kraus "Diese Lesung ist im par. membr. und im Sinnzusammenhang kaum möglich."[32] The text of the Vorlage of LXX is as a rule regarded as the original.[33]

This is probably a name with universal rather than national associations[34] so that Jacob refers here to a theological entity and not to Israel as a political unit.[35] In the Book of Psalms and in the prophetic literature from the exile onwards it is a designation of the whole of Israel and often of an ideal Israel separated from the political and social realities of the age; it may also refer to the exilic or post-exilic community regarded as the eschatological people of God.[36]

The Massoretes point אביר in two different ways, with or without dagesh, and many scholars suggest that this is an artificial device to distinguish between אביר as "bull" and as "strong", since only the latter could be applied to Yahweh.[37] This theological bias is partly based on the opposition to the golden calves of Jeroboam I, 1 Kgs 12:25-33.[38] It is also emphasized that the pointing without dagesh is only employed when the word is part of a name of God.[39] Thus the distinction is not simply between a metaphorical and a literal meaning. On the other hand, both of the roots mean "strong, powerful"[40] and only the context

---

[24] See e.g. Ollenburger, **Zion**, p. 41 and n. 116.

[25] See 5.9.1 and Ollenburger, **Zion**, p. 41 and n. 113, p. 42. See especially Ps 132:5-8.

[26] Wildberger, **Jesaia**, p. 63, Ollenburger, **Zion**, p. 41 and n. 114.

[27] Freedman, **Divine Names**, p. 65.

[28] The similarity between these names is also obvious from the identical translation thereof in the Book of Psalms, θεὸς Ιακωβ. Another similar title, "the God of Israel", is much more frequent.

[29] Kapelrud, אביר, col. 45.

[30] Wanke, **Zionstheologie**, p. 58.

[31] Cf. Wanke, **Zionstheologie**, p. 55.

[32] Kraus, **Psalmen**, p. 342. According to BHS and Kraus, LXX reads פני אלהי יעקב. See also Wanke, **Zionstheologie**, p. 55 n. 42. 2 Hebrew MSS and Peshitta also had אלהי יעקב. Kraus, op. cit., p. 342, BHK, BHS.

[33] See e.g. Anderson, **Psalms**, p. 204.

[34] Weiss, **Bible**, p. 351.

[35] Wanke, **Zionstheologie**, p. 57, Anderson, **Psalms**, p. 175.

[36] Wanke, **Zionstheologie**, pp. 57-58.

[37] Thus **Erwin**, p. 79. See also Kapelrud, אביר, cols. 44-45.

[38] Kapelrud, אביר, col. 45. For the theological opposition to Jeroboam's cult, see e.g. Ringgren, עגל, cols. 1059-1061. Regarding the character of these calves, see Anderson, **Psalms**, p. 742 with references.

[39] Schmid, אביר, col. 26. See also the lexica.

[40] See HAL and Schmid, אביר, cols. 25, 27.

decides to what the term refers. The pointing by the Massoretes was probably intended to distinguish between "mighty" when it refers to God and "mighty" when it is used of men, not between "mighty" and "bull".[41]

Even though both Baal and El could have the designation "bull", other terms are employed in these cases.[42] אביר as a designation of the Lord may have a Canaanite background, since, although it never occurs as an name of Baal or El, it is in some texts clearly associated with Baal.[43] That the name originally meant "the Bull of Jacob", (see HAL) is, however, improbable since the basic meaning of the word is not "bull" but "strong", "powerful".[44] The original meaning of the term clearly suggests that the name of the Lord is to be translated "the Strong One of Israel" and not "the Bull of Israel",[45] even though associations with the meaning "bull" can hardly be excluded. But since animal names in metaphorical meaning, not least אביר, as a rule occur in a negative context, i.e. with reference to persons who are opposed to Yahweh, cf. 1 Sam 21:8; Job 24:22; 34:20; Ps 76:6; Lam 1:15, this sense was surely not intended in MT.

5.1.3   The equivalents of the term in the literal sense and as a metaphor

אביר does not refer to a specific animal. It could be used of horses, Judg 5:22; Jer 8:16; 47:3; 50:11, as well as bulls, Ps 22:13; 50:13; Is 34:7.[46] It was thus not exclusively connected with the bull.[47] The LXX translators were were well aware that the word sometimes referred to a "bull". See Ps 21 (22):13; 49 (50):13; 67 (68):31; Is 34:7 and Jer 27 (50):11 which have ταῦρος. In Jer 26 (46):15 אביר is, according to HR, rendered by ἇπις, but either the expression ὁ Ἇπις; ὁ μόσχος reflects אביר in the sense of bull[48] or the LXX translation is based on a different word division, which is the most probable solution. The translator in that case read נסחף "be cut down", "washed away" as נס "fled" and חף as "Apis".[49] Kapelrud suggests that even though the Hebrew word means "strong one", it also contains a reference to the Apis bulls of the Egyptians.[50] Others surmise that it refers to Pharaoh or maybe warriors.[51] ἱππασία "horse-riding", "chariot-driving", "cavalry" is employed in Jer 8:16.[52] In Is 10:13 K the translator has misunderstood the Hebrew

---

[41] This is rightly emphasized in Briggs, **Psalms II**, p. 473. There may even be a simple grammatical motivation for the difference. Schmid, אביר, col. 27 with references.

[42] See Anderson, **Psalms**, p. 742 with references, Freedman, **Divine Names**, p. 65, Ollenburger, **Zion**, p. 41 and n. 115.

[43] Ollenburger, **Zion**, p. 41 and n. 115.

[44] See Kapelrud, אביר, cols. 43-44, Süring, **Horn-Motif**, pp. 15-17. But cf. ibid., p. 33. Among the cognate languages it is only in Ugaritic that the term mostly refers to a bull.

[45] Gunkel, **Psalmen**, p. 344, Anderson, **Psalms**, p. 880. Cf. ibid., p. 880, where he quotes a statement of A. Alt implying that it is an expression of "bull-mania" to translate the name as "the Bull of Jacob". The interpretation of אביר as "bull" in the divine name is, however, not altogether abandoned. See Miller, **Animal Names**, p. 181 n. 20, Schmid, אביר, col. 27.

[46] See Miller, **Animal Names**, p. 180.

[47] Kapelrud, אביר, col. 44.

[48] See BHS, Ziegler, **Ieremias**. See also Schmid, אביר, col. 26. Rahlfs also incorporates ὁ ἐκλεκτός since it is documented by the whole manuscript tradition. In Ziegler it is included within brackets. This may be a type of double translation which is part of the translation technique in LXX Isaiah or it may be a sign of recensional activity. See above. Cf. Söderlund, **Jeremiah**, pp. 268-269 n. 29.

[49] See BHK, HAL, Thompson, **Jeremiah**, p. 690 n. 1, Carroll, **Jeremiah**, p. 768, Söderlund, **Jeremiah**, pp. 268-269 n. 29.

[50] Kapelrud, אביר, col. 44. This interpretation must be based on the rendering of the LXX.

[51] See Schmid, אביר, col. 26 and Carroll, **Jeremiah**, p. 768.

[52] See BHS, Ziegler, **Ieremias**. Rahlfs has ἱππασίας ἵππων. But the last word is evidently a gloss for the unusual ἱππασία. See LSJ, McKane, **Isaiah**, p. 192 with references, Söderlund, **Jeremiah**, p.

בְּאַבִּיר and rendered it by πόλις, which probably reflects בירה in his Hebrew text.[53]

The LXX translators also knew the meaning "strong", "powerful" of אַבִּיר. It is thus rendered by ἰσχυρός, Judg 5:22 B; Lam 1:15, δυνατός, Judg 5:22 A.[54] This meaning does not occur in the Book of Psalms. In Ps 75 (76):6, where אבירי לב "the stouthearted" is rendered by πάντες οἱ ἀσύνετοι τῇ καρδία "all the witless ones",[55] the translator probably read כל-בערי לב in his Hebrew text.[56] It may be a theological correction with the implication that for God even the mighty are weak.[57] The same Hebrew phrase, אבירי לב, in Is 46:12 is translated by οἱ ἀπολωλεκότες τῆν καρδίαν "senseless ones".[58] ἰσχυρός or δυνατός (including cognates) are thus not exclusively employed for אביר as a divine name. On the other hand, ἰσχυρός is the ordinary rendering of אל in Theodotion.[59]

Animal names are frequently employed metaphorically for different types of leaders in the OT, mostly in a negative context.[60] This is also the case with אביר in 1 Sam 21:8; Job 24:22; 34:20; Ps 76:6; Is 10:13 K; Lam 1:15. Cf. Jer 46:15.[61] In Ps 68:31 both the meanings "strong" and "bull" are in play.[62]

The rendering of the term when it refers to divine beings

אביר is translated with ἄγγελος in Ps 77 (78):25. The text of MT is not easy to interpret: לחם אבירים אבל איש "bread of the mighty, man did eat" is rendered by ἄρτον ἀγγέλων ἔφαγεν ἄνθρωπος "bread of angels, man did eat" (Erwin) in LXX. The Targum and Peshitta have a similar understanding, while Aquila, Theodotion and Quinta have a rendering ἄρτων δυναστῶν, which is probably dependent on Gen 49:24 in LXX.[63] Even though the equivalent is unique in the LXX it is a reasonable interpretation.[64] Cf. the parallel with דגן שמים "the grain of heaven" in 78:24. Cf. 105:40; Wisd 16:20 and John 6:31.[65] It refers to angels, as in Ps 102 (103):20 where גברי כח is rendered by δυνατοὶ ἰσχύι. Cf. Wisd 16:20 ἀγγέλων τροφή, 19:21 ἀμβροσία τροφή. See also 5 Esra 1:19. A reference I have not been

---

[53] 268 n. 28. HR has an obelus. Cf. Trommius.

Cf. Trommius. This rendering is common in LXX. It occurs 10x, according to Santos, **Index**. BHK with hesitation suggests ערים. Thus also Ottley, **Isaiah II**, p. 161, Gray, **Isaiah**, p. 202. But this proposal is not convincing. The same understanding is reflected in Peshitta. See van der Kooij, **Textzeugen**, pp. 287–288.

[54] Sometimes ἀδύνατος is employed, according to HR, e.g. Job 24:22; 34:20, but both are contested. אבירים may even have been rendered by θύμος in 24:22. Cf. HR. For another solution, see Budde, **Hiob**, pp. 145–146.

[55] See LSJ "void of understanding", "witless". Cf. Schmid, אבר, col. 27. Cf. the inadequate translation by Brenton.

[56] See BHS. Cf. Briggs, **Psalms II**, p. 169. See Ps 93 (94):8 where בער is rendered by ἄφρων.

[57] Thus Schmid, אבר, col. 27. In MT it refers to the brave fighter. Schmid, אבר, col. 26. Cf. the parallelism with "men of war".

[58] Mozley, p. 126, Ziegler, **Untersuchungen**, p. 127. BHS suggests a Vorlage אבדי לב.

[59] See Venetz, **Quinta**, p. 87.

[60] Miller, **Animal Names**, pp. 180–186, Watson, **Poetry**, p. 268. The same is true for many Ugaritic texts. Miller, op. cit., pp. 178–180.

[61] Anderson, **Psalms**, p. 568, Miller, **Animal Names**, p. 180, Kapelrud, אביר, col. 45, Schmid, אביר, col. 26. Cf. Watson, **Poetry**, p. 268, who also mentions Ps 68:31. This is probably right, even though the text may be corrupt. See Anderson, **Psalms**, p. 497, Kraus, **Psalmen**, p. 628. Cf. Briggs, **Psalms II**, p. 104.

[62] Schmid, אביר, col. 26, Kapelrud, אביר, col. 44.

[63] See Erwin, p. 84, Venetz, **Quinta**, pp. 95–96.

[64] See HAL, Baetgen, **Psalmen**, p. 426, Briggs, **Psalms II**, pp. 184–185, 193, Gunkel, **Psalmen**, p. 344, Bentzen, **Fortolkning**, p. 448, Kraus, **Psalmen**, p. 709.

[65] Schmid, אביר, col. 27, Kapelrud, אביר, col. 45.

able to verify.[66]

The translation of 'ĕlohîm in plural meaning

A similar interpretation of אלהים when it refers to a plurality is evidenced in the LXX. ἄγγελος is sometimes employed as a translation of אלהים, especially in its plural function. See e.g. Ps 96 (97):7; 137 (138):1. Cf. 8:6.[67] In these cases a theological motive may have played a part, and the angels were introduced as a substitute for God, 8:3, or for gods, 97:7; 138:1, although other interpretations are also possible. This applies especially to 137 (138):1.[68] This rendering often occurred when the translators did not want to identify אלהים with the God of Israel or with pagan gods.[69] There was a Hebrew precedent for this interpretation since אלהים in Gen 32:29–30 is called מלאך in Hos 12:5. The term בני אלהים could also be understood as "angels", Gen 6:2; Job 1:6; 2:1.[70]

אלוה, אל, אלהים are usually rendered by θεός in LXX when they refer to pagan gods, but sometimes other more or less neutral equivalents are employed, such as ἄρχων "ruler" and πάτραρχος "tutelary god". They may also be replaced by equivalents expressing a negative view of the pagan gods such as εἴδωλον "image", "idol", γλυπτός "carved image", βδέλυγμα "abomination". On the other hand, the neutral counterpart θεός was sometimes employed for Hebrew terms derogatory of pagan gods, such as אליל "worthless" and עצב "image", "idol". Notwithstanding that LXX sometimes resembles a "monotheistic Targum on the Hebrew text",[71] the opposite also applies. LXX in fact reflects a development which can be seen in the Hebrew text itself, even though LXX and MT demonstrate different stages in the process.[72] Thus the theological exegesis on the part of the translators in this regard does not represent an autonomous theological conception based on the attitudes prevalent in their religious milieu, but reflects and further develops tendencies inherent in the Hebrew text itself.

5.1.4 Preliminary conclusions regarding the translation technique

The translation of אביר in LXX varies widely. The translators did not strictly distinguish between the term when it was employed as a name of God and its use in other connections. Thus ἰσχυρός or δυνατός render אביר when it refers to a horse in Judg 5:22 and cognate terms are used in Gen 49:24; Is 49:26, where it is a name of God in LXX.

אביר probably means "strong" and it is so understood by the LXX translators. Frequently, however, the reference rather than the meaning of the term is reflected in LXX. Thus ταῦρος is a common rendering when the word relates to bulls and once, when it refers to divine beings, it is translated by "angels". The equivalent in Ps 131 (132):2, 5 and Is 60:16 θεός may be due to the same reasoning, but it is more likely that the frequent use of the similar phrase "the God of Jacob" with an identical translation and the parallel with יהוה have influenced the rendering. The

---

[66] See Gunkel, **Psalmen**, p. 344.

[67] See BHS, Rahlfs, Dodd, **Bible**, pp. 21–24, **Erwin**, pp. 86–89.

[68] See e.g. Kraus, **Psalmen**, pp. 1088–1089.

[69] See Dodd, **Bible**, p. 22.

[70] Cf. Deut 32:8 where the Vorlage of LXX had בני אל or בני אלהים. See BHK, BHS, Rahlfs and Dodd, **Bible**, p. 22 n. 1. The same is true for the Targum, according to BHS, and Symmachus, Vetus Latina, according to BHK, as well as 4QDeut-q. Wittstruck, **Deuteronomy**, pp. 58, 399–400. But, according to Field, Symmachus reflects the text of MT.

[71] Dodd, **Bible**, pp. 23–24.

[72] Cf. Dodd, **Bible**, p. 23.

parallelism between יהוה and אלהים frequently occurs in MT. The LXX translators were aware that אביר often referred to bulls and may therefore have considered it metaphorical. Consequently it cannot be excluded that the choice of equivalent in these cases was based on theological exegesis. But the suggested interpretation accords better with the more or less identical translation of the term as a divine name in Gen 49:24; Is 49:26, and with reference to a horse in Judg 5:22. It is thus not probable that theological exegesis accounts for the rendering of אביר as a designation of God. That the difference in spelling of the term in MT as a divine name and in other connections is based on theological considerations can be excluded, since other interpretations which are more adequate exist.

5.2 THE TRANSLATION OF 'EBEN AS A DIVINE NAME

5.2.1 The divine name in Gen 49:24

The studies concerning the translation of metaphorical names in LXX have paid no attention to אבן, possibly because the existence of this designation is disputed. אבן, in contrast to צור and סלע, means stone.[73] אבן occurs as a divine name in MT in two places, Gen 49:24 and Is 8:14. For the rendering of אבן in Is 8:14, see 3.1.1. In Gen 49:24, a verse that presents serious textual and exegetical problems, the phrase אבן ישראל, rendered by ὁ κατισχύσας Ισραηλ, stands in parallel with אביר יעקב, translated by δυνάστου Ιακωβ. The former is probably a variant of the comparatively common expression אל ישראל.

> yet his bow remained unmoved, his arms were made agile by the hands of the Mighty One of Jacob (by the name of the Shepherd, the Rock of Israel) (MT).

> But their bow and arrows were mightily consumed, and the sinews of their arms were slackened by the hand of the mighty one of Jacob; thence is he that strengthened Israel (LXX).

Dahood categorically denies the existence of אבן as a divine name and emends the text.[74] Freedman suggests, with reference to Ps 80:2, that it is a secondary form of בן with prosthetic aleph. Then the phrase "Shepherd of the sons of Israel" stands in parallel with "Mighty One of Jacob".[75]

A certain confusion in the interpretation of Gen 49:24 is attested in the old versions.[76] BHK suggests that the LXX translator may have read עזר instead of אבן. The reference to LXX is dropped in BHS. But the rendering of אבן by ὁ κατισχύσας "he that strengthened", is within the limits of the translation technique of inanimate divine metaphorical names in LXX. It is not exactly identical with the terms for protection and refuge employed in the Book of Psalms, but the choice of equivalent was probably influenced by the parallelism. ὁ κατισχύσας is equivalent to אבן rather than רעה "shepherd". This means that the divine metaphor רעה was not in the Vorlage of the LXX since רעה as a divine name, which in fact seldom occurs in MT, is mostly rendered literally by ποιμήν with cognates, Ps 22 (23):1, 79 (80):2, or by the participle of τρέφειν, "to feed", Gen 48:15. This is in line with the

---

[73] It is never employed for a rock or a mountain. Cullman, πέτρα, p. 95 n. 7. The conceptual similarity with שׁדי is emphasized in Knowles, **Rock**, p. 315 n. 17.

[74] See Dahood, **Gen 49:24**, p. 1006. For a more probable interpretation that eliminates אבן as a divine name, see van der Woude, צור, col. 542. He asserts that אבן is a corruption of בני.

[75] Freedman, **Divine Names**, p. 65 and n. 35. See also van der Woude, צור, col. 542.

[76] Dahood, **Gen 49:24**, pp. 1003-1007. See also the less plausible interpretation of LXX in Procksch, **Genesis**, p. 274. For a description of the relation between LXX and MT in v. 24, see Gunkel, **Genesis**, pp. 485-486, Procksch, op. cit., pp. 273-274.

translation technique in this regard in LXX. The last-mentioned is a unique equivalent in LXX as a whole. The employment in Gen 48:15 and Ps 23:1 may reflect a later usage than Gen 49:24, since in these cases an individual speaks of Yahweh as his shepherd. In Ps 79 (80):2 the same phrase as in Gen 49:24 occurs, רעה ישראל "the shepherd of Israel", but is rendered by ὁ ποιμαίνων τὸν Ισραηλ. רעה is never equivalent to κατισχυειν or ἰσχύειν in LXX as a whole. In fact designations of God which refer to the activities of man seem, in contrast to names of God based on nature, to be rendered literally in LXX. The term "shepherd" is also very rare as a divine name, especially in view of the frequent use of "shepherd" as a metaphor in connection with Yahweh.[77] This may be a consequence of the frequent employment of רעה as a name for gods in the countries surrounding Israel.[78] That kings have had the same designation in both Israel and the Ancient Near East generally may have played a part, since there was theological opposition to the deification of kings in Israel.

It is probable that אבן and רעה are Hebrew variants. רעה may be a gloss from Ps 80:2 for the extremely unusual divine name "stone",[79] but a development in the opposite direction is also possible, i.e. that a scribe wanted to increase the similarity in the synonymous parallelism by replacing רעה with אבן as a divine name.[80] In any case both possibilities are in line with the supposition that theological tensions could exist regarding both of these designations.

5.2.2   The background for the term as a divine name

אבן can be used in a variety of contexts, e.g. of a single stone, of precious stones, but also of stone as a building material or as a weapon. Sometimes it refers to a plummet or to hailstones. The referent may even be a certain weight.[81] A sacral use of the term, including its Aramaic counterpart, is also conspicuous. It is employed of a stone altar, 1 Sam 6:14; 14:33, of stones marking a grave or a frontier, but also of approved cultic stones, Gen 28:18; 35:14, and polemically against gods of stone, idols, Deut 4:28; Jer 2:27; Ez 20:32; Dan 5:4, 23.[82] Cf. also Hab 2:19.

The metaphorical use of אבן is rare and where it occurs has negative associations. As a metaphor the term mostly denotes a hard, insensitive heart, Ez 11:19; 36:26. That the quality of firmness and hardness is connected with אבן is evident from the simile in Job 6:12 "Is my strength the strength of stones...?"

The occurrence of אבן as a divine name, in contrast to צור, is very restricted, despite its cultic use, especially in older traditions.[83] The explanation may be that the polemics by the prophets against idolatry sometimes inveigh against the worship of sacred stones, מצבות, which are regarded as signs of Canaanite influence, Lev 26:1; Deut 16:22, and against the idols of stone, Is 37:19; Jer 2:27; 3:9; Ez 20:32.[84] The meaning of the ordinary metaphor and another obvious reason (size) made אבן, contrary to צור and סלע, less suitable for the most common sense of the inanimate divine metaphors, shelter and refuge.

[77] Jeremias, ποιμήν, p. 486:1-22, Beyreuther, **Hirte,** p. 698.

[78] See Beyreuther, **Hirte,** p. 698.

[79] Westermann, **Genesis III,** p. 272. Cf. Gunkel, **Genesis,** p. 486, Weippert, שדד, col. 881. This interpretation is also indirectly supported by LXX.

[80] Westermann, **Genesis III,** p. 249.

[81] See HAL, Kapelrud, אבן, cols. 50-52.

[82] HAL, van der Woude, צור, col. 540, Kapelrud, אבן, cols. 52-53. Cf. Schwarzenbach, **Geographische Terminologie,** pp. 120-121. For the use of אבן in OT generally, see especially Kapelrud, אבן, cols. 50-53, van der Woude, op. cit., cols. 540-541.

[83] Cf. Gamberoni, מצבה, cols. 1068-1069.

[84] See Kapelrud, אבן, cols. 52-53. For the polemics against the מצבה, see Gamberoni, מצבה, cols. 1071-1074.

5.3   THE TRANSLATION OF QEREN AS A DIVINE NAME

5.3.1   The equivalents of the term as a divine name

A metaphor of considerable interest for evaluating which factors influence the
non-literal translation of metaphorical divine names in LXX is קרן "horn", since this
metaphorical name of God is always rendered literally in LXX. Yahweh is twice
called "horn of my salvation" in the parallel texts, Ps 18:3 (= 2 Sam 22:3), i.e. one
to whom man can turn in order to be protected from his enemies. This title is
used in connection with other divine names for protection and refuge. It is translated differently from the rest of the designations of God in Ps 17 (18):3, which
have not been rendered literally:

> The LORD is my rock, and my fortress, and my deliverer, my God, my
> rock, in whom I take refuge, my shield, and the horn (קרן) of my
> salvation, my stronghold (MT).

> The Lord is my firm support,[85] and my refuge, and my deliverer; my
> God is my helper, I will hope in him; he is my defender, and the horn
> (κέρας) of my salvation, and my helper[86] (LXX).

The literal translation in Ps 17 (18):3 of one of many divine metaphors in LXX, and
that in a context where all the other metaphors have equivalents which are taken
from a cultic vocabulary, equivalents which are more or less in accord with the
metaphorical meaning, the point of similarity, is unexpected indeed. The Greek of
2 Sam 22:3 has a somewhat different character. See 3.1.1.

The use of קרן as a divine name seems to be characteristic of a certain epoch
in the history of Israel, since Ps 18 and 2 Sam 22 are dated to the 10th century by,
inter alia, Freedman.[87] קרן is an old designation of God which may have been
replaced by other Hebrew terms in the course of time. There are signs in the
transmission of these parallel texts that make this a possible development. Thus
Delekat's suggestion that Ps 18:47 (= 2 Sam 12:47) originally read וירום קרן ישעי,
where קרן was later replaced by אלוהי in Ps 18:47 and by אלהי צור in 2 Sam 22:47
is possible,[88] but not supported by any of the versions. The main reasons for this
proposal are of course the combination of רום and קרן (see below) and that this
name only occurs in the expression קרן ישעי in 2 Sam 22:3; Ps 18:3.

Horns were commonly used to depict strength and might of both gods and
human beings in the world around Israel.[89] Since קרן was employed as a name of
other gods[90] and frequently occurs as a symbol for the power of the gods in
Egypt and in Babylon, both early and in Hellenistic times,[91] the theological
motivation for avoiding a literal translation would have been strong, if the translators were eager to emphasize the uniqueness of Yahweh.

---

[85] Or "strength", "steadfastness". See LSJ.

[86] Two different words for "helper" are employed in this verse.

[87] Freedman, **Divine Names**, pp. 96-97.

[88] See Delekat, **Asylie**, pp. 379-380. Maybe it is original also in other places, where a similar combination occurs. Ibid., p. 380.

[89] Foerster, κέρας, p. 668:20-22 and n. 3, 4. It was, for example, used for priests, kings and soldiers.
Süring, **Horn-Motif**, p. 292. See also ibid., pp. 192-264, for examples.

[90] See particularly Süring, **Horn-Motif**, pp. 125-192 for a detailed presentation. Cf. Tallqvist,
Akkadische Götterepitheta, p. 144.

[91] Lurker, **Symbole**, p. 158.

5.3.2 The meaning of the term as a metaphor

קרן as a metaphor clearly denotes "strength" and "power",[92] but perhaps also "pride" and "dignity".[93] As an ordinary metaphor קרן is mostly derived from the horns of an animal, probably a wild bull, rather than the horn of an altar.[94] See especially Deut 33:17 and Ps 92:11, where the metaphorical use of קרן is connected with the wild ox, or the wild bull. On the other hand, the Psalmist may have compared himself with the horn of an altar in Ps 92:11b, although not as a place of refuge, "(But thou hast exalted my horn like that of the wild ox;) thou hast poured over me fresh oil." Primarily the expression refers to the festival joy.[95]

The involvement of animal imagery is confirmed by the sense of the metaphor, "power", and also accords with verbs used in connection with קרן. See e.g. Zech 2:4, with חרד hiphil "to terrify", which is often connected with animals, cf. Deut 28:26; Jer 7:33; Is 17:2 and Nah 2:12, נשא "lift up", which may here suggest the horn of an ox, and זרה "scatter", a word employed of Israel as the warrior flock in Ps 44:12.[96] On the other hand, זרה is mostly employed for the dispersion of Israel, without relation to animal metaphors, especially in Ezekiel and Jeremiah. As a metaphor קרן often occurs in the phrase רום קרן "to lift the horn".[97] That this phrase is taken from the horn of an animal is obvious.[98] There is an explicit comparison in Ps 92:11: "But thou hast exalted my horn like that of the wild ox."

The word as a metaphor has both positive and negative associations. The wicked is forbidden to lift up his horn, Ps 75:5, 6, since only God has the right to exalt or trample down the horn of men. It is a sign of arrogance when man himself lifts his horn.[99] When קרן is employed in connection with the righteous it has a strong positive meaning: God will lift their horns, Ps 89:18; 148:14, or their horns are lifted, 112:9. It is used especially of the king; God will lift the horns of his Messiah, 1 Sam 2:10, or by God's name shall David's horn be exalted, 89:25.[100] The meaning of this phrase, "to give power", is most easily seen in 1 Sam 2:10 "he will give strength to his king, and exalt the power (literally "lift the horn") of his anointed." See also Ps 92:11.

Certain passages even suggest that the lifting of the horn is a visible sign of success, Ps 112:9-10, and that it sometimes refers to progeny. See particularly Deut 33:16-17; 1 Chr 25:5; Ps 132:17.[101] In 132:17 God promises to "make a horn to sprout to David". A slightly different wording is used here, אצמיח קרן, which means, in more general terms, "to give salvation" or "to give blessing".[102]

---

[92] HAL, Lurker, **Symbole**, p. 158. See e.g. 1 Sam 2:10; Jer 48:25. For further examples, see HAL and Süring, **Horn-Motif**, p. 105.

[93] Anderson, **Psalms**, p. 549, Süring, **Horn-Motif**, p. 105. It is also a symbol of fertility. Ibid., p. 295. If evidence from the surrounding countries are taken into account the metaphorical meaning is extended considerably. Ibid., p. 453.

[94] Briggs, **Psalms I**, p. 151, Anderson, **Psalms**, p. 155, Stähli, קרן, col. 756.

[95] Briggs, **Psalms II**, p. 285, Dahood, **Psalms II**, p. 337, Kraus, **Psalmen**, p. 812.

[96] Cf. Porter, **Metaphors**, p. 66 and n. 18, p. 67 and n. 25-27. See also Dan 7:10-13, ibid., p. 66 and n. 19, 20, and Dan 8:4 which has נגח piel "to charge". Ibid., p. 76.

[97] The same expression was employed by the Babylonians. Gunkel, **Psalmen**, p. 327 with references. The picture of the raised horn is also evidenced in Greek. Bertram, **Sprachschatz**, p. 91.

[98] Süring less convincingly argues that this connection should not be taken for granted. Süring, **Horn-Motif**, pp. 343-345.

[99] Foerster, κέρας, p. 669:8-15. Cf. also Süring, **Horn-Motif**, p. 105.

[100] See Foerster, κέρας, p. 669:15.

[101] See McCarter, **1 Samuel**, pp. 71-72.

[102] Note the parallel "arrange a lamp". Cf. Kraus, **Psalmen**, p. 1066. See also 1 Kgs 11:36 and Ez 29:21. The reference is probably to a future Messianic king. See Briggs, **Psalms II**, p. 472.

5.3.3 The background for the use of the term as a divine name

What is the background for the use of קֶרֶן as a designation of God. קֶרֶן in literal sense mostly signifies the horns of an animal. See, for example, Ps 22:2; 92:11. Another important referent is the horns of an altar, protrusions at the four corners.[103] This usage is especially frequent in Ex and Lev. In the Book of Psalms it only occurs in 118:27. A horn could also be a receptacle for oil, 1 Sam 16:1, 13; 1 Kgs 1:39, or refer to a hill-side,[104] Is 5:1, or rays of brightness, Hab 3:4.[105]

The use of קֶרֶן with reference to the horns of an altar to which a criminal could flee in order to save his life, i.e. as a place of shelter[106] is interesting. It may underlie קֶרֶן as a divine name, since it is used in Ps 17 (18):3 with other metaphors for protection and the expression "horn of my salvation" is in line with Yahweh as he who grants protection.[107] The religious function of the altar also suggests a concept easily transferred to Yahweh. In that case the metaphorical use of קֶרֶן as a divine name has a different background from the use as an ordinary metaphor. Others surmise that animal imagery also lies behind the use of קֶרֶן as a name of God.[108] It may also be the image of a mountain top, Is 5:1, or a tower or a tall building, Lam 2:3, (note the parallelism with v. 2) which would explain its use as a divine name,[109] but this is less probable.

The meaning of the Hebrew word as an ordinary metaphor fits the metaphorical use of κέρας in Greek.[110] κέρας was employed as a metaphor for power in LXX in Deut 33:17: κέρατα μονοκέρωτος τὰ κέρατα αὐτοῦ "his power is like the power of an unicorn".[111] It is obviously a question of a living metaphor in MT. Note that the context supports the animal imagery "His firstling bull has majesty, and his horns are the horns of a wild ox; with them he shall push the peoples, all of them, to the ends of the earth."[112] It is also a living metaphor in Ps 21 (22):22 "Save me from the mouth of the lion, my afflicted soul from the horns of the wild oxen" which in LXX is rendered by "Save me from the lion's mouth; and regard my lowliness from the horns of the unicorns."

The Greek word is, according to Bertram, employed as a metaphor in LXX more or less independently of the Hebrew Vorlage in Jer 31:12 and Amos 6:13,[113] but this may not be taken for granted. Bertram's discussion is based on an inferior text; the Old Greek of Jer 31 (48):12 probably had a different term, κέρασμα

---

[103] This feature was probably unique for Israel. Süring, **Horn-Motif**, p. 324 and n. 1. For the appearance of these horns, see pictures in Keel, **Bildsymbolik**, pp. 127–128, Pritchard, **Pictures**, p. 192, Galling, **Reallexikon**, p. 8, **Altar**, Biblisches Historisches Handwörterbuch, pp. 63–65. It was probably not based on animal imagery as was previously maintained. Süring, **Horn-Motif**, pp. 297–298, 308–312.

[104] Cf. KBL, HAL "Berghalde" (slope of a hill). Others suggest "Ausläufer eines Berges" (spur of a mountain), Wildberger, **Jesaia**, p. 168, "steilen Berg" (a steep mountain), Schwarzenbach, **Geographische Terminologie**, p. 20.

[105] See e.g Süring, **Horn-Motif**, p. 460. Other interpretations are also possible. Ibid., pp. 374–383.

[106] See e.g. Wolff, **Joel**, p. 239. Cf. 1 Kgs 1:50–53 and 2:28–34 as well as Amos 3:14. Cf. Süring, **Horn-Motif**, pp. 323–324. For a detailed description of the function of the institution of asylum in Israel, see Delekat, **Asylie**, pp. 270–342. This institution is only evidenced in Israel and not in the adjacent cultures. Süring, op. cit., pp. 324–325.

[107] See HAL. For a comprehensive discussion, see Süring, **Horn-Motif**, pp. 326–331. Cf. KBL where the only metaphorical meaning noted is "might".

[108] E.g. Anderson, **Psalms**, p. 155. Cf. Süring, **Horn-Motif**, pp. 441–443. Then it would have the metaphorical meaning "might" also as a designation of God. See e.g. RSV, HAL, Albrektson, **Lamentations**, p. 89 and n. 6.

[109] Thus Baetgen, **Psalmen**, p. 50, McCarter, **1 Samuel**, p. 71. For a discussion regarding the meaning of קֶרֶן here, see Süring, **Horn-Motif**, pp. 336–340.

[110] Bertram, **Sprachschatz**, p. 90. Cf. Süring, **Horn-Motif**, pp. 450–451.

[111] See Foerster, κέρας, p. 668:28–34. Cf. the perhaps misleading rendering by Brenton "his horns are the horns of an unicorn."

[112] See the criteria for a living metaphor in **Beekman, Callow**, pp. 133–136.

[113] Bertram, **Sprachschatz**, p. 91.

"mixture".[114] The situation is different in Amos 6:13: "Have we not by our own strength taken Karnaim for ourselves?" is in LXX rendered by "Have we not possessed horns by our own strength?" According to Bertram, "horn" is a metaphor "ascendency" here: "Wird nicht auf unserer Stärke unsere Machtstellung beruhen?"[115] But the rendering of LXX might as well be regarded as a literal Verlegenheitsübersetzung for an unknown place-name as a Greek metaphor.

Even where there is no reference to a literal horn of an animal, κέρας can denote physical might and power in non-biblical Greek, although κέρας as a metaphor does not signify physical bravery.[116]

5.3.4   Preliminary conclusions regarding the translation technique

קרן is nearly always translated by κέρας in LXX as a whole, not only when it has a literal referent,[117] but also when it is used in metaphorical sense.[118] קרן as a verb in a way reflects the semantical meaning of the ordinary metaphor "become great, wealthy and important". The cognates also have a similar meaning. See HAL.

We may conclude that neither theological bias prompted by the use of the name for other gods nor the fear that a literal translation would suggest that Yahweh could be identified with a horn seem to have influenced the choice of equivalent here. Even though κέρας is employed in a metaphorical sense in Greek "power", "strength", it is not to be taken for granted that this is also the metaphorical meaning of the Hebrew. On the other hand, the translator may have understood קרן in the sense of "strength" here, as do some modern interpreters, even though the equivalent diverges from the usual lexical choices for this type of metaphorical divine names and κέρας never renders a non-metaphorical word for strength in LXX. Another factor which may have influenced the translators is that קרן is often employed as a live metaphor in MT. See 6.4.3.

5.4   THE TRANSLATION OF 'OZ AS A DIVINE NAME

5.4.1   The equivalents of the name in LXX

The equivalents of the name in the Psalms

Inasmuch as עז is sometimes employed as a divine name in MT and not least since it has equivalents in common with other divine names I shall try delineate its relation to the designations of God previously discussed. There are different opinions as to where the term should be understood as a designation of God.

The renderings of עז as a name of God, in my opinion, in LXX are varied, βοηθός, 27 (28):7; 58 (59):18; 80 (81):2, βοήθεια, 61 (62):8, κραταίωμα, 27 (28):8, κραταιός, 70 (71):7, δύναμις, 45 (46):2; 139 (140):8, ἰσχύς, 60 (61):4; 117 (118):14, and maybe κράτος, 58 (59):10.[119] עז is not recognized as a designation of God in 59:10 in HAL and this is also true for the text of MT. עזי in MT, contrary to LXX:s עזו, cannot be understood as a divine name, but the text is obviously

---

[114] See Ziegler, Ieremias, and LSJ.

[115] Bertram, Sprachschatz, p. 90.

[116] See Foerster, κέρας, pp. 668:22-24, 669:2-7. But cf. Bertram, Sprachschatz, p. 91. It is often employed in later Judaism for the creation of power. Foerster, op. cit., p. 669:16-25. For the use in NT, see ibid., pp. 669:30-671:10.

[117] As a horn or a bugle it is rendered by σάλπιγξ in Dan 3:5, 7, 10, 15. In Ez 27:15 it is employed for the teeth of an elephant and therefore translated by ὀδούς.

[118] In Job 16:15 it is translated by σθένος "strength" as a metaphor. Bertram, Sprachschatz, p. 91.

[119] For κράτος as a divine name here, see Michaelis, κράτος, p. 906:14-15.

corrupt.[120] The LXX text can be interpreted with reference to the Psalmist. Cf. the twisted translation of τὸ κράτος μου, πρὸς σὲ φυλάξω by Brenton "I will keep my strength, looking to thee". But the parallel expression in v. 18, which is regarded as a direct address to God in LXX, unequivocally favours the same interpretation of v. 10; the same is true of משגב, which in both verses occurs in synonymous parallelism with עז, and is rendered by a common designation of God in LXX, ἀντιλήμπτωρ. In 88 (89):18 עז is employed in close connection with Yahweh, even though it cannot be regarded as a divine name, according to our interpretation: "For thou art the glory of their strength". It is rendered by δύναμις in LXX.

The differences in the renderings do not depend on the character of the Hebrew. Thus the combination of divine names has not affected the choice of equivalents e.g. צור-עזי, 62:8, מחסי-עז, 71:7, עז ישועתי, 140:8 and מגדל-עז, 61:4. The equivalents are not distinguished in any way from the passages where the term occurs alone. מגדל is, apart from Ps 61:4, not employed as a divine name, even though it is used in close connection with the Lord in Prov 18:10, where it is interpreted from its etymology. It is literally rendered here in conformity with קרן, but contrary to the usual technique in LXX as a whole.

The equivalents of the name outside LXX Psalms

Outside the Book of Psalms a similar picture can be seen, thus βοηθός is used in Ex 15:2, otherwise ἰσχύς, Is 49:5; Jer 16:19, or δόξα, Is 12:2. ἰσχύς may have been employed in Jer 16:19 on account of the succeeding βοήθεια. See the LXX text: Κύριε ἰσχύς μου καὶ βοήθειά μου καὶ καταφυγή μου. In Is 49:5, where it might perhaps be regarded as a divine name, the context was evidently crucial for the choice of equivalent since the servant's weakness is emphasized in 49:4, before Yahweh gives him strength, while his power is reflected in v. 6:

> But I said, "I have laboured in vain, I have spent my strength (כחי) for nothing and vanity; yet surely my right is with the LORD, and my recompense with my God." And now the LORD says, who formed me from the womb to be his servant, to bring Jacob back to him, and that Israel might be gathered to him, for I am honoured in the eyes of the LORD, and my God has become my strength (עזי) (Is 49:4–5 MT).

> Then I said, I have laboured in vain, I have given my strength (τὴν ἰσχύν μου) for vanity and for nothing: therefore is my judgment with the Lord, and my labour before my God. And now, thus saith the Lord that formed me from the womb to be his own servant, to gather Jacob to him and Israel. I shall be gathered and glorified before the Lord, and my God shall be my strength (μοι ἰσχύς) (LXX).

Two different terms for "might" have only one Greek equivalent, and thus v. 5 refers back to v. 4. The words for "gather" are also the same in the Greek contrary to the Hebrew.

The context may have been decisive also for the rendering of Is 12:2 since δόξα stands there in conjunction with αἴνεσις "praise" so that the meaning "strength" may have been somewhat out of place. The Hebrew term here is part of a standard formula, עזי וזמרת יה, which only occurs in poetical sections of the OT. In order to stand on firmer ground, we shall investigate how this expression was understood generally. The meaning of the Hebrew is not self-evident.[121] The two

---

[120] Most scholars read עזו with versiones and some Hebrew manuscripts. Cf. v. 18. See e.g. Briggs, **Psalms II**, pp. 53, 56, Gunkel, **Psalmen**, p. 254, Michel, **Tempora**, p. 153, Anderson, **Psalms**, p. 438.
[121] See the different interpretations presented in Loewenstamm, **Strength**, pp. 464–465.

most probable interpretations are "refuge and protection"[122] or "my strength and my glory".[123]

The phrase is interpreted differently in LXX in all the places where it occurs in MT, Ex 15:2; Ps 117 (118):14 and Is 12:2: βοηθὸς καὶ σκεπαστὴς "helper and protector", Ex 15:2, ἰσχύς μου καὶ ὕμνησίς μου "my strength and my song", Ps 117 (118):14, ἡ δόξα μου καὶ ἡ αἴνεσίς μου "my glory and my praise", Is 12:2. Only the rendering in Ps 117 (118):14 accords with a traditional interpretation of the Hebrew.

The meaning of ʿoz I and II

Apart from the places where it refers to a bulwark or a fortress, עז has two different meanings. For this reason the word is often divided into separate roots, עז I "power", "strength" and עז II "refuge", "protection".[124] The differences between the lexica concerning which passages to include in עז II "refuge" are great.[125] It is thus very hard to single out places where this meaning of the word occurs in the Book of Psalms.[126] When עז is employed as a divine name it is mostly regarded as עז II.[127] But perhaps all instances save 62:8 can be interpreted as עז I.[128]

At least three factors contradict the suggestion that the LXX translators only tried to reflect the meaning of עז I and II in their renderings of the divine names. עז II should in that case have been rendered by καταφυγή or a synonym. The places where the LXX translators use words for strength are not expected in the context and by no means coincide with the suggested classification in the lexica, even if the differences between them are taken into account. Furthermore, terms which appear as equivalents to other metaphorical divine names are often used, for example, κραταίωμα and βοηθός, which are far from adequate translations of עז in any sense of the word and which never render עז in other connections. This implies that, apart from the Psalms' translator, at least the translators of Exodus and Isaiah regarded עז as a metaphor from inanimate nature. See also the discussion below. But if this is the case, what made semantically accurate renderings suitable to be employed as common equivalents for divine metaphorical names? The most probable answer is that עז, contrary to other designations of God, seldom refers to a fortress, while the meaning "strength" is very common.

---

[122] Craigie, **Ps XXIX**, pp. 145–146.

[123] Loewenstamm, **Strength**, p. 470. Cf. ibid., p. 468. The text is emended to זמרתי.

[124] The division is suggested by, inter alia, KBL, HAL, even though the latter is more restricted in the inclusion of passages under the second root. Lisowsky, on the other hand, records the meaning "refuge" under the ordinary root. Note also the occurrences included in **Tsevat**, p. 15 and n. 59, Hugger, **Zuflucht**, p. 90. For the meaning "refuge", see also Wagner, עזז, cols. 1–2, 5–7. The suggestion of a Hebrew root עזד "warrior" or "patience", "consolation", with reference to two Arabic words, can hardly be relevant here since ־ in the divine names is as a rule regarded as a suffix in LXX and no Greek equivalents adequately reflect these interpretations. See Loewenstamm, **Strength**, p. 465 with references.

[125] Cf. **Tsevat**, p. 15 and n. 59.

[126] See the discussion in Hugger, **Zuflucht**, pp. 89–90. Cf. HAL, p. 762.

[127] See HAL, Hamp, **Ps 8,2b. 3**, p. 118. Cf. Gunkel, **Psalmen**, pp. 87, 254.

[128] See HAL, Hamp, **Ps 8,2b. 3**, p. 118. Cf. Hugger, **Zuflucht**, p. 89. Note that 70 (71):7, which is not recognized as a divine name in HAL, is recorded as עז I.

5.4.2 The equivalents of the term as a metaphor and in the literal sense

A prerequisite for the metaphorical use of words is that they are employed also in a literal sense.[129] In a few cases עז has literal referents, "bulwark" Prov 21:22; Amos 3:11; 5:9, "firmament", "heaven" Ps 8:3.[130] Note the context, especially the use of "city", in Prov 21:22, the parallel with "fortress" in Amos 5:9,[131] and the commentators generally. In Jer 51:53 עז qualifies מרום, and it is not a noun "fortress". Cf. HAL.

The word can of course have a literal referent in the Hebrew, even though the LXX translators have interpreted it differently. But the understanding in LXX is the determining factor for the evaluation of the translation technique. עז in Ps 8:3 is rendered by αἶνος "praise", a unique interpretation in LXX, probably a guess from the context. In Jer 28 (51):53; Amos 3:11 and 5:9 LXX has the standard equivalent ἰσχύς which, however, is ambiguous. It can be used in a literal as well as a metaphorical sense.[132] In Amos 3:11 it should probably be interpreted as "strength". Cf. the translation by Brenton "bring down thy strength out of thee". The same might be true for Amos 5:9, but the meaning "fortress" can perhaps be intended here contrary to the rendering by Brenton, "strength".

The LXX translators have only once an indisputably literal equivalent to עז, ὀχύρωμα, Prov 21:22. But even though ὀχύρωμα is employed only in a literal meaning in ordinary Greek[133] it is used at least once in LXX in a metaphorical sense, Prov 10:29.[134] This word is also probably used metaphorically in Prov 12:11, without counterpart in the Hebrew, and with an uncertain counterpart in 12:12.[135]

Thus although עז in MT obviously has literal referents, it can only by way of exception be regarded as a metaphor in LXX, since it cannot be excluded that many translators recognized merely the most common senses of the word. The rendering of עז "might" in Ps 131 (132):8 with ἁγίασμα may, however, indicate that it could have literal referents in the eyes of the translator of LXX Psalms: "Arise, O LORD, and go to thy resting place, thou and the ark of thy might" (עזך). The translation by Brenton is misleading: "Arise, O Lord, into thy rest; thou, and the ark of thine holiness" (τοῦ ἁγιάσματός σου). The Greek word probably means "sanctuary" here.[136] Certain equivalents in LXX also make it probable that a metaphorical sense of the word was recognized.

The most common equivalents of עז in ordinary sense, without distinction between I and II, are ἰσχύς and δύναμις. ἰσχύς is often used for the strength of God, especially in connection with the exodus from Egypt where MT employs both עז and כח, notwithstanding that the word had more or less disappeared in the

---

[129] "Metaphor" is used in the sense of a so-called referential metaphor which is based on a concrete image. See Watson, **Poetry**, p. 264.

[130] See e.g. HAL. Another suggestion is "bulwark", "fortress". See BDB, Hamp, **Ps 8,2b. 3**, pp. 118-119 and n. 16. This interpretation requires that the three first words of v. 3 are connected with v. 2. Ibid., p. 119 and n. 20. Cf. Anderson, **Psalms**, p. 102, where "fortress" is understood as a poetic name for "heaven". The ordinary sense of the word "strength" can, however, not be excluded here. Craigie, **Psalms**, p. 105.

[131] The translation of RSV in Amos 5:9 "strong" is misleading. But cf. Hamp, **Ps 8,2b. 3**, p. 117, who has a similar understanding.

[132] See LSJ. Cf. Zobel, מעוז, col. 1021.

[133] It means "stronghold", "fortress" or "prison". See LSJ.

[134] Cf. Heidland, ὀχύρωμα, p. 590:28-29.

[135] See BHS, Rahlfs and HR. For a suggested Vorlage, see BHK. The metaphorical use in Prov 12:11, 12 is not discussed by Heidland, ὀχύρωμα, p. 590:28-29, but two other cases are noted, 2 Sam 22:2; Job 19:6. Gerleman, contrary to the meaning in MT, suggests a literal sense of ὀχύρωμα in LXX of Job 19:6. Gerleman, **Job**, p. 67.

[136] Cf. Ps 77 (78):54; 113 (114):2, as well as many places in 1-2 Chr and Daniel. See also the meanings recorded in LSJ.

[137] It was common in the older Greek literature. Grundmann, ἰσχύω, p. 400:17-18.

Hellenistic world.[137] δύναμις is less frequently used in this connection.[138]

δύναμις is seldom an equivalent to עז outside the Book of Psalms. It is as a rule a translation of חיל. This is an expected counterpart, since they have the meanings "army", "powers of war" and maybe "wealth" in common.[139] δύναμις is also frequently employed in connection with God, particularly his power and strength. See HR. But it is also the ordinary rendering of עז and therefore not exclusively so employed. This trait is even more pronounced if the use of δύναμις and ἰσχύς in other connections are taken into consideration. Both ἰσχύς and δύναμις have many Hebrew equivalents. ἰσχύς is as a rule equivalent to כח but can also render מעוז, albeit never as a divine name.[140]

κράτος is mostly employed for the strength and power of God, but is found only in a few books in LXX, outside the Apocrypha. It occurs but once in the Pentateuch, but became more common in the Apocrypha, in the intertestamental Jewish literature and in the NT. This term is frequently attested in Greek literature.[141]

ἰσχύς and δύναμις as well as κράτος are employed when עז is given to man by Yahweh, 28 (29):11; 67 (68):29, 36; 85 (86):16, cf. 61 (62):12, while τιμή is used when עז is attributed to God, 28 (29):1; 95 (96):7. Once δόξα is employed in the same sense, 67 (68):35. The choice of vocabulary probably has a theological motivation; man cannot ascribe עז in the sense of "strength" to God.[142] At least it is the question of a conscious act of interpretation of the text, contrary to a mechanical word-substitution.[143] Craigie's suggestion that the semantic meaning of עז is "strength", "might", when it is inputed to God, Ps 29:1, and "refuge", "protection", when it is refers to man, 29:11,[144] is, however, more or less contrary to the choice of equivalents in LXX. עז is thus rendered with much freedom in LXX Psalms.[145]

5.4.3 Preliminary conclusions regarding the translation technique

The translation of עז as a name of God varies. The equivalents mostly reflect the ordinary meaning of the term but a rendering that is more or less in line with the metaphorical sense of the word is also employed. At least to a certain degree the rendering of the term as a divine name accords with the translation technique adopted for the metaphors previously discussed.

βοηθός is as we have seen the most common translation. It could be regarded as the main equivalent, since other terms are sometimes employed when βοηθός occurs in the proximity. This is the case with δύναμις in 45 (46):2:

> God is our refuge (לנו מחסה) and strength, (עז) a very present help (עזרה) in trouble (MT).

> God is our refuge (ἡμῶν καταφυγὴ) and strength, (δύναμις) a help (βοηθός) in the afflictions that have come heavily upon us (LXX).

---

[138] Grundmann, ἰσχύω, p. 400:17-25 and n. 2, Grundmann, δύναμαι, pp. 292-293 n. 33.

[139] For the use of δύναμις in LXX, see HR and Grundmann, δύναμαι, p. 288:1-5.

[140] Cf. HR, Grundmann, ἰσχύω, p. 400:20-25.

[141] Michaelis, κράτος, pp. 905:45-46, 906:54-57, 907:16-908:8. See also HR. It often occurs in connection with ἰσχύς and δύναμις. Ibid., p. 906:15-19.

[142] This distinction is evidently not made by all of the LXX translators. See 1 Chr 16:28.

[143] Note that, for example, ברך is translated in the same way, whether it is attributed to the Lord or to man. For an interesting discussion of the differences in the meaning of certain words when they are applied to Yahweh and to the worshipper of the Lord, see Loewenstamm, **Strength**, p. 468.

[144] Craigie, **Ps XXIX**, p. 146.

[145] Cf. **Mozley**, p. 16.

In 27 (28):8 κραταίωμα, which is a common alternative rendering of metaphorical divine names in the Book of Psalms, is probably used for variation since the combination βοηθός μου καὶ ὑπερασπιστής μου as a divine name is encountered in v. 7 (rendering עזי ומגני). It is true that βοηθός would perhaps have been more expected. See 6.3.1.

To give an adequate picture of the translation technique it must be emphasized that עזר, which as a rule is rendered by βοηθός, has priority, whether or not it is a divine name. Thus if both עז and עזר should occur close to each other as divine names, עזר not עז would be rendered by βοηθός. Ps 45 (46):2 is the only example of this combination.

Contrary to the translation of these names of God generally in the Psalter, good semantic equivalents, which also render עז in the sense of "strength", are sometimes employed, for example, κραταίωμα, κραταιός, δύναμις, ἰσχύς, and maybe κράτος. In exceptional cases this applies when βοηθός occurs in close proximity but often no such reason can be found. That βοήθεια is used instead of βοηθός in 61 (62):8 is a consequence of the constructus relation. צור-עזי is rendered by ὁ θεὸς τῆς βοηθείας. On the other hand, terms which are common divine names, for example, βοηθός and κραταίωμα, are employed but they never render עז, except as a divine name; not even when it occurs in close connection with God. The translator thereby consciously preserves the exclusiveness of these terms.

κράτος as a translation of עז, 58 (59):10; 61 (62):12; 85 (86):16; 89 (90):11, always refers to God in the Book of Psalms. This is also true of this term generally. The same picture is valid for NT where κράτος is never used for the power and might of men.[146] Thus κράτος, βοηθός and κραταίωμα are in fact cultic terms which pertain exclusively to God. The equivalents have thus many affinities with the choice of vocabulary previously discussed, with the exception that κράτος is not exclusively reserved for divine names.

Contrary to the case with the divine names discussed in chapter 3, equivalents of עז in LXX with reference to material objects are sometimes employed as divine names. Thus ἰσχύς is used both as a divine name, Ps 60 (61):4 and when the Hebrew term denotes a fortress, Amos 3:11; 5:9. In these cases the LXX translator may, however, have regarded it as a general word for strength. The translator of the Psalter probably understood the metaphorical character of עז, but outside the Book of Psalms the literal referent of the word is hardly ever reflected. Both ἰσχύς and δύναμις are employed when עז refers to God and also when it is a more or less abstract word for strength. It is unlikely that the LXX translator tried to reflect עז II "refuge" with his renderings.

It cannot be excluded that theological motivations played a part in the choice of vocabulary. The recognition and worship of power was an essential factor in the Hellenistic milieu, not least in Egypt. Epithets such as κράτος and δύναμις could thus perhaps be theologically offensive. On the other hand, Jews often had to face the accusation that Yahweh was a god without power,[147] which could increase their zeal to proclaim his might to the Gentile world. Some of the equivalents in LXX also contradict such a motivation.

---

[146] van der Osten-Sacken, κράτος, col. 780.

[147] See Urbach, **Sages I,** pp. 86–96.

5.5 THE TRANSLATION OF 'ZR AS A DIVINE NAME

5.5.1 The equivalents of the name in LXX

עֹזֵר "helper", עֵזֶר "help" and עֶזְרָה "help", apart from being common designations of God, have βοηθός as their main equivalent, a word often employed as a variant rendering of divine metaphorical names. It thus has a terminological connection with the names hitherto investigated. A further reason for the inclusion of a discussion of the root עזר in this dissertation is that it can serve as a test of whether the translation of divine names which are based on man's activities follows the same principles as those which derive from material objects. See 6.4.1. This could help us to understand the extent to which the character of the metaphor decides the choice of equivalents in LXX.

The root עזר is a designation of God in Deut 33:7, 29; Ps 10:14; 27:9; 30:11; 33:20; 40:18; 46:2; 54:6; 63:8; 70:6; 94:17; 115:9, 10, 11.[148] In Deut 33:7; Ps 10:14; 27:9; 30:11 and 63:8 it is the question of the actualization of Yahweh as עזר. But the term is always translated by βοηθός with cognates. עזר often occurs in close connection or in parallel with other divine names, אֱלֹהֵי יִשְׁעִי, Ps 27:9, מְפַלֵּט, 40:18; 70:6, מָגֵן, Deut 33:29; Ps 33:20; 115:9, 10, 11. In the latter cases the meaning may be "protection", rather than "help", "helper",[149] but no such distinction is seen in the choice of equivalents in the Septuagint. It is part of a longer phrase in Ps 46:2, עֶזְרָה בְצָרוֹת נִמְצָא מְאֹד, which is mostly understood as "a very present help in trouble". In that case it could hardly be described as a divine name. But in light of the parallel with two other designations of God, מַחְסֶה וָעֹז, the expression may be interpreted as two divine names "help in troubles" and "very present".[150] In the LXX interpretation "a help in the afflictions that have come heavily upon us" עזרה is not looked upon as a name of God.

Thus עזר is always rendered by βοηθός with cognates as a divine name, whether it occurs alone or in combination with other names of God. The same is as a rule true when it refers to men.

The meaning and distribution of 'zr I and II

To complicate the picture we must also try to distinguish between two different words, since עזר has a homonymous root meaning "hero", "warrior" as a noun, which is cognate with an Ugaritic root with similar significance,[151] and "to strengthen", "to fight" as a verb. There are great differences in the evaluation of which passages are to be regarded as examples of this word.

The reason for including a discussion of the two different roots of the term is that this division is by now well-established. It is included in both ThWAT and HAL,[152] and some LXX translators may have recognized the homonym. If this was a widespread understanding of the meaning of the word in LXX, it would have obvious consequences for the evaluation of the translation technique.

עזר II as a verb occurs in 1 Kgs 1:7; 1 Chr 12:22; 2 Chr 20:23,[153] or in 1 Chr 5:20; 2 Chr 26:15; Dan 11:34; Ps 28:7 and maybe in 1 Chr 12:18, 22; 2 Chr 20:23; 26:7; 28:23; 32:3, 8; Ps 46:6; 118:13,[154] and as a noun in 2 Sam 18:3 (emend.); Ps

---

[148] Cf. Lipiński, עזר, cols. 18-19.

[149] Lipiński, עזר, col. 19.

[150] See e.g. Weiss, **Bible**, pp. 320-322.

[151] See especially Miller, **Ugaritic**, pp. 159-161.

[152] For discussions, see the references in Miller, **Ugaritic**, p. 160 n. 5, Lipiński, עזר, col. 14.

[153] Thus Lipiński, עזר, col. 20.

[154] Thus HAL. Miller also includes 2 Chr 28:23; Is 41:6; Dan 11:34 and Zech 1:15 as possible examples of this root. See too the discussion of these passages in Miller, **Ugaritic**, pp. 169-172. He also suggests further examples which are less convincing. Ibid., pp. 173-174.

89:20, and maybe also in 1 Chr 12:1; Jer 47:4; Ez 30:8; 32:21.[155] The alternation in the textual transmission between noun and participle can be seen in Ps 89:20 in MT compared with 4QPs-89. See also Ps 124:8 and Is 44:2 in MT and 1QIs-a. The different vocalization of the word in MT is thus more or less artificial,[156] which is evidenced in the Hebrew text transmission as well as in LXX. This means that no distinction should be made between the noun and the participle. In HAL only 1 Chr 12:1 (conj.) and Ps 89:20 are included, but some other examples, Job 9:13; Ez 12:14; 30:8; 32:21, which, however, could also be interpreted as עזר I, are suggested. Miller, apart from the examples previously cited, notes Deut 33:26; Judg 5:23; 2 Sam 18:3; Job 31:21; Ps 33:20; 115:9, 10, 11 and Nah 3:9 as possible examples of עזר II.[157] Ps 89:20 is, according to Miller, one of the earliest and most obvious examples of עזר II with the meaning "hero".[158] Cf. his translation "I set a (young) hero over the mighty; I raised up a young warrior from the people."

The recognition of עזר II as a noun is by now more or less universally accepted, but the existence of a verbal form is less certain, especially since it has not as yet been found in Ugaritic. Other proposed homonyms have not been accepted in the lexica and have no relevance for this study.[159] It is hard to distinguish between the two roots since the difference in meaning is not particularly marked, i.e. "helper" and "warrior".[160] Both of the roots are as a rule employed in a military context.[161] Furthermore, they belong to closely related semantic fields.[162]

God is often the subject of the verb and as a rule the term "helper" refers to him.[163] This is not least the case in the Book of Psalms. Apart from the phrase אֵין עֹזֵר, which describes a desperate situation, see e.g. Ps 22:12; 72:12; 107:12,[164] God is always identified as he who helps. עזר II, which often occurs in prophetic texts, Second Isaiah, Ezekiel, Zechariah, and in post-exilic psalms, but also in Job and Chronicles, is especially frequent in the Psalms of confidence.[165] Most of the passages which have been cited as examples of עזר II are from relatively late texts.[166]

The equivalents of 'zr I and II in LXX

עזר is as a rule rendered in LXX by βοηθός with derivatives, which suggests that the LXX translators based their translation on the ordinary sense of the word. A semantically accurate translation of the term under discussion clearly dominates.[167] This is the case both for passages where the term is a divine name and where it is not, and applies to the Book of Psalms as well as to other biblical books.

On the other hand, עזר II was probably known to at least the translator of Chronicles and possibly to the LXX translator of Daniel, e.g. 1 Chr 5:20; 2 Chr 25:8;

---

[155] Lipiński, עזר, col. 20.
[156] See Lipiński, עזר, col. 17. Cf. Miller, **Ugaritic**, p. 165.
[157] Miller, **Ugaritic**, pp. 164-168.
[158] Miller, **Ugaritic**, p. 165.
[159] For examples, see Barr, **Philology**, pp. 139-140, 332.
[160] Cf. Miller, **Ugaritic**, p. 175, Bergmann, עזר, col. 257.
[161] Cf. Lipiński, עזר, cols. 17-20.
[162] Miller, **Ugaritic**, pp. 174-175.
[163] Lipiński, עזר, cols. 15, 17-19.
[164] Cf. Lipiński, עזר, col. 18. Here God is in fact the implicit "helper".
[165] Bergmann, עזר, cols. 257-259.
[166] Miller, **Ugaritic**, p. 175. For a suggested explanation of this phenomenon, see ibid., p. 175.
[167] The explanation that the translators had no intention of expressing the semantic meaning of עזר when it is employed as a divine name, and therefore βοηθός could as well reflect עזר II is not applicable here.

26:7. Cf. Dan 11:34.[168] These passages are rendered by ἰσχύειν with cognates. In some cases a different Vorlage cannot be excluded, e.g. 1 Chr 5:20; 2 Chr 25:8.[169] But the same rendering occurs in cases where none has suggested any other meaning than "help", "helper", 2 Chr 14:10; 28:23, which indicates that the translator, who often employs the traditional equivalent, βοηθός, recognized two different roots, even though he sometimes made the wrong choice. This is not astonishing since the uncertainty concerning where to find the two roots also pervades modern discussions.

Some of the proposed cases of עזר II refer to places where the Hebrew word is a divine name, Deut 33:29; Ps 33:20; 115:9, 10, 11, but in none of these has the translator departed from his regular equivalent.

5.5.2   Preliminary conclusions regarding the translation technique

עזר is always rendered by a term which reflects the literal meaning of the word. βοηθός is thus employed whether it is the question of God or man as the helper. Only the traditional meaning of עזר is recognized by the LXX translators, with the possible exception of the translator of Chronicles, and there is no adequate rendering of עזר II when it may be regarded as a divine name.

Other divine names, which are based on the activities of man, i.e. what may be called anthropological metaphors, such as מפלט, ישע, רעה, גאל, also have semantically accurate equivalents and the same is true for non-metaphorical names, which are more or less abstract entities, such as בוז. Thus the anthropomorphic imagery when employed as a divine name is as a rule translated literally in contrast to when the image refers to material objects. This is often in opposition to the result if only linguistic factors were entailed. Anthropomorphic imagery which reflects Yahweh in his helping and saving activity would in fact more often become dead metaphors than the imagery with material objects with a similar meaning. See 6.4.3. It is thus probable that ideological motives were involved in the choice of equivalents. This does not mean that the anthropomorphic metaphors always have a stereotyped equivalent, but only that the equivalents reflect the literal meaning of the word. See, for example, מפלט, which as a rule is rendered by ῥύστης, 17 (18):3, 49; 69 (70):6; 143 (144):2, but once has ὑπερασπιστής, 39 (40):18, as equivalent without any obvious reason. But the alternative rendering as well as the ordinary translation is a good semantic equivalent to the Hebrew word in question, in contrast to what is the case with the inanimate metaphorical divine names under discussion.

5.6   THE TRANSLATION OF MĀRÔM AS A DIVINE NAME

5.6.1   The term as a divine name in MT

מרום in literal sense means "height" and maybe "heaven", in plural "the height of heaven" and probably occurs as a divine name in a few cases.[170] It is mostly employed in a poetical context and refers to the height of the mountains, to hills as well as towns, and could thus be used generally of high places as well as of the abode of God. In Ps 92:9 it may be employed as a divine name, "Most

---

[168] See especially Allen, **Chronicles I**, p. 127 with references. Cf. Miller, **Ugaritic**, pp. 168-173.

[169] Miller, **Ugaritic**, pp. 169, 173. But since there was a tendency to confuse עזר and עוד in LXX it may sometimes prove to be question of a pseudo-variant. Cf. Allen, **Chronicles I**, p. 127 and n. 3, 4.

[170] Anderson, **Psalms**, p. 492, Stähli, רום, cols. 757-758. This evaluation contradicts that in HAL which does not note any occurrence.

High":[171] ואתה מרום לעלם יהוה is rendered by σὺ δὲ ὕψιστος εἰς τὸν αἰῶνα, κύριε in LXX. MT is as a rule interpreted as in RSV "but thou, O Lord, art on high for ever". מרום is thus mostly regarded as an accusative of place,[172] but, for example, Anderson does not reject the interpretation in LXX, where in his opinion it is considered more or less as a divine name.[173] The LXX translator renders it by the designation of God (see below) ὕψιστος "Most High", "the Highest".[174] The translation of LXX by Brenton is misleading "But thou, O Lord, art most high for ever". It is a rendering of the meaning of the Hebrew rather than the wording of the Greek.

מרום in 56:3 is as a rule understood as an adverbial accusative "proudly":[175] שאפו שוררי כל היום כי רבים לחמים לי מרום "my enemies trample upon me all day long, for many fight against me proudly". But it could as well be regarded as a designation of Yahweh in line with the interpretation in Vulgate, Aquila, the Targum and Quinta. Otherwise the adverbial use of the Hebrew word is confined to Ps 56:3.[176] It may even be part of a composite divine title אלהי מרום "God on high", Mic 6:6, where מרום is rendered by ὕψιστος. See Table 4. The vocative אלהים in Ps 56:2 is balanced by the locative מרום "O Exalted" in v. 3.[177] Baetgen's objection that if it is a divine name the phrase in Micah ought to have been employed is thus not decisive.[178] According to Baetgen, the enemies, as a sign of their arrogance, have a high position in a princely court.[179] The text of MT may be corrupt and some scholars therefore suggest that מרום should be moved to v. 4.[180]

The interpretation of LXX accords with the understanding of Baetgen here, even though it reflects a different vocalization:[181] "Mine enemies have trodden me down all the day, for there are many warring against me from the dawning of the day" (LXX). Dahood less convincingly interprets מרום as a name of God in MT also in Ps 7:8; 10:5; 75:6; Is 38:14 and Jer 31:12.[182]

The term used in connection with God

This designation may sometimes be used in apposition to God, i.e. "God, the exalted", Job 25:2; Ps 7:8; 68:19; 102:20.[183] But in none of these passages is it regarded as a divine name in LXX, which has ὕψος, Ps 7:8; 67:19; 101:20, or ὕψιστος, Job 25:2. See 5.6.2. It has been suggested that מרום is used in Is 32:15;

---

[171] Thus Bertram, ὕψος, p. 616:8-11 with references, Dahood, **Psalms II**, p. 337. Note also that Briggs, contradicting his discussion of Ps 92:9, regards it as a name of God in his commentary. Compare Briggs, **Psalms I**, p. 58, **Psalms II**, p. 34 with ibid., p. 285.

[172] See Gunkel, **Psalmen**, p. 409, Anderson, **Psalms,** p. 663.

[173] Cf. Anderson, **Psalms**, p. 663.

[174] Cf. Baetgen, **Psalmen**, p. 164, Briggs, **Psalms II**, p. 34, Bertram, **Sprachschatz**, p. 93, Bertram, ὕψος, pp. 615:32-33, 616:8-11. It is not probable that LXX reflects a different Vorlage מרֹמָם. See Kraus, **Psalmen**, p. 810. Cf. Bertram, ὕψος, p. 616 n. 28.

[175] Briggs, **Psalms II**, pp. 31, 34, Anderson, **Psalms,** p. 421.

[176] Baetgen, **Psalmen**, p. 164, Briggs, **Psalms II**, pp. 31, 34, Dahood, **Psalms II**, p. 43. Regarding Aquila, see also Bertram, ὕψος, p. 616:9. Cf. Reider, Turner, **Index**, pp. 247, 309.

[177] Thus Dahood, Review of HAL, p. 356. For the division of stereotype phrases, see e.g. Miller, **Parallelism**, passim.

[178] Baetgen, **Psalmen**, p. 164.

[179] Baetgen, **Psalmen**, p. 164 who refers to Eccles 10:6. Cf. Stähli, רום, col. 758, BDB.

[180] Baetgen, pp. 636-637, Baetgen, **Psalmen**, p. 165, Briggs, **Psalms II**, p. 34, Dahood, **Psalms II**, p. 43. Cf. Mozley, pp. XIX, 93. Gunkel does not accept any of the interpretations and deletes מרום. Gunkel, **Psalmen**, p. 243. The same is true for Kraus. Kraus, **Psalmen**, p. 566. See also BHS.

[181] See BHK, Mozley, pp. XIX, 93, Wutz, **Psalmen**, p. 140. In BHS a dittography of מ is suggested.

[182] Dahood, **Psalms I**, pp. XXXVII, 44-45, 63, ibid., **Psalms II**, p. 212.

[183] Cf. 92:9. See Stähli, רום, cols. 757-758.

38:14; 58:4 to replace the ordinary name of God.[184] Cf. 32:15 "until the Spirit is poured upon us from on high, and the wilderness becomes a fruitful field", 38:14 "My eyes are weary with looking upward. O Lord, I am oppressed; be thou my security!", 58:4 "Fasting like yours this day will not make your voice to be heard on high." But even if this is true it is not reflected in LXX which has ὑψηλός, 32:15, ὕψος 38:14, and κραυγή "crying", 58:4.[185] See the translation in LXX: "until the Spirit shall come upon you from on high, and Chermel shall be a desert" (32:15), "for mine eyes have failed with looking to the height of heaven to the Lord, who has delivered me, and removed the sorrow of my soul" (38:14), "wherefore do ye fast to me as ye do this day, so that your voice may be heard in crying?" (58:4). On the other hand, in Is 57:15, which in MT refers to the abode of God, מרום has been understood as a name of God in LXX[186] and is therefore rendered by ὕψιστος, in analogy with רם "high" in the first part of the verse.

> For thus says the high and lofty One who inhabits eternity, whose name is Holy: "I dwell in the high and holy place" (MT).

> Thus saith the Most High, who dwells on high for ever, Holy in the holies, is his name, the Most High resting in the holies (LXX).

In LXX, contrary to MT, מרום is evidently seen as a name of God in Ps 74 (75):6 and maybe in 72 (73):8. מרום stands in parallel with צור (emended text) as a divine name in 74 (75):6,[187] and is rendered by ὕψος. The Hebrew in 73:8-9 may have been understood as a chiastic construction in LXX, and therefore also as a divine name. Note especially the parallel between "speak unrighteousness against the sky", rendered by ἀδικίαν εἰς τὸ ὕψος ἐλάλησαν in LXX,[188] and "set their mouth against heaven",[188] which is translated by ἔθεντο εἰς οὐρανὸν τὸ στόμα αὐτῶν. The parallel between 8a and b, and 9a and b is obvious also in the Greek. Cf. the probably misleading translation of v. 8-9 by Brenton: "They have taken counsel and spoken in wickedness: they have uttered unrighteousness loftily. They have set their mouth against heaven, and their tongue has gone through upon the earth."

ὕψος is perhaps a designation of God in 2 Kgs 19:22 in LXX since εἰς ὕψος stands in parallel with εἰς τὸν ἅγιον τοῦ Ισραηλ. The translation by Brenton "and against whom hast thou lifted up thy voice, and raised thine eyes on high? Is it against the Holy One of Israel?" is probably inadequate.[189] The parallelism is not as obvious in MT "Against whom have you raised your voice and haughtily lifted your eyes? Against the Holy One of Israel!"

5.6.2 The Most High as a divine name in LXX

The most natural equivalent for מרום as a divine name is ὕψιστος, especially since it is used for עליון as a name of God. See 5.8.2. Apart from a few cases where it is a place-name, ὕψιστος is, more or less exclusively employed as a designation of God.[190]

---

[184] Stähli, רום, col. 758 with references.

[185] LXX has a different Vorlage. See e.g. BHK.

[186] Stähli, רום, col. 758, Bertram, ὕψος, p. 616:8-11 with references. Cf. Seeligmann, Isaiah, p. 102, Ottley, Isaiah I, p. 291, who translates "the Lord, the highest".

[187] MT is corrupt. Bertram, ὕψος, p. 601:24-26. See 3.1.1. The understanding of Kraus, who takes צור as a divine name here, accords with this interpretation, even though he translates למרום with "zur Höhe". Kraus, Psalmen, pp. 683-686. Cf. Anderson, Psalms, p. 549.

[188] Cf. Bertram, ὕψος, p. 601:17-20.

[189] See Bertram, ὕψος, p. 601:16-17.

[190] Bertram, ὕψος, p. 615:32-33. Job 25:2 is an exception. It is there used in a local sense, "heaven".

This term was at first purely poetic, but later used in a religious sense.[191] In Sirach it is, if κύριος is excluded, the most common name of God.[192] It has, apart from עליון, also other Hebrew equivalents in Sirach. Even יהוה is sometimes rendered with this equivalent, e.g. 12:2; 43:2; 48:5.[193]

ὕψιστος was a very popular divine name in the Apocrypha and Pseudepigrapha, and in Hellenistic Jewry as a whole, not least in syncretistic circles.[194] This name was also employed for divine beings in the countries surrounding Israel, particularly as a designation of Zeus.[195] Thus the employment of ὕψιστος was potentially theologically dangerous since it was a common syncretistic designation of a god, but therefore also an opportunity for missionary advances in the Hellenistic world.[196]

5.6.3   The referents of the Greek equivalents

No pattern in the usage of ὕψος can be detected. It is employed both as an abstract and a concrete term. As a metaphor it often has a positive meaning, "loftiness", "sublimity".[197] When it occurs in literal sense it is associated with all types of referent, mountains, 2 Kgs 19:23; Is 37:24; Jer 51:53, high places, Job 39:18; Is 37:23; Hab 2:9, as well as God's abode, heaven, Ps 7:8; 17:17; 55:3; 72:8; 74:6; 101:20; 143:7; Is 38:14; Lam 1:13. It is also employed metaphorically of high social position, Job 5:11; Eccles 10:6.[198] Opinions differ as to the referent of Job 39:18; Is 37:23 and Jer 51:53 but this does not change the general picture that ὕψος is mostly employed in the literal sense.

ὑψηλός in the sense of "elevated", "impressive" was often used in connection with God in LXX, Ps 98:2; 112:4; 137:6, but never as equivalent of מרום. In Lam 3:41 it is, according to Bertram, used without counterpart in MT.[199] But in fact it renders אל, in the Hebrew and is thus clearly employed as a divine name there.[200] It also has literal referents, a town, or a hill, Prov 9:3,[201] or refers more generally to a high place, Is 22:16. In metaphorical sense it can be employed of men in a prominent social position, Is 24:4,[202] or of God's abode, Ps 92:4; Is 32:15; 33:5; Jer 32:16.[203]

---

[191] Bertram, ὕψος, p. 613:13-14.

[192] It occurs 44x in B, but 21-22x we have no Hebrew counterpart. Baudissin, **Kyrios I**, p. 425 and n. 1, Bertram, ὕψος, p. 616:13-17. Cf. Zobel, עליון, col. 151.

[193] Baudissin, **Kyrios I**, p. 419, Bertram, ὕψος, p. 616:14-16. Cf. Baudissin, **Kyrios I**, p. 425 and n. 1, pp. 464-465. Greek Sirach was extremely free in the rendering of different designations of God in the Hebrew. For a full treatment of the divine names and epithets in Sirach, see Baudissin, **Kyrios I**, pp. 405-438. See also the examples in Urbach, **Sages I**, p. 78 n. 53. ὕψιστος has in fact become a proper name in this book. Bertram, **Gottesnamen**, p. 241.

[194] Bertram, ὕψος, pp. 616:20-617:20 with references. Cf. Urbach, **Sages I**, pp. 78-79.

[195] Bertram, ὕψος, pp. 613:10-614:4 with references. See also 5.8.2.

[196] Bertram, **Sprachschatz**, p. 93. The tendency to venerate a most high god was one of the ways in which Greek piety approached monotheism. It thus met Jewish monotheism half-way so to speak. Bertram, ὕψος, p. 617 n. 41. The word seems to have been avoided by Philo, possibly on account of its syncretistic character. Bertram, **Gottesnamen**, p. 241. On the other hand, it refers to God in the NT. Ibid., p. 241, Bertram, ὕψος, pp. 613:10-614:4 with references.

[197] Bertram, ὕψος, pp. 600:10-601:5.

[198] See HAL, Stähli, רום, cols. 757-758. Stähli rightly suggests the meaning "arrogance" of the Hebrew in Ps 73:8; 75:6 and regards Is 38:14 more or less as a divine name. Ibid., col. 758. Concerning 73:8, see also Kraus, **Psalmen**, pp. 663, 668. Cf. Bertram, ὕψος, p. 601:17-18.

[199] Bertram, ὕψος, p. 601 and n. 14.

[200] See especially Albrektson, **Lamentations**, p. 155.

[201] See Stähli, רום, col. 757 and HAL.

[202] Stähli, רום, col. 758. Text-critical problems are involved here. See BHK, HAL.

[203] See HAL. Stähli suggests "the height of heaven" in Is 32:15.

Even though a literal translation of מרום prevails, LXX has twice used a name of the referent rather than reflected the semantic meaning of the Hebrew word. Thus ὄρος is employed in Jer 38 (31):12[204] and οὐρανός in Is 24:18, 21.

5.6.4   Preliminary conclusions regarding the translation technique

מרום is seldom employed as a divine name in MT, but is not peculiar to the OT. At least cognate terms are sometimes employed as divine names in countries surrounding Israel, which can be clearly seen in some theophoric personal names.[205] The notion of elevated, exalted gods was widespread in the ancient religious world of the Semites. This implies that מרום is an ancient name of God, but the relation between the frequency of the word in the literal sense and as a divine name may contradict this evaluation. While it is common in the literal sense only in a few cases does it occur as a divine name. See 6.3.2. The LXX translators have more often understood this term as a name of God. In these cases מרום is not exclusively rendered by words which are only employed as names of God. Once it is rendered by ὕψος, Ps 75 (76):6, where it is regarded as a divine name in LXX. The designation in Ps 91:9; Is 57:15, ὕψιστος, is a common name of gods in the Hellenistic world and also used for other titles of God in MT. See 5.8.2. ὕψος, which may refer directly to God in 2 Kgs 19:22; Ps 72:8; 74:6, has as a rule literal referents.

מרום is only rendered by terms which well reflect the semantic meaning of the Hebrew word when it is interpreted as a divine name in LXX. The translation technique thereby resembles that of the anthropological metaphors. One of the equivalents is nearly always used as a designation of God. The others are often employed in the literal sense. Thus although they sometimes render divine names the equivalents do not constitute a group of words reserved for such titles as was the case with the inanimate metaphorical designations of God previously discussed.

5.7   THE TRANSLATION OF SHADDAY AS A DESIGNATION OF GOD

5.7.1   The equivalents of the term as a designation of God in MT

Another designation of God of interest for my investigation is שדי, which, however, does not have a metaphorical character in MT. שדי thus only occurs as a designation of God and is not employed in literal sense in MT. Thus it deviates from the names or epithets hitherto investigated in this dissertation. It is in the first place included as a test of the limits for the choice of translation technique as regards metaphorical designations of God. שדי occurs both as a divine name, 40x, and as a name or an epithet in the expression אל שדי, 8x.[206] An etymological exegesis, built on Rabbinic methods, derives שדי from שֶ and דַי in late biblical Hebrew and the meaning is "he who suffices" or "he who is sufficient".[207] This may be the reason for the translation ἱκανός "the Mighty One", a rendering which always betrays influence from the Hexaplaric recension, Job 21:15; 31:2; 40:2,[208] or

---

[204] LXX may here reflect a different Vorlage, הר, since Vetus Latina, the Targum and Vulgate also have the same interpretation. See BHK.

[205] Baudissin, Kyrios III, pp. 77–81.

[206] Weippert, שדי, col. 873.

[207] Cooke, Ezekiel, p. 115, Dodd, Bible, p. 15, Bertram, Hikanos, p. 21 and n. 5, p. 22, Tov, Septuagint, p. 49.

[208] See Rahlfs and Dhorme, Job, pp. 313–314, 450, 614. In Ez 1:24 codex A has ἱκανός. These variants are probably taken from Theodotion. Cooke, Ezekiel, p. 27, Weippert, שדי, col. 874.

the Kaige recension, Ruth 1:20, 21. Thus the rendering in Ruth cannot be adduced in a discussion of the equivalents in LXX, which were common in older literature.[209] This is also the regular rendering in Aquila, Theodotion and Symmachus and was probably known to Paul.[210]

The designation אל שדי, which is more or less confined to the Pentateuch, is as a rule rendered by θεός μου, or θεός with another possessive pronoun, Gen 17:1; 28:3; 35:11; 43:14; 48:3; 49:25[211] and Ex 6:3, and once by θεὸς Σαδδαι, Ez 10:5. Dodd suggests that etymological considerations were the main reason for this rendering, i.e. the translator interpreted the word as a combination of של as a relative pronoun and די in the meaning "of me" in analogy with Aramaic. Thus the term could be understood as "the God who is mine".[212] The equivalent could also reflect the technique employed in the rendering of metaphorical designations of God generally in LXX. It may be a substitute for the less acceptable phrase θεὸς θεός, since θεός is the main equivalent for both of the words in LXX. See below. On the other hand, an alternative rendering for שדי would have been expected.

Bertram's suggestion that the translation of the designation is characteristic for the LXX concept of God as a personal God,[213] i.e. "my God", "our God", is unnecessary in view of the background for the choice of equivalents of divine names or epithets in LXX and the mechanical substitution of the second θεός when the same word occurs in close proximity with a different hyponym. In this case the deficient knowledge of the meaning of the obscure archaic term may have affected the choice of equivalents,[214] but the rendering of metaphorical divine names in LXX generally suggests that this was not the main reason. This evaluation is strengthened if Joel 1:15, a passage where the translator did not recognize שדי as a divine name, is taken into consideration. He then employs a common translation for the noun שד "violence", "destruction", ταλαιπωρία "trouble".

Since שדי often occurs when God shows his power against his enemies, Is 13:6; Joel 1:15, or at least with more or less negative connotations, Ruth 1:20; 21; Job 5:17; 6:4; 15:25; 21:20; 23:16; 27:2, the derivation from שדד "devastate", "lay waste", "overpower", is not impossible. The name would then have the sense "powerful", "violent",[215] but the proposal that this derivation is supported by the rendering in some parts of the LXX, παντοκράτωρ, is hardly adequate.[216] Both the meaning of the verb, with its associations with violence and devastation,[217] and the choice of counterparts,[218] clearly contradict this interpretation. Not even in Is 13:6; Joel 1:15, which are based on this popular etymology, do the LXX translators reflect this connection. The ordinary rendering of the Hebrew verb, ταλαιπωρεῖν, which as a rule means "to do hard work", "endure hardship" or "suffer" and seldom "to distress", "to trouble" (see LSJ), implies a clear softening of the original since the word is rather focused on the experience of mischief and evil, rather than the wreaking of violence and destruction.[219]

---

[209] See e.g. Bertram, **Gottesvorstellung**, p. 513. Cf. Dodd, **Bible**, p. 15 and n. 1.

[210] Dodd, **Bible**, pp. 15–16. Cf. 2 Cor 3:5–6.

[211] Emended text with 3 Hebrew MSS, the Samarian Pentateuch and LXX. See e.g. BHK, Freedman, **Divine Names**, p. 64.

[212] Dodd, **Bible**, p. 14. For the use of Aramaic in LXX, see Olofsson, **LXX Version**, p. 29 and n. 239, 241.

[213] Bertram, **Gottesvorstellung**, p. 511, Bertram, **Hikanos**, p. 22. For the background in the OT, see Baudissin, **Kyrios III**, pp. 557–561.

[214] Dodd, **Bible**, p. 14.

[215] Bertram, **Gottesvorstellung**, pp. 508–509 and n. 3, Weippert, שדי, col. 875. Cf. Baudissin, **Kyrios III**, p. 122 n. 1.

[216] For this suggestion, see Dodd, **Bible**, p. 14 n. 1.

[217] Weippert, שדי, cols. 875–876. The same is true for שד. See Bertram, **Gottesvorstellung**, p. 503 and the examples on pp. 503–508.

[218] See the translation equivalents in Santos, **Index** and Bertram, **Gottesvorstellung**, pp. 508, 513.

[219] Cf. Bertram, **Gottesvorstellung**, pp. 505–506. See also LSJ.

The rendering of the term in the Book of Job

The most common translation of the name is παντοκράτωρ, but this equivalent is confined to the Book of Job. Bertram suggests that this choice had a theological motivation and reflects the universal demand for the OT revelation in the Hellenistic world.[220]

שדי is often found in the Book of Job, 31x, and is there translated in the Old Greek, apart from παντοκράτωρ, 15x, by κύριος, 9x, and once by the combination κύριος παντοκράτωρ, Job 15:25.[221] Once a paraphrastic translation occurs, ὁ τὰ πάντα ποιήσας, 8:3, that is not out of place in the context. In 27:10 αὐτοῦ, referring to κύριος, is used, probably on account of the frequency of the ordinary terms for God in the context. The deviating equivalent ὑλώδης "woody", "muddy" in Job 29:5, depends on a different hyponym.[222]

The employment of παντοκράτωρ as equivalent of שדי is not found in any specific semantic context. But this term is as rule used when שדי and אלהים, אל,אלוה, which are often rendered by κύριος, occur in parallel in the Book of Job.[223] παντοκράτωρ is with three exceptions, 32:8; 33:4; 37:22 (23), only used when κύριος stands in parallel or in close proximity (= within the same verse) and κύριος never renders שדי if the latter term occurs in parallel.

It is possible to explain most of these exceptions. In 32:8 some commentators suggest a wording with אלוה, following Symmachus.[224] The phrases רוח אלוה and נשמת שדי would in fact constitute a perfect parallel.[225] Dhorme, perhaps rightly, argues for MT as the original text here,[226] but this does not affect the issue. The equivalent in the Old Greek must in that case be conjectured.

> But it is the spirit (רוח היא) in a man, the breath of the Almighty, (נשמת שדי) that makes him understand (32:8 MT).

> but there is a spirit (πνεῦμά ἐστιν) in mortals; and the inspiration of the Almighty (πνοὴ δὲ παντοκράτορός) is that which teaches (LXX).

The choice of the alternative equivalent in 33:4 does not depend on a parallel with κύριος. On the other hand, שדי occurs in parallel with אל in MT, which in this case, contrary to the ordinary rendering, is translated by θεῖος. Either the translator did not want κύριος as parallel with θεῖος or Rahlfs' text does not reflect the Old Greek or his text does not come from one and the same period of the transmission history of the Greek text. The identical rendering of the Hebrew expression in 27:3 favours the former solution.

> The spirit of God (רוח אל) has made me, and the breath of the Almighty (נשמת שדי) gives me life (33:4 MT).

---

[220] Bertram, **Gottesvorstellung**, pp. 512–513.

[221] For a possible reason for this combination, see Baudissin, **Kyrios I**, p. 253, Bertram, **Gottesvorstellung**, p. 512. Cf. Weippert, שדי, col. 874.

[222] Regarding the context of this verse, see Bertram, **Hikanos**, pp. 25–26. Different suggestions regarding the Vorlage of the Greek term are given in Gerleman, **Job**, p. 20, Dhorme, **Job**, p. 417.

[223] Baudissin even implies that this translation was always intended by the translator. Baudissin, **Kyrios I**, p. 254. אל and אלוה in particular are so rendered in Job, 38x (20x in B). Baudissin, **Kyrios I**, pp. 253–254, 469.

[224] See Budde, **Hiob**, pp. 201–202, Hölscher, **Hiob**, p. 78. See also BHK. Cf. also the parallel expression in 33:4. Bertram, **Gottesvorstellung**, p. 512.

[225] Cf. 27:3. See Budde, **Hiob**, p. 205. This parallel is strengthened by the fact that שדי is always associated with אל and cognates. The only exceptions in Job are 22:23, 25; 24:1; 32:8.

[226] See Dhorme, **Job**, p. 476, who refers to 27:3.

The Divine Spirit (πνεῦμα θεῖον) is that which formed me, and the breath of the Almighty (πνοὴ δὲ παντοκράτορος) that which teaches me (LXX).

That a different Greek text with the ordinary rendering, κύριος, was original or at any rate once existed as a parallel, could be suspected in 37:23 since שדי occurs there in parallel with אלוה, which is misread as אלה in LXX.[227]

The principles behind the translation of Job 22:25 is complicated since שדי is rendered by παντοκράτωρ because of the employment of κύριος in v. 26, which, however, translates שדי. Thus even with the text at our disposal the choice of equivalents reflects a striving for variation. But παντοκράτωρ would have been expected in v. 26, since שדי, אלוה occur in parallel, but the latter is oddly translated by τὸν οὐρανόν, probably in order to avoid the appearance of anthropomorphism:[228]

and if the Almighty is your gold, and your precious silver; then you will delight yourself in the Almighty, and lift up your face to God (Job 22:25-26 MT).

So the Almighty shall be thy helper from enemies, and he shall bring thee forth pure as silver that has been tried by fire. Then shalt thou have boldness before the Lord, looking up cheerfully to heaven (LXX).

Therefore the exceptions to the translation technique under discussion may only be apparent or could be given a reasonable explanation since the use of παντοκράτωρ can even in most of these cases depend on the variation with κύριος in an earlier form of the Greek.[229] This translation policy also reflects an aspect of the composition of the Hebrew, the skilful variation in the distribution of divine names in Job.[230] κύριος must therefore be regarded as the main equivalent, even though παντοκράτωρ is the most common rendering. This indirectly confirms that the choice of κύριος as equivalent to שדי as a divine name depends on the frequently attested parallelism between שדי and אל, אלוה. The same technique as we have seen concerning the inanimate divine metaphorical names is evidenced here. See 6.3.1. But the choice of παντοκράτωρ, as alternative equivalent, may be partly explained by etymological speculations.[231] On the other hand, it is also the main rendering of another metaphorical designation of God, צבאות. The equivalents in the Book of Job are thereby connected with the renderings of metaphorical names generally. Another manifestation of the deliberate composition technique is that Yahweh is only employed in the prologue and the epilogue of Job[232] since Job's opponents, as heathens, would not use the name of the God of Israel in their conversation.

The rendering of the term in the Book of Psalms

The translation in the Psalter partly deviates from the pattern seen in the Book of Job. The parallelism between שדי and עליון, rendered by ὕψιστος, may explain the designation ὁ θεὸς τοῦ οὐρανοῦ in Ps 90 (91):1. In this case the semantic meaning of the synonymous parallel may have influenced the rendering. On the other hand, the same main equivalent, θεός, is the base of the rendering. A

---

[227] See e.g. Budde, **Hiob**, p. 239, Dhorme, **Job**, p. 572.

[228] Dhorme, **Job**, p. 340. Cf. Bertram, **Gottesvorstellung**, p. 513 n. 1.

[229] Cf. Driver, Gray, **Job**, p. XLIII.

[230] See the examples in Dhorme, **Job**, pp. LXVII–LXVIII.

[231] Cf. Bertram, **Gottesvorstellung**, p. 512.

[232] Baudissin, **Kyrios I**, p. 469, Dhorme, **Job**, p. LXX.

Vorlage with שדי אל cannot be excluded either.

Erwin sees a theological motive for the rendering of שדי by τὸν ἐπουράνιον "the Heavenly One" in Ps 67 (68):15. This translation "seems to echo the transcendentalizing tendency of the Alexandrian Synagogue".[233] The equivalent here is in fact unique in LXX,[234] nor does it correspond to the rendering of metaphorical names of God in the Book of Psalms or in LXX as a whole.[235] But MT is hardly understandable and may be corrupt.[236] For the LXX translator (and the modern interpreter) it is difficult to understand the meaning of the Hebrew in v. 12-20. It cannot merely be assumed that he interpreted שדי as a name of God in this context:

> Even if ye should lie among the lots, ye shall have the vings of a dove covered with silver, and her breast with yellow gold. When the heavenly One scatters kings upon it, they shall be made snow-white in Selmon (67:14-15 LXX).

5.7.2   The background for the term as a designation of God in MT

The meaning and etymology of שדי are highly controversial[237] and the varied, partly conditional renderings in the versions suggest that they did not know the right meaning either.[238]

The most adequate solution is that the term is derived from the cognate Akkadian word shaddu "mountain", which sometimes refers to deities.[239] This may be the background for the usage in MT too. But it is probably not a loan-word directly from the Akkadian, but rather an Assyrian coinage.[240] Freedman asserts that shaddu was replaced by Hebrew צור, with a similar meaning, during the monarchy, and was revived in the late seventh century in a period of national nostalgia.[241] This is another reason for a discussion of this designation of God, because the metaphorical character may well have been recognized by the LXX translators even though the term does not occur in the literal sense in MT.[242]

---

[233] Erwin, p. 61. He finds the same bias in the translation of שדי in 90 (91):1. Ibid., pp. 61-62.

[234] It occurs a few times in the Apocrypha, 2 Macc 3:39; 3 Macc 6:28 A; 7:6; 4 Macc 4:11 A, R; 11:3 S and once in Dan 4:26 A, but also as a variant of οὐράνιος. See Traub, οὐρανός, p. 539:23-26.

[235] Cf. Bertram, **Gottesvorstellung**, p. 511. See also Gunkel, **Psalmen**, p. 289, Bertram, **Hikanos**, p. 24 and n. 14.

[236] Cf. Baetgen, **Psalmen**, pp. 205-206, Briggs, **Psalms II**, pp. 100, 108, and Gunkel, **Psalmen**, p. 289.

[237] For different suggestions, see Weippert, שדי, cols. 875-880. Cf. Dodd, **Bible**, p. 14 n. 1, Bertram, **Gottesvorstellung**, pp. 508-509 n. 3, Wanke, **Zionstheologie**, pp. 40-58, Anderson, **Psalms**, p. 490. For a hypothetical tradition-historical background of the term, see Stolz, **Kult**, pp. 157-163.

[238] See Dodd, **Bible**, pp. 14-16, Weippert, שדי, cols. 874-875.

[239] Dodd, **Bible**, p. 14 n. 1, Anderson, **Psalms**, p. 490. It is a name of e.g. Enlil. Cf. Stolz, **Kult**, pp. 161, 163, Knowles, **Rock**, p. 315.

[240] Weippert, שדי, cols. 878-879. Many other suggestions regarding the background of שדי exist but none withstands a critical examination. Weippert, op. cit., cols. 875-877, 879-880.

[241] Freedman, **Divine Names**, pp. 63-64, 71. Cf. Knowles, **Rock**, p. 315 and n. 17. This is strengthened by the fact that they never occur in the same texts. See Tables 3 and 4. That צור, contrary to שדי, never occurs as a divine title in the Ugaritic texts and that it was not associated with patriarchal religion in the OT, speak in the same direction. Ibid., 63-64, 71.

[242] Cf. Freedman, **Divine Names**, pp. 71, 93.

5.7.3 Preliminary conclusions regarding the translation technique

Outside the Book of Job when שדי occurs as a name of God it is rendered by
θεός, Num 24:4, 16; Is 13:6. θεός is evidently the main rendering of שדי as a
divine name in the Old Greek, replaced by κύριος in Job, depending on the choice
of translation for אל with cognates in that book. παντοκράτωρ is the most
common rendering in Job for the sake of variation, since it is only used when the
ordinary translation of אל with cognates in Job, κύριος, occur in parallel. The few
exceptions are probably due to text critical considerations. This accords with the
fact that θεός with a personal pronoun is the ordinary rendering of אל שדי.

The choice of main equivalent implies that the metaphorical character of the
designation was recognized by the LXX translators since, as we have seen,
inanimate divine metaphorical names tend to have equivalents which do not reflect
the semantic meaning of the word in the literal sense. Furthermore, θεός is also
the main equivalent of צור as a divine name, which may have a similar meaning to
שדי. It is also possible that the LXX translators only reflected the denotation of
the word since they did not know the meaning of the Hebrew. שדי does not even
occur with a literal referent in MT, but only as a designation of God. The alternative rendering is not included among the traditional equivalents of divine
metaphorical names generally, albeit it occurs as the main equivalent of another
epithet of God, צבאות. It is also evidenced, even though seldom, as a designation
of gods in the Hellenistic world.[243] It is characteristic that the translators replaced
the Hebrew word by "ihnen geläufige Gottesbezeichnungen".[244]

5.8 THE TRANSLATION OF ῾ELYÔN AS A DESIGNATION OF GOD

5.8.1 The origin and the distribution of the title

עליון is mostly employed as a designation of God in the OT, 31x,[245] but sometimes
also refers to Israel, Deut 26:19; 28:1, or the king, Ps 89:28.[246] Thus we may have
here an example of the phenomenon that divine names could be employed of the
king of Judah as Yahweh's representative on earth. But note that the Lord
proclaims the king as עליון. It is in these passages perhaps not a name at all, but
rather an adjective "high".[247] This distinction between the Hebrew word as a
designation of God and its use in other connections is also reflected in the
renderings of LXX, which has ὑπεράνω, Deut 26:19; 28:1, or ὑψηλός, Ps 88 (89):28.
Thus equivalents which are not employed for the word as a name or epithet of
Yahweh are used.

עליון as a designation of God is used almost exclusively in poetic texts, particularly the Psalter, but also in Num 24; Deut 32; 2 Sam 22; Is 14 and Lamentations.
In Gen 14 it twice (out of four passages) occurs in a poetical context, 14:19, 20. In
fact two thirds of the occurrences (21 out of a total of 31) are located to the Book
of Psalms.

It is an archaic royal title for Yahweh, which is not confined to a specific
Gattung. Although it is particularly common in Hymns it also occurs in Laments
and Wisdom psalms. Most of the examples are concentrated to the post-exilic

---

[243] At least once it is a designation of Zeus. See SEG 31 (1981), p. 242 nos. 946 with references. Cf.
SEG 26 (1976–77), p. 350 nos. 1456. A connection with the equivalents of צור in the Targum is
evidenced since the Hebrew term in Deut 32 is consistently interpreted as "Mighty One", "Almighty".
Cf. Knowles, Rock, p. 321 n. 29.

[244] Bertram, Gottesvorstellung, p. 513. See also ibid., p. 511.

[245] See e.g. Wanke, Zionstheologie, p. 46 and Lisowsky.

[246] Briggs, Psalms II, p. 268. Cf. Anderson, Psalms, p. 642, Kraus, Psalmen, p. 791.

[247] See e.g. Lisowsky. Cf. RSV.

"Sängerpsalmen".[248] This designation is connected with the cult in the Jerusalem temple,[249] which may be one of the reasons for the distribution pattern. מרום and עליון are semantically closely related. Both mean "the High One" or "the One who dwells on high". This is clearly reflected in LXX Psalms where they have the equivalent ὕψιστος in common, even though מרום is probably also rendered by ὕψος as a divine name. See 5.6.1. Save when it occurs as a name of God, עליון is used as a title in three different forms in the OT; in the phrases אל עליון, Gen 14 (4x); Ps 78:35, or אלהים עליון, 78:56 with par., or יהוה עליון, 7:18; 47:3; 97:9.[250] אל עליון is probably the oldest form of the divine epithet.[251] Apart from these passages in the Book of Psalms and Gen 14 it is always an independent noun.[252]

The frequent parallelism between עליון and אל, Num 24:16; Ps 73:11; 78:17–18; 107:11, cf. 57:3; 77:10–11, may depend on the technique of breaking up composite phrases, including designations of God.[253] The name sometimes occurs in parallel with שדי, Ps 91:1, cf. Num 24:16, and אלהים, Ps 46:8, cf. 78:35, or יהוה, 7:18; 18:14; 21:8; 78:35; 83:19; 91:9; 92:2. The parallels and the interchangeability between different designations of God imply that in post-exilic texts they had lost much of their specific meaning and were merely employed as general names of God.[254]

This state of affairs is clearly evidenced in Ps 46 where עליון, v. 5, is used in one and the same psalm together with אלהי צבאות, v. 8, 12, and אלהי יעקב, v. 8, 12, in a way which clearly suggests that they are to be regarded as synonymous expressions. Cf. the translation in RSV "There is a river whose streams make glad the city of God, the holy habitation of the Most High", v. 5, "The LORD of hosts is with us; the God of Jacob is our refuge", v. 8, 12. Since מרום and עליון never occur in close proximity in LXX as names or epithets of God it is hard to say whether a translation technique such as we have demonstrated concerning inanimate divine names has been followed. When they occur in one and the same psalm as designations of God, but not in close proximity, Ps 91 (92):2, 9, both are rendered by ὕψιστος.

The universal power of עליון is often underlined, Deut 32:8; Ps 7:18; 9:3; 18:14; 92:2. Typical expressions are "the Lord is the Most High over the whole earth"; cf. 83:19; 97:9, or "the Most High is a great king over all the earth"; cf. 47:3. It is also used to emphasize that God is enthroned in heaven or that he created heaven and earth. The name also often occurs in texts where יהוה is honoured as king.[255]

עליון as a divine name is not peculiar to the OT; it is also attested as a name of a Syr.-Canaanite deity.[256] Moreover, it has clear affinities with certain names of El in Ugaritic.[257] This is a usage that belongs already to the pre-Israelite period and then designated the highest god in a pantheon.[258]

---

[248] Wanke, **Zionstheologie**, pp. 51–52, Zobel, עליון, cols. 136–137, Bertram, ὕψος, pp. 615:8–12, 616:4–6. The designation was probably employed during a long period. Ibid., p. 53. The same concentration to these psalms can be seen as regards the designation יהוה צבאות in the Psalter. Wanke, **Zionstheologie**, p. 46.

[249] Wanke, **Zionstheologie**, pp. 46, 52–53, Zobel, עליון, cols. 134, 137.

[250] יהוה may not be original here. See BHK, BHS. Cf. Wanke, **Zionstheologie**, p. 47 n. 22. See also Gunkel, **Psalmen**, p. 426, Kraus, **Psalmen**, p. 97. עליון is perhaps an adjective "high" in this verse instead of a title of God. Anderson, **Psalms**, p. 689. Note the parallelism with "you are exalted". This is evidently the original usage. See especially ibid., p. 362. It is regarded as a divine epithet or a divine name in LXX.

[251] Zobel, עליון, cols. 135–136.

[252] See Wanke, **Zionstheologie**, p. 47.

[253] See e.g. Dahood, **Psalms II**, p. XXXIX, Watson, **Poetry**, p. 30.

[254] Cf. Wanke, **Zionstheologie**, p. 48.

[255] Kraus, **Psalmen**, pp. 97–98, Zobel, עליון, cols. 137–138. Both עליון and שדי are universal names of God. Bertram, **Gottesvorstellung**, p. 511.

[256] See especially Dodd, **Bible**, p. 11, Bertram, ὕψος, p. 614:6–15 and n. 12–14. For the previous history of the term in Israel, see Bertram, op. cit., pp. 614:15–615:23.

[257] Regarding the connection with El and Baal, see Zobel, עליון, cols. 141–145.

[258] See e.g. Anderson, **Psalms**, p. 362, Kraus, **Psalmen**, p. 201. Regarding the religio-historical

In the Old Testament it is as a rule clearly identified with the Lord, even though in the underlying traditions it may have referred to a Canaanite god.[259] The employment of עליון as an independent designation of God is due to the common break-up of composite divine titles which is reflected in the frequent parallelism between El and Älyon.

5.8.2   The rendering of the term in LXX

In LXX this designation of God is always, whether as an epithet or a name of God, rendered by ὕψιστος, which can mean "the highest among others" or "the High One".[260] ὕψιστος was a common name for gods in the Hellenistic world. Thus many inscriptions with this title exist from the Hellenistic period, both pagan and Jewish.[261] The equivalent is in line with the universal character of the epithet. Most examples of the usage of ὕψιστος in a Jewish or pagan context can be found in SEG. Zeus was sometimes worshipped under the epithet Ζεὺς ὕψιστος in the Hellenistic world.[262]

עליון and ὕψιστος are thus sometimes employed as names or epithets for pagan gods. This is seldom the case with the other designations of Yahweh in Greek which have been discussed.[263] On the other hand, the influence from LXX and Judaism is in fact often the basis for the usage outside the OT, both in Jewish and pagan circles.

5.8.3   Preliminary conclusions regarding the translation technique

The equivalent in LXX, ὕψιστος, reflects the semantic meaning of the Hebrew term, contrary to what is the case with the inanimate metaphorical divine names, but in line with the anthropomorphic metaphors and the non-metaphorical desig-nations of God generally. It is always employed as a designation of God even when it has other Hebrew hyponyms. In this respect it has affinities with equiva-lents of the first investigated metaphorical names of God.

We cannot decide whether the same kind of variation as we have seen for many other names or epithets would have been employed since עליון never stands in parallel with מרום, which has the same main equivalent. See 6.3.1. The LXX translators clearly distinguished between עליון as a designation of God and as a

---

background of עליון, see Wanke, **Zionstheologie**, pp. 49–54, Anderson, **Psalms**, pp. 99–100, 357–358, 362, Zobel, עליון, cols. 141–145.

[259] See especially Wanke, **Zionstheologie**, pp. 46–54, Zobel, עליון, col. 136. It is unlikely that the original form of the expression, אל עליון, refers to two different gods, El and Älyon, at least in the OT texts. See ibid., pp. 50–51 with references. Cf. Anderson, **Psalms**, pp. 357–358.

[260] Dodd, **Bible**, pp. 12–13.

[261] See e.g. Dodd, **Bible**, pp. 11–13.

[262] See Dodd, **Bible**, p. 12, SEG 31 (1981), nos. 946, p. 242, which probably refers to Zeus but may also be of Jewish origin. See also nos. 1080, pp. 290–291, nos. 1069, p. 285, SEG 32 (1982), nos. 1679, pp. 467–468, which refer to the Cretan Zeus. Regarding the cult of Zeus Hypsistos, see further the reference in nos. 1599, p. 445. For the use of ὕψιστος as a designation of God in a pagan context generally, see SEG 26 (1976–1977), nos. 422, p. 110, nos. 962, p. 249, nos. 1355–1356, pp. 326–327. This word is also used in inscriptions of Jewish or Christian origin. See SEG 29 (1979), nos. 1400, p. 351, SEG 33 (1983), nos. 1049, p. 317, nos. 1475, p. 385, SEG 32 (1982), nos. 790, pp. 218–219, 263, nos. 1049, p. 317, nos. 1326, pp. 395–396. In nos. 1263, pp. 351–352, and nos. 1573, pp. 438–439, Ps 90:1 is quoted. The same is true for SEG 29, nos. 1606, p. 403. See also the examples of both Jewish and pagan usage in **Enermalm-Ogawa**, pp. 124–126.

[263] The only exception in this regard is perhaps παντοκράτωρ, which is used as a designation of Hermes, see SEG 33, nos. 736, pp. 216–217, and for Zeus, see SEG 32, nos. 1254, p. 347.

term used in connection with man, exactly as was the case with מגן. The distribution of the Hebrew term implies that in many passages it has lost much of its specific sense and thus can hardly be distinguished from other designations of God, but this is not reflected in the equivalents of LXX.

5.9 THE TRANSLATION OF YHWH ṢĔBĀʾÔT IN LXX

5.9.1 The origin and the distribution of the title

יהוה צבאות is a very common title of God in the OT, being found as many as 279-287x in MT.[264] The distribution pattern is remarkable; יהוה צבאות is absent from the Pentateuch and Ezekiel, seldom employed in the Deuteronomistic history of the monarchy (1-2 Sam, 1-2 Kgs), but very frequent in Is 1-39, Jeremiah, Haggai, Zechariah and Malachi.[265] This designation was thus especially common during and just after the exile, but it was less frequent before the exile and in the later books of the OT,[266] although in some books from the same period it occurs seldom or not at all. The reason for these anomalies in the distribution of the title is obscure.

Different theories have been proposed to explain this state of affairs. The title could per se recall its origin, which according to one theory, is vitiated mythical powers, and therefore, contain a potentially offensive aspect.[267] Therefore it was seldom, or never employed by those who emphasized the validity of the first commandment. Baumgärtel points out that it would have been an anomaly to speak about God in the terminology of the Zion-tradition, whereby Yahweh is "the Lord of hosts, who is enthroned on the cherubim", when the leading people are in exile and Yahweh has left the Jerusalem temple.[268] Cf. Ez 10-11. The absence of the title in Ezekiel and in the Deuteronomistic history is, however, best explained by T. Mettinger, who emphasizes that these literary complexes have a distinct terminology of their own as regards the presence of the Lord with the stress on different aspects. Thus the "glory" and the "name" were better suited to a description of the presence of Yahweh in an exilic situation.[269]

The title was originally employed in the traditions concerning the ark of the covenant in Shiloh, traditions which were later incorporated in the temple traditions of Jerusalem.[270] It is hard to say whether it is a pre-Israelite title which has been taken over by the Israelites or if it is a genuine Israelite term.[271] Mettinger's discussion concludes that Sabaoth is not of pre-Israelitic origin, but is an Israelite creation, originating from Shiloh where the El qualities of Yahweh played an important part. Thus the original form of the title would have been אל צבאות. It may then together with אל עליון have served as twin titles for Yahweh as the supreme head of the divine assembly.[272] It had its formative Sitz im Leben in the context of the temple cult.[273] This is also easily seen by its use in non-formulaic

---

[264] For the different figures given, see Wanke, **Zionstheologie**, pp. 40-41 with references, Mettinger, **Dethronement**, p. 12 and n. 3, Mettinger, **Sabaoth**, pp. 109, 112, 122-123, 128-135, Zobel, צבאות, col. 878.

[265] See e.g. Baumgärtel, **Gottesnamen**, p. 14, Mettinger, **Dethronement**, p. 12.

[266] van der Woude, צבא, col. 499.

[267] See e.g. van der Woude, צבא, cols. 506-507.

[268] Baumgärtel, **Gottesnamen**, pp. 27-29.

[269] See Mettinger, **Dethronement**, pp. 14-16, 78-79, 115, 132-134.

[270] See e.g. Wanke, **Zionstheologie**, p. 41 and n. 3, 4 with references, von Rad, **Theology I**, p. 18 and n. 11, Kraus, **Psalmen**, pp. 98-99, van der Woude, צבא, col. 506, Mettinger, **Dethronement**, p. 13 and n. 14. For a more comprehensive discussion, see ibid., pp. 19-24. Cf. 1 Sam 1:3, 11; 4:4; 2 Sam 6:2, 18.

[271] van der Woude, צבא, col. 506.

[272] Mettinger, **Sabaoth**, pp. 130-135.

[273] Mettinger, **Sabaoth**, pp. 122-123.

language, especially in the prophets, where it is virtually confined to contexts where the ark or Zion, as the home of the ark, play a major role.[274]

יהוה צבאות occurs 15x in the Book of Psalms, being restricted to eight psalms, 24; 46; 48; 59; 69; 80; 84; 89. In Ps 80 it occurs 4x, v. 5, 8, 15, 20. It is thus especially common in Songs of Zion and in Royal psalms.[275] It is, however, surprisingly rare in the Book of Psalms in light of the close connection between this title and Zion. This is probably because the designation is often employed in an unreflected way of God, free from its original cultic context, not least in the Psalter.[276] It often stands in parallelism with general divine titles such as "God of Jacob", 46:8; 84:9, "God of Israel", 69:7. Cf. also 59:6.

The referential meaning of the title is not certain. At least six different suggestions regarding the denotation of צבאות have been submitted. It can refer to the armies of Israel, the stars, the vitiated mythical natural powers of Canaan, the heavenly council, all beings on earth as well as in heaven; but it may also simply be understood as an abstract plural, the Almighty.[277] The latter understanding is most open to different shades of meaning.[278] All these interpretations encounter linguistic and semantic difficulties,[279] but the last-mentioned corresponds best to the actual use in the OT,[280] even though the title probably had more than one interpretation in OT times.[281] These interpretations derive from different aspects of the term צבא in the OT,[282] since it sometimes refers to the armies of Israel, cf. Ex 7:4; 12:41; Ps 44:10, or in the expression צבא השמים to the heavenly armies, hosts of angels, 1 Kgs 22:19 par.; Neh 9:6; Dan 8:10, cf. Ps 103:21; 148:2 emend.,[283] or stars, in a negative meaning, as objects of worship, Deut 4:19; 17:3; 2 Kgs 17:16; 21:3, 5; 23:4, 5; Jer 8:2; 19:13; Zeph 1:5, cf. 2 Chr 33:3; Is 24:41, or countless stars, Jer 33:22.[284] It is also sometimes employed of cultic services.

The denotations "stars" or "army" seldom occur in books where יהוה צבאות is employed as a divine title. The use of the term as a designation of God is clearly adversatively correlated to its employment in the literal sense.[285] The same is more or less true for the names or epithets discussed in chap. 3 as well. This can hardly be a coincidence. In most of the books where the word in its ordinary sense is used it is never a designation of God, e.g. the Pentateuch (90x),[286] Josh (5x), Judg (4x), 2 Chr (12x), Neh (2x), Job (3x) and Dan (6x). If the literal sense of the word is employed in books where this term also appears as a divine title, e.g. 1-2 Sam, 1-2 Kgs, 1 Chr, Is, Jer, the occurrences are sporadical where the title is

---

[274] Janzen, Jeremiah, p. 163.

[275] See Anderson, Psalms, p. 35, van der Woude, צבא, col. 506, Mettinger, Dethronement, p. 13.

[276] Cf. Wanke, Zionstheologie, pp. 41-46, 107.

[277] See HAL. See also van der Woude, צבא, cols. 504-506. Cf. von Rad, Theology I, p. 19, Anderson, Psalms, p. 206, Mettinger, Sabaoth, pp. 109-110.

[278] Wanke, Zionstheologie, p. 43. For a criticism of the theory of an abstract plural, see Mettinger, Sabaoth, p. 127 n. 70.

[279] Kraus, Psalmen, p. 99. The original meaning of the designation is veiled in obscurity.

[280] Wanke, Zionstheologie, p. 43, van der Woude, צבא, cols. 505-506. For a different opinion, see Mettinger, Sabaoth, pp. 123-128, who rather suggests that the title is as a rule to be connected with Yahweh as king and his divine council.

[281] von Rad, Theology I, p. 19, Wanke, Zionstheologie, p. 43 and n. 15, Anderson, Psalms, p. 206. See also HAL.

[282] The connection with the ordinary word is as a rule taken for granted, but it is not universally accepted. Cf. the reference in Mettinger, Sabaoth, p. 123 and n. 53.

[283] In all these cases, except Neh 9:6, it is in fact probably the question of the divine council of Yahweh. See Mettinger, Sabaoth, p. 124. Cf. HAL.

[284] See especially van der Woude, צבא, cols. 501-502. For further examples, see HAL.

[285] For a description of the distribution pattern in this respect in statistical terms, see van der Woude, צבא, cols. 498-499. Cf. the statistics regarding the distribution of the divine title in LXX in Mettinger, Dethronement, p. 12, who has identical figures, save that 2 Kgs 19:31 Q is not included, since it is probably not the original reading. Ibid., p. 52.

[286] Num has in fact 77 occurrences of צבא, but not a single example of the term as a divine title.

common and vice versa. The Book of Psalms is, apart from perhaps 1-2 Sam, the only book where the term often occurs both in the literal sense and in a divine title, although never in one and the same psalm,[287] see Ps 44:10; 60:12; 68:13; 108:12 (armies) and 33:6; 103:21; 148:2 (stars or angels). This suggests that the authors or editors of OT books did not want associations from the literal sense to intrude in the meaning of the expression as a divine title. The only cases where the exact form of the term as a designation of God, i.e. צבאות, occurs in literal sense are 1 Kgs 2:5; 1 Chr 27:3, and Ps 68:13.

The earliest understanding of the long form of the title,[288] יהוה אלהי צבאות, may have been that it referred to the God of the armies of Israel.[289] This interpretation is hardly adequate for the majority of the passages, which occur in the prophetic writings.[290] Later on it may have denoted God as he who reigns over the host of heaven, i.e. the supernatural beings.[291] This is, according to Mettinger, the basic meaning of the title.[292]

It must be emphasized that even if the designation יהוה אלהי צבאות originally had connotations of the God who ruled over the armies of Israel or the heavenly beings, these are never identified with him. He is their ruler. Thus it is hardly probable that a theological tension is reflected in the rendering of the title in LXX because of the risk that Yahweh will be identified with the original reference of this designation. This also applies to the shorter, more common form of the title, according to the traditional understanding of the phrase, which is the most natural.[293] The interpretations that presuppose an identity between Yahweh and צבאות (see above) are not convincing.[294]

5.9.2   The equivalents of the title in LXX

Three types of translation of יהוה צבאות are evidenced in LXX. In Isaiah צבאות is always (56x), and in 1 Sam nearly always, e.g. 1:3, 11; 15:2; 17:45, transcribed by Σαβαωθ, but never outside these books. This equivalent is only employed in books where the title seldom occurs in formulas. See especially Is 1-39 where 46 out of the 56 occurrences are in a non-formulaic language.[295] Sometimes Σαβαωθ occurs without counterpart in MT, but, apart from Josh 6:17, this only applies to books where it is the main equivalent of צבאות as a designation of God, e.g. 1 Sam 1:20; Is 5:25; 7:7; 22:17; 23:11; 45:14. In certain manuscripts it also occurs in Is 14:22 (S); 19:17 (R); 21:6 (the fourth corrector of S). κύριος τῶν δυνάμεων is, apart from the Book of Psalms and 2 Kgs, only employed in the Hexaplaric witnesses and not in the Old Greek.[296] This equivalent is, according to HR, employed in 1-2 Sam (2x), 1-2 Kgs (2x), Amos (1x), Zechariah (1x) and Jeremiah (1x).[297]

[287] Cf. the statistics in van der Woude, צבא, cols. 498-499.

[288] Briggs asserts that this is the original form, Briggs, Psalms I, pp. 217-219, others rather suggest that it is an interpretation of the short title. von Rad, Theology I, pp. 18-19, Anderson, Psalms, p. 206, Mettinger, Sabaoth, p. 127 and n. 69. A complete list of the different forms of this title can be found in van der Woude, צבא, col. 499.

[289] See 1 Sam 17:45. Caird, Language, p. 234. Cf. Briggs, Psalms I, pp. 217-218, 219, Dodd, Bible, p. 16, Kraus, Psalmen, pp. 98-99.

[290] von Rad, Theology I, p. 19, Anderson, Psalms, p. 206.

[291] Dodd, Bible, p. 16.

[292] Mettinger, Sabaoth, pp. 123-127.

[293] See van der Woude, צבא, col. 504, Mettinger, Sabaoth, pp. 110, 127-128 and n. 70-73.

[294] For references, see van der Woude, צבא, col. 504, Mettinger, Sabaoth, p. 110.

[295] See Baumgärtel, Gottesnamen, pp. 1, 9, 25. Cf. Zobel, צבאות, col. 889.

[296] van der Woude, צבא, col. 507. See also Janzen, Jeremiah, p. 216 n. 19. The title is included in the text of Rahlfs in Zech 7:4.

[297] Cf. Dodd, Bible, p. 17. Exact references in, for example, Zobel, צבאות, col. 878. For the occurrences in the Book of Psalms, see below.

παντοκράτωρ is used in 2 Sam (4x), 1 Kgs (1x), 1 Chr (4x, one without counterpart in the Hebrew), Jeremiah (15x, including two without counterpart in the Hebrew), Hosea (1x), Amos (10x, including three without counterpart in the Hebrew), Micah (1x), Nahum (2x), Habakkuk (1x), Haggai (9x, including one without counterpart in the Hebrew), Zechariah (58x, including eight without counterpart in the Hebrew) and Malachi (17x, including three without counterpart in the Hebrew).[298] This equivalent coincides with an alternative rendering of שדי in the Book of Job. In nearly all of the books where it occurs, except 1 Kgs, this is the only or the dominant equivalent. The Minor Prophets has probably one translator and may thus from point of view of the translation technique be regarded as a unity.[299]

The Book of Jeremiah

The employment of צבאות as a designation of God is especially frequent in Jeremiah, with 82 occurrences. In as many as 74x or 70x it is the question of formulaic language.[300] The evaluation of the translation technique in the Book of Jeremiah is more complicated, but if differences between MT and LXX depend on the Hebrew, as is likely, παντοκράτωρ is the dominant, if not the only, equivalent of צבאות as a designation of God. It is very often excluded in the translation. That only 10[301] out of 82 occurrences have a counterpart in LXX depends on the Vorlage rather than on the translation technique. Maybe only six occurrences of this title in MT are original.[302]

The dominant formula in which this title occurs is כה אמר יהוה צבאות, with different additions. According to Janzen and Baumgärtel, it occurs 55 times.[303] The same formula, but without צבאות, is even more common in Jeremiah, occurring 85x, and in the Vorlage of LXX as many as 120x.[304] Both these formulas are rendered by τάδε λέγει κύριος (63x) in the first 29 chapters of Jeremiah LXX, i.e. with the verb in the present tense, while from chap. 30 to the end of the book they are translated by οὕτως εἶπεν κύριος (68x).[305] The most common explanation of this state of affairs is that two different translators were at work.[306] An alternative suggestion is that an editor revised the second part of the book, but not the first.[307] This is perhaps the more convincing suggestion since the rendering of the formula in the first part of the book accords with the translation in LXX as a whole. In fact only Isaiah and 1, 2 Chr employ both of the

---

[298] The statistics are based on HR. Thus the individual figures are not entirely reliable, but the general picture can be trusted. Söderlund has the most correct figures, but the relation to MT is not mentioned there. See Söderlund, Jeremiah, p. 163 and n. 10-12.

[299] This is the usual understanding, but it cannot be excluded that two translators were at work. Cf. Baumgärtel, Gottesnamen, p. 17.

[300] Janzen, Jeremiah, p. 163, Mettinger, Sabaoth, p. 12 and n. 4. The different figures depend on Mettinger's inclusion of צבאות as an address in the free usage. Cf. ibid., p. 12 n. 4.

[301] See Janzen, Jeremiah, p. 75, Mettinger, Dethronement, p. 12 n. 6. Cf. also Söderlund, Jeremiah, pp. 213-214. I have found only nine examples.

[302] Janzen, Jeremiah, p. 80. All the others may derive from secondary literary contexts.

[303] See Baumgärtel, Gottesnamen, pp. 14, 16-18, Janzen, Jeremiah, p. 163. Baudissin reckons with 54 examples, including passages where אלהי is added. Baudissin, Kyrios II, p. 76.

[304] Janzen, Jeremiah, p. 75.

[305] For the statistics, see Ziegler, Ieremias, p. 92. But cf. Söderlund whose figures are not identical. Söderlund, Jeremiah, p. 168.

[306] See Thackeray, Grammar, p. 11, Söderlund, Jeremiah, p. 153.

[307] Cf. Ziegler, Ieremias, p. 128 n. 1. But his discussions on the whole rather presuppose the classical interpretation. For a description of Ziegler's ambiguity in this respect, see Söderlund, Jeremiah, p. 154 and n. 2. It is probable that a later editor wanted the choice of translation to conform to the ordinary rendering of the particle and the verb separately in LXX. Cf. Söderlund, Jeremiah, p. 169.

renderings.[308]

The new translation policy of the formula is introduced in chap. 30 in MT.[309] A few exceptions to this policy exist. The texts of Rahlfs and Ziegler have the combination οὕτως λέγει in 23:16; 42:13.[310] 23:16 is remarkable also because here צבאות is reflected in LXX. A formula with a similar meaning, נאם יהוה צבאות, sometimes occurs, 7x.[311] Similar expressions with אדני instead of יהוה and with the combination of both are included. נאם יהוה appears 175x in MT, agreeing with LXX in 102x, but LXX has eight additional occurrences. In 17 cases the omission in LXX is in a context which does not occur in this version.[312] This means that 65x LXX did not have the phrase נאם יהוה in their original.[313] The only difference in the translation of this formula from the preceding one is that as a rule it is rendered without τάδε or οὕτως, 2:19; 27 (50):31; 30 (49):5; 37 (30):8. Sporadically φησί, 30:15 (49:26), οὕτως 32:14 (25:28),[314] or ὅτι τάδε, 8:4,[315] are employed.

Thus these two formulas seems to have been standardized in LXX. On the other hand, the translator of Jeremiah has the ordinary rendering of the last-mentioned phrase in LXX as a whole, except that צבאות is as a rule reflected in the translation.

The cases where צבאות are not rendered in LXX often occur in these two formulas. There are a few exceptions. Apart from the text already mentioned, παντοκράτωρ is employed in 5:7; 32:13 (25:27); 39 (32):14 and 51 (44):7.[316] Once, 29:19 (49:18), the title is an addition in relation to MT.

In non-formulaic language it is sometimes (three out of eight cases in MT) rendered by παντοκράτωρ, 15:16, 28 (51):5, 40 (33):11, and once it is added, 39:19 (32:18).[317] A similar picture is seen as regards the rarer formula יהוה צבאות שמו. Only three times does LXX reflect the title under discussion, 27 (50):34; 28 (51):57 (see above); 38:36 (31:35).[318] The combination of יהוה צבאות with אלהי ישראל is never reflected in LXX,[319] but when the same formula lacks צבאות it is always reflected (14x).[320]

It is probable that LXX sometimes or always has a different Vorlage in these cases, since it is more or less universally admitted that the LXX of Jeremiah, at least as regards size and sequence, reflects a shorter, probably more original

---

[308] Söderlund, Jeremiah, p. 168.

[309] Thackeray suggested that the turning point was in chap. 29, but this is hardly the case, even though the textual transmission there is somewhat unstable. Thackeray, Grammar, p. 11.

[310] A variant reading, εἶπεν O–233 L', which occurs in both passages, makes the text conform to the rendering of the formula in the second part of Jeremiah, i.e. it accords with the translation technique in Jer 42:13 but not in 23:16. The manuscript 233 is clearly influenced by the Lucianic recension. Ziegler, Ieremias, p. 84. The Lucianic recension twice has οὕτως εἶπεν instead of τάδε λέγει, 13:1; 17:19, but as a rule the change goes in the opposite direction, 24x. See Ziegler, Ieremias, p. 92. On the other hand, in 44 cases the texts are identical with the Old Greek.

[311] See Lisowsky, Baumgärtel, Gottesnamen, p. 1, Janzen, Jeremiah, p. 163. Jer 51:57, where a combination of the two formulas נאם יהוה צבאות and יהוה צבאות שמו is employed, is not part of this sum.

[312] Janzen, Jeremiah, pp. 82–83.

[313] Tov, Vorlage, p. 87.

[314] The expression seems to be moved from v. 29 in the Hebrew to v. 28. See Ziegler, Ieremias, BHK, BHS.

[315] It is hard to say whether the Greek renders the phrase at the end of 8:3 in MT or another in the beginning of 8:4. See Ziegler, Ieremias and BHS.

[316] Ziegler, Ieremias, and Baudissin, Kyrios II, p. 76 n. 1.

[317] HR wrongly suggests that it reflects צבאות here. For the relation between free and formulaic use in Jer, see Baumgärtel, Gottesnamen, p. 1. If the title as an address is included in the free usage the relation is 3 out of 12. See Janzen, Jeremiah, pp. 79–80, 166.

[318] There are seven occurrences of this phrase in MT or eight if the longer formula in 46:18 is included. See HR, Ziegler, Ieremias and Baudissin, Kyrios II, p. 76 and n. 2, Janzen, Jeremiah, p. 79.

[319] It occurs in fact as many as 34 times in MT. Janzen, Jeremiah, p. 157, Tov, Vorlage, p. 82.

[320] Janzen, Jeremiah, p. 157.

Hebrew text than MT.[321] Söderlund asserts that this is a overinterpretation since each reading has to be evaluated on its own merits, but admits that there is a strong case for the proposal that צבאות did not occur in the Vorlage of LXX, where it was excluded in the translation.[322]

5.9.3 The character of the equivalents in LXX

The usual equivalent of צבאות in LXX, παντοκράτωρ, also dominates in apocryphal and pseudepigraphical literature.[323] The meaning is probably "one who exercises all power", "one who rules over the world", rather than "almighty" in the absolute sense of the word.[324] It is sometimes employed as a divine name or epithet in non-biblical literature. In this respect it is in line with ὕψιστος, which is a common name or epithet of gods in the Hellenistic world.

The referent of δύναμις in the title under discussion is uncertain. It may denote powers of war, but could also refer to subordinate supernatural beings, who are more or less to be identified with angels.[325] δύναμις, as a common rendering of חיל, has the meaning "power", "strength".[326] Other meanings are "property", "function", "attribute". The equivalent in the Book of Psalms may have been employed since the translator did not want to be too specific in the interpretation of the Hebrew designation of God. He has avoided the military term στρατιά, which often renders this Hebrew word in LXX.[327] It only occurs as a designation of God in variant readings. See e.g. Amos 6:14 L, C. The choice of equivalent in LXX Psalms coincides with the rendering in Quinta, a version which Venetz regards as a later stage within the Kaige group.[328] This suggests that the Book of Psalms is associated with a Palestinian milieu of interpretation and has some connection with the Kaige recension,[329] but the other arguments for this theory[330] are not convincing.[331]

Both when referring to an army, 43 (44):10; 59 (60):12; 67 (68):13; 107 (108):12, and to angels or stars, 32 (33):6; 102 (103):21; 148:2, צבא is rendered by δύναμις in LXX Psalms. Thus the equivalent, as a divine title, is in line with the more or less stereotyped translation of צבא. The rendering in the Book of Psalms in this case well reflects the semantic meaning of the epithet, contrary to most of the previously investigated metaphorical titles of God. On the other hand, the translation accords with the rendering of anthropological designations of God in LXX

---

[321] See especially Janzen, **Jeremiah**, passim. This is confirmed by 4QJer-b. Even though it is only preserved in fragments and has a text that sometimes does not agree with either MT or LXX, it clearly evidences a short Hebrew text of Jeremiah, akin to that of the LXX. Ibid., pp. 173–184. Cf. Tov, **Vorlage**, pp. 73–76.

[322] Söderlund, **Jeremiah**, p. 214.

[323] van der Woude, צבא, col. 507.

[324] Dodd, **Bible**, p. 19, Michaelis, κράτος, p. 914 n. 10, 11.

[325] Dodd, **Bible**, pp. 17–19, van der Woude, צבא, col. 507.

[326] Cf. the discussion in Flashar, pp. 105–107.

[327] Dodd, **Bible**, p. 17. In non-biblical Greek it can sometimes mean "crowd", without military connotations. Bauernfeind, στρατεύομαι, p. 702:28–30. στρατιά, which is the second most common rendering, is never employed in the Psalter. Cf. Santos, **Index**, Dodd, **Bible**, p. 16.

[328] Venetz, **Quinta**, p. 90. For the relation between Quinta and the Kaige recension, see also ibid., pp. 57–72. The same equivalent is employed in the Kaige recension. Evidently the revisers reproduced the terminology of the Greek Psalter. Munnich, **Révision**, p. 216. It is a common technique in the revision to use one of the equivalents in LXX, particularly from the Psalter. Ibid., pp. 205, 218.

[329] Munnich, **La Septante**, pp. 77, 86. See also Munnich, **Révision**, p. 216. He points out that στρατιά is a name of God in Amos 6:14; Zech 1:3; 7:4. Munnich, **La Septante**, p. 77 n. 4. But apart from Zech 7:4, it is the question of variant readings.

[330] See especially Venetz, **Quinta**, pp. 51–57. Cf. van der Kooij, **Origin**, pp. 68–71.

[331] Munnich, **La Septante**, passim.

generally.

The knowledge of the term ṣābā' in the ordinary sense in LXX

Which denotations of צבא were known to the LXX translators? צבא when it refers to a star is occasionally rendered by ἀστήρ, Jer 8:2; Dan 8:10, or ἄστρον, Is 34:4; 45:12. Sometimes a more general equivalent is employed, κόσμος, Gen 2:1; Deut 17:3; Is 24:21 and 40:26.[332] στρατιά is employed twice in Jeremiah, Jer 7:18; 8:2.[333] Other referents are mostly reflected such as "army service", "warfare", παράταξις, 11x, πόλεμος with cognates, Num 31:32, 36, 53; Deut 24:5, 1 Chr 12:37; 2 Chr 26:13, "army", "warriors", δύναμις, 125x, στρατιά, 21x, "cultic service", λειτουργία with cognates, 8x. The word in the sense "cultic service" only occurs in the Book of Numbers.[334] δύναμις is the only equivalent to occur both as a designation of God and in the meaning "army", "warriors".

Thus the LXX translators were as a rule acquainted with the referents of the word in the literal sense, with the possible exception of "the heavenly council of Yahweh", i.e. angels, since it is rendered by the general term δύναμις, 2 Chr 18:18; Ps 102 (103):21; 148:2, but also by στρατιά, 1 Kgs 22:19; 2 Chr 33:3, 5; Neh 9:6; Hos 3:14.

5.9.4   Preliminary conclusions regarding the translation technique

The translation of יהוה צבאות has as a rule no connection with the rendering of צבא in the ordinary sense in the same book, with the exclusion of the Book of Psalms. This is in line with the translation of inanimate metaphorical designations of God generally, but contrary to the rendering of anthropological metaphors. In books where the word does not occur in a title of God, δύναμις is a frequently employed equivalent. This is especially the case in the Pentateuch, 1-2 Sam, 1-2 Kgs and 1-2 Chr. Evidently, the LXX translators knew the connection between its use in a divine name or epithet and the ordinary sense of צבא. They were familiar with the different denotations of the word, but consciously never chose equivalents reflecting these denotations.

This title thus seems to differ from the earlier investigated designations of God since no common approach characterizes LXX as a whole. The differences are more between than within the books, but the picture is more complicated than that. Three equivalents, which may reflect three different understandings of the term, two of which coincide with modern interpretations, δύναμις and παντοκράτωρ, are evidenced in LXX. The last-mentioned could also be understood as an equivalent which bears no relation to the literal meaning of the Hebrew, but accords with the metaphorical sense. But this is less probable for two reasons; it is the ordinary, and mostly the only, equivalent in the books under discussion, and metaphors (if this is to be regarded as a metaphor) employed as designations of God which are based on the activities of man, i.e. "army", tend to be translated literally in LXX as whole. The rendering may then be used as an argument for the interpretation of the word as an abstract plural.[335] On the other hand, if the translators interpreted the term in the title as, for example, "star" this argument loses all of its validity. This is, however, less probable in light of the equivalents in LXX.

---

[332] The meaning in Gen 2:1 is disputed. See HAL.

[333] The rendering in Jer 8:2 is part of a double translation. See Rahlfs, BHK, BHS.

[334] Bauernfeind asserts that this is the reason for the use of the phrase as a divine title, but this is hardly probable. Bauernfeind, στρατεύομαι, p. 705:20 with references.

[335] Cf. van der Woude, צבא, col. 505.

Baumgärtel's theory that this designation of God in Jeremiah, Isaiah and the Minor Prophets is a later addition in LXX to conform to MT, and thus does not represent the Old Greek, is impossible.[336] Baumgärtel asserts that the divine title יהוה צבאות was problematic for the Alexandrian Jewish community so that the translator(s) of Jeremiah rendered it only by $\kappa\acute{\upsilon}\rho\iota o\varsigma$. Moreover, the designations of God were, according to him, simplified in the service of the synagogue.[337]

Even though deviations from a semantic point of view are easily seen in the rendering of divine metaphorical names or epithets in LXX they are hardly ever quantitative, i.e. in the form of additions or subtractions. The variety of Greek equivalents does not indicate that the Alexandrian community had problems with this title, since one equivalent was as a rule employed in the Old Greek, $\pi\alpha\nu\tau o\kappa\rho\acute{\alpha}\tau\omega\rho$. This is true also for the Book of Jeremiah. $\delta\acute{\upsilon}\nu\alpha\mu\iota\varsigma$ represents, as we have seen, a later stage within the textual history of LXX, with the probable exclusion of the Psalter.[338] The transcription $\Sigma\alpha\beta\alpha\omega\theta$, which is more or less confined to Isaiah, is probably an individual understanding on the part of the translator of Isaiah,[339] who sometimes diverges from the usual translation pattern of the divine names or epithets. Proto-Isaiah is the only prophet in which the title is predominantly employed in free contexts. Otherwise it had become a mere residuum as a stylistic feature of prophetic speech.[340] That only in books where the free use is dominant (including when it is employed as an address to God) do other equivalents than $\pi\alpha\nu\tau o\kappa\rho\acute{\alpha}\tau\omega\rho$ occur suggests that linguistic factors influenced the choice of vocabulary.

---

[336] Cf. Baumgärtel, **Gottesnamen**, pp. 14, 16-18. See Janzen, **Jeremiah**, pp. 163, 167-170.

[337] Baumgärtel, **Gottesnamen**, p. 15.

[338] Cf. Janzen, **Jeremiah**, p. 169. The Kaige recension adopts the equivalent chosen in LXX Psalms. Munnich, **Révision**, p. 216.

[339] This usage is divergent and therefore hard to explain. Janzen, **Jeremiah**, p. 169. The occurrence in Josh and the five instances in 1-2 Sam suggest that his understanding was not unique. It is hardly the reflection of recensional activity. Maybe it is a representation of the Massoretic pointing, since the words of the title are, according to Dodd, in apposition and not in constructus relation in MT. Dodd, **Bible**, pp. 16-17.

[340] Janzen, **Jeremiah**, p. 165.

Chapter VI

BACKGROUND FOR THE TRANSLATION OF DIVINE NAMES OR EPITHETS IN LXX

6.1 THE INFLUENCE OF SPEAKER, GENRE AND FUNCTION

6.1.1 The influence of the speaker in the texts

Eichhorn's theory that the speaker in the texts containing the inanimate metaphorical names of God which are discussed in chap. 3 in this dissertation is always professionally connected with the temple, a person institutionally engaged in the transmission of the Lord's revelation in the traditions from the Jerusalem temple, or is to be identified with the king is by no means universally accepted.[1] But his explicit suggestions regarding the speaker make it easy to compare his proposals with the equivalents in LXX.

The possibility that the speaker could influence the choice of equivalents in the LXX is admittedly not great. On the other hand, a difference in vocabulary when God is the subject and not man can sometimes be demonstrated in this version. Thus it cannot be excluded that a similar translation technique is employed, for example, when the king is the speaker and not common cultic functionaries or ordinary Israelites. The speaker in the psalms under discussion is the king, 2 Sam 22:2-3; Ps 18:3; 89:27 and 144:1-2, or a cultic prophet, Ps 27:1; 28:1, 8; 42:10?; 59:10-12, 17-18; 62:3, 7-9; 73:26; 75:6; 91:2; 142:6; Jer 16:19; 17:17; Hab 1:12, or a post-exilic levitical temple singer or a teacher, Ps 9:10?; 19:15; 27:3; 31:3-5; 42:10?; 43:2 (or maybe a "cultic prophet"); 71:3, 7; 78:35; 91:2, 9; 142:6, or a wisdom teacher, loyal to the law, 37:39; 91:2, 9; 94:22.[2]

In many passages other opinions have also been submitted concerning the identity of the speaker.[3] But, even if the only distinction made is between the king as speaker and others, the one more or less secure basis of division,[4] it is evident that the speaker in the psalms under discussion did not influence the translation equivalents chosen. See e.g. Tables 3 and 4.

6.1.2 The influence of the genre or function of the texts

Another question concerns whether the genre has affected the choice of equivalents in LXX in the investigated passages.[5] The names occur in many different literary forms, in Didactic poems, Deut 32:4, 18, 30-31, 37; Ps 78:35, a Torah psalm, 19:15, in Individual laments, 28:1; 31:3; Hab 1:12, a Hymn, Nah 1:7 Songs of confidence, Josh 25:4; Is 26:4, a Salvation poem, Is 30:29, in Prophetic liturgies, 1 Sam

---

[1] It is perhaps the weakest point in Eichhorn's discussion. See Kraus, **Psalmen,** p. 374. Cf. **Eichhorn,** pp. 25-26 and passim.

[2] Even Eichhorn has difficulty in distinguishing between different groups of post-exilic cultic functionaries. **Eichhorn,** p. 123.

[3] See e.g. the review of Croft, **Identity,** JSOTSup 44 (1987) by L.C. Allen in JBL 108 (1989), pp. 335-337.

[4] But. cf. Allen's review of Croft, **Identity,** p. 336.

[5] For convenience sake the designations of the different Gattungen are built on the understanding of Eichhorn. **Eichhorn,** passim.

2:2; Jer 16:19; Joel 4:16, in a Prophetic speech, Ps 75:6, or in a Prophetic confession, Is 8:14. It is not possible to detect an influence from the Gattungen on the equivalents in LXX, i.e. the equivalents are not distributed according to the different literary forms of the text. The singular employment of an alternative rendering for צוּר in 18 (19):15 has nothing to do with the fact that it is regarded as a Torah psalm.[6]

The divine metaphors are not rendered in a different manner if they occur in a description of a theophany. Cf. Ps 18; 144:1-2 and Is 30:29. The translators' main motivation for the choice of equivalents can thus hardly have been fear that the metaphor would be regarded as a literal description of the form of God. See 1.1. The occurrence of the metaphors in current prophetic proclamations, Is 17:10; 30:29; Ps 75:6 (emended text), or in theological reflections concerning their meaning when applied to Yahweh, Deut 32; Ps 78:35, did not affect the renderings. The same is true for the description of how Yahweh takes action against the enemies of his people in Ps 18; 31; 71; 91; 144, or steps forward for the salvation of his people, while he destroys those that rise up against him, Nah 1:2-10, or when the term occurs in a representation of his primeval struggle against his enemies, Ps 46, 48, or when the prophet insists that Yahweh is characterized by מחסה, even though he punishes his own people, Jer 17:14-18. Cf. Ps 14.

6.2   THE TRANSLATION OF DIVINE NAMES IN OTHER GREEK VERSIONS

6.2.1   The translation in Aquila

We have seen that the inanimate metaphorical names which were examined in the first part of my dissertation are rendered with terms which are more or less exclusively employed as divine names in LXX Psalms, and mostly used in connection with God in LXX as a whole. See 4.1. Now I shall investigate whether the other Greek versions follow a similar translation technique or whether LXX unique in this respect. In other words, does the translation technique in LXX reflect an exegetical tradition which continued in the first centuries A.D.?

The statistics of the renderings in Aquila are based on many different sources since one, unfortunately, cannot rely upon the information in the concordance by Reider and Turner. It has serious methodical shortcomings in addition to wrong information and many misprints.[7] Thus I have tried to confirm the information there by other, more reliable, sources. This is especially the case with the renderings of divine names or epithets in the Book of Psalms.

צוּר is in Aquila rendered by both στερεός and πέτρα. στερεός is the ordinary rendering in the Book of Psalms, whether or not divine names are at issue, 17 (18):32, 47; 26 (27):5; 27 (28):1; 30 (31):3; 61 (62):8; 88 (89):27 are divine titles, while 60 (61):3; 88 (89):44, are ordinary metaphors.[8] The same is true for occurrences outside the Psalter, Deut 8:15; 32:4, 15, 31 (twice); 2 Sam 2:16; Is 8:14; 30:29; Hab 1:12.[9] πέτρα is used in Judg 7:25; Ps 77 (78):16; Is 48:21 (twice).[10] The reason for the use of two equivalents is hard to see since στερεός renders the term not only when it refers to divine names, but also when it applies to literal rocks, Deut 8:15, and to ordinary metaphors, Ps 60 (61):3. Venetz suggests that

---

[6] This is also a disputed designation. See e.g. Mays, **Torah-Psalms**, pp. 3, 5. For a proposal regarding the choice of equivalent here, see 6.3.1.

[7] See especially Tov, **Corrections**, p. 164. See also the detailed corrections on pp. 164-174. Furthermore, it does not discuss the problematical cases. Cf. e.g. Hyvärinen, **Aquila**, p. 14.

[8] Mercati, **Hexapli**, pp. 5, 9, 31, Venetz, **Quinta**, p. 141. Cf. Schenker, **Hexapla**, pp. 135, 168, 253-255, 437 and Reider, Turner, **Index**, p. 221. The statistics of Dell'Acqua, **Roccia**, p. 435 is not reliable.

[9] See Venetz, **Quinta**, p. 141, Reider, Turner, **Index**, p. 221, Field I, II, ad loc. This is probably because סלע is as a rule translated by πέτρα.

[10] Reider, Turner, **Index**, p. 191. Cf. Field I, II, ad loc. Is 48:21 is not noted in **Field**.

theological reasons were involved in the choice of vocabulary here in Aquila (and Quinta), since στερεός is employed for סלע as a name of God in LXX and also once used as a designation of God for אדיר, 1 Sam 4:8.[11] This is hardly convincing since the divine names or epithets are as a rule literally rendered and no distinction is made between a metaphorical and a literal sense of the Hebrew words in Aquila, with מעון as a possible exception. See below. סלע is always rendered by πέτρα both as a divine name, Ps 17 (18):3; 30 (31):4; 41 (42):10; 70 (71):3, and in the literal sense, 139 (140):6.

The ordinary rendering of מגן, θυρεός, is employed whether it is the question of a designation of God, as in Ps 17 (18):31; 27 (28):7; 32 (33):20,[12] a metaphor connected with God, 17 (18):36,[13] or with man (the king), 46 (47):10, or 83 (84):10, or literal shields, Is 37:33; Ez 27:10; Nah 2:4.[14] Another equivalent of מגן is ἀσπίς, Prov 6:11; Jer 26 (46):3 syr., 9,[15] which is employed in the literal sense in Jer 46, but as a metaphor in Prov 6:11.

Both מעון and מעונה in the sense of "lair" are rendered by κατοικητήριον in Aquila, thus reflecting the literal meaning of the Hebrew term, 1 Sam 2:32 (the meaning of the Hebrew word here is disputed and the text is probably corrupt, see 3.6.2); Jer 9:11 (10) syr.; Songs 4:8.[16] οἰκητήριον is used for מעון as the dwelling of God in Ps 67 (68):6 and as a divine name in 90 (91):9.[17] This may reflect a conscious distinction between a literal meaning and the use of the term in connection with God: the abode of God could not be translated with the same word as was employed for a den of animals. On the other hand, the terms employed are more or less synonyms, even though οἰκητήριον is less frequently attested. See LSJ.

מצודה II is always rendered literally by ὀχύρωμα, 1 Sam 22:4; 24:23; 2 Sam 5:7, 17; 70 (71):3; Ps 30 (31):3-4; 65 (66):11; Job 39:28.[18] מצודה I (in HAL) is correctly rendered by ἀμφίβληστρον in Ez 12:13.[19] Thus Aquila, contrary to LXX, distinguished between the two roots of מצודה. See 3.7.2.

For משגב, which is only used as a name of God in the extant fragments of Aquila, he employs a singular word which is not found in the other versions, or for that matter in Greek literature per se, ὑπερέπαρσις, "excessive exaltation" (LSJ).[20] This equivalent is employed in 9:10 syr. (twice); 45 (46):8; 47 (48):4, but in 45 (46):12, without apparent reason (46:8 and 46:12 are identical in the Hebrew), the

---

[11] Venetz, **Quinta**, p. 143.

[12] The ascription of ὑπερασπιστής in 32 (33):20 to Aquila is probably not correct. Reider, Turner, **Index**, p. 244. See Mercati, **Hexapli**, p. 5, Schenker, **Hexapla**, pp. 400–404, especially p. 403. The rendering in O.G. 398 is probably from Quinta, who often has equivalents to divine names or epithets identical with those in LXX. Regarding the translation in 17 (18):31, 36 and 27 (28):7, see Mercati, **Hexapli**, pp. 3, 5. All references in Dell'Acqua, **Roccia**, p. 435 are hardly correct.

[13] The ascription of ὑπερασπισμός in 17 (18):36 to Aquila, built on O.G. 398, in Reider, Turner, **Index**, p. 244, and Field II, ad loc. is wrong. Aquila has in fact his ordinary translation. See Mercati, **Hexapli**, p. 5. Cf. Saiz, **Simaco**, p. 596. Regarding the Hexaplaric fragments in Ottobonianus Graecus 398 (O.G. 398), see Schenker, **Hexapla**, pp. 23–31.

[14] See Reider, Turner, **Index**, p. 114 and Freedman, O'Connor, מגן, cols. 650–654, Field II, ad loc. See also HR, p. 663. Nah 2:4 is only noted in Reider, Turner, op. cit. מגן in Job 41:7 has been subjected to different interpretations. Probably it refers to scales of a crocodile, but a metaphorical sense is not impossible. See 3.3.2.

[15] See Field II, pp. 321, 706, Reider, Turner, **Index**, ad loc. The equivalent in 26 (46):9 is only based on cod. 86. See Field II, p. 706.

[16] See Field I, p. 492, and Field II, pp. 418, 596. Cf. Reider, Turner, **Index**, p. 132.

[17] Field II, pp. 200, 249.

[18] For all of these passages, see Reider, Turner, **Index**, p. 181, HR. Regarding 30 (31):3-4, see Mercati, **Hexapli**, p. 31, Schenker, **Hexapla**, pp. 253–257. The term in 66:11 is thus interpreted as מצודה II in Aquila.

[19] See Field II, p. 797.

[20] Caird suggests that ἐις ὑπερέπαρσιν here means "to raise her to safety". Caird, **Lexicon**, p. 150.

term ὑπερεπαρτής, a word that does not even occur in LSJ, is employed.[21] Thus it is probable that the literal meaning of the Hebrew word was not recognized by Aquila. But it cannot be excluded that the etymological translation technique took the upper hand, even though he was aware of the literal sense of the word.[22]

מחסה is translated by ἐλπίς, 45 (46):2; 61 (62):8; 90 (91):9.[23] It is obvious that Aquila did not interpret מחסה as "refuge", "place of refuge", as in that case καταφυγή would have been used. It is in fact not even regarded as a metaphor since the word is never understood in the literal sense in Aquila. The same is true for the LXX.

מעוז is not interpreted as "fortress". It is as a rule rendered by κραταίωμα, whether it occurs in a literal sense, Judg 6:26; Dan 11:10, 38, or as a divine name, Ps 26 (27):1; 27 (28):8; 30 (31):3, 5 and Jer 16:19.[24] Once it is rendered by δικαίωμα, Prov 10:29. The Hebrew term is employed in close connection with Yahweh.[25]

מגדל is always rendered literally by πύργος, exactly as in LXX, even when it is a divine name, 60 (61):4.[26] The rendering μεγαλύνειν in Is 30:25 depends on a deviant vocalization from that of MT.[27] קרן is, in accordance with LXX, always translated literally by κέρας with cognates in Aquila.[28] Both עליון and מרום are rendered by ὕψιστος, even though מרום sometimes has ὕψος or ὕψωμα and עליון sometimes ὑψηλός, as equivalent.[29]

In conclusion one may state that Aquila, in line with his translation technique, employs literal stereotyped equivalents and his departures from his regular rendering are not due to a special treatment of divine names or epithets. Thus Aquila does not distinguish between the usage of words as metaphorical divine names or epithets and the usage in other contexts. The equivalents in Aquila are particularly important for the evaluation of the metaphorical character of these Hebrew words in the beginning of the second century A.D., since some of the names or epithets may have gone out of use in literal meaning. In that case the literal sense of the word could have been unknown to the translators of LXX.

6.2.2   The translation in Quinta

Quinta as a rule employs στερεός as equivalent of צור, 17 (18):32, 47; 27 (28):1; 30 (31):3; 88 (89):27,[30] but not exclusively. It is once employed for סלע, 30 (31):4. But צור is rendered by στερρότης, when it is not a divine name, 88 (89):44.[31] Quinta

---

[21] See Mercati, **Hexapli**, pp. 77, 79, Field II, pp. 98, 168. Cf. Reider, Turner, **Index**, p. 24.

[22] Cf. Reider, Turner, **Index**, p. 311.

[23] Regarding 45 (46):2, see Mercati, **Hexapli**, p. 75, Venetz, **Quinta**, p. 55 and n. 29, 61 (62):8 Venetz, **Quinta**, p. 55 and n. 30, Field II, pp. 192, 249, 90 (91):9, Venetz, **Quinta**, pp. 54–55 and n. 19, 31. For these passages, see also Reider, Turner, **Index**, pp. 78, 278.

[24] Regarding Judg 6:26, see Field I, p. 422, Jer 16:19 Field II, p. 616, Dan 11:10, 38 Field II, pp. 930, 932, Ps 26 (27):1 Schenker, **Hexapla**, p. 124, 27 (28):8 Mercati, **Hexapli**, p. 11, 30 (31):3, 5 Mercati, **Hexapli**, p. 31, Schenker, **Hexapla**, pp. 253–255, 259. It has manuscript support from both O.G. 398 and Cod. 1098. See also Field II, p. 132. Concerning the rendering of Aquila outside the Psalter, see also Reider, Turner, **Index**, p. 140.

[25] Field II, p. 330, Reider, Turner, **Index**, p. 59.

[26] See Field II, p. 190, Reider, Turner, **Index**, pp. 208, 270.

[27] See Field II, p. 489, Reider, Turner, **Index**, pp. 153, 270.

[28] Thus Reider, Turner, **Index**, pp. 133, 308. But, according to Süring, Aquila employs a different equivalent in 1 Kgs 2:28. Süring, **Horn–Motif**, p. 469.

[29] Thus Reider, Turner, **Index**, ad loc.

[30] Mercati, **Hexapli**, pp. 5, 9, 31, Venetz, **Quinta**, p. 140. Probably the same equivalent occurs in 27 (28):1, supported by cod. 264 and O.G. 398. Ibid., p. 140. See also Schenker, **Hexapla**, p. 168. The equivalent to 31:3 in Dell'Acqua, **Roccia**, p. 435 is evidently wrong.

[31] See Venetz, **Quinta**, pp. 140, 142. In MT it probably has the sense of "flint" צר here. The rendering

and Aquila have similar equivalents, even though a difference may exist in the rendering of צור as a metaphor and in literal meaning.[32]

מעוז is as a rule rendered by ὑπερασπιστής, 27 (28):8; 30 (31):5,[33] but once by κραταίωμα, 26 (27):1.[34] The translation in 30 (31):3, κατοικητήριον, reflects מעון instead of מעוז. See 3.6.1. ὑπερασπιστής is also used for מגן, 17 (18):31, 36; 27 (28):7; 32 (33):20.[35] Quinta has taken over the equivalent in LXX of מעוז and מגן, notwithstanding that one and the same equivalent is used for both of these Hebrew words. The translations of משגב and מצודה also follow the rendering in LXX. Thus they are translated by ἀντιλήμπτωρ, 45 (46):8, 12[36] and καταφυγή, 30 (31):3, 4.[37]

6.2.3   The translation in Symmachus

Symmachus has many different equivalents for צור as a divine name, including the literal rendering πέτρα, 93 (94):22 syr.; 113 (114):8 syr.[38] The equivalents are wholly different from those in LXX.[39] They can best be described as a mixture of literal and non-literal renderings. Interestingly enough, when Symmachus has a term among the equivalents which render metaphorical designations of God in LXX, κραταίωμα, 61 (62):3,[40] it is never employed for צור in LXX. πέτρα is the only equivalent of סלע in conformity with Aquila.[41] It is employed when the Hebrew word occurs as a divine name, 17 (18):3; 30 (31):4; 41 (42):10; 70 (71):3, but also when it refers to a literal rock, even though the language is figurative, 140 (141):6.

משגב is always rendered literally by ὀχύρωμα "fortress",[42] despite the fact that it is only employed as a name of God in the Book of Psalms. This is the same term as Aquila employs for מצודה, except in Ez 12:13, where it has a different meaning. See 3.7.2. Thus the literal senses of both of these Hebrew words were probably known in the time of Aquila and Symmachus. Remarkably enough, מצודה is rendered by καταφυγή in agreement with LXX in 30 (31):3, 4; 70 (71):3,[43] where it is a divine name. In Ps 65 (66):11, where מצודה may have a different meaning, "prison", πολιορκία "siege", "besieging" (LSJ) is used. For the understanding of the Hebrew word here in LXX, see 3.7.2.

מחסה occurs only as a designation of God in the Book of Psalms and is often rendered by ἀφοβία, 60 (61):4; 61 (62):9 syr.; 90 (91):9; 93 (94):22 syr., sometimes by πεποίθησις, 45 (46):2; 70 (71):7,[44] words which are never divine names or epithets in other versions. The renderings are also in line with the suggestion that מחסה was not interpreted as "place of refuge" in LXX or in Aquila, Quinta or Symmachus.

---

in 30 (31):4 is also confirmed by Schenker, **Hexapla**, pp. 256-257. In 48 (49):15 צור in the sense of "rock" (Q), צורה or maybe "fashion" (Q) or ציר "idol" (K), is rendered by ἰσχύς.

[32] See the discussion in Venetz, **Quinta**, pp. 140-144.

[33] Mercati, **Hexapli**, pp. 11, 31, Estin, **Psautiers**, pp. 63, 71.

[34] See Schenker, **Hexapla**, p. 124.

[35] Mercati, **Hexapli**, pp. 3, 5, 11, Schenker, **Hexapla**, pp. 182, 183, 400-404.

[36] Mercati, **Hexapli**, pp. 77, 79, Venetz, **Quinta**, p. 57.

[37] Mercati, **Hexapli**, p. 31, Venetz, **Quinta**, p. 57.

[38] See Saiz, **Simaco**, p. 568.

[39] It is true that φύλαξ occurs, Deut 32:31; Ps 28:1, but this term is only used in the Kaige recension. Cf. Saiz, **Simaco**, p. 714, Dell'Acqua, **Roccia**, p. 435.

[40] Here it is a retranslation from the Syriac. Saiz, **Simaco**, pp. 537, 714.

[41] Saiz, **Simaco**, pp. 568, 693.

[42] See Saiz, **Simaco**, pp. 561, 681.

[43] See Saiz, **Simaco**, pp. 534, 680. For 30 (31):3, 4, see also Mercati, **Hexapli**, p. 31. For v. 4, see also Schenker, **Hexapla**, p. 256.

[44] See Saiz, **Simaco**, pp. 477, 566, 675.

As a divine name מגן has the equivalents ὑπερασπιστής, 17 (18):31; 27 (28):7; 32 (33):20; 58 (59):12; 83 (84):10, or ὑπερασπισμός, 83 (84):12.[45] When מגן occurs in the literal sense it is rendered by ἀσπίς, 34 (35):2; 75 (76):4.[46] This is the only clear example of a conscious distinction between an inanimate metaphorical divine name and a literal rendering in Symmachus' Psalms. On the other hand, in many cases only the divine names or epithets are preserved in the texts of Symmachus.

מעוז exclusively occurs as a name of God in the Psalter, but every passage has a new equivalent, maybe for stylistic reasons. On the other hand, many renderings hardly reflect the semantic meaning of the Hebrew word; cf. 26 (27):1 σθένος, 42 (43):2 σωτηρία, others are extremely rare words such as ἀηττησία "invincibility" in 30 (31):5,[47] or ἐνίσχυσις "Bekräftigung", "Bestätigung", 27 (28):8.[48] None of the renderings are among the usual equivalents to divine names or epithets in LXX.

As regards מעון, no distinction between this term as a name of God, 70 (71):3; 90 (91):9, and as signifying God's dwelling, 25 (26):8; 67 (68):6, can be seen and the word always has a new equivalent.[49] The words employed here are hardly synonyms. Where מעון refers to God's dwelling a word for a palace rather than a commoner's abode is employed, for example, ἀνάκτορον "palace", "temple" (LSJ), 25 (26):8, and βασίλειον "kingly dwelling", "palace" (LSJ), 67 (68):6. Regarding the rendering in 70 (71):3, see 3.6.1.

Variation is thus a characteristic trait in the translation of these names or epithets in Symmachus. This is especially significant for צור, מעון and מעוז. The choice of equivalents, with the exception of the renderings of מגן, does not depend on whether or not the Hebrew word is a designation of God and the variation between the equivalents does not seem to reflect a shyness of repetition. Symmachus has no special technique in the translation of inanimate metaphorical names or epithets; some of them are stereotypically rendered, others display unwarranted variations in the equivalents employed. מצודה is the only name of God of which Symmachus has employed the same equivalent as in LXX.

6.2.4   The relation between LXX and the versions

Despite the great differences in the choice of equivalents between the Greek versions only Quinta partly adopts the approach of the LXX concerning the inanimate metaphorical designations of God. Quinta follows the renderings of מעוז, מגן, משגב and מצודה in LXX, but not of צור or סלע. Even though מחסה is rendered by καταφυγή in conformity with LXX in 45 (46):2, this is not the ordinary equivalent in LXX. Symmachus employs καταφυγή as a rendering of מצודה, and Aquila ἐλπίς as equivalent to מחסה in accordance with LXX. Otherwise the differences are the most striking feature. Thus the general, systematic approach in LXX to the rendering of divine names or epithets, which suggests that a common exegetical outlook in this regard characterized this, in other respects, disparate translation, is not reflected in Aquila or Symmachus, and only partly in Quinta. Theodotion is so fragmentary that it is hard to draw more definite conclusions.[50]

---

[45] Saiz, Simaco, pp. 596, 673. Regarding 17 (18):31 and 27 (28):7, see also Mercati, Hexapli, pp. 3, 11. In 17 (18):36; 46 (47):10 ὑπερασπισμός is employed when it is used in close connection with God. Regarding 17 (18):36, see also Mercati, Hexapli, p. 5.

[46] Saiz, Simaco, pp. 475, 673. In 35:2 the text contains figurative language where God is described as a warrior.

[47] See Saiz, Simaco, p. 679. Cf. LSJ (suppl.).

[48] Saiz, Simaco, p. 679, Schenker, Hexapla, pp. 185-189. The ascription of ἐνίσχυσις to Sexta in O.G. 398 is not correct. Ibid., p. 188. It does not even occur in LSJ and may be chosen on account of the alliteration of the Hebrew. Ibid., p. 189. The translation of the Greek term is taken from Schenker, op. cit., p. 189.

[49] Saiz, Simaco, p. 679.

[50] None of the equivalents for the group of inanimate metaphorical designations of God in LXX,

If a widespread exegetical tradition lies behind the choice of renderings in LXX this seems to have gradually waned, since the approach of LXX in this regard was not followed by the later Greek translations. On the other hand, both Peshitta and the Targum often had renderings comparable to those in LXX in the Book of Psalms, but the Targum particularly does not follow a consistent translation technique.[51] Even though the translation techniques in Peshitta and the Targum in the Book of Psalms are similar inasmuch as they often or usually avoid a literal rendering of these names or epithets, the semantic meaning of the equivalents, especially in the Targum, tend to be "strength" rather than "help" or "protection".[52] The Targum of the Book of Psalms is very late and therefore hardly the best comparison material. Regarding Peshitta opinions differ as to whether, and if so to what extent, it is dependent on the Septuagint in the Psalter.[53] Furthermore, the Targumic traditions are probably dependent on the Septuagint and not vice versa.[54]

6.3   THE TRANSLATION OF METAPHORICAL DESIGNATIONS OF GOD IN LXX

6.3.1   The translation technique

The type of equivalents employed in LXX as counterparts to inanimate names or epithets of God adequately reflects the metaphorical meaning of these designations in general terms. All the Hebrew names under discussion have positive connotations since they are as a rule used of Yahweh as helper, saviour and protector. None of them is negative per se and the same is true for their Greek counterparts. Some of the main equivalents are obviously chosen in order to retain the relationship with the ordinary rendering of the cognate Hebrew verb, e.g. מגן, מחסה, מרום. Otherwise in LXX as a whole the translators seem to have avoided equivalents to the term in the literal sense. צבאות is an exception. This only applies to the Book of Psalms. מחסה is evidently not regarded as a metaphor in LXX nor in the other versions, but understood as an abstract term, "hope", "expectation".

The main equivalent of מגן is connected with the literal meaning of the term through the choice of the counterpart ὑπερασπιστής, which incorporates ἀσπίς, a term for a shield. This is, however, not the most common rendering of מגן in the literal sense in LXX. Certain renderings have probably been chosen with reference to words which frequently stand in parallel with these divine metaphors, e.g. θεός as a translation of צור and κύριος as a rendering of שדי.

Even though the choice of the main equivalents can sometimes be explained by an etymological translation technique as well as by the connection with certain aspects of the Hebrew words in question in context this is not the case with the alternative equivalents. But the bewildering picture of the renderings of individual passages, especially in the Book of Psalms, are only partly apparent, since as we

---

however, were included as a rendering of Theodotion in Saiz, **Simaco**. But מעוז and סלע were obviously rendered by κραταίωμα, 30 (31):3, 4. Regarding 30 (31):3, see Schenker, **Hexapla**, pp. 253-256, 431. Cf. Dell'Acqua, **Roccia**, p. 435.

[51] This observation is based on the investigation of Erwin, who has the text of the London Polyglott, and his text may thus not be completely reliable. It is also hard to know whether his selection of texts comprises representative exponents of the translation technique of the Targum in this respect. **Erwin,** pp. 5, 56–78, especially pp. 62 and n. 2, pp. 63–65, 67. Note e.g. the literal translation of צור in 31:3 and 71:3. Cf. Dell'Acqua, **Roccia**, p. 423.

[52] **Erwin,** pp. 64, 69, 70, 73–75. This is confirmed by Schwarzenbach, **Geographische Terminologie,** pp. 114, 185, as regards צור and סלע. For a more comprehensive presentation of the equivalents in Peshitta and the Targum, see Dell'Acqua, **Roccia,** pp. 421-430.

[53] Cf. e.g. **Berg**, passim.

[54] See e.g. Brown, **Loan-words,** pp. 197, 216.

have demonstrated, nearly all of the divine names or epithets have a certain equivalent that is used in ordinary cases. סלע has no standard equivalent, which explains why the choice of translation in the individual passages is more or less haphazard. The same is to a certain degree also true for עז and אביר. If only translation units are considered, even צבאות has in fact one main, but hardly any alternative equivalents.

The diversified renderings, especially in the Book of Psalms, are ultimately due to two conflicting tendencies. One is the choice of the same main equivalent for אלהים, אל, אלוה and צור, for מגן and מעוז, as for מעון and מצודה, and to a certain degree also for עזר and עז. See Tables 1 and 2. Another is the tendency to employ an alternative rendering, which for the most part is identical with the main equivalent or one of the alternative equivalents of other divine metaphorical names or epithets. The alternative equivalents are as a rule only employed when the use of the main rendering would result in the repetition of the same word in close proximity. This is the case in, for example, 17:3; 61:9; 77:35; 88:27; 90:2; 93:22. The technique is especially rigid when a Greek designation of God would have been repeated without an intervening divine metaphor. Cf. 77:35. Sometimes the occurrence of a cognate verb seems to be enough to effect the change. See 90:2. But such is not always the case. See, for example, Ps 69 (70):6 ὁ θεός βοήθησόν μοι βοηθός μου, where the verb renders חוש, which in fact is usually translated differently in LXX Psalms. 17 (18):32 is an exception, since צור is rendered by θεός, although this term is employed for אלהים in the same verse.

On the other hand, the main rendering of one and same divine title is often kept even if it is repeated within the same verse or adjacent verses, with or without intervening divine metaphors. See 30 (31):3-4; 58 (59):17-18; 113:17-19 (115:9-11). The equivalents of משגב in 9:10 are an exception. The same is true for the renderings of מחסה in 61 (62):8-9. See Table 3. What I have described here is the standard pattern. In many cases an alternative rendering is chosen without apparent reason; this happens sometimes when the term is used alone, 3:4; 42 (43):2 (presumably here because of a different derivation); 51 (52):9, sometimes when it is connected with other divine names or epithets, 18 (19):15; 93 (94):22; 118 (119):114. See Table 3. Thus the employment of standard equivalents together with the desire for variation governed the choice of renderings in individual passages and not semantic accuracy or contextual factors. The technique of having an identical rendering of parallels in the Hebrew seems to have had less influence on the choice of equivalents. See e.g. סלעי ומצודתי, 18:3; 31:4; 71:3, which is translated by στέρεωμά μου καὶ καταφυγή μου, 17:3; 70:3, and κραταίωμά μου καὶ καταφυγή μου, 30:4, although the whole passage in the Hebrew, 31:2-4, is also a close parallel to 71:3.

What, inter alia, seems strange in view of the above-mentioned translation technique, is that the translators have not tried to give each of the divine names or epithets a specific equivalent, since the number of Greek equivalents of the inanimate divine metaphorical names or epithets is in parity with their Hebrew counterparts, at least in the Book of Psalms. The need for alternative renderings is the obvious outcome of the translation technique employed. But the number of alternative renderings, especially for משגב and מחסה, is harder to explain, since the choice of one alternative equivalent instead of the other does not seem to be governed by the same factors as the choice of alternative renderings per se, i.e. there is no main alternative equivalent which would yield to a second alternative if the same word occurred in close proximity. The translation technique with variation in the equivalents is particularly consistent as regards צור as a name of God, but the renderings of שדי also follow a strict pattern. This technique in the translation of צור may even be employed in the recensions of LXX in 2 Sam 22,[55] even though other alternative equivalents are chosen.

---

[55] The Proto-Lucianic recension is here, according to many scholars, basically identical with the Old Greek.

The non-employment of $\theta\epsilon\acute{o}\varsigma$ in 18 (19):15 is astonishing; an alternative rendering of צור as a divine name never otherwise occurs without being preceded or succeeded by $\theta\epsilon\acute{o}\varsigma$, translating אלהים with cognates. It may well be that the preceding $\kappa\acute{v}\rho\iota o\varsigma$ is not original, even though no Greek variant with $\theta\epsilon\acute{o}\varsigma$ has been found. יהוה and אלהים often alternate in the Book of Psalms, especially as a consequence of recensional activity. Thus I propose that $\theta\epsilon\acute{o}\varsigma$, albeit not a reading in existing Greek manuscripts, may be the original rendering in view of the oscillation between the two names of the God of Israel in both Hebrew and Greek, not least in the Psalter.

Nearly all of the words which are the main equivalents for inanimate divine names or epithets, e.g. $\theta\epsilon\acute{o}\varsigma$, $\acute{v}\pi\epsilon\rho\alpha\sigma\pi\iota\sigma\tau\acute{\eta}\varsigma$, $\dot{\epsilon}\lambda\pi\acute{\iota}\varsigma$, $\kappa\alpha\tau\alpha\phi\upsilon\gamma\acute{\eta}$, $\dot{\alpha}\nu\tau\iota\lambda\acute{\eta}\mu\pi\tau\omega\rho$, are employed as alternative renderings of other metaphorical designations of God, but $\beta o\eta\theta\acute{o}\varsigma$ and $\kappa\rho\alpha\tau\alpha\acute{\iota}\omega\mu\alpha$ are only used as alternative renderings among these metaphors. This can partly be explained by the fact that $\beta o\eta\theta\acute{o}\varsigma$ is the main equivalent of עזר in LXX Psalms, whether it is a divine name or not, even though $\beta o\eta\theta\acute{o}\varsigma$ is nearly always used in connection with God in LXX. $\kappa\rho\alpha\tau\alpha\acute{\iota}\omega\mu\alpha$ is employed for different divine names, without being the main equivalent of one specific name. Alternative equivalents are not always synonyms to the ordinary rendering of the Hebrew words. See Table 1. The reason for the non-use of $\kappa\acute{v}\rho\iota o\varsigma$, except for the Book of Job and Is 17:10, is probably that this word was more or less exclusively reserved for the Tetragrammaton, especially in the first two parts of the Hebrew canon, the Law and the Prophets.[56]

The employment of the same equivalent for different divine names or epithets is in line with Wanke's suggestion that from the exile onwards different designations of God were used more or less indiscriminately in the Book of Psalms.[57] It is not out of the question that these names or epithets had partly lost their specific semantic meaning in the eyes of the LXX translator and were regarded as general designations of God with positive connotations.

The picture as regards the translation technique outside the Book of Psalms is not as clear, partly because the occurrences of the inanimate metaphorical names or epithets are few, with the exception of צור and צבאות. These metaphors are frequently misunderstood by the LXX translator, especially if they refer to man or to other gods. They are then used ironically in MT, an irony which as a rule is not recognized by the translator. Of the inanimate divine names צור and מגן both have a main equivalent, which is identical with the ordinary rendering of these names in LXX Psalms. This is also true for the more or less non-metaphorical names or epithets, עליון and שדי, as well as for the anthropological metaphor, עזר. The rest of the inanimate metaphorical divine names or epithets that occur outside the Book of Psalms are so rare that one cannot speak of a main rendering. Designations which both are frequently used and have an ordinary rendering, which is also employed for other Hebrew terms, so that variation as a translation technique could be employed, e.g. צור and שדי, show the same type of systematic variation in the translation when confronting an identical equivalent as characterizes the designations of God in the Psalter.

The distribution pattern of the group of names or epithets under discussion in the Book of Psalms is interesting. They are evenly spread in the first three books and in a few psalms of the fourth, viz. 89–94, but seldom occur in the rest of the Psalter and מעוז does not appear at all. This state of affairs is difficult to explain; it may relate to the history of the Psalter, since the order of the psalms in the three first books is similar in all Psalter manuscripts, while confusion reigns regarding the order in the last two books in the Qumran material, which suggests that these were added later.[58]

---

[56] Baudissin, **Kyrios I**, pp. 453–454 and passim. In the Book of Psalms too $\kappa\acute{v}\rho\iota o\varsigma$ is with few exceptions only equivalent to יהוה. Ibid., pp. 454–456.

[57] Wanke, **Zionstheologie**, pp. 44–46, 48–49, 54, 58.

[58] See Wilson, **Qumran**, pp. 386–387.

6.3.2 The translation as a reflection of a tendency in the Hebrew

LXX only develops further a tendency to reserve a certain vocabulary for the poetic sections of the OT which can be observed in the Massoretic text itself.[59] This is not least the case with words used as divine names. Thus מצודה, מגן, סלע, צור, and מעון, which in MT are commonly employed in a literal sense, have as names of God always been rendered by words which are only used in connection with Yahweh in LXX. The same is true for מעוז and מנוס, even though the words occur as often in metaphorical as in literal meaning. While מצודה, מעוז, מגן, סלע, צור and מעון are the most common words for "rock", "shield", "fortress" and "abode", מחסה, משגב and עז are seldom employed in a literal sense. This may be due to the existence of other Hebrew words with a similar literal meaning, e.g. מבצר, מצודה and בירה. Regarding the use of מחסה in the literal sense, see below.

It could be a chronological development, which would suggest that the literal employment of certain words used as designations of God disappears in the course of time. The literal use of words, which are also employed as inanimate metaphorical designations of God, gradually diminishes. This does not mean that the terms as divine names only occur in late texts, or that texts where, for example, משגב, עז and מצודה are employed in the literal sense are comparatively early, but may suggest that terms which are mostly employed in the literal sense are late-comers, while the ancient divine names or epithets are seldom or not at all used in the literal sense in the OT. These were at least partly a common heritage from the cultural environment of the Ancient Near East.

Originally all the terms under discussion were probably employed both in a literal sense and as divine names or epithets on Israelite soil. This evaluation is strengthened by the fact that שדי is never used in the sense of "mountain" in OT, even though the metaphorical character of the word seems to be confirmed by the equivalents in LXX, while צור and סלע, which may have replaced שדי as a divine name or epithet in certain texts from the OT,[60] are frequently employed in the literal sense. This accords with the suggestion that the temple rock is the most important background for the use of these terms as divine names, see 3.1.2; this would be even more probable if it could be shown that צור as a divine name does not precede the period of the monarchy.[61]

The inanimate metaphorical divine names as a rule belong to the time of the monarchy and the names with a similar meaning do not supersede each other, with the possible exception of מעוז, which seems to supersede an older name of God, מעון. This suggestion is supported by the fact that they never occur in the same texts (see Tables 3 and 4) and are confused in Hebrew texts and in the old versions more often than would be expected from the graphical similarity.[62] It is perfectly in line with this proposal that מעון seldom occurs in the literal sense, except when it refers to the abode of God, i.e. heaven or the Jerusalem temple, while מעוז is much more frequent in the meaning "fortress" or the like. Hugger's proposal that also משגב and מצודה were replaced is possible but hardly probable.[63]

---

[59] See e.g. **Tsevat**, passim.

[60] See especially Freedman, **Divine Names**, p. 71. See 6.2.1. Note that they never occur in the same texts. Ibid., p. 71 and chart C. The exception in chart B.1, Ps 78, is not correct. See also Tables 3 and 4 in this dissertation. צור, סלע are often employed in literal sense, but the relation between literal and metaphorical use are different; צור is often used as a name of God but that is not the case with סלע.

[61] This is also clearly suggested by the texts in which it occurs. Freedman, **Divine Names**, pp. 71, 93. See also chart C in the same article. The oldest text is perhaps Deut 32, which may go back to the end of the time of Judges. Cf. Freedman, **Divine Names**, pp. 55, 79, 96, Knowles, **Rock**, p. 321 n. 28. This could explain the unusual connotations of צור in this chapter. A development in the significance of the metaphor may thus have taken place.

[62] Cf. Wutz, **Transkriptionen**, p. 223.

[63] Hugger, **Zuflucht**, pp. 90–91. Note that they sometimes occur in one and the same context in the

Two possible exceptions to this development must be mentioned, אבן and
אביר. They both occur as divine names in an ancient text, Gen 49:24, but are also
frequently employed in the literal sense. The reflection of אבן in the Vorlage of
LXX, see 5.2.1, does not mean that this was the original text. The text of MT is
evidently corrupt and several proposals regarding the original wording have been
put forward. If this is a 'late' designation of God it probably replaced the older
רעה ישראל for theological reasons. Freedman asserts that אביר יעקב is a name
of God from the early monarchy tied to the traditions of Jerusalem.[64]

Freedman's investigations clearly indicate that שדי and עליון are the oldest of
the names or epithets included in our discussion.[65] Eichhorn's suggestion
regarding the names, which we investigated in chap. 3, that the oldest phase in the
employment of divine metaphorical names or epithets is when the king is the
speaker is not impossible. Most of these designations of God seem to have been
royal prerogatives from the beginning. In that case צור, סלע and מצודה would be
the oldest divine names in our texts,[66] while מעוז, מעון, משגב and מחסה are
late-comers. But his opinion is not really compatible with the suggested development of a poetic vocabulary, with the divine names or epithets as a central
component, even though it supports Hugger's proposal that מצודה in the sense of
"fortress" in a non-poetic context had gone out of use in the late period of kings
and during the exile,[67] and had been replaced by מעוז and משגב. The distribution
of the names or epithets in different books of the Bible seems to be reversely
correlated to their literal employment. This does not pertain only to צבאות, but
seems to be a general trait that applies to most, if not all, of these names or
epithets.

The terms in Qumran and in rabbinical Hebrew

The said development, if it continued after the translation of LXX, could have the
result that the literal meaning of the metaphorical names or epithets under
discussion would be further diminished or even wholly disappear in late Hebrew.
This is also often the case.

סלע, מגן and צור are, as expected, employed in the literal sense also in
rabbinical Hebrew. The meaning of the Hebrew words is based on the combination
of Lewy and Dalman. צור is, however, probably only used in the metaphorical
sense in the Qumran texts. See 1QH 8:23; 11:15; 4QDibHam-a 5:19. In the two
last-mentioned it appears as a designation of God.[68] סלע has literal referents, but
is also used as a metaphor in the Qumran texts. In 1QH 9:28 the term is more or
less a name of God.[69] The meaning "shield" of מגן dominates in the Qumran
manuscripts but the word is also used metaphorically in 1QH 6:27.[70] מעון seems to
be especially employed with reference to the dwelling of God, God's abode. The
profane meaning in biblical Hebrew "hiding-place of animals", "den" is not
evidenced at all. מצודה is only employed in the sense of "net", "trapping tackle",
"hunting", "watch-tower", i.e. as מצודה I. In the form of מצודת the literal meaning
of מצודה II once occurs in a quotation from Judg 6:2, but otherwise the ordinary
root in MT on which the divine name is based seems to have disappeared.[71] The

---

Psalter.

[64] Freedman, **Divine Names**, p. 65.

[65] Freedman, **Divine Names**, pp. 90–92.

[66] Cf. **Eichhorn**, p. 113.

[67] Hugger, **Zuflucht**, pp. 101–102. The literal meaning was, however, not completely forgotten, as can
be seen by the rendering in Aquila. See 6.2.1.

[68] Fabry, צור, col. 983.

[69] Haag, סלע, col. 880.

[70] Freedman, O'Connor, מגן, cols. 655–656.

[71] In 1QH 9:28-29, however, מנוס, משגב, מצודה, סלע, עז are used as divine titles. Cf.

term מחסה, written מחסא, only means "compassion", "pity", "mercy" and not "place of refuge". Both מעוז and משגב have disappeared altogether in rabbinical Hebrew. In the Qumran texts the literal significance of מעוז has vanished. The term means "power", "strength" in 1QH 8:24, 32, 33, and "shelter", "refuge" in 1QH 8:27; 10:23, 32.[72] עז is only employed in the sense of "strength" and never as "fortress".[73]

Thus both the texts from Qumran and the late Hebrew material support the said development. 'The other side of the coin', that the words are commonly employed as divine names or epithets, is, however, only partly evidenced. The literal use of מעוז and משגב, "fortress", in modern Hebrew does not contradict the description given here since its vocabulary is consciously based on the traditional terminology of the Bible. A more detailed chronology of the usage of divine metaphorical names or epithets is hard to compile, chiefly because the dating of the individual texts is highly controversial. If Delekat's suggestion that many of the divine metaphorical names or epithets have been replaced by more common-place names of God during the textual transmission is right the decision becomes even more precarious.

6.4   THE BACKGROUND FOR THE CHOICE OF TRANSLATION TECHNIQUE

6.4.1   The translation of different types of designations of God

The Hebrew terms under discussion, which are used as divine names or epithets are of different types; most are inanimate objects, one refers to man, one has no literal referent and one may denote an animal. One or two of the terms are only employed as designations of God. Generally anthropomorphic metaphors are the most common in the Bible.[74] Moreover, the language of human relationships furnishes the most natural vocabulary for the designations of God, but metaphors are also frequently drawn from both animal life and inanimate nature.[75] But animals are never used as divine names,[76] even though Yahweh is sometimes depicted as, for example, a lion or an eagle, either explicitly, or implicitly.

The equivalents of the investigated divine names or epithets, are as a rule, words which are exclusively employed as designations of God or in close connection with God in LXX. These designations include Greek words which are not semantically related, or poorly related, to the literal meaning of the Hebrew terms they render, but also others that are semantically accurate equivalents. Non-literal equivalents are as a rule employed for the inanimate divine metaphors.

LXX appears to distinguish between inanimate objects and anthropomorphic expressions as metaphorical divine names or epithets. The last-mentioned, contrary to the inanimate objects, are rendered by terms which reflect the literal meaning of the Hebrew. עזד is the only example in our selection of metaphors but the tendency is easily recognized in LXX generally.[77] A similar picture can be seen as regards the non-metaphorical designations of God. Two exceptions must be mentioned, δύναμις, as the rendering of צבאות, and ὕψιστος, as an equivalent of מרום, both of which are semantically accurate hyponyms, despite the fact that these Hebrew terms may refer to inanimate objects. The first-mentioned is in the Old Greek as a rule confined to the Book of Psalms. It also deviates from the

---

Dell'Acqua, **Roccia**, p. 441.

[72] See Zobel, מעוז, cols. 1026–1027, Wagner, עזז, cols. 13–14.

[73] Wagner, עזז, col. 13.

[74] Caird, **Language**, pp. 173–174.

[75] Caird, **Language**, pp. 174, 177.

[76] For a possible exception, see 5.1.

[77] For more examples, see 5.5.2. עזז is divergent because it is an exception to the non-usage of equivalents of inanimate metaphorical names or epithets for anthropological metaphors.

ordinary translation technique of inanimate metaphorical names or epithets because the same equivalent is employed when the word has its literal meaning and when it is a divine name. It is thus not invariably a divine name, as is the case with the other example and the names or epithets in this group generally. An influence from the Kaige recension can perhaps not be ruled out. See 5.9.3.

The equivalents of עז as a divine name seem to reflect the characteristics of both the inanimate metaphorical designations of God and the non-metaphorical designations since it is sometimes translated literally and sometimes with an equivalent from the vocabulary reserved for inanimate metaphorical names or epithets. On the other hand, the noun may sometimes be derived from עוז and have the meaning "refuge". See 5.4.1. But if the LXX translator recognized this sense of the word he would rather have rendered it by καταφυγή.

Metaphorical and non-metaphorical names or epithets

To make a distinction between Hebrew metaphorical and non-metaphorical designations of God is not easy, and even less so if the translators' understanding of these words is taken into account. The metaphorical character[78] varies both between the Hebrew words per se, according to modern lexica and dictionaries and in the understanding of LXX. If the interpretation in the individual books is considered the picture becomes even more complicated. All the investigated divine names or epithets, except שדי and עליון, are also used in a literal sense in MT. שדי probably had the literal meaning "mountain" from the beginning, but no traces of this use can be found in the OT. But in the interpretation in LXX, looked upon as a unity, we have no clear indications that מחסה was regarded as a metaphor, and the same may be true for עז, even though the metaphorical character of the last-mentioned is perhaps indicated by the type and distribution of the equivalents. The translator of the Book of Psalms was probably acquainted with the already translated Old Testament books, but the Psalter text itself does not prove that he knew of a literal meaning of מצודה II, which does not, according to the majority of scholars, occur in that sense in the Book of Psalms. On the other hand, he probably had such a knowledge because there are many indisputable cases with a literal referent outside the Book of Psalms which are so understood also by the LXX translators. מצודה I "hunting-net" may occur once in the Book of Psalms and the translator at least understood that the term must have a literal meaning, even though the rendering may be a guess from the context. See 3.7.2.

משגב is only employed in the literal sense in Is 25:12; 33:16 and Jer 48:1 but the meaning here is not recognized by the translators. Thus, even though it is possible that the translator of the Book of Psalms was familiar with the LXX of Isaiah,[79] his translation is of little help for recognizing a literal sense of משגב. This implies that משגב had become a cultic term and thus the literal meaning of the word had gone out of use when the translator of Isaiah made his translation.[80]

The same type of reasoning is of course applicable to the other books of the LXX. Particularly in cases where the Hebrew word in question only occurs a few times in a literal meaning in a certain book it cannot merely be assumed that the literal significance was recognized by the translator of a different book, if indications to the contrary cannot be found in the book itself. The fact that the metaphorical character of some of the designations of God cannot be taken for granted in the interpretation of the LXX implies that it was not only the image or

---

[78] With the term metaphor I mean a "referential metaphor", a metaphor which is based on something tangible. See Watson, **Poetry**, p. 264.

[79] This is taken for granted in **Flashar**, pp. 181-182, but questioned by Seeligmann, **Isaiah**, pp. 71-74, who emphasizes that the dependence was reversed.

[80] This evaluation is strengthened by the rendering in Aquila, which does not reflect the literal meaning of the term. See 6.2.1.

the fact that the word has a literal referent from inanimate nature, offensive for the theology of the translators, which affected the choice of equivalents. Rather a certain vocabulary was created for divine names and epithets generally. On the other hand, it is possible to argue from the fact that a certain translation technique was employed for the inanimate metaphorical designations of God that these were regarded as metaphors also in LXX. This applies, for example, to משׂגב since it is translated by a term which is frequently used for other metaphorical divine names. See 4.1.

6.4.2   Theological motivations for the rendering of divine names

The motivations for the use of theological exegesis have seldom been defined explicitly in the investigation of divine names even though three reasons for a non-literal rendering can be discerned. One is that the use of inanimate objects as designations of God are derogatory for God's transcendence and majesty. Cf. Erwin who speaks of the "reluctance of the translator(s) to place God in a direct relationship to sensuous things".[81] Another is that any name of God that in literal meaning was an inanimate object could be interpreted literally by ignorant Jews or heathens, especially if these objects were regarded as the embodiment of gods in other religions.[82] A further reason is that if the expression, literally interpreted or not, coincides with a term employed in other religions for their gods, it could create doubts regarding the exclusiveness of Yahweh and his character, especially in a missionary situation.[83]

This attitude could also be based, albeit not explicitly stated by Erwin, on the first commandment, as interpreted in Jewish tradition. In many cases all of these factors could be involved. Theological motivations for the choice of equivalents cannot be excluded in LXX and not least as regards צור and סלע they are probable. See 3.1, 3.2 and below in this dissertation.

6.4.3   The influence of linguistic factors

The topic, the image and the point of similarity

The theological motivation is, however, hardly the only explanation for the choice of translation technique in LXX; there are also linguistic factors involved. These have rarely if ever attracted the attention they deserve. An important aspect that has been overlooked in connection with the rendering of inanimate metaphorical divine names or epithets in LXX is the character of the metaphors in terms of the relation between topic, image and point of similarity.[84]

A metaphor can be described as the overlap of two word meanings.[85] It could also be said that the metaphor works by applying to the primary subject a system of associated implications characteristic of the secondary subject.[86] The interaction

---

[81] Erwin, p. 68.

[82] Cf. Erwin, pp. 65, 76–77.

[83] This was not least the case in Egypt. Cf. Erwin, pp. 66–68.

[84] I have here employed the terminology of a common description of the components of a metaphor. See e.g. Beekman, Callow, pp. 127–131. Other terms, with the same reference, which are sometimes employed are tenor, vehicle and point of comparison. See Watson, Poetry, p. 263. Since "tenor" and "vehicle" are sometimes used for "topic" and "point of similarity", I have avoided these terms which can create terminological confusion. See e.g. Black, Metaphor, p. 294 n. 23.

[85] See Watson, Poetry, p. 263.

[86] Black speaks of the primary (principal) and the secondary (subsidiary) subject, which are more or less to be equated with the topic and the image. Black, Metaphor, pp. 286–287.

view of metaphors as described by M. Black,[87] albeit often regarded as a general theory, is best applicable to creative, live metaphors of some complexity which are highly developed[88] and part of a metaphor system. It is therefore well suited for the animal imagery of Dan 7, 8.[89] Yet it should not be used for the study of metaphorical designations of God in the language of prayer, since it would lead to exaggerated interpretations.[90] The characteristics which are emphasized in this section can be intuitively comprehended by any translator and do not presuppose that the LXX translators had an understanding of modern translation theory. It is not in any way anachronistic.

The terminology chosen fits a substitution or comparison view of metaphors[91] which are rightly criticized as general theories concerning the nature of metaphors. But when it comes to the metaphorical names or epithets under discussion this is an adequate terminology since these are trivial metaphors, not creative metaphors or complex metaphors and rarely part of any metaphor system. In these cases the substitution or comparison views of metaphors are, according to Black, often the most adequate.[92] If, for example, "rock" should be used in a new context where it functions as a creative metaphor the interaction view of metaphor could adequately be applied in a discussion of the metaphor.[93]

The point of similarity, or as it sometimes is termed, the ground,[94] is seldom explicitly marked in these names or epithets in MT,[95] but the topic is as a rule explicit, and also underlined in the texts, i.e. Yahweh, Elohim or other ordinary names of God always precede the metaphor or stand on the same line in the Book of Psalms. Thus that the metaphor refers to God is as a rule clearly marked. This is also true for the names or metaphors studied in chap. 5 of this dissertation. In 91:1 עליון and שדי precede יהוה and אלהי in v. 2. But in v. 9 יהוה and עליון are in parallel with each other. מגן in 119:114 is mentioned before "my God" in v. 115, but not before the address in v. 108 "Lord", who is also referred to in v. 114 "your word". The stress is thus as a rule placed on the topic rather than on the image, i.e. in this case it is the Lord who is emphasized and not that he is called a rock, a shield and so on.[96]

The degree of correspondence between image and topic and between image and point of similarity is probably fairly high. It is easy to associate a fortress, a shield and a rock with the theme "protection" and that Yahweh protects his people accords with his character as revealed in many OT texts. It is, however, not as high as in the anthropomorphic metaphors with a positive point of similarity, e.g. God is described as the one who helps and teaches.[97] A metaphor that consists of an image with a comparison of low correspondence was probably a live metaphor, since literalism, i.e. that the metaphor could be completely substituted by a non-metaphoric word or expression, can hardly arise if the correspondence is low,

---

[87] Black, **Metaphor**. For a handy summary of Black's theory, see Porter, **Metaphors**, pp. 4–6.

[88] See Black, **Metaphor**, pp. 280–281, 292, 294 n. 23. For the meaning of "development", see below.

[89] See the dissertation of P. Porter. Porter, **Metaphors**, p. 4.

[90] Cf. Nielsen, **Håb**, p. 65.

[91] Cf. Beekman, **Callow**, p. 127.

[92] See Black, **Metaphor**, p. 292. He suggests that metaphors could be classified as substitution, comparison, or interaction metaphors, but these are hardly different kinds of metaphor but metaphors in different contexts. One and the same metaphor can very well be a live metaphor in certain contexts and dead in others. See e.g. the discussion in Nielsen, **Håb**, pp. 64–68.

[93] Nielsen, **Håb**, p. 65. But this only applies to the Hebrew metaphor. What is of importance in my investigation is also, and in fact especially, the understanding of the metaphor in LXX.

[94] Watson, **Poetry**, p. 263.

[95] The fact that the inanimate divine metaphorical names mostly or exclusively stand for protection is, contrary to MT, emphasized in the rendering of the LXX.

[96] In the New Testament it sometimes occurs that neither the topic, nor the point of similarity of a metaphor are explicit. The image is of course always more or less explicit, otherwise one cannot speak about a metaphor. See **Beekman, Callow**, pp. 138–140.

[97] Cf. Caird, **Language**, p. 154.

as when God is depicted as a "spring", Jer 2:13, or a "bird-catcher", Hos 7:12.[98]

The development of the metaphor is a factor that works in the opposite direction. A metaphor is said to be highly developed if other metaphors from the same area of origin occur in the vicinity or if it is presented in minute detail in order to drive home a message.[99] A different type of development can be said to have taken place when an expression which explains the meaning of the metaphor occurs in connection with the actual metaphor and thereby actualizes the image. This is the case in some of the passages discussed. See e.g. Ps 18:3 "my rock where I take refuge". In Deut 32:37-38 there is a clear allusion to the literal sense "rock". See 3.1.1. But usually the metaphors are not developed in the actual texts. A factor which works in the same direction is the occurrence of similes for God based on the same term as was used for the metaphorical epithet, since the image is then also stressed. But similes based on the epithets under discussion never occur.[100]

Metaphors belonging to metaphor systems[101] lend themselves more readily to a high development. But there are hardly any examples thereof in my material, even though מגן may be included in a military metaphor system. Cf. Ps 35:1-3. This is not the case with משגב and מעוז, although they are often used in a literal sense in a military context. This especially applies to the last-mentioned. See 3.4.2. A low correspondence as well as a high development keep metaphors alive. The accumulation of different metaphors, which often occurs in the case of divine epithets, e.g. Ps 18:3 par.; 31:3-4; 71:3; 144:1-2, impels the reader to emphasize the topic and the point of similarity rather than the image.[102] This is not least the case when the images are taken from different spheres of life, as often happens in my texts. Cf. Ps 18:3 "The LORD is my rock, and my fortress, my deliverer, my God, my rock in whom I take refuge, my shield and the horn of my salvation, my stronghold", where metaphors from at least four fields are combined; nature, defences, weapons and animals (or maybe altars as a place of asylum).

The point of similarity is particularly emphasized if all the metaphors are congruent in meaning. This applies to the accumulation of divine metaphors in the Book of Psalms. See, for example, Ps 18:3 where all the metaphors reinforce the underlying semantic parameters of "rock", i.e. "firm", "protective".[103] The stress on the point of similarity automatically makes the image less prominent. From this it is evident that the image is the factor which has received the least attention in the text of MT and this may be reflected in the rendering of LXX.

The frequency of the terms

Another factor that may have contributed to the lexicalized character[104] of the divine names or epithets under discussion is that most of the metaphors are only rarely employed in the literal sense in the OT. They are often part of a psalm-language and therefore seldom used in profane contexts. Not only the frequency of the terms in the literal meaning is an important factor in this respect, but also the frequency of the metaphors[105] per se and in relation to the literal use. If the

---

[98] Caird, **Language**, pp. 155, 189.

[99] This is sometimes described as an extended metaphor. Watson, **Poetry**, p. 269.

[100] An alternative word for shield, צנה, is employed at least once as a simile in connection with God. Cf. Ps 5:13.

[101] A group of metaphors linked together by their common area of origin, such as farming, warfare, family, sport, law. Caird, **Language**, p. 155.

[102] Cf. Caird, **Language**, p. 190.

[103] Watson, **Poetry**, p. 265. This function is called "reinforcement of parameters". Ibid., p. 265.

[104] A worn out or dead metaphor is sometimes labelled a lexicalized metaphor. Watson, **Poetry**, p. 264.

[105] Cf. **Beekman, Callow**, pp. 134-135.

term was often employed both as a metaphor and literally it could make the image more conspicuous even though this factor is probably less significant, which can be seen by the frequency of "heart", "eyes" as dead metaphors in Hebrew, in Greek and in English. On the other hand, a metaphor which is seldom employed in the literal sense or from the point of view of the translator, known in the literal sense, easily becomes a dead metaphor. That the last-mentioned relation has changed in the course of time towards an infrequent use of the literal sense of the words under discussion we have seen earlier in this dissertation. The frequency of the metaphor per se and in relation to the literal use affects the 'living conditions' of the image. A term that frequently occurs as a metaphor, especially if it is always employed in the same sense, is rapidly worn out.

Not only the Hebrew metaphors wear out, as a similar development could be suggested concerning the Greek equivalents. κύριος, the most common designation of God in LXX, apart from θεός, is reserved for Yahweh and Yahweh is always rendered by κύριος in the older part of the LXX books but the Scriptures tend to use this name also for other Hebrew terms, and to translate Yahweh with other names. This is sporadically evidenced in the Psalter, Daniel, 1 Esdras, the additions to Esther, but is especially marked in Sirach, Proverbs and Job. The choice of translation equivalents probably reflects a process where the semantic meaning of the Greek term has been blurred,[106] since it is hardly probable that the distinctive character of יהוה has been expunged. Thus a certain interaction between the Hebrew terms and their Greek counterparts, which has facilitated the interchange of different equivalents, cannot be excluded.

Traditional divine names or epithets from the Ancient Near East

The life of a metaphor would also be influenced if it was part of a traditional cultic language from the Near East,[107] which more or less mechanically may have been taken over by the Israelites. In that case the metaphors were probably in common use in worship for a long time before they were written down in the OT. This of course wears them out. If the divine names or epithets were part of a traditional language the possibility that the metaphors were dead is increased.[108]

On the other hand, if they belong to traditions with which people were familiar the metaphors were kept alive. This may be the case with צור and סלע, which are probably connected with traditions concerning the sacred rock in the temple of Jerusalem. But the relation between the temple rock and these Hebrew metaphors is not emphasized in the context of the divine names, even though references to the temple rock in Jerusalem may occur in two texts where צור is an ordinary metaphor, Ps 27:5; 61:5.[109] The frequent employment of both of them in the literal sense could also keep them alive.

None of the divine names or epithets is a creative metaphor[110] in the text of the Hebrew. This is understandable since the liturgical language, not least the language of prayer, is as a rule traditional. On the other hand, in certain cases

---

[106] Cf. Baudissin, Kyrios I, pp. 438-480, ibid., Kyrios II, pp. 15-17.

[107] Divine names or epithets tended to be metaphorical also in Akkadian texts. Watson, Poetry, p. 266. Certain of the names or epithets or at least types of divine designation have also been found in countries surrounding Israel, e.g. עליון, שדי, אביר, מגן, צור.

[108] For the term and the function of a dead metaphor, see Beekman, Callow, pp. 131-133, Caird, Language, pp. 66-67, 152-153, 191.

[109] See 3.1.2. Cf. Delekat, Asylie, p. 379, who says that it never occurs as a divine name "mit klarem Bezug auf einen konkreten Felsen". But cf. Deut 32:37-38; Is 17:10; 26:4; 30:29. Ibid., p. 379. If the connection with the original tradition is reinforced in the texts in which the metaphors occur they are much more easily kept alive.

[110] An invention by the poet himself or a worn-out expression provided with a new twist. Watson, Poetry, pp. 264-265. Cf. Caird, Language, pp. 152, 191, Nielsen, Håb, p. 67.

where the metaphor is employed in an ironical sense it may be described as creative, since it is then provided with a new twist. This applies to צוּר, Deut 32:31, 37; Is 8:14; Jer 2:27; 21:13; 31:9; 51:25, see 3.1.1 and maybe אֶבֶן, Is 8:14, see 5.2, מַחְסֶה, Is 28:15, see 3.5.2, and מָעוֹן, Jer 21:13, see 3.6.3. The irony has not influenced the equivalents in LXX, probably because it was never noticed by the translators.

The metaphorical designations in the eyes of the translators

We may conclude that from the point of view of the Hebrew many of the metaphors under discussion were probably dead or worn out, but this does not automatically mean that they were dead for the translators too,[111] since their understanding of the character of the Hebrew also depends on their familiarity with the language. If they only understood it as foreigners, they may not have recognized the character of the metaphors. A person less versed in a language is wont to interpret the metaphors more literally than one for whom Hebrew is the mother tongue. One can only speculate regarding the translators' knowledge of Hebrew in this respect.[112]

An additional factor must also be taken into account, the translation technique. Thus the rendering of the inanimate divine metaphors must be seen in relation to the translation technique of the individual LXX translator, since the primary sense of a term may be reflected in the translation even though it was not spontaneously called to mind by the translator, since his translation technique may have demanded a literal rendering of the Hebrew metaphors.[113]

6.4.4   The evaluation of different factors of influence

The employment of non-figurative renderings of inanimate divine metaphors, which for the most part were dead in the Hebrew, is with few exceptions the rule in LXX as a whole. This would a priori suggest that the main reason for the choice of equivalents for these names or epithets was that the metaphors were dead, but the same fact calls for an explanation of the consistent translation technique, since there are great differences between the LXX translators as regards the degree of literality, including the non-figurative rendering of metaphors. A theory of worn out metaphors as the best or the only explanation of this state of affairs is also contradicted inasmuch as stereotyped equivalents exist for these metaphors, the rules laid down for the choice of alternative renderings are rather mechanical, and the same translation technique in this respect can be seen in LXX as a whole.

If the metaphors were completely dead this could perhaps imply that they were interchangeable in the Hebrew and the same is true for the equivalents in the Greek, but this is not an adequate description of the situation. The interchangeability of terms presupposes that the point of similarity of the divine metaphors is identical or that the translator so understood them. But this is hardly always the case, even though the theme of protection clearly dominates in the choice of equivalents. It would have been most natural if some of the metaphors were translated literally and some figuratively, since there are features which suggest that certain of the metaphors were more living than others. This applies to צוּר and

---

[111] The meaning of the metaphor also depends on the interpretation of the reader or listener, whose understanding defines the character of the metaphor. Cf. Nielsen, **Håb**, p. 56.

[112] See the discussion in Olofsson, **LXX Version**, pp. 28–32 with references.

[113] Cf. Olofsson, **LXX Version**, pp. 16–20. For example, the translation of Aquila can hardly tell us anything about how he understood the character of the biblical metaphors since his philosophy of translation demanded a literal rendering.

to a certain extent also to סלע. A purely linguistic explanation of the renderings of the names or epithets of God to some extent demands that these have in the Book of Psalms worn out more than other metaphors, because we only have sporadic examples of a free translation of dead metaphors, e.g. לב, נפש, בשר and יד, in the more literally translated parts of the LXX, including the Book of Psalms. This may of course partly depend on different translators' understanding of the degree to which the metaphors are living. In the evaluation of this situation one must also take into account the fact that many literal equivalents were also used as metaphors in the Greek. This is the case with, inter alia, $\kappa\alpha\rho\delta\iota\alpha$, $\psi\upsilon\chi\acute{\eta}$ and $\sigma\acute{\alpha}\rho\xi$. They all had an extensive metaphorical use in Greek, with meanings similar to those of their counterparts in the Hebrew.

An explanation based on linguistic factors only is less probable also because the development of the translation technique is not straightforward in the LXX,[114] nor in the other Greek versions. For example, Symmachus and Theodotion break the development towards a strictly literal translation and some parts of the Septuagint which were translated later display an extremely free translation technique. The growing tendency towards literalism, not least in the recensions of the LXX, depends on many different factors.[115] But it has no connection with the development of the Hebrew tongue, especially not that Hebrew ceased to be a living language in Palestine and Egypt.[116]

6.4.5   The milieu of the inanimate metaphorical designations of God

The milieu and the text of MT and LXX

Bertram's suggestion that the names discussed in chap. 3 had a Sitz im Leben in the liturgy of the synagogue accords with certain of the observed phenomena, e.g. that semantic accuracy is not the primary aim in the translation of these names, that they are to a certain extent interchangeable in both MT and LXX, that one of the reasons for the making of LXX was probably the need for a text for use in the liturgy.[117]

The strongest argument for the proposed Sitz im Leben, the synagogue prayers or more generally, the liturgy of the synagogue, is that it could give a reasonable explanation of the unity of approach in LXX concerning the divine names or epithets, as well as the use of a certain vocabulary exclusively for certain metaphorical designations of God, which are unexpected in view of the great differences as regards translation techniques and choice of equivalents between LXX books. Not only the general translation technique but also the treatment of ordinary metaphors in the individual books are far from uniform. Even though the translators worked independently of each other and were separated in time and some maybe also in space, the collective experience of being a loyal Jew and the attachment to the services of the synagogue probably constituted a bond.[118]

Although the Hagiographa, according to the usual understanding, were excluded from the lectionary of the synagogue, the psalms of the Psalter, as prayers or

---

[114] See Olofsson, **LXX Version**, p. 8 n. 72, 73.

[115] See Barr, **Typology**, pp. 324-325.

[116] Cf. Olofsson, **LXX Version**, p. 8 and n. 72, 73, p. 29 and n. 237. Not least the circles around Rabbi Akiba, with which Aquila was probably associated, were affected by a revival of the Hebrew language.

[117] Olofsson, **LXX Version**, p. 9 and n. 77. Liturgical notes are also sometimes reflected in the text of LXX. Olofsson, op. cit., pp. 9-10 and n. 85, 86.

[118] Olofsson, **LXX Version**, pp. 3-4, 9, and n. 77. This was a bond that in fact even connected the divine services of Judaism and Christianity, since it is universally admitted that a continuity exists between the liturgy of the Christian church and that of the synagogue, which in turn was partly modelled on the temple service. Werner, **Bridge I**, pp. 18-21, 22-26.

chants, played an important role in the early Jewish liturgy.[119] The Psalter, where most of the inanimate divine metaphorical names or epithets occur and where the unified approach is most visible, was in fact of paramount importance generally for the structure and development of the temple service as well as the synagogue service.[120] There are also indications that some sort of regular psalm lesson, either chanted or read, was employed in the ancient synagogue[121] in connection with the readings of the Pentateuch.[122] This does not change the fact that the most prominent role was played by the texts of the Pentateuch, and a less prominent by the prophetic corpus. Even though an official, consecutive reading of the Pentateuch cannot be proved before the first century A.D. some texts were evidently in use in the Jewish liturgy from early pre-Christian time. One of these texts is Deut 32, where both עליון and צור are employed as designations of God.[123]

A few psalms in LXX have superscriptions with liturgical designations which indicate that they were used in the temple service.[124] Even though Pietersma probably rightly regards them as additions to the original text[125] they may testify to the use of the Psalter in the liturgy of the synagogue. But only two of the psalms with superscriptions that include extra-Massoretic additions in LXX were later employed regularly in the service of the synagogue, 91 (92); 92 (93).[126] Ps 91 (92) together with many other psalms was used on the sabbath, which is in line with the wording of the superscription in both LXX and MT.[127]

Certain facts speak against the proposed Sitz im Leben: that hardly any counterparts to the names or epithets are found in rabbinic literature or in the Targums, which are closely connected with the synagogue, the scarcity of some of the terms, viz. ἀντιλήμπτωρ, ὑπερασπισμός, κραταίωμα, per se (see 4.1, 4.2), and in the NT, that the other Greek translations show no clear influence thereof (see 6.2), even though at least Aquila was closely connected with the synagogue.[128] This explanation does not imply that whole text passages have been assimilated to the synagogue liturgy,[129] or that the text of the Septuagint consists of isolated readings from the service of the synagogue, later revised and declared to be the authentic version.[130] It only suggests that the choice of a specific vocabulary employed by the translators for the designations of God under discussion has been influenced by the names or epithets used in the prayers of the synagogue or by the synagogue service generally.

The milieu and the linguistic and theological factors

Bertram's suggestion concerning the Sitz im Leben of these names (see 4.2) has thus much in its favour, even though no proofs can be adduced that the individual words per se were employed in the service of the synagogue. The linguistic explanation and the proposed Sitz im Leben by no means exclude each other. Only the absence of a literal translation could be at least partly explained by the

[119] Werner, Bridge I, p. 55.
[120] Werner, Bridge I, pp. 133, 144-148 and passim.
[121] Werner, Bridge II, pp. 73-74, 98.
[122] Beyerlin, Ps 52, p. 126 and n. 312, Werner, Bridge II, pp. 97-100 with references. For a more comprehensive discussion see Arens, Gottesdienst, pp. 160-202.
[123] See Patte, Hermeneutic, p. 36 and n. 30.
[124] See Olofsson, LXX Version, p. 9 n. 80-82.
[125] Pietersma, David, pp. 214, 219-226. Cf. Pietersma, Manuscripts, pp. 52-53 n. 1.
[126] Cf. Werner, Bridge I, p. 145.
[127] See BHK, BHS. Cf. van der Kooij, Origin, p. 73.
[128] But in the synagogue of Palestine Aramaic was of course the language that would have influenced Aquila rather than Greek.
[129] Cf. Olofsson, LXX Version, p. 10 and n. 86, 87.
[130] Cf. Seeligmann, Isaiah, pp. 1-2, Olofsson, LXX Version, p. 10, n. 87, pp. 40-41.

suggestion of worn out metaphors, which were perhaps especially common as regards the divine names or epithets, because of the frequent employment of the terms in the temple service, while the actual choice of equivalents was influenced by the prayer language of the synagogue.

In this case theological considerations also obviously played a part, but not mainly as local theological biases on the part of the translators from a conjectured anachronistic Philo-like milieu, not even as a reflection of a anti-anthropomorphic development, evidenced in later books of the OT, in the Apocrypha and in pseude-pigraphical literature. Rather they are the continuation of a development, which can be seen in rudimentary form in the Hebrew text itself, to reserve certain words for inanimate divine metaphorical names or epithets and some other designations of God. Tsevat's statistics point towards the existence of a poetic sublanguage in the Hebrew OT of which the divine metaphorical names or epithets are a part. The question of whether this is reflected, or perhaps even further developed, in LXX is outside the scope of this dissertation, but would be an interesting object for research. On the other hand, few of the equivalents of the inanimate divine names discussed in chap. 3 were in non-biblical Greek especially reserved for religious use. See 4.2. In fact the opposite seems to have been the case; they are as a rule words devoid of religious connotations, and some of them also occur very seldom, and were perhaps on that account suitable for inclusion in a group of names or epithets of Yahweh, since they lacked specific associations to pagan religions. Thus theological motivations cannot be excluded for the choice of this specific vocabulary.

Otherwise it cannot be shown to be a general objective of the LXX translators to avoid words which were frequently employed in other religions. ὕψιστος and παντοκράτωρ are good examples in this respect, even though their employment in Hellenistic literature may well have been strongly influenced by the usage in LXX. The Septuagint had a tremendous influence on the Hellenistic literature, inasmuch as the terms qualifying God in LXX are very often used in the Hellenistic Jewish writings. This is in fact the case with most of the divine names or epithets as well as with words which denote the activities or qualities of God generally. Only one fourth of the words employed for God in the Hellenistic Jewish literature do not occur in the LXX.[131] The terms that cannot be found in LXX are as a rule formal variants of expressions which are used in the Greek Bible. Furthermore, the most common divine names or epithets occur in the Septuagint.[132] Thus Jews who wrote original works in Greek were for the most part content to use the religious vocabulary found in LXX, but this, at least as regards the inanimate divine names, is a vocabulary that was often for the first time employed in a religious sense in LXX.

---

[131] Marcus, **Divine Names**, pp. 46-47.

[132] Marcus, **Divine Names**, p. 48.

Chapter VII

SUMMARY

The diverse examples of theological exegesis, i.e. anti-anthropomorphisms and theological toning down, which have been scrutinized in this dissertation could in most cases be otherwise explained. A reluctance to translate expressions for seeing God literally can indeed be evidenced in LXX, but the choice of equivalents is rarely based on conscious theological exegesis, being rather a reflection of the translators' linguistic conception of the expressions in question. A certain influence from the Pentateuch translation as well as the unconscious search for theological consistency within the Scriptures also played an important part. Thus although theological factors are probably involved here it is hardly a question of a deliberate theological exegesis on the part of the translator; the situation is far more complicated.

My investigation does not confirm theories which have been submitted regarding the influence of different types of theological toning down in LXX Psalms. The equivalents in LXX on which these theories are based in fact often accord with the usual understanding of the Hebrew terms in question in the Book of Psalms and sometimes in LXX as a whole, whether or not it is a question of designations of God. The LXX translator seldom knew the exact meaning of the words and then used a generic term from which the reader could at least infer his understanding of the text. Often it is a question of favourite words intended to disguise the translator's deficient knowledge of the Hebrew. They are not always guesses based on the context since some of these favourite words hardly fit the meaning of the terms therein. This is even more pronounced as regards another remedy for the translator's linguistic shortcomings, the Verlegenheitsübersetzung, which at the same time to some degree reflects his fidelity to the Hebrew text. Guesses would have given a much more readable translation.

There are cases in my material where the possibility that some kind of theological exegesis was involved cannot be excluded, but the motivation for the rendering which have been given are not always adequate. No general pattern of theological toning down can be discerned, at least if the examples of Erwin and Fritsch are taken as representative examples of theological exegesis. The methodical insights are the most important for this section of my dissertation. I believe that my presuppositions regarding the best methodology for an investigation of theological exegesis, which are stated in the general introduction, have to some degree been validated in this study of selected examples from other scholars. Even though these methodical presuppositions are more or less obvious they are in fact sometimes overlooked in the investigations of theological exegesis. The methodology has often been the Achilles' heel of such studies. Apart from giving simpler and better explanations to certain renderings in LXX which have been understood as manifestations of theological exegesis this method can also help to select those examples of the translators' theological bias which may prove to be valid.

We have been able to demonstrate a marked difference in the translation between the Hebrew words from the sphere of inanimate nature when they are divine epithets or names and when they occur in other connections in LXX as a whole. This dissimilarity as a rule does not depend on a deficient knowledge of the literal meaning of the terms. It is also evident that the equivalents in LXX are not chosen in order to express the significance of the word as metaphor and even less its literal meaning. On at least two occasions, however, the metaphorical sense of the Greek terms seem to have played a part in the choice of equivalent. In the case of "rock" as a name of God, a literal translation could have conveyed a misleading impression of the meaning of the metaphor while "horn" in Greek adequately expresses the metaphorical sense of the Hebrew. The literal translation of "horn", which is an exception to the rule that the inanimate metaphorical names are rendered freely in LXX, can thus be plausibly explained. Why "tower" as a divine name, 60 (61):4, is translated literally is harder to comprehend.

The translation of divine titles in LXX Psalms is as we have seen not stereotypical, even though an ordinary rendering is used in most cases. But the reason for a non-employment of the main rendering is as a rule easily recognized. The most important motive is the endeavour to have different Greek equivalents for Hebrew terms when they occur in parallel or in conjunction with each other, terms which normally had one and the same equivalent. The technique is also sometimes employed when a Hebrew term occurs twice in close proximity or in parallel. This trait is also to a certain degree visible outside the Psalter, but can only be demonstrated as regards a few of the names or epithets, because most of these designations of God occur only sporadically outside LXX Psalms.

The background of the meaning of the terms as metaphors often derives from their function when they are employed in a literal sense. They are often concerned with "protection", "refuge", mostly as a refuge from enemies but are also used for defence in a cultic sense, e.g. the temple rock. The "rock" occurs also as a hiding place from enemies. It is probable that especially the "rock-metaphor" is tied to specific religious traditions, not least the so-called Zion tradition. Connections between "the rock" and cultic practices are also evidenced to a certain degree.

Most of the terms under discussion occur very seldom in a literal meaning; they are more or less confined to a metaphorical use and to poetical language. This is a trait that is further developed in LXX. Thus a certain vocabulary is created in the translation that is reserved for inanimate metaphorical divine names or epithets. These are with few exceptions rendered by terms which are only used in connection with God in LXX, even though most of the Hebrew equivalents are also employed in a literal sense in MT. The distribution of the names or epithets in different books of the Bible seems to be reversely correlated to their literal employment. On the other hand, few of the equivalents of the inanimate divine names or epithets are reserved in non-biblical Greek for a religious use. On the contrary, they are often employed in a profane context. This may also be one of the reasons why they were selected. Some of the names or epithets in LXX are used as designations for other gods, but the reason for this state of affairs may as well be that LXX has influenced the usage in a Jewish-Hellenistic context as vice versa.

The equivalents in LXX could reflect a chronological development in the vocabulary of the Hebrew language, since the literal use of words, which are also employed as inanimate metaphorical divine names or epithets, seems to be gradually diminishing. In that way the point of similarity, rather than the image, is stressed. The most ancient divine names or epithets, are seldom or never used in a literal sense in the OT. These were evidently a heritage from the cultural milieu of the Ancient Near East. Some of the other titles of God also have counterparts in the countries surrounding Israel and may have been borrowed at a later date, but they may as well be genuine Israelite designations. Most of the inanimate metaphorical divine names or epithets probably belong to the period of the monarchy. Some of the terms, which are seldom used in a literal sense in LXX, have lost their literal meaning in late Hebrew, but not all of them are employed as divine names or epithets. A few of the words have in fact disappeared altogether in rabbinical Hebrew. On the other hand, a change in the frequency of use of different senses of these Hebrew words can hardly be the principal explanation for the choice of equivalents in LXX. In that case the other Greek versions would show a similar translation technique (with the possible exception of Aquila). But, apart from Quinta, which seems to have some connections with LXX, this is definitely not the case. It is true that the technique of Peshitta and the Targum shows similarities with LXX, but Peshitta and the Targums depend on the LXX to a certain degree, at least in the Book of Psalms, and the written Targums are often late and therefore may not be the best comparison material.

A distinction is obviously made between inanimate objects and anthropomorphic expressions as metaphorical divine names or epithets. The anthropomorphic metaphors, unlike those based on inanimate nature, are rendered by terms which reflect the literal meaning of the Hebrew. The same is of course true for the non-metaphorical designations of God. But it is not always possible to distinguish between Hebrew metaphorical and non-metaphorical designations of God, and even less so if the translators' understanding of these words is taken into account. Some of the names, e.g. מחסה, עז, משגב, were perhaps not regarded as metaphors in LXX. Animals are never used as divine names or epithets, even though Yahweh is sometimes depicted with imagery taken from the animal world. The metaphorical language in general in the OT is frequently drawn from animal life and from inanimate nature, but the language of human relationships furnishes the most natural vocabulary for divine metaphorical names or epithets. All these factors weaken a purely linguistic explanation of the choice of equivalents in LXX. See below.

Two kinds of theological motives may have been involved in the rendering of the divine names or epithets under discussion. One is based on the similarity or identity with archaic or contemporary titles of divine beings outside the religion of Israel, which could create doubts regarding the exclusivity of Yahweh, the other is based on a tendency to emphasize his transcendence, and thereby free him from associations with material objects. These motives are understandable in the religio-cultural situation of Jewry in the diaspora with its strong missionary ambitions, and also compatible with a religious development within Jewish religion in the last centuries B.C.

But theological motives are not the only reason for the translation technique in LXX, linguistic factors are also involved. Thus the point of similarity and the topic rather than the image of the metaphor are as a rule emphasized in the actual texts. Furthermore, the correspondence between the point of similarity of the metaphor and the topic is often close, and the same is true for the image and the point of similarity. The metaphors are seldom developed in the texts and do not serve as similes for God. They are rarely part of a metaphor system. Clusters of metaphors are common. In the Book of Psalms in particular divine metaphors from different spheres of life are accumulated. All these factors contribute to the conclusion that the metaphors in question are in most passages not creative, living images, but more or less stereotypes for the protection and help of God. This is further emphasized through the interchangeability of some of the terms. As regards צור and סלע the situation is different, since these terms are tied to living religious traditions and sometimes used ironically with reference to man or to other gods. The first-mentioned has also sometimes retained the connection with a literal rock in the Hebrew text. Both are frequently employed in a literal sense. These are factors which keep metaphors alive. Thus these linguistic factors cannot per se explain the common translation technique for all the names or epithets throughout LXX. But they may well have contributed to the choice of non-literal equivalents.

Bertram's suggestion that the Sitz im Leben of these designations of God is the prayer language of the synagogue has much in its favour, even though no proofs that the individual words per se were employed therein can be given. First and foremost it can explain that the same pattern is visible in LXX as a whole, despite the differences in translation technique between the individual books. The linguistic factors, the theological exegesis and the proposed Sitz im Leben do not in any way rule out each other. They can all contribute to a better understanding of the translation technique of the LXX in this regard.

7.1 ABBREVIATIONS

AASF	Annales Academiae Scientiarum Fennicae
AB	The Anchor Bible
AJSL	American Journal of Semitic Languages & Literatures
AnBib	Analecta Biblica
ASV	The American Standard Version
ATD	Das Alte Testament Deutsch
AltAbh	Alttestamentliche Abhandlungen
BA	Biblical Archaeologist
BASOR	Bulletin of the American Schools of Oriental Research
BEThL	Bibliotheca Ephemeridum Theologicarum Lovaniensium
Bib	Biblica
BO	Bibliotheca Orientalis
BKAT	Biblischer Kommentar Altes Testament
BulSeptStud	Bulletin of the International Organization for Septuagint and Cognate Studies
BZ	Biblische Zeitschrift
BWAT	Beiträge zur Wissenschaft vom Alten (und Neuen) Testament
CollBiblLat	Collectanea Biblica Latina
CBQ	Catholic Biblical Quarterly
CBQMS	Catholic Biblical Quarterly. Monograph Series
ConBib.OT	Coniectanea Biblica. Old Testament Series
ConBib.NT	Coniectanea Biblica. New Testament Series
DissHumLitt	Dissertationes Humanarum Litterarum
EJ	Encyclopedia Judaica
GrRByz	Greek, Roman and Byzantine Studies
HAT	Handbuch zum Alten Testament
HKAT	Handkommentar zum Alten Testament
HSM	Harvard Semitic Monographs
HUBP	The Hebrew University Bible Project
HUCA	Hebrew Union College Annual
HUCAMon	Hebrew Union College Annual Monographs
ICC	The International Critical Commentary
JbProtTheol	Jahrbücher für Protestantische Theologie
JBL	Journal of Biblical Literature
JBLMon	Journal of Biblical Literature. Monograph Series
JerB	The Jerusalem Bible
JQR	Jewish Quarterly Review
JSocStud	Jewish Social Studies
JSOT	Journal for the Study of the Old Testament
JSOT Suppl	Journal for the Study of the Old Testament. Supplement Series
JSS	Journal of Semitic Studies
JStJud	Journal for the Study of Judaism
JTS	Journal of Theological Studies
KAT	Kommentar zum Alten Testament
KHAT	Kurzer Handkommentar zum Alten Testament
LUÅ	Lunds Universitets Årsskrift
MSU	Mitteilungen des Septuaginta-Unternehmens der Akademie der Wissenshaften in Göttingen
NCB	New Century Bible
NEB	The New English Bible
NICOT	The New International Commentary on the Old Testament
OBO	Orbis Biblicus Orientalis
OTL	Old Testament Library
OTS	Oudtestamentische Studien
PAAJR	Proceedings of the American Academy for Jewish Research
RB	Revue Biblique

RSV	The Revised Standard Version
SBL	Society of Biblical Literature
RQ	Revue de Qumran
SeptCogStud	Septuagint and Cognate Studies
SEÅ	Svensk Exegetisk Årsbok
SubsB	Subsidia Biblica
TEV	Good News Bible. The Bible in Today's English Version
TextEstCisn	Textos y Estudios del Seminario Filologico 'Cardenal Cisneros' de la Biblia Poliglota Matritense de l'Instituto 'Arias Montano'
TFor	Theologische Forschung
TThSt	Trier Theologische Studien
UF	Ugarit-Forschungen
WBC	Word Biblical Commentary
VT	Vetus Testamentum
VTS	Supplements to Vetus Testamentum
WeltOr	Welt des Orients
WestThJ	Westminster Theological Journal
ZAW	Zeitschrift für die alttestamentliche Wissenschaft
ZNT	Zeitschrift für die neutestamentliche Wissenschaft

Table 1

Ordinary and alternative equivalents in the Psalter

Hebrew	OE	AE	AE	AE
צור	θεος 13	βοηθος 4	βοηθεια 1	αντιλημπτωρ 1
סלע	στερεωμα 2	κραταιωμα 1	αντιλημπτωρ 1	
מגן	υπερασπιστης 10	αντιλημπτωρ 2		
מעוז	υπερασπιστης 5	βοηθος 1	κραταιωμα 1	
מחסה	ελπις 7	βοηθος 2	καταφυγη 1	αντιλημπτωρ 1
מעון	καταφυγη 2	υπερασπιστης 1		
מצודה	καταφυγη 6			
משגב	αντιλημπτωρ 9	καταφυγη 2	βοηθος 1	
אביר	θεος 2			
קרן	κερας 1			
מרום	υψιστος 1	υψος 2		
עז	βοηθος 3	ισχυς 2	δυναμις 2	κραταιωμα 1
עז		κραταιος 1	βοηθεια 1	
עזר	βοηθος 9			
עזרה	βοηθος 3			
עליון	υψιστος 21			
צבאות	δυναμις 15			
שדי	ο θεος του ουρανου 1		ο επουρανιος 1	

Remarks:

Column markings:

OE = It is the ordinary equivalent of the term as a divine name or epithet.

AE = It is an alternative equivalent of the term as a divine name or epithet.

The statistics includes also divine names or epithets in LXX regardless of whether they are such epithets in MT, but not designations of God in MT which are interpreted in a different way in LXX.

Emendations based on LXX are also included. βοηθος can only tentatively be regarded as an ordinary equivalent of עז. עזר in the Tables refers to both עֵזֶר and עֹזֵר.

Table 2

Ordinary and alternative equivalents outside the Psalter

Hebrew	OE	AE	AE	AE
צור	θεος 7	φυλαξ 4	κυριος 1	μεγας 1
צור		δικαιος 1	κτιστης 1	
מגן	υπερασπιστης 2			
מעוז	βοηθος 2	βοηθεια 1		
מחסה		σκεπη 1		
אביר		ισχυς 1	θεος 1	δυναστος 1
אבן		ο κατισχυσας 1		
קרן	κερας 1			
עז	βοηθος 1	ισχυς 2	δοξα 1	
עזר	βοηθος 2			
מרום	υψιστος 2	υψος 1		
אל שדי	ο θεος μου 7	θεου Σαδδαι 1		
שדי	θεος 3	παντοκρατωρ 16 κυριος παντοκρατωρ 1		
שדי	(κυριος 10)	ο τα παντα ποιησας 1		
עליון	υψιστος 10			
צבאות	παντοκρατωρ 127			
	(σαβαωθ 61)			
	(δυναμις 7)			

Remarks:
Column markings:
See Table 1.
Comments:
δικαιος may be based on a different *Vorlage*. See Table 4. κυριος is the ordinary equivalent in the Book of Job, while σαβαωθ and δυναμις are the ordinary equivalents in Isaiah and the Psalter. The use of the term alternative equivalent does not *per se* imply that an ordinary equivalent of the metaphor exists.

Table 3

Renderings of divine names and epithets in the Psalter

Passage	Hebrew	Greek	DE	OE	AE	SC	Comment
3:4	מגן	αντιλημπτωρ			X		
7:18	עליון	υψιστος	X		X		
9:3	עליון	υψιστος	X		X		
9:10	משׂגב	καταφυγη		X			Var.
9:10	משׂגב	βοηθος		X			Var.
9:35 (10:14)	עזר	βοηθος	X		X		Lit.
13 (14):6	מחסה	ελπις	X				
17 (18):3	סלע	στερεωμα	X				
17 (18):3	מצודה	καταφυγη	X				
17 (18):3	צור	βοηθος		X			Var.
17 (18):3	מגן	υπερασπιστης	X				
17 (18):3	קרן	κερας	X		X		Lit.
17 (18):14	עליון	υψιστος	X		X		
17 (18):31	מגן	υπερασπιστης	X				
17 (18):32	צור	θεος	X				
17 (18):47	צור	θεος	X				
18 (19):15	צור	βοηθος		X			Greek
20 (21):8	עליון	υψιστος	X		X		
23 (24):10	צבאות	δυναμις	X		X		Lit.
26 (27):1	מעוז	υπερασπιστης	X				
26 (27):9	עזרה	βοηθος	X		X		Lit.
27 (28):1	צור	θεος	X				
27 (28):7	עז	βοηθος	X?				
27 (28):7	מגן	υπερασπιστης	X				
27 (28):8	עז	κραταιωμα		X?	X		
27 (28):8	מעוז	υπερασπιστης	X				
29 (30):11	עזר	βοηθος	X?		X		Lit.
30 (31):3	צור	θεος	X				
30 (31):3	מעוז	υπερασπιστης	X				
30 (31):3	מצודה	καταφυγη	X				
30 (31):4	סלע	κραταιωμα		X?			
30 (31):4	מצודה	καταφυγη	X				
30 (31):5	מעוז	υπερασπιστης	X				
32 (33):20	עזר	βοηθος	X		X		Lit.
32 (33):20	מגן	υπερασπιστης	X				
36 (37):9	מעוז	υπερασπιστης	X				
39 (40):18	עזרה	βοηθος	X		X		Lit.
39 (40):18	מפלט	υπερασπιστης		X			
41 (42):10	סלע	αντιλημπτωρ		X?			Cont.
42 (43):2	מעוז	κραταιωμα		X?			Der.?

Passage	Hebrew	Greek	DE	OE	AE	SC	Comment
45 (46):2	מחסה	καταφυγη			X		Heb.
45 (46):2	עז	δυναμις			X?	X	Lit.
45 (46):2	עזרה	βοηθος	X			X	De.?, Lit.
45 (46):5	עליון	υψιστος	X			X	
45 (46):8	צבאות	δυναμις	X			X	Lit.
45 (46):8	משגב	αντιλημπτωρ	X				
45 (46):12	צבאות	δυναμις	X			X	Lit.
45 (46):12	משגב	αντιλημπτωρ	X				
46 (47):3	עליון	υψιστος	X			X	
47 (48):4	משגב	αντιλαμβανεσθαι			X		Voc.?
47 (48):9	צבאות	δυναμις	X			X	Lit.
49 (50):14	עליון	υψιστος	X			X	
51 (52):9	מעוז	βοηθος			X		
53 (54):6	עזר	βοηθειν	(X)				Voc.*
55 (56):3	מרום	υψος	X			X	De.?, Lit.
56 (57):3	עליון	υψιστος	X			X	
58 (59):6	צבאות	δυναμις	X			X	Lit.
58 (59):10	עז	κρατος	X		X?	X	
58 (59):10	משגב	αντιλημπτωρ	X				
58 (59):12	מגן	υπερασπιστης	X				
58 (59):17	משגב	αντιλημπτωρ	X				
58 (59):18	עז	βοηθος	X?				
58 (59):18	משגב	αντιλημπτωρ	X				
60 (61):4	מחסה	ελπις	X				
60 (61):4	מגדל	πυργος	X			X	Lit.
60 (61):4	עז	ισχυς			X?	X?	Lit.
61 (62):3	צור	θεος	X				
61 (62):3	משגב	αντιλημπτωρ	X				
61 (62):7	צור	θεος	X				
61 (62):7	משגב	αντιλημπτωρ	X				
61 (62):8	צור	θεος	X				
61 (62):8	עז	βοηθεια			X?		
61 (62):8	מחסה	ελπις	X				
61 (62):9	מחסה	βοηθος			X		Heb., Var.
62 (63):8	עזרה	βοηθος	X			X	Lit.
67 (68):15	שדי	τον επουρανιον			X?		?
68 (69):7	צבאות	δυναμις	X			X	Lit.
69 (70):6	עזר	βοηθος			X?	X	Lit.
70 (71):3	צור	θεος	X				
70 (71):3	מעון%	υπερασπιστης	X				מעוז
70 (71):3	מצודה	οχυρος					Greek
70 (71):3	סלע	στερεωμα	X?				
70 (71):3	מצודה	καταφυγη	X				
70 (71):7	מחסה	βοηθος	X				
70 (71):7	עז	κραταιος			X?		Var.?

Passage	Hebrew	Greek	DE	OE	AE	SC	Comment
72 (73):8	מרום	υψος	X?		X?	X	Lit.
72 (73):11	עליון	υψιστος		X	X		
72 (73):26	צור	θεος		X			
72 (73):28	מחסה	ελπις		X			
74 (75):6	מרום	υψος	X		X?	X	Lit.
74 (75):6	צואר%	θεος	X	X			צור
76 (77):11	עליון	υψιστος		X	X		
77 (78):17	עליון	υψιστος		X	X		
77 (78):35	צור	βοηθος			X		Var.
77 (78):35	עליון	υψιστος		X	X		
77 (78):56	עליון	υψιστος		X	X		
79 (80):5	צבאות	δυναμις		X		X	Lit.
79 (80):8	צבאות	δυναμις		X		X	Lit.
79 (80):15	צבאות	δυναμις		X		X	Lit.
79 (80):20	צבאות	δυναμις		X		X	Lit.
80 (81):2	עז	βοηθος	X?				
81 (82):6	עליון	υψιστος		X	X		
82 (83):19	עליון	υψιστος		X	X		
83 (84):2	צבאות	δυναμις		X		X	Lit.
83 (84):4	צבאות	δυναμις		X		X	Lit.
83 (84):9	צבאות	δυναμις		X		X	Lit.
83 (84):10	מגן	υπερασπιστης	X	X			Man
83 (84):12	מגן	αληθεια					*
83 (84):13	צבאות	δυναμις		X		X	Lit.
86 (87):5	עליון	υψιστος		X	X		
88 (89):9	צבאות	δυναμις		X		X	Lit.
88 (89):27	צור	αντιλημπτωρ			X		Var.
88 (89):44	צור	βοηθεια	X?	X?			
89 (90):1	מעון	καταφυγη		X			
90 (91):1	עליון	υψιστος		X	X		
90 (91):1	שׁדי	ο θεος του ουρανου					?
90 (91):2	מחסה	αντιλημπτωρ			X		Var., Int.?
90 (91):2	מצודה	καταφυγη		X			
90 (91):9	מחסה	ελπις		X			
90 (91):9	עליון	υψιστος		X	X		
90 (91):9	מעון	καταφυγη		X			
91 (92):2	עליון	υψιστος		X			
91 (92):9	מרום	υψιστος	X?	X	X		
91 (92):16	צור	θεος		X			
93 (94):17	עזרה	βοηθειν		(X)			Voc.*
93 (94):22	משׂגב	καταφυγη			X		
93 (94):22	צור	βοηθος			X		Var.
93 (94):22	מחסה	ελπις		X			
94 (95):1	צור	θεος		X			
96 (97):9	עליון	υψιστος		X	X		

Passage	Hebrew	Greek	DE	OE	AE	SC	Comment
106 (107):11	עליון	υψιστος	X	X			
113:17 (115:9)	עזר	βοηθος	X			X	Lit.
113:17 (115:9)	מגן	υπερασπιστης	X				
113:18 (115:10)	עזר	βοηθος	X			X	Lit.
113:18 (115:10)	מגן	υπερασπιστης	X				
113:19 (115:11)	עזר	βοηθος	X			X	Lit.
113:19 (115:11)	מגן	υπερασπιστης	X				
117 (118):7	עזר	βοηθος	X?	X		X	Lit.
117 (118):14	עז	ισχυς			X?	X	Lit.
118 (119):114	מגן	αντιλημπτωρ		X			
131 (132):2	אביר	θεος	X				
131 (132):5	אביר	θεος	X				
139 (140):8	עז	δυναμις			X?	X	Lit.
141 (142):6	מחסה	ελπις	X				
143 (144):1	צור	θεος	X				
143 (144):2	מצודה	καταφυγη	X				
143 (144):2	משגב	αντιλημπτωρ	X				
143 (144):2	מגן	υπερασπιστης	X				

Remarks:

Column markings:

SC = It is a semantically correct translation of the vehicle of the metaphor.

DE = It is a divine epithet or a divine name in LXX but not in MT.

(X) = The equivalent is a cognate term to the ordinary equivalent.

X? = The notation in the Table is disputable.

Comments:

De.? = It may be interpreted as a divine epithet or a divine name in MT but not in LXX.

Var. = The choice of an alternative equivalent depends on the desire for variation.

Heb. = The choice of equivalent probably depends on the Hebrew construction.

Der. = The word may here have been derived from a different root than from the usual.

Cont. = The choice of an alternative equivalent depends on the context.

Lit. = The equivalent for the word as a divine epithet or a divine name also occurs as a literal rendering of the term.

Voc. = The rendering in LXX is built on a different vocalization.

Text. = LXX may have had a hyponym different from the one in MT, which is marked by %. Retroversions are given when they are obvious or probable and in that case "Text." as comment is omitted.

Int. = The passage is treated differently in LXX in such a way that it cannot be used as an indication of how these metaphors were treated when they refer to man or gods.

Greek = A different Greek text from the one in Rahlfs may be the original text.

Man = The Hebrew word refers to man in MT but it is a divine epithet or a divine name in LXX.

* = It is a divine epithet or a divine name in MT but not in LXX.

The statistics includes divine names or epithets in LXX in MT as well as in MT. The traditional understanding and derivation of some of the Hebrew terms is a matter of dispute. Thus עזר "helper" has probably an homonym, עזר II "hero, warrior". LXX as a rule did not recognize עזר II. מגן has also a homonym, labelled מגן II "giver" or maybe "suzerain". עז and מעוז in MT can be derived from both עז and עוז. מָעוֹז and עז could thus mean "refuge". Regarding the understanding of these words in LXX, see 3.4.3 and 5.4.1.These meanings *can* be used to explain certain renderings of these terms as a designation of God.

Table 4

Renderings of divine names and epithets outside the Psalter

Passage	Hebrew	Greek	DE	OE	AE	SC	Comment
Gen 14:18	עליון	υψιστος	X		X		
Gen 14:19	עליון	υψιστος	X		X		
Gen 14:20	עליון	υψιστος	X		X		
Gen 14:22	עליון	υψιστος	X		X		
Gen 17:1	אל שדי	θεος μου	X				
Gen 28:3	אל שדי	θεος μου	X				
Gen 35:11	אל שדי	θεος μου	X				
Gen 43:14	אל שדי	θεος μου	X				
Gen 48:3	אל שדי	θεος μου	X				
Gen 49:24	אביר	δυναστος			X		
Gen 49:24	אבן	κατισχυειν					*
Gen 49:25	את% שדי	θεος μου	X				אל שדי
Ex 6:3	אל שדי	θεος μου	X				
Ex 15:2	עז	βοηθος	X?				
Num 24:4	שדי	θεος	X				
Num 24:16	עליון	υψιστος	X		X		
Num 24:16	שדי	θεος	X				
Deut 32:4	צור	θεος	X				
Deut 32:8	עליון	υψιστος	X		X		
Deut 32:15	צור	θεος	X				
Deut 32:18	צור	θεος	X				
Deut 32:30	צור	θεος	X				
Deut 32:31	צור	θεος	X				
Deut 32:37	צור	θεος	X				
Deut 33:7	עזר	βοηθος	X		X		Lit.
Deut 33:27	מעונה	σκεπασις					Lit.*
Deut 33:29	מגן	υπερασπιζειν	(X)				Voc.?*
Deut 33:29	עזר	βοηθος	X		X		Lit.
Ruth 1:20	שדי	ικανος				X?	K., Greek
Ruth 1:21	שדי	ικανος				X?	K., Greek
1 Sam 2:2	צור%	δικαιος			X		צדיק?
2 Sam 22:2	סלע	πετρα				X	K, Lit.
2 Sam 22:2	מצודה	οχυρωμα				X	K,
2 Sam 22:3	צור	φυλαξ			X		K, Var.
2 Sam 22:3	מגן	υπερασπιστης	X	X			
2 Sam 22:3	קרן	κερας			X	X	Lit.
2 Sam 22:3	משגב	αντιλημπτωρ	X				
2 Sam 22:14	עליון	υψιστος	X		X		
2 Sam 22:31	מגן	υπερασπιστης	X		X		
2 Sam 22:32	צור	κτιστης			X		Var.

Passage	Hebrew	Greek	DE	OE	AE	SC	Comment
2 Sam 22:33	מעוז	κατοικητηριον					Voc.?*
2 Sam 22:36	מגן	υπερασπισμος	X				De.?
2 Sam 22:47	צור	φυλαξ			X		K., Var.
2 Sam 23:3	צור	φυλαξ			X		K, Var.
2 Kgs 19:22	מרום	υψος	X?			X	Lit.
Job 5:17	שדי	παντοκρατωρ			X	X?	Var.
Job 6:4	שדי	κυριος		X			
Job 6:14	שדי	κυριος		X			
Job 8:3	שדי	ο τα παντα ποιησας				X?	Var.
Job 8:5	שדי	παντοκρατωρ			X	X?	Var.
Job 11:7	שדי	παντοκρατωρ			X	X?	Var.
Job 13:3	שדי	κυριος		X			
Job 15:25	שדי	κυριος παντοκρατωρ			X		Var.
Job 21:15	שדי	....					
Job 21:20	שדי	κυριος		X			
Job 22:3	שדי	κυριος		X			
Job 22:17	שדי	παντοκρατωρ			X	X?	Var.
Job 22:23	שדי	κυριος		X			
Job 22:25	שדי	παντοκρατωρ			X	X?	Var.
Job 22:26?	שדי	κυριος		X			
Job 23:16	שדי	παντοκρατωρ			X	X?	Var.
Job 24:1	שדי	κυριος		X			
Job 27:2	שדי	παντοκρατωρ			X	X?	Var.
Job 27:10	שדי	αυτου (κυριος)		X			Var.
Job 27:11	שדי	παντοκρατωρ			X	X?	Var.
Job 27:13	שדי	παντοκρατωρ			X	X?	Var.
Job 29:5	שדי	υλωδης					Text.*
Job 31:2	שדי	....					
Job 31:35	שדי	κυριος		X			
Job 32:8	שדי	παντοκρατωρ			X	X?	Var.
Job 33:4	שדי	παντοκρατωρ			X	X?	Var.
Job 34:10	שדי	παντοκρατωρ			X	X?	Var.
Job 34:12	שדי	παντοκρατωρ			X	X?	Var.
Job 35:13	שדי	παντοκρατωρ			X	X?	Var.
Job 37:22 (23)	שדי	παντοκρατωρ			X	X?	Var.
Job 40:2	שדי	παντοκρατωρ			X	X?	Var.
Prov 2:7	מגן	υπερασπιζειν		(X)			Voc.?*
Prov 14:26	מחסה	ερεισμα		?			De.?, Var.
Prov 30:5	מגן	υπερασπιζειν		(X)			Voc.?*
Is 1:24	אביר	ισχυς				(X)	*
Is 8:14	אבן	λιθος				X	Lit.*?
Is 8:14	צור	πετρα				X	Lit.?
Is 12:2	עז	δοξα				X?	
Is 13:6	שדי	θεος		X			
Is 14:14	עליון	υψιστος			X	X	

Passage	Hebrew	Greek	DE	OE	AE	SC	Comment
Is 17:10	צור	κυριος			X		Var.
Is 17:10	מעוז	βοηθος	X				
Is 25:4	מעוז	βοηθος	X				
Is 25:4	מחסה	σκεπη				X	
Is 26:4	צור	μεγας		X?			
Is 27:5	מעוז	ενοικειν					De.?
Is 30:29	צור	θεος	X				
Is 44:8	צור	θεος?	X				
Is 49:5	עז	ισχυς			X?	X	Lit.
Is 49:26	אביר	ισχυς				X	
Is 57:15	מרום	υψιστος	X	X		X	
Is 60:16	אביר	θεος	X?				
Jer 16:19	עז	ισχυς			X?	X	Lit.
Jer 16:19	מעוז	βοηθεια	X				
Jer 17:17	מחסה	φειδεσθαι					Der.*
Lam 3:35	עליון	υψιστος	X		X		
Lam 3:38	עליון	υψιστος	X		X		
Ez 1:24	שדי	....					
Ez 10:5	אל שדי	θεου Σαδδαι		X			
Joel 1:15	שדי	παλαιπωρια					*
Joel 3 (4):16	מחסה	φειδεσθαι					Der.*
Joel 3 (4):16	מעוז	ενισχυειν	X				*
Mic 6:6	מרום	υψιστος	X		X		
Nah 1:7	מעוז%	υπομενειν	X				De.?, Text.
Hab 1:12	צור	πλασσειν					Der.*

Remarks:
Column markings:
See Table 3.
Comments:
K. = The rendering reflects the *Kaige* recension.
For further symbols, see Table 3. צבאות as a designation of God is not included in this Table.
For a discussion of the renderings in LXX, see 5.9.2.

Table 5

Renderings of the terms as ordinary metaphors in the Psalter

Passage	Hebrew	Greek	RM	RG	CG	SC	Comment
7:11	מגן	βοηθεια			X	X	
17 (18):36	מגן	υπερασπισμος		X			(OA)
45 (46):2	עזרה	βοηθος	X			X	De.?, Lit.
46 (47):10	מגן	κραταιος	X				
55 (56):3	מרום	υψος	X			X	De.?, Lit.
59 (60):9	מעוז	κραταιωσις	X	X			(OA)
77 (78):25	אביר	αγγελος	X				
88 (89):19	מגן	αντιλημψις	X	X			
88 (89):28	עליון	υψηλος	X				
88 (89):44	צור	βοηθεια	X?				
88 (89):19	מגן	αντιλημψις	X	X			
107 (109):9	מעוז	αντιλημψις	X	X			

Remarks:
Column markings:
RM = The metaphor refers directly to man in MT.
RG = The metaphor refers directly to pagan gods or angels in MT.
CG = The metaphor is used in close connection with God without being a name or an epithet of God in MT.

Comments:
OA = The equivalent is identical with the ordinary or an alternative equivalent of the word as a designation of God. For further symbols, see Table 3.

(OA) = The equivalent is a cognate term to the ordinary or an alternative equivalent of the word as a designation of God.

The metaphors designated De.? has been included both here and in Table 6. Only metaphors which refer to man or pagan gods or is used in close connection with God are included in this Table. צבא as a designation of an army is, however, not included.

Table 6

Renderings of the terms as ordinary metaphors outside the Psalter

Passage	Hebrew	Greek	RM	RG	CG	SC	Comment
Deut 26:19	עליון	υπερανω	X				
Deut 28:1	עליון	υπερανω	X				
Deut 32:31	צור	θεος			X		
Deut 32:37	צור	θεος			X		
Deut 33:26	עזר	βοηθος				X	
1 Sam 21:8	אביר	?	X				
2 Sam 22:36	מגן	υπερασπισμος			X		(OA), De.?
Prov 2:7	מגן	υπερασπιζειν			X	X?	(OA), Voc.?
Prov 14:26	מחסה	ερεισμα			?		De.?, Var.
Job 24:22	אביר	αδυνατος	X				
Job 34:20	אביר	αδυνατος	X				
Is 10:13	אביר%	πολις	X				Text.
Is 27:5	מעוז	ενοικειν					De.?#
Is 31:9	סלע	πετρα	X	X?		X	OA, Int.#
Is 32:2	סלע	?	X	X?			Int.#
Is 51:1	צור	πετρα	X		X?		
Jer 21:13	צור	Σορ	X?				Voc.#
Jer 46:15	אביר%	ο μοσχος ?	X?				
Lam 1:15	אביר	ισχυρος	X				
Nah 1:7	מעוז%	υπομενειν		X			De.?, Text.

Remarks:
Column markings:
See Table 5.
Comments:
For further symbols, see Table 3.
= Contrary to MT the word does not directly refer to man or gods in LXX.
Divine epithets or divine names in MT which are rather understood as in close connection with God in LXX have been included both here and in Table 4. The metaphors designated De.? has been included here as well as in Table 5. Only ordinary metaphors which refer to man or is used in close connection with God are included.

WORKS CONSULTED

A. Texts, Translations and Reference Works.

Arndt, W.F., Gingrich, F.W., A Greek-English Lexicon of the NT, Chicago, Cambridge 1957 (cit.: Arndt, Gingrich).

Baumgartner, W., Hartmann, B., Kutscher, E.Y., Hebräisches und aramäisches Lexicon zum Alten Testament, Leiden 1967 ff (cit.: HAL).

Biblia Hebraica ..., ed. R. Kittel, 3rd ed., Stuttgart 1937 (cit.: BHK).

Biblia Hebraica Stuttgartensia ..., ed. K. Elliger, W. Rudolph, Stuttgart 1968-1976 (cit.: BHS).

Brown, F., Driver, S.R., Briggs, C.A., A Hebrew and English Lexicon of the Old Testament ..., Oxford 1907, reprint Oxford 1977 (cit.: BDB).

Camilo dos Santos, E., An Expanded Hebrew Index for the Hatch-Redpath Concordance to the Septuagint, Jerusalem 1973 (cit.: Santos, Index).

Dalman, H., Aramäisch-neuhebräisches Handwörterbuch zu Targum, Talmud und Midrasch, 2:e Aufl., Frankfurt am Main 1922 (cit.: Dalman).

Eissfeldt, O., Einleitung in das Alte Testament, 3:e Aufl., Tübingen 1964 (cit.: Eissfeldt, Einleitung).

Galling, K., Biblisches Reallexikon, HAT, Erste Reihe 1, 2:e Aufl., Tübingen 1977 (cit.: Galling, Reallexikon).

Ieremias, Baruch, Threni, Epistula Ieremiae, Septuaginta. Vetus Testamentum Graecum ... XV, ed. J. Ziegler, Göttingen 1957 (cit.: Ziegler, Ieremias).

Hatch, E., Redpath, H.A.A., A Concordance to the Septuagint ..., 3 vols., Oxford 1892-1906 (cit.: HR).

Holladay, W.L., A Concise Hebrew and Aramaic Lexicon of the Old Testament, Grand Rapids, Michigan 1976 (cit.: Hol).

Jastrow, M., A Dictionary of the Targumim, the Talmud Babli and Yerushalmi and the Midrashic Literature, 2 vols., New York 1950 (cit.: Jastrow).

Koehler, L., Baumgartner, W., Lexicon in Veteris Testamenti Libros ..., Leiden 1953 (cit.: KBL).

Lewy, L., Wörterbuch über die Talmudim und Midraschim, 4 vols., 2:e Aufl. 1924, reprinted in Darmstadt 1963 (cit.: Lewy).

Liddell, H.G., Scott, H., Jones, H.S., A Greek-English Lexicon, 9th ed., Oxford 1940, incl. a suppl. by E.A. Barber, Oxford 1968, reprinted 1978 (cit.: LSJ).

Lisowsky, G., Rost, L., Konkordanz zum hebräischen Alten Testament, 2:e Aufl., Stuttgart 1958 (cit.: Lisowsky).

Mandelkern, S., Veteris Testamenti Concordantiae Hebraicae atque Chaldaicae, Graz 1955 (cit.: Mandelkern).

Mercati, I.C., Psalterii Hexapli Reliquiae ..., Rome 1958 (cit.: Mercati, Hexapli).

Oliver, A., A Translation of the Syriac Peshito Version of the Psalms of David ..., Boston 1861 (cit.: Oliver, Syriac Psalms).

Origenis Hexaplorum quae supersunt ..., 2 vols., ed. F. Field, Oxonii 1867–1875 (cit.: Field I, II).

Preisigke, F., Kiessling, E., Wörterbuch der griechischen Papyrusurkunden ..., 1928 ff (cit.: Preisigke I–).

Pritchard, J., The Ancient Near East in Pictures. Relating to the Old Testament, Princeton, New Jersey 1954 (cit.: Pritchard, Pictures).

Reider, J., Turner, N., An Index to Aquila. Greek–Hebrew, Hebrew–Greek, Latin–Hebrew with the Syriac and Armenian Evidence, VTS 12 (1966) (cit.: Reider, Turner, Index).

Septuaginta id est Vetus Testamentum Graece iuxta LXX interpretes, ed. A. Rahlfs, 2 vols., Stuttgart 1935 (cit.: Rahlfs).

Septuaginta, Vetus Testamentum Graecum Auctoritate Academiae Scientiarum Gottingensis editum X, ed. A. Rahlfs, Göttingen 1931 (cit.: Rahlfs, Psalmi).

Supplementum Epigraphicum Graecum, eds. H.W. Pleket, R.S. Stroud, Germantown, Maryland, Alphen aan den Rijn, Amsterdam 1977 ff (cit.: SEG).

The Book of Isaiah I, II, HUBP, ed. M.H. Goshen–Gottstein, Jerusalem 1975, 1981 (cit.: Goshen–Gottstein, Isaiah).

The Book of Isaiah. According to the Septuagint I ..., ed. R.R. Ottley, 2nd ed., Cambridge 1909 (cit.: Ottley, Isaiah I).

The Book of Isaiah. According to the Septuagint II ..., ed. R.R. Ottley, Cambridge 1906 (cit.: Ottley, Isaiah II).

Thackeray, H.S:tJ., A Grammar of the Old Testament in Greek according to the LXX. 1. Introduction, Orthography and Accidence, Cambridge 1909 (cit.: Thackeray, Grammar).

The Interpreter's Dictionary of the Bible, 4 vols., Nashville, Tenn. 1962 (cit.: IDB).

The Interpreter's Dictionary of the Bible. Supplementary Volume, Nashville, Tenn. 1976 (cit.: IDB Suppl.).

The Septuagint Version of the Old Testament, with an English Translation ..., Anonymous translator and date, but obviously based on the translation of L.C.L. Brenton, London 1844, reprinted 1978 (cit.: Brenton).

Theologisches Handwörterbuch zum Alten Testament, eds. E. Jenni, C. Westermann, 2 vols., München, Zürich 1971 (cit.: THAT).

Theologisches Wörterbuch zum Alten Testament, eds. G.J. Botterweck, H. Ringgren, Stuttgart 1974 ff (cit.: ThWAT).

Theologisches Wörterbuch zum Neuen Testament, eds. G. Kittel, G. Friedrich, Stuttgart 1933 ff (cit.: ThWNT).

Trommius, A., Concordantiae graecae versionis vulgo dictae LXX interpretum, 2 vols., Amsterdam, Utrecht 1718 (cit.: Trommius).

B. Commentaries

Allen, L.C., The Books of Joel, Obadiah, Jonah and Micah, NICOT, London 1976 (cit.: Allen, Joel).

Anderson, A.A., The Book of Psalms, 2 vols., NCB, London 1972 (cit.: Anderson, Psalms).

Baetgen, D.F., Psalmen, HAT 2:2, Göttingen 1892 (cit.: Baetgen, Psalmen).

Bentzen, A., Fortolkning til de gammaltestamentlige salmer, København 1939 (cit.: Bentzen, Fortolkning).

Briggs, C.A., Briggs, E.G., A Critical and Exegetical Commentary on the Book of Psalms, vol. I, ICC, Edinburgh 1906 (cit.: Briggs, Psalms I).

Briggs, C.A., Briggs, E.G., A Critical and Exegetical Commentary on the Book of Psalms, vol. II, ICC, Edinburgh 1907 (cit.: Briggs, Psalms II).

Bright, J., Jeremiah ..., AB 21, New York 1965 (cit.: Bright, Jeremiah).

Budde, K.F.R., Das Buch Hiob, Göttingen 1913 (cit.: Budde, Hiob).

Carroll, R.P., Jeremiah: A Commentary, OTL, London 1986 (cit.: Carroll, Jeremiah).

Childs, B.S., Exodus. A Commentary, OTL, London 1974 (cit.: Childs, Exodus).

Cooke, G.A., The Book of Ezekiel, ICC, Edinburgh 1936 (cit.: Cooke, Ezekiel).

Craigie, P.C., Psalms 1–50, WBC 19, Waco, Texas 1983 (cit.: Craige, Psalms).

Craigie, P.C., The Book of Deuteronomy, NICOT, Grand Rapids, Michigan 1976 (cit.: Craigie, Deuteronomy).

Dahood, M., Psalms 1–50, AB 16, Garden City, New York 1966 (cit.: Dahood, Psalms I).

Dahood, M., Psalms 51–100, AB 17, Garden City, New York 1968 (cit.: Dahood, Psalms II).

Dhorme, E., A Commentary on the Book of Job, London 1967 (cit.: Dhorme, Job).

Driver, S.R., Gray, G.B., The Book of Job, ICC, Edinburgh 1921 (cit.: Driver, Gray, Job).

Duhm, B., Das Buch Jesaia übersetzt und erklärt, 4:e Aufl., Göttingen 1922 (cit.: Duhm, Jesaia).

170

Duhm, B., Die Psalmen, KHAT 15, Freiburg, Göttingen 1899 (cit.: Duhm, Psalmen).

Elliger, K., Deuterojesaja. 1. Teilband Jesaja 40,1–45,7, BKAT 11:1, Neukirchen–Vluyn (cit.: Elliger, Deuterojesaja).

Giesebrecht, F., Das Buch Jeremia übersetzt und erklärt, HKAT 3:2, 2:e Aufl., Göttingen 1907 (cit.: Giesebrecht, Jeremia).

Gordis, R., The Book of Job: Commentary, New Translation and Special Notes, New York 1978 (cit.: Gordis, Job).

Gray, G.B., Critical and Exegetical Commentary on the Book of Isaiah I–XXXIX, ICC, Edinburgh 1912, second impression 1928 (cit.: Gray, Isaiah).

Gunkel, H., Genesis, HAT 1:1, Göttingen 1901 (cit.: Gunkel, Genesis).

Gunkel, H., Die Psalmen …, GHAT 2:2, 4:e Aufl., Göttingen 1926 (cit.: Gunkel, Psalmen).

Habel, N., The Book of Job, Cambridge 1975 (cit.: Habel, Job).

Herkenne, H., Das Buch der Psalmen übersetzt und erklärt, Die Heilige Schrift des Alten Testaments 5:2, Bonn 1936 (cit.: Herkenne, Psalmen).

Hillers, D.H., Micah, Hermeneia, Philadelphia 1984 (cit.: Hillers, Micah).

Holladay, W.L., Jeremiah 1, Hermeneia, Philadelphia 1986 (cit.: Holladay, Jeremiah).

Hyatt, J.P., Exodus, NCB, London 1971 (cit.: Hyatt, Exodus).

Hölscher, G., Das Buch Job, HAT 17, Tübingen 1937 (cit.: Hölscher, Hiob).

Kaiser, O., Der Prophet Jesaia. Kapitel 13–39, ATD 18, Göttingen 1973 (cit.: Kaiser, Jesaia).

Kissane, E.J., The Book of Job, Dublin 1939 (cit.: Kissane, Job).

Kissane, E.J., The Book of Psalms …, Dublin 1953 (cit.: Kissane, Psalms I).

Kissane, E.J., The Book of Psalms …, Dublin 1964 (cit.: Kissane, Psalms II).

Kittel, D.R., Die Psalmen …, KAT 13, 3:e und 4:e Aufl., Leipzig & Erlangen 1922 (cit.: Kittel, Psalmen).

Kraus, H.-J., Psalmen. 2 vols., BKAT 15:1-2, 5:e Aufl., Neukirchen–Vluyn 1978 (cit.: Kraus, Psalmen).

McCarter, P.K.Jr., 1 Samuel …, AB 8, New York 1980 (cit.: McCarter, 1 Samuel).

McCarter, P.K.Jr., 2 Samuel …, AB 9, New York 1984 (cit.: McCarter, 2 Samuel).

McKane, W., A Critical and Exegetical Commentary on Jeremiah 1, ICC, Edinburgh 1986 (cit.: McKane, Jeremiah).

Oesterley, W.O.E., Psalms, 2 vols., London 1939 (cit.: Oesterley, Psalms).

Pope, M.H., Job, AB 15, 3rd ed., New York 1973 (cit.: Pope, Job).

Pope, M.H., Songs of Songs, AB 7C, New York 1977 (cit.: Pope, Songs).

Procksch, O., Die Genesis übersetzt und erklärt, KAT 1, Leipzig 1913 (cit.: Procksch, Genesis).

Procksch, O., Jesaia I übersetzt und erklärt, KAT 9, Leipzig 1930 (cit.: Procksch, Jesaia I).

Rudolph, W., Jeremia, HAT I, 12, 3:e verbesserte Aufl., Tübingen 1968 (cit.: Rudolph, Jeremia).

Rudolph, W., Joel-Amos-Obadja-Jona ..., KAT 13:2, Gütersloh 1971 (cit.: Rudolph, Joel).

Rudolph, W., Micha-Nahum-Habakuk-Zephanja ..., KAT 13:3, Gütersloh 1975 (cit.: Rudolph, Micha).

Skinner, J., A Critical and Exegetical Commentary on the Book of Genesis, ICC, 2nd ed., Edinburgh 1930 (cit.: Skinner, Genesis).

Smith, H.P., A Critical and Exegetical Commentary on the Books of Samuel, ICC, Edinburgh 1891 (cit.: Smith, Samuel).

Smith, J.M.P., Waard, W.H., Bewer, J.A., A Critical and Exegetical Commentary on Micah ..., ICC, Edinburgh 1911, second impression 1928 (cit.: Smith, Waard, Bewer, Micah).

Thompson, J.A., The Book of Jeremiah, NICOT, Grand Rapids, Michigan 1980 (cit.: Thompson, Jeremiah).

Weiser, A., Die Psalmen, ATD 14-15, 5:e Aufl., Göttingen 1959 (cit.: Weiser, Psalmen).

Westermann, C., Genesis. Kapitel 37-50, BKAT 10:3, Neukirchen-Vlujn 1982 (cit.: Westermann, Genesis III).

Wildberger, H., Jesaia, BKAT 10:1-3, Neukirchen-Vlujn 1972-1982 (cit.: Wildberger, Jesaia).

Wolff, H.-W., Dodekapropheton 2. Joel, Amos, BKAT 14:2, Neukirchen-Vluyn 1969 (cit.: Wolff, Joel).

Volz, P., Der Prophet Jeremia übersetzt und erklärt, KAT 10, Leipzig, Erlangen 1922 (cit.: Volz, Jeremia).

Wutz, F.X., Die Psalmen textkritisch untersucht, München 1925 (cit.: Wutz, Psalmen).

Zimmerli, W., Ezechiel, 2 vols., BKAT 13:1-2, Neukirchen-Vluyn 1969 (cit.: Zimmerli, Ezechiel).

C. General Works

Aejmelaeus, A., Parataxis in the Septuagint. A Study of the Renderings of the Hebrew Coordinate Clauses in the Greek Pentateuch, AASF, DissHumLitt 31, Diss. Helsinki 1982 (cit.: Aejmelaeus, Parataxis).

Albrektson, B., Studies in the Text and Theology of the Book of Lamentations, Studia Theologica Lundensia 21, Lund 1963 (cit.: Albrektson, Lamentations).

Allen, L.C., Review of Croft, S.J.L., 'The Identity of the Individual in the Psalms', JSOT Suppl 44 (1987), JBL 108 (1989), pp. 335–337.

Allen, L.C., The Greek Chronicles. The Relation of the Septuagint of I and II Chronicles to the Massoretic Text. Part I: The Translator's Craft, VTS 25 (1974) (cit.: Allen, Chronicles I).

Altar, Biblisch Historisches Handwörterbuch, eds. B. Reicke, L. Rost, 4 vols., cols. 63–65, Göttingen 1962–1979.

Altman, A., 'God: Attributes of God', EJ 7, cols. 664–669 (cit.: Altman, God).

Arens, A., Die Psalmen im Gottesdienst des Alten Bundes. Eine Untersuchung zur Vorgeschichte des christlichen Psalmengesanges, TThSt 11, Trier 1961 (cit.: Arens, Gottesdienst).

Arieti, J.A., 'The Vocabulary of Septuagint Amos', JBL 93 (1974), pp. 338–347 (cit.: Arieti).

Baetgen, F., Der Textkritische Wert der Alten Übersetzungen zu den Psalmen, JbProtTheol 8 (1882) (cit.: Baetgen).

Balz, H., Schneider, G., ὀχύρωμα, Exegetisches Wörterbuch zum NT, Band II, col. 1356 (cit.: Balz, Schneider, ὀχύρωμα).

Barnes, W.E., 'The Recovery of the Septuagint', JTS 36 (1935), pp. 123–131 (cit.: Barnes, Recovery).

Barr, J., Comparative Philology and the Text of the OT, Oxford 1968 (cit.: Barr, Philology).

Barr, J., 'Doubts about Homoeophony in the Septuagint', Textus 12 (1985), pp. 1–77 (cit.: Barr, Homoeophony).

Barr, J., The Semantics of Biblical Language, Oxford 1961 (cit.: Barr, Semantics).

Barr, J., 'Theophany and Anthropomorphism in the Old Testament', VTS 7, Congress Volume, Oxford 1959, pp. 31–38 (cit.: Barr, Theophany).

Barr, J., 'The Typology of Literalism in Ancient Biblical Translations', MSU 15, pp. 279–325, Göttingen 1979 (cit.: Barr, Typology).

Barr, J., 'Seeing the Wood for the Trees? An Enigmatic Ancient Translation ...', JSS 13 (1968), pp. 11–20 (cit.: Barr, Wood).

Baudissin, W.W.Graf, Kyrios als Gottesname im Judentum und seine Stelle in der Religionsgeschichte ... I–III, Giessen 1926–1929 (cit.: Baudissin, Kyrios I–III).

Bauernfeind, O.D., στρατεύομαι ..., ThWNT VII, pp. 701–713 (cit.: Bauernfeind, στρατεύομαι).

Baumgärtel, F., 'Zu den Gottesnamen in den Büchern Jeremia und Ezechiel', Verbannung und Heimkehr ..., ed. A. Kuschke, Tübingen 1961, pp. 1–29 (cit.: Baumgärtel, Gottesnamen).

Beekman, J., Callow, J., Translating the Word of God. With Scripture and Topical Indexes, Grand Rapids, Michigan 1974 (cit.: Beekman, Callow).

Begrich, J., 'Die Vertrauensäusserungen im israelitischen Klageliede des Einzelnen und in seinem babylonischen Gegenstück', ZAW N.F. 5 (1928), pp. 221–260 (cit.: Begrich, Vertrauensäusserungen).

Behm, J., θύω, ThWNT III, pp. 180–190 (cit.: Behm, θύω).

Berg, J.E., The Influence of the LXX upon the Peshitta Psalter, New York 1895 (cit.: Berg).

Bergmann, U., עזר, THAT II, cols. 256–259 (cit.: Bergmann, עזר).

Bertram, G., 'Der Sprachschatz der Septuaginta und der des hebräischen Alten Testaments', ZAW 57 (1939), pp. 85–101 (cit.: Bertram, Sprachschatz).

Bertram, G., 'Hikanos in den griechischen Übersetzungen des AT:s als Wiedergabe von schaddaj', ZAW N.F. 29 (1958), pp. 20–31 (cit.: Bertram, Hikanos).

Bertram, G., στερεός ..., ThWNT VII, pp. 609–615 (cit.: Bertram, στερεός).

Bertram, G., 'Theologische Aussagen im griechischen Alten Testament: Gottesnamen', ZNT 69 (1978), pp. 239–246 (Bertram, Gottesnamen).

Bertram, G., ὕψος ..., ThWNT VIII, pp. 600–619 (cit.: Bertram, ὕψος).

Bertram, G., 'Vom Wesen der Septuaginta-Frömmigkeit', WeltOr 2 (1954–1959), pp. 274–284 (cit.: Bertram, Frömmigkeit).

Bertram, G., 'Zur Prägung der biblischen Gottesvorstellung in den Griechischen Übersetzungen des AT ...', WeltOr 2 (1954–1959), pp. 502–513 (cit.: Bertram, Gottesvorstellung).

Beyerlin, W., Der 52. Psalm. Studien zu seiner Einordnung, BWAT Sechste Folge, Heft 11, Stuttgart, Berlin, Köln, Mainz 1980 (cit.: Beyerlin, Ps 52).

Beyreuther, E., 'Hirte', Begriffslexikon zum NT, Band II, Wuppertal 1969, pp. 697–700 (cit.: Beyreuther, Hirte).

Bjørndalen, A.J., Untersuchungen zur allegorischen Rede der Propheten Amos und Jesaja, Diss. Oslo 1982 (mimeographed) (cit.: Bjørndalen, Rede).

Black, M., 'Metaphor', Proceedings of the Aristotelian Society, N.S. 55 (1954–1955), pp. 273–294 (cit.: Black, Metaphor).

Borse, U., τὸ ἱερόν, Exegetisches Wörterbuch zum NT, Band II, cols. 429–431 (cit.: Borse, τὸ ἱερόν).

Braude, W.G., The Midrash on Psalms, Yale Judaica Series XIII, 2 vols., New Haven 1959 (cit.: Braude, Midrash).

Brock, S.P., 'The Phenomenon of Biblical Translation in Antiquity', Alta: The University of Birmingham Review 2:8 (1969), pp. 69–102, reprinted in Jellicoe, Studies, pp. 541–571 (cit.: Brock, Phenomenon).

Brock, S.P., 'The Phenomenon of the Septuagint', The Witness of Tradition. Papers read at the joint British–Dutch Old Testament Conference held at Woudschoten 1970, OTS 17 (1972), Leiden, pp. 11–36 (cit.: Brock, Septuagint).

Brooke, G.J., Exegesis at Qumran. 4Q Florilegium in its Jewish Context, JSOT Suppl 29, Sheffield 1985 (cit.: Brooke, Qumran).

Brown, J.P, 'The Septuagint as a Source of Loan-Words in the Targums', Bib 70 (1989), pp. 194–216 (cit.: Brown, Loan-Words).

Büchsel, F., βοηθέω ..., ThWNT I, p. 627 (cit.: Büchsel, βοηθέω).

Bultmann, R., ἐλπίς, ThWNT II, pp. 515–520, 525–531 (cit.: Bultmann, ἐλπίς).

Caird, G.B., 'Ben Sira and the Dating of the Septuagint', Papers presented to the Fifth International Congress on Biblical Studies held at Oxford 1973, ed. E.A. Livingstone, Studia Evangelica 7 (1982), Berlin, pp. 95–100 (cit.: Caird, Ben Sira).

Caird, G.B., The Language and Imagery of the Bible, Duckworth Studies in Theology, London 1980 (cit.: Caird, Language).

Caird, G.B., 'Towards a Lexicon of the Septuagint II', Septuagintal Lexicography, ed. R.A. Kraft, rev. ed., SeptCogStud 1, pp. 133–152, Missoula, Montana 1975 (cit.: Caird, Lexicon).

Chester, A., Divine Revelation and Divine Titles in the Pentateuchal Targumim, Tübingen 1986 (cit.: Chester, Revelation).

Churgin, P., 'The Targum and the Septuagint', AJSL 50 (1933–34), pp. 41–65 (cit.: Churgin).

Craigie, P.C., 'Psalm XXIX in the Hebrew Poetic Tradition', VT 22 (1972), pp. 143–151 (cit.: Craigie, Ps XXIX).

Cullman, O., πέτρα, ThWNT VI, pp. 94–99 (cit.: Cullman, πέτρα).

Dahl, N.A., Segal, A.F., 'Philo and the Rabbis on the Names of God', JStJud 9 (1978), pp. 1–28 (cit.: Dahl, Segal, Philo).

Dahood, M., 'Gen 49:24', Bib 40 (1959), pp. 1002–1007 (cit.: Dahood, Gen 49:24).

Dalbert, P., Die Theologie der hellenistisch–jüdischen Missions-Literatur unter Ausschluss von Philo und Josephus, TFor 4, Hamburg 1954 (cit.: Dalbert).

Daniel, S., Recherces sur le Vocabulaire du Culte dans la Septante, Études et Commentaires 61 (1966), Paris (cit.: Daniel).

Davies, G.H., 'Psalm 95', ZAW 85 (1973), pp. 183–195 (cit.: Davies, Psalm 95).

Delekat, L., Asylie und Schutzorakel am Zionheiligtum. Eine Untersuchung zu den privaten Feindpsalmen ..., Leiden 1967 (cit.: Delekat, Asylie).

Dell'Acqua, A.P., 'La metafora biblica di Dio come roccia e la sua soppressione nelle antiche versioni', Ephemerides Liturgicae 91 (1977), pp. 417–453 (cit.: Dell'Acqua, Roccia).

Dodd, C.H., The Bible and the Greeks, London 1934 (cit.: Dodd, Bible).

Dohmen, Ch., מזבח, ThWAT IV, cols. 787–801 (cit.: Dohmen, מזבח).

Eichhorn, D., Gott als Fels, Burg und Zuflucht. Eine Untersuchung zum Gebet des Mittlers in den Psalmen, Europäische Hochschulschriften 23:4, Bern, Frankfurt am Main 1972 (cit.: Eichhorn).

Enermalm–Ogawa, A., Un Langage de prière juif en grec …, ConBib.NT 17, Uppsala 1987 (cit.: Enermalm–Ogawa).

Erwin, H.M., Theological Aspects of the Septuagint of the Book of Psalms, Diss. Princeton Theological Seminary, Princeton, New Jersey 1962 (mimeographed) (cit.: Erwin).

Fabry, H.–J., נס, ThWAT V, cols. 468–473 (cit.: Fabry, נס).

Fabry, H.–J., עזר, ThWAT VI, cols. 20–21 (cit.: Fabry, עזר).

Fabry, H.–J., צור, ThWAT VI, cols. 973–983 (cit.: Fabry, צור).

Feldman, L.H., 'The Orthodoxy of the Jews in Hellenistic Egypt', JSocStud 22 (1960), pp. 215–237 (cit.: Feldman).

Flashar, M., 'Exegetische Studien zum LXX–Psalter', ZAW 32 (1912), pp. 81–116, 161–189, 241–269 (cit.: Flashar).

Foerster, W., κέρας, ThWNT III, pp. 668–671 (cit.: Foerster, κέρας).

Foerster, W., ὄρος, ThWNT V, pp. 475–486 (cit.: Foerster, ὄρος).

Freedman, D.N., 'Divine Names and Titles in Early Poetry', Magnalia Dei. The Mighty Acts of God. Essays on the Bible and Archaelogy in Memory of G.E. Wright, eds. F.M. Cross, W.E. Lemke and P.D. Miller, Jr., New York 1976, pp. 55–107 (cit.: Freedman, Divine Names).

Freedman, D.N., O'Connor, P., מגן, ThWAT IV, cols. 646–659 (cit.: Freedman, O'Connor, מגן).

Fritsch, C.T., 'Studies in the Theology of the Greek Psalter', Zalman Shazar Jubilee Volume, ed. B.Z. Luria, 1973, pp. 741–729 (cit.: Fritsch, Studies).

Fritsch, C.T., The Anti-Anthropomorphisms of the Greek Pentateuch, Princeton 1943 (cit.: Fritsch, Pentateuch).

Gamberoni, J., חסה, ThWAT III, cols. 71–83 (cit.: Gamberoni, חסה).

Gamberoni, J., מצבה, ThWAT IV, cols. 1064–1074 (cit.: Gamberoni, מצבה).

Gard, D.H., The Exegetical Method of the Greek Translator of the Book of Job, JBLMon 8, Philadelphia, Pennsylvania (cit.: Gard, Job).

Gehman, H.S., 'Adventures in LXX Lexicography', Textus 5 (1966), pp. 102–109 (cit.: Gehman, Adventures).

Gerhardsson, B., 'The Hermeneutic Program in Matthew 22:37–40', Jews Greeks and Christians. Religious Cultures in Late Antiquity. Essays in Honor of W.D. Davies, eds. R. Hamerton-Kelly, R. Scroggs, Leiden 1976 (cit.: Gerhardsson, Program).

Gerleman, G., Studies in the Septuagint I: The Book of Job, LUÅ N.F. 1, 43, 2, Lund 1946 (cit.: Gerleman, Job).

Goitein, S.D., 'מאון – A Reminder of Sin', JSS 10 (1965), pp. 52–53 (cit.: Goitein, מאון).

Goshen-Gottstein, M.H., 'The Textual Criticism of the Old Testament: Rise, Decline, Rebirth', JBL 102 (1983), pp. 365–399 (cit.: Goshen-Gottstein, Textual Criticism).

Goodenough, E.R., 'Philo Judaeus', IDB, pp. 796–798 (cit.: Goodenough, Philo).

Greenspoon, L., 'The Use and Abuse of the Term "LXX" and Related Terminology in Recent Scholarship', BulSeptStud 20 (1987), pp. 21–29 (cit.: Greenspoon, LXX).

Grundmann, W., δύναμαι ..., ThWNT II, pp. 286–318 (cit.: Grundmann, δύναμαι).

Grundmann, W., ἰσχύω ..., ThWNT III, pp. 400–405 (cit.: Grundmann, ἰσχύω).

Haag, E., סלע, ThWAT V, cols. 872–880 (cit.: Haag, סלע).

Hamerton-Kelly, R.G., 'Some Techniques of Composition in Philo's Allegorical Commentary with special Reference to de Agricultura ...', Jews, Greeks and Christians. Religious Cultures in Late Antiquity. Essays in Honor of W.D. Davies, eds. R. Hamerton-Kelly, R. Scroggs, Leiden 1976, pp. 45–56 (cit.: Hamerton-Kelly, Allegorical Commentary).

Hamp, V., 'Ps 8,2b. 3', BZ 16 N.F. (1972), pp. 115–120 (cit.: Hamp, Ps 8,2b. 3).

Harl, M., Dorival, G., and Munnich, O., La Bible Greque des Septante ..., Éditions du cerf – Éditions du C.N.R.S. 1988 (cit.: Harl, Dorival, Munnich, Septante).

Harrison, R.K., Introduction to the Old Testament, Grand Rapids, Michigan 1969 (cit.: Harrison, Introduction).

Hartberger, B., An den Wassern von Babylon ...: Psalm 137 auf dem Hintergrund von Jeremia 51, der biblischen Edom-Traditionen und babylonischer Originalquellen, Frankfurt am Main 1986 (cit.: Hartberger, Psalm 137).

Heater, H., A Septuagint Translation Technique in the Book of Job, CBQMS 11 (1982), Washington (cit.: Heater, Job).

Heidland, H.W., ὀχύρωμα, ThWNT V, pp. 590–591 (cit.: Heidland, ὀχύρωμα).

Herrmann, A., 'Dolmetschen im Altertum. Ein Beitrag zur antiken Kulturgeschichte', Beiträge zur Geschichte des Dolmetschens von K. Thieme, A. Herrmann, E. Glässer, Schriften des Auslands- und Dolmetscherinstituts ..., Band I, München 1956, pp. 25–59 (cit.: Herrmann, Dolmetschen).

Hugger, P., Jahwe meine Zuflucht. Gestalt und Theologie des 91. Psalms, Münsterschwarzacher Studien 13 (1971) (cit.: Hugger, Zuflucht).

Janzen, J.G., Studies in the Text of Jeremiah, HSM 6, 1973, Cambridge, Mass. (cit.: Janzen, Jeremiah).

Jellicoe, S., Studies in the Septuagint: Origins, Recensions and Interpretations, New York 1974 (cit.: Jellicoe, Studies).

Jellicoe, S., The Septuagint and Modern Study, Oxford 1968 (cit.: Jellicoe, Septuagint).

Jeremias, J., ποιμήν ..., ThWNT VI, pp. 484-501 (cit.: Jeremias, ποιμήν).

Jevons, F.B., 'Anthropomorphism', Encyclopaedia of Religion and Ethics, ed. J. Hastings, 12 vols., Edinburgh 1908-1926, pp. 573-578 (cit.: Jevons, Anthropomorphism).

Johannessohn, M., Der Gebrauch der Präpositionen in der Septuaginta, MSU 3:3, Berlin 1925 (cit.: Johannessohn, Präpositionen).

Kapelrud, A.S., אביר, ThWAT I, cols. 43-46 (cit.: Kapelrud, אביר).

Kapelrud, A.S., אבן, ThWAT I, cols. 50-53 (cit.: Kapelrud, אבן).

Katz, P., 'Zur Übersetzungstechnik der Septuaginta', WeltOr 2 (1954-1959), pp. 267-273 (cit.: Katz, Übersetzungstechnik).

Keel, O., Die Welt der Altorientalischen Bildsymbolik und das Alte Testament ..., Zürich, Einsiedeln, Neukirchen 1972 (cit.: Keel, Bildsymbolik).

Klein, M.L., Anthropomorphisms and Anthropopathisms in the Targumim of the Pentateuch ..., Jerusalem 1982 (cit.: Klein, Pentateuch).

Klein, M.L., 'Converse Translation: A Targumic Technique', Bib 57 (1976), pp. 515-537 (cit.: Klein, Converse Translation).

Knowles, M.P., '"The Rock, his Work is Perfect": Unusual Imagery for God in Deuteronomy XXXII', VT 39 (1989), pp. 307-322 (cit.: Knowles, Rock).

Koenig, J., L'Herméneutique analogique du Jüdaïsme antique d'après les témoins textuels d'Isaïe, VTS 33, Leiden 1982 (cit.: Koenig, L'Herméneutique).

Koester, H., History, Culture and Religion of the Hellenistic Age. Vol 1: Introduction to the New Testament, Philadelphia, Berlin, New York 1980 (cit.: Koester, Hellenistic Age I).

van der Kooij, A., 'Accident or Method? On "Analogical" Interpretation in the Old Greek of Isaiah and in 1QIs-a', BibOr 43 (1986), pp. 366-376 (cit.: van der Kooij, Accident).

van der Kooij, A., Die Alten Textzeugen des Jesajabuches. Ein Beitrag zur Textgeschichte des Alten Testaments, OBO 35, Freiburg, Göttingen 1981 (cit.: van der Kooij, Textzeugen).

van der Kooij, A., 'On the Place of Origin of the Old Greek of Psalms', VT 33 (1983), pp. 69-74 (cit.: van der Kooij, Origin).

Lee, J.A.L., A Lexical Study of the Septuagint Version of the Pentateuch, SeptCogStud 14, Chico, Mass. 1983 (cit.: Lee, Pentateuch).

Levy, B.B., 'Review of Klein, Pentateuch', JBL 104 (1985), pp. 708-709.

Lipiński, E., עזר ..., ThWAT VI, cols. 14-20 (cit.: Lipiński, עזר).

Loewenstamm, S.E., 'The Lord is my Strength and my Glory', VT 19 (1969), pp. 464-470 (cit.: Loewenstamm, Strength).

Loretz, O., 'מֹגָן אִישׁ in Proverbia 6:11 und 24:34', UF 6 (1974), pp. 476–477 (cit.: Loretz, אִישׁ מֹגָן).

Loretz, O., 'Psalmenstudien III', UF 6 (1974), pp. 175–210 (cit.: Loretz, Psalmenstudien III).

Loretz, O., 'Psalmenstudien IV: Stichometrische und Textologische Probleme in den Thronbesteigungs-psalmen', UF 6 (1974), pp. 211–240 (cit.: Loretz, Psalmenstudien IV).

Lurker, M., Wörterbuch biblisher Bilder und Symbole, München 1973 (cit.: Lurker, Symbole).

Marcus, R., 'Divine Names and Attributes in Hellenistic Jewish Literature', PAAJR 1931–1932, Philadelphia 1932, pp. 43–120 (cit.: Marcus, Divine Names).

Marcus, R., 'Jewish and Greek Elements in the LXX', Louis Ginzberg Jubilee Volume … 1 (English section), 1945, pp. 227–245 (cit.: Marcus, Elements).

Marmorstein, A., 'Philo and the Names of God', JQR N.S. 22 (1931–1932), pp. 295–306 (cit.: Marmorstein, Names).

Marmorstein, A., The Old Rabbinic Doctrine of God I: The Names and Attributes of God, London 1927 (cit.: Marmorstein, Doctrine).

Martin, M., The Scribal Character of the Dead Sea Scrolls, vol 1, Bibliothèque du Muséon 44, Louvain 1958 (cit.: Martin, Character).

Mays, J.M., 'The Place of the Torah-Psalms in the Psalter', JBL 106 (1987), pp. 3–12 (cit.: Mays, Torah-Psalms).

McGregor, L.J., The Greek Text of Ezekiel. An Examination of Its Homogeneity, Septuagint and Cognate Studies Series 18, Atlanta, Georgia 1985 (cit.: McGregor, Ezekiel).

McNamara, M., 'Targums', IDB Suppl., pp. 856–861 (cit.: McNamara, Targums).

Meier, H., Die Metapher. Versuch einer zusammenfassenden Betrachtung ihrer linguistischen Merkmale, Abhandlung der Universität Zürich, Winterthur 1963 (cit.: Meier, Metapher).

Melamed, E.Z., 'Break-up of Stereotype Phrases as an Artistic Device in Biblical Poetry', Scripta Hierosolymitana 8 (1961), pp. 115–153 (cit.: Melamed, Break-up).

Mettinger, T.N.D., 'YHWH SABAOTH-The Heavenly King on the Cherubim Throne', Studies in the Period of David and Solomon and Other Essays …, ed. T. Ishida, pp. 109–138, Tokyo 1982 (cit.: Mettinger, Sabaoth).

Mettinger, T.N.D., The Dethronement of Sabaoth: Studies in the Shem and Kabod Theologies, ConBib.OT 18, Lund 1982 (cit.: Mettinger, Dethronement).

Metzger, M., 'Himmlische und Irdische Wohnstatt Jahwes', UF 2 (1970), pp. 139–158 (cit.: Metzger, Wohnstatt).

Michaelis, W., κράτος …, ThWNT III, pp. 905–914 (cit.: Michaelis, κράτος).

Michaelis, W., ὁράω …, ThWNT V, pp. 315–382 (cit.: Michaelis, ὁράω).

Michaelis, W., πύργος, ThWNT VI, pp. 953–956 (cit.: Michaelis, πύργος).

Michel, M., Tempora und Satzstellung in den Psalmen, Abhandlingen zur Evangelischen Theologie I, Bonn 1960 (cit.: Michel, Tempora).

Miller, P.D., 'Animal Names as Designations in Ugaritic and Hebrew', UF 2 (1970), pp. 177–186 (cit.: Miller, Animal Names).

Miller, P.D., 'Ugaritic gzr and Hebrew ʿzr II', UF 2 (1970), pp. 159–175 (cit.: Miller, Ugaritic).

Mozley, F.W., The Psalter of the Church. The Psalms Compared with the Hebrew, with Various Notes, Cambridge 1905 (cit.: Mozley).

Munnich, O., 'Contribution à l'étude de la première révision de la Septante', Aufstieg und Niedergang der Römischen Welt 2, 20 1, Berlin 1987, pp. 190–220 (cit.: Munnich, Révision).

Munnich, O., 'La Septante des Psaumes et le groupe kaige', VT 33 (1983), pp. 75–89 (cit.: Munnich, La Septante).

Muraoka, T., 'The Greek Texts of Samuel–Kings: Incomplete Translations or Recensional Activity', Abr–Nahrain 21 (1982–1983), pp. 28–49 (cit.: Muraoka, Samuel–Kings).

Nida, E.A., Taber, C.R., The Theory and Practice of Translation, Helps for Translators 8. Prepared under the Auspices of the United Bible Societies, Leiden 1974 (cit.: Nida, Taber).

Nielsen, K., For et træ er der håb, Bibel og historie 8, Afhandling Aarhus Universitet, Køpenhavn 1985 (cit.: Nielsen, Håb).

O'Connell, K.G., 'Greek Versions (minor)', IDB Suppl., pp. 377–381 (cit.: O'Connell, Greek Versions).

Ollenburger, B.C., Zion the City of the Great King. A Theological Symbol of the Jerusalem Cult, JSOT 41, Sheffield 1987 (cit.: Ollenburger, Zion).

Olofsson, S., The LXX Version. A Guide to the Translation Technique of the Septuagint, ConBib.OT 30, Stockholm 1990 (cit.: Olofsson, LXX Version).

Olofsson, S., 'The Translation of Jer 2,18 in the Septuagint. Methodical, Linguistic and Theological Aspects', Scandinavian Journal of the Old Testament 2 (1988), pp. 169–200 (cit.: Olofsson, Jer 2,18).

Olsson, B., Structure and Meaning in the Fourth Gospel, ConBib.NT 6, Lund 1974 (cit.: Olsson, Structure).

Orlinsky, H.M., 'Review of Fritsch, Pentateuch', The Qrozer Quarterly 21 (1944), pp. 156–160.

Orlinsky, H.M., 'Studies in the Septuagint of Job', HUCA 28 (1957), pp. 53–74 (cit.: Orlinsky, Job).

Orlinsky, H.M., 'The LXX: its Use in Textual Criticism', BA 9 (1946), pp. 22–34 (cit.: Orlinsky, The LXX).

180

Orlinsky, H.M., 'The Septuagint as Holy Writ and the Philosophy of the Translators', HUCA 46 (1975, ed. 1976), pp. 89-114 (cit.: Orlinsky, Holy Writ).

Orlinsky, H.M., 'The Treatment of Anthropomorphisms and Anthropopathisms in the Septuagint of Isaiah', HUCA 27 (1956), pp. 193-200 (cit.: Orlinsky, Isaiah).

van der Osten-Sacken, P., κράτος, Exegetisches Wörterbuch zum Neues Testament II, col. 780 (cit.: van der Osten-Sacken, κράτος).

Ottley, R.R., A Handbook to the Septuagint, Leiden 1929 (cit.: Ottley, Handbook).

Pace, S., 'The Stratigraphy of the Text of Daniel and the Question of Theological Tendenz in the Old Greek', BulSeptStud 17 (1985), pp. 15-35 (cit.: Pace, Daniel).

Patte, D., Early Jewish Hermeneutic in Palestine, SBL Diss. Series 22, Missoula Montana 1975 (cit.: Patte, Hermeneutic).

Pietersma, A., 'David in the Greek Psalms', VT 30 (1980), pp. 213-226 (cit.: Pietersma, David).

Pietersma, A., Two Manuscripts of the Greek Psalter ..., AnBib 77, Rome 1978 (cit.: Pietersma, Manuscripts).

Plantin, H., 'Leviternas veckodagspsalmer i templet', SEÅ 48 (1983), pp. 69-76 (cit.: Plantin, Veckodagspsalmer).

Polak, F.H., 'Jer 23:29 – An Expanded Colon in the LXX', Textus 11 (1984), pp. 119-123 (cit.: Polak, Jer 23:29).

Porter, P.A., Metaphors and Monsters: A Literary-Critical Study of Daniel 7 and 8, ConBib.OT 20, Lund 1983 (cit.: Porter, Metaphors).

Preuss, H.D., מעונה, מעון, ThWAT IV, cols. 1027-1030 (cit.: Preuss, מעון).

Prijs, L., Jüdische Tradition in der Septuaginta, Leiden 1948 (cit.: Prijs).

Procksch, O., ἅγιος ..., ThWNT I, pp. 87-97, 101-116 (cit.: Procksch, ἅγιος).

Rabin, Ch., 'The Translation Process and the Character of the Septuagint', Textus 6 (1968), pp. 1-26 (cit.: Rabin, Character).

von Rad, G., Old Testament Theology, vol. 1 ..., English ed., Edinburgh 1962 (cit.: von Rad, Theology I).

Reindll, J., נוס ..., ThWAT V, cols. 307-315 (cit.: Reindll, נוס).

Rengstorf, K.H., ἐλπίς, ThWNT II, pp. 520-525 (cit.: Rengstorf, ἐλπίς).

Ringgren, H., עגל, עגלה, ThWAT V, cols. 1056-1062 (cit.: Ringgren, עגל).

Ringgren, H., עוד, ThWAT V, cols. 1130-1131 (cit.: Ringgren, עוד).

Roberts, B.J., The Old Testament Text and Versions. The Hebrew Text in Transmission and the History of the Ancient Versions, Cardiff 1951 (cit.: Roberts).

Sailhamer, J.H., The Translational Technique of the Greek Septuagint for the Hebrew Verbs and Participles in Psalms 3–41, Diss. Los Angeles 1981 (mimeographed) (cit.: Sailhamer).

Busto Saiz, J.R., La traduccion de Simaco en el libro de los Salmos, Madrid 1978, TextEstCisn 22, Madrid 1978 (cit.: Saiz, Simaco).

Schenker, A., Psalmen in den Hexapla ..., Studi e Testi 295, Rome 1982 (cit.: Schenker, Hexapla).

Schmid, H.H., אביר, THAT I, cols. 25–27 (cit.: Schmid, אביר).

Schrenk, G., ἱερός ..., ThWNT III, pp. 221–284 (cit.: Schrenk, ἱερός).

Schunck, K.-D., מצודה ..., ThWAT IV, cols. 1081–1085 (cit.: Schunck, מצודה).

Schüpphaus, J., בלע, ThWAT I, cols. 658–661 (cit.: Schüpphaus, בלע).

Schwarzenbach, A., Die Geographische Terminologie im Hebräischen des Alten Testamentes, Abhandlung zur Erlangung der Doktorwürde der Philosophischen Fakultät I der Universität Zürich, Leiden 1954 (cit.: Schwarzenbach, Geographische Terminologie).

Seeligmann, I.L., The Septuagint Version of Isaiah. A Discussion of its Problems, Mededelingen en verhandelingen 9 van het Vooraziatisch-Egyptisch Genootschap "Ex Oriente Lux", Leiden 1948 (cit.: Seeligmann, Isaiah).

Shunary, J., 'Avoidance of Anthropomorphism in the Targum of Psalms', Textus 5 (1966), pp. 133–144 (cit.: Shunary, Psalms).

Skehan, P.W., 'Qumrân and Old Testament Criticism', Qumrân. Sa piété, sa théologie et son milieu, BEThL 46 (1978), ed. M. Delcor, Paris, Louvain, pp. 163–182 (cit.: Skehan, Qumrân).

Soffer, A., 'The Treatment of Anthropomorphisms and Anthropopathisms in the Septuagint of Psalms', HUCA 38 (1957), pp. 85–107 (cit.: Soffer).

Stolz, F., Strukturen und Figuren im Kult von Jerusalem. Studien zur altorientalischen, vor- und frühisraelitischen Religion, Berlin 1970 (cit.: Stolz, Kult).

Strack, H., Billerbeck, P., 'Exkurs über den Memra Jahves', Kommentar zum Neuen Testament aus Talmud und Midrash, vol. 2, München 1924, pp. 302–333 (cit.: Strack, Billerbeck).

Stähli, H.-P., רום, THAT II, cols. 753–761 (cit.: Stähli, רום).

Süring, M.L., The Horn-Motif ..., Diss., Andrews University Seminary Doctoral Dissertation Series vol. IV, Berrien Springs, Michigan 1980 (cit.: Süring, Horn-Motif).

Swete, H.B., An Introduction to the OT in Greek, Cambridge 1900 (cit.: Swete, Introduction).

Söderlund, S., The Greek Text of Jeremiah. A Revised Hypothesis, JSOT Suppl 14 (1986) (cit.: Söderlund, Jeremiah).

Tallquist, K.L., Akkadische Götterepitheta, Helsingfors 1938 (cit.: Tallquist, Götterepitheta).

Talmon, S., 'Aspects of the Textual Transmission of the Bible in the Light of Qumran Manuscripts', Textus 4 (1964), pp. 95–132 (cit.: Talmon, Aspects).

Talmon, S., 'The Ancient Hebrew Alphabet and Biblical Text Criticism', Mélanges Dominique Barthélemy. Études Bibliques offertes à l'occasion de son 60-e Anniversaire, OBO 38, Freiburg, Göttingen 1981, pp. 497–530 (cit.: Tov, Alphabet).

Talshir, Z., 'Linguistic Development and the Evaluation of Translation Technique in the Septuagint', Scripta Hierosolymitana 31 (1986), pp. 301–320 (cit.: Talshir, Development).

Thackeray, H.S:tJ., Some Aspects of the Greek Old Testament, London 1927 (cit.: Thackeray, Aspects).

Thackeray, H.S:tJ., The Septuagint and Jewish Worship, The Schweich Lectures 1920, London 1921 (cit.: Thackeray, Worship).

Toombs, L.E., 'Bathing', IDB, pp. 365–366 (cit.: Toombs, Bathing).

Tov, E., 'Computor Assisted Analysis of the Translation Technique of the LXX', Early version of article published by the Israel Academy of Sciences, 1984 (cit.: Tov, Analysis).

Tov, E., 'Did the Septuagint Translators Always Understand their Hebrew Text', De Septuaginta, Studies in Honour of John William Wevers on his sixty-fifth Birthday, eds. A. Pietersma, C. Cox, Missisauga, Ontario 1984, pp. 53–70 (cit.: Tov, Septuagint Translators).

Tov, E., 'Die griechischen Bibelübersetzungen', Aufstieg und Niedergang der Römischen Welt 2, 20 1, Berlin 1987, pp. 121–189 (cit.: Tov, Bibelübersetzungen)

Tov, E., 'Exegetical Notes on the Hebrew Vorlage of the LXX of Jeremiah 27 (34)', ZAW 91 (1979), pp. 73–93 (cit.: Tov, Vorlage).

Tov, E., 'Some Corrections to Reider–Turner's Index to Aquila', Textus 8 (1973), pp. 164–174 (cit.: Tov, Corrections).

Tov, E., 'Studies in the Vocabulary of the Septuagint – The Relation between Vocabulary and Translation Technique', Tarbiz 47 (1978), English summary, pp. I-II (cit.: Tov, Studies).

Tov, E., 'The Growth of the Book of Joshua in the Light of the Evidence of the LXX Translation', Scripta Hierosolymitana 31 (1986), pp. 321–339 (cit.: Tov, Joshua).

Tov, E., 'The Impact of the LXX Translation of the Pentateuch on the Translation of the other Books', Mélanges Dominique Barthélemy. Études Bibliques offertes à l'occasion de son 60-e Anniversaire, OBO 38, Freiburg, Göttingen 1981, pp. 577–592 (cit.: Tov, Impact).

Tov, E., The Text-Critical Use of the Septuagint in Biblical Research, Jerusalem Biblical Studies 3, Jerusalem 1981 (cit.: Tov, Septuagint).

Tov, E., 'Three Dimensions of LXX Words', RB 83 (1976), pp. 529–544 (cit.: Tov, Dimensions).

Traub, H., οὐρανός ..., ThWNT V, pp. 496–501, 509–543 (cit.: Traub, οὐρανός).

Trebolle, J., 'Redaction, Recension, and Midrash in the Books of Kings', BulSeptStud 15 (1982), pp. 12–35 (cit.: Trebolle, Redaction).

Tsevat, M., A Study of the Language of the Biblical Psalms, SBL, Philadelphia 1955 (cit.: Tsevat).

Urbach, E.E., The Sages: Their Concepts and Beliefs I, II, Jerusalem 1975, 1979 (cit.: Urbach, Sages I, II).

Venetz, H.-J., Die Quinta des Psalteriums. Ein Beitrag zur Septuaginta- und Hexaplaforschung, Hildesheim 1974 (cit.: Venetz, Quinta).

Wacholder, B.Z., Eupolemus. A Study of Judaeo-Greek Literature, HUCAMon 3, Cincinnati, New York, Los Angeles, Jerusalem 1974 (cit.: Wacholder).

Wagner, S., עדד ..., ThWAT VI, cols. 1–14 (cit.: Wagner, עדד).

Walter, N., 'Jüdisch-hellenistische Literatur vor Philon von Alexandrien (unter Ausschluss der Historiker)', Aufstieg und Niedergang der Römischen Welt 2, 20 1, Berlin 1987, pp. 67–120 (cit.: Walter, Literatur).

Wanke, G., Die Zionstheologie der Korachiten in ihrem traditionsgeschichtlichen Zusammenhang, Berlin 1966 (cit.: Wanke, Zionstheologie).

Watson, W.G.E., Classical Hebrew Poetry ..., JSOT Suppl 26, Sheffield 1984 (cit.: Watson, Poetry).

Weippert, W., שדי, THAT II, cols. 873–881 (cit.: Weippert, שדי).

Weiss, M., The Bible from Within. The Method of Total Interpretation, Jerusalem 1984 (cit.: Weiss, Bible).

Weissert, D., 'Alexandrian Analogical Word-Analysis and Septuagint Translation Techniques ...', Textus 8 (1973), pp. 31–44 (cit.: Weissert).

Werblowsky, R.J.Z., 'Anthropomorphism', EJ 3, cols. 50–56 (cit.: Werblowsky, Anthropomorphism).

Werner, E., The Sacred Bridge ..., London, New York 1959 (cit.: Werner, Bridge I).

Werner, E., The Sacred Bridge ..., London, New York 1984 (cit.: Werner, Bridge II).

Wevers, J.W., 'Barthélemy and Proto-Septuagint Studies', BulSeptStud 21 (1988), pp. 23–34 (cit.: Wevers, Proto-Septuagint).

Wevers, J.W., 'Text History and Text Criticism of the Septuagint', Göttingen Congress Volume 1977, VTS 29, Leiden 1978, pp. 392–402 (cit.: Wevers, Text History).

Wevers, J.W., 'The Use of Versions for Text Criticism: The Septuagint', La Septuaginta en la Investigación contemporánea: V congreso de la IOSCS, TextEstCisn 34, Madrid 1985, pp. 15–24 (cit.: Wevers, Versions).

Wevers, J.W., 'Weapons and Implements of War', IDB, pp. 820–825 (cit.: Wevers, Weapons).

Wiegand, C., 'Der Gottesname צור u Seine Deutung in dem Sinne Bildner oder Schöpfer in der Alten Jüd Lit', ZAW 10 (1890), pp. 85-96 (cit.: Wiegand, Gottesname).

Wigtil, D.N., The Translation of Religious Texts in the Greco-Roman World, Diss. in partial fulfillment of the Requirement for the Degree of Doctor in Philosophy, University of Minnesota 1980 (cit.: Wigtil, Religious Texts).

Wiklander, B., Prophecy as Literature. A Text-Linguistic and Rhetorical Approach to Isaiah 2-4, ConBib.OT 22, Stockholm 1984 (cit.: Wiklander, Prophecy).

Wilson, G.H., 'The Qumran Psalms Manuscripts and the Consecutive Arrangement of Psalms in the Hebrew Psalter', CBQ 45 (1983), pp. 377-388 (cit.: Wilson, Qumran).

Wittstruck, T.K., The Greek Translators of Deuteronomy, Diss Ph.D., Ann Arbor, Michigan 1972 (cit.: Wittstruck, Deuteronomy).

Wittstruck, T.K., 'The So-Called Anti-Anthropomorphisms in the Greek text of Deuteronomy', CBQ 38 (1976), pp. 29-34 (cit.: Wittstruck, Anti-Anthropomorphisms).

van der Woude, A.S., עדד, THAT II, cols. 252-256 (cit.: van der Woude, עדד).

van der Woude, A.S., צבא, THAT II, cols. 498-507 (cit.: van der Woude, צבא).

van der Woude, A.S., צור, THAT II, cols. 538-543 (cit.: van der Woude, צור).

Würtwein, E., Der Text des Altes Testaments. Eine Einführung in die Biblia Hebraica, vierte, erweiterte Aufl., Stuttgart 1973 (cit.: Würtwein, Text).

Wutz, F.X., Die Psalmen textkritisch untersucht, München 1925 (cit.: Wutz, Psalmen).

Wutz, F.X., Die Transkriptionen von der Septuaginta bis zu Hieronymus, BWAT 9, Zweite Folge. Lieferung 1-2, Stuttgart 1925-1933 (cit.: Wutz, Transkriptionen).

Wutz, F.X., Systematische Wege von der Septuaginta zum hebräischen Urtext, Eichstätter Studien I:1, Stuttgart 1937 (cit.: Wutz, Wege).

Ziegler, J., Untersuchungen zur LXX des Buches Isaias, AltAbh 12:3, Münster W. 1934 (cit.: Ziegler, Untersuchungen).

Zlotowitz, B.M., The Septuagint Translation of the Hebrew Terms in Relation to God in the Book of Jeremiah, KTAV 1980 (cit.: Zlotowitz, Jeremiah).

Zobel, H.-J., מעוז, ThWAT IV, cols. 1019-1027 (cit.: Zobel, מעוז).

Zobel, H.-J., עליון, ThWAT VI, cols. 131-151 (cit.: Zobel, עליון).

Zobel, H.-J., צבאות, ThWAT VI, cols. 876-892 (cit.: Zobel, צבאות).

INDICES

INDEX OF AUTHORS

194

INDEX OF PASSAGES. QUMRAN TEXTS

INDEX OF PASSAGES. APOCRYPHA AND PSEUDEPIGRAPHA

INDEX OF PASSAGES. THE NEW TESTAMENT